War, Revenue, and State Building

War, Revenue, and State Building

Financing the Development of the American State

Sheldon D. Pollack

Cornell University Press

Ithaca and London

First published 2009 by Cornell University Press
First printing, Cornell Paperbacks, 2009
Printed in the United States of America

Library of Congress Cataloging-in-Publication Data

Pollack, Sheldon David.
    War, revenue, and state building : financing the development of the
American state / Sheldon D. Pollack.
        p. cm.
    Includes bibliographical references and index.
    ISBN 978-0-8014-4792-1 (cloth : alk. paper) — ISBN 978-0-8014-7586-3
(pbk. : alk. paper)
    1. Revenue—United States—History.   2. Revenue—Europe—
History.   3. Finance, Public—United States—History.   4. Finance,
Public—Europe—History.   5. War—Economic aspects—United
States—History.   6. War—Economic aspects—Europe—
History.   I. Title.

    HJ2362.P69   2009
    336.02'73—dc22

2009013056

Cornell University Press strives to use environmentally responsible
suppliers and materials to the fullest extent possible in the publishing of
its books. Such materials include vegetable-based, low-VOC inks and
acid-free papers that are recycled, totally chlorine-free, or partly composed
of nonwood fibers. For further information, visit our website at www.
cornellpress.cornell.edu.

Cloth printing   10 9 8 7 6 5 4 3 2 1
Paperback printing   10 9 8 7 6 5 4 3 2 1

Contents

Acknowledgments

A great many people assisted me in this project as well as my academic studies over the years. I thank Paul Quirk of the University of British Columbia, Stephen Newman of York University, William T. Bluhm of the University of Rochester, and Theodore J. Lowi of Cornell University for their many courtesies and support over the years. Youssef Cohen of New York University and Edward J. Harpham of the University of Texas at Dallas both read substantial portions of the manuscript and provided advice that greatly improved it. I thank them for the time and effort they contributed. Gerald Turkel and Leslie Goldstein, my colleagues at the University of Delaware, read portions of the manuscript and offered valuable suggestions. I also greatly benefited from the insights and comments of the participants at the July 2007 conference on Historical Perspectives on Tax Law and Policy, cosponsored by the UCLA School of Law and the UCLA Center for Economic History. In particular, Joseph Thorndike of the University of Virginia (and Tax Analysts) and Ajay Mehrotra of Indiana University provided useful suggestions that improved my arguments.

I thank Roger Haydon, my editor at Cornell University Press, for his helpful comments and criticisms. Karen Laun ably supervised the editing of the manuscript. The two anonymous readers for Cornell University Press went far beyond the call of duty and provided me with extraordinarily detailed and helpful analysis and comments. They saved me from many embarrassing errors and omissions, and greatly improved the finished work. Jack Rummel, copyeditor for Cornell University Press, and Eileen Pollack of the University of Michigan, greatly improved this book through their careful work in editing the text. Harriet Kennedy, my research assistant at the University of Delaware, aided me in preparing the manuscript. The University of Delaware provided generous financial support. Bobby Gempesaw and Tom Apple, academic deans at the University of Delaware, supported my research over the years, for which I am grateful. The research librarians at the Morris Library of the University of Delaware assisted me in locating books and documents. In particular, Rebecca Knight was always gracious and helpful in tracking down resources, especially obscure government documents. I thank her for all her assistance over the years.

Last, I thank my family. I am greatly indebted to my children, Alyssa and Seth, and my wife, Patti Werther. Without their support, I never would have been able to complete such a time-consuming undertaking. Finally, I thank my parents, Wilma and Abraham Pollack, for all their support. Alas, my father died before publication. This book is dedicated to them.

INTRODUCTION

The revenue of the state is the state. In effect all depends upon it,
whether for support or reformation.

—EDMUND BURKE, *Reflections on the Revolution in France* (1790)

The fiscal history of a people is above all an essential part of its general
history. An enormous influence on the fate of nations emanates from
the economic bleeding which the needs of the state necessitates.

—JOSEPH A. SCHUMPETER, "The Crisis of the Tax State" (1918)

In a relatively short time, the American state developed from a weak,
highly decentralized confederacy comprised of the thirteen former English colonies into the foremost global superpower. The central argument
of this book is that this remarkable institutional transformation would not
have been possible but for the revenue raised through a particularly efficient system of public finance originally devised by national political leaders during the Civil War and subsequently resurrected and perfected in the
early twentieth century. The revenue from this system of public finance
facilitated an extraordinary expansion of the apparatus of the American
state—in particular, the military forces and social welfare programs of the
American state. Conversely, the limited ability of the national government to raise revenue during the late eighteenth and early nineteenth
centuries severely inhibited the development of the American state during this formative period. For decades after the founding of the republic,
political leaders struggled to cope with the restrictions imposed on the

revenue-raising capacity of the American state by its archaic constitutional design, which preserved virtually all of the powers of the local state governments at the expense of the newly created national government. This was particularly true with respect to its fiscal and military powers. Nevertheless, during successive periods of war and crisis, political leaders eventually expanded these powers, and in doing so, effected a fundamental reconstitution of the American state.

The essential connection between public revenue and institutional development was not unique to the United States. Indeed, an extensive literature suggests that the development of the European state was linked to, and ultimately dependent on, the ability of its rulers to use the coercive powers of the state to successfully extract revenue from society. Yet despite compelling evidence of a connection between revenue and state development in Europe, the subject has been given only peripheral attention in the emerging body of scholarship on the development of the American state. This is unfortunate. In North America, as in Europe, public revenue has been a critical factor influencing state development.

Revenue is critical to state development because modern states, with their powerful armies and vast bureaucracies, require enormous revenue. Without that revenue, maintenance of state institutions, let alone expansion, is impossible. Every exercise of state power requires revenue, and the more developed the state, the more revenue is required. At the same time, when the revenue-raising capacity of a state is in jeopardy, there arises the distinct possibility of institutional decay and perhaps even regime collapse. Writing in 1788, Alexander Hamilton, soon to become the first treasury secretary of the impoverished American state, affirmed the importance of this vital commodity when he observed: "A nation cannot long exist without revenue."[1] During the critical period of instability that beset the young republic in the years immediately following the American Revolution, Hamilton had witnessed firsthand and was justly dismayed by the debilitating consequences of a deficient system of public revenue. Later, at

---

1. Alexander Hamilton, Federalist Paper No. 12, in James Madison, Alexander Hamilton, and John Jay, *The Federalist Papers* (New York: New American Library, 1961), 96. In Federalist Paper No. 30, Hamilton similarly observed: "Money is, with propriety, considered as the vital principle of the body politic; as that which sustains its life and motion and enables it to perform its most essential functions." Ibid., 188.

the helm of Treasury, he would dedicate himself to resolving the constant revenue shortages and fiscal instability that plagued the early American state and inhibited its development.

Rulers and Revenue Strategies

That states consume enormous revenue is hardly a revelation. A simple glance at the budget of any contemporary state will confirm this. Less obvious and ultimately more interesting is *how* rulers go about acquiring that revenue. In one sense, the story is the same everywhere: rulers use the coercive powers of the state to extract revenue from society. Dall Forsythe describes this vital process of revenue extraction as follows: "'Extraction' is an ugly but necessary term that neatly summarizes the complex strategies governments adopt to assure themselves adequate flows of revenue.... Rulers cannot develop a central state apparatus without some degree of capacity to extract revenues from the subject population of a nation."[2] State development requires vast amounts of revenue, and rulers and their functionaries wield the coercive powers of the state to extract that revenue from the population under their control. To be sure, states do more than just extract revenue from society, but this is the prerequisite for every other exercise of state power.

If revenue extraction invariably requires the use of the coercive powers of the state, rulers nevertheless possess considerable discretion in deciding *how* to deploy those powers in raising that revenue. This is what I refer to as a *revenue strategy*. Revenue strategies vary widely from state to state. The revenue strategy that ultimately emerges in any particular state is the product of a complicated calculus of decision making by rulers, with input from bureaucrats, private individuals, interest groups, and political parties, and influence exerted by numerous economic and social factors unique to each state. Whether a state has strong representative bodies, an independent legislature, a democratic political process, or a liberal political culture will influence the type of revenue strategy adopted by its rulers. Exogenous factors such as military threats from foreign competitor states also

---

2. Dall W. Forsythe, *Taxation and Political Change in the Young Nation, 1781–1833* (New York: Columbia University Press, 1977), 1.

influence the revenue strategy of rulers. Complicating the equation is the wide variety of methods that states potentially can use to extract revenue from society. These range from outright conquest (plunder and pillage), to more subtle forms of revenue extraction such as tribute, colonialism, imperialism, as well as a wide assortment of taxes, imposts, assessments, and user fees. The European monarchies relied on revenue generated by the "royal domains" (state-owned land, mineral mines, and monopolies on commodities such as salt, tobacco, and alcohol).[3] Modern states also derive revenue from state-owned industries and entrepreneurial ventures conducted for profit—some more successfully than others.[4]

Ultimately, the choice of a revenue strategy depends on the specific circumstances, history, and needs of a state. This accounts for the great variation in revenue strategies employed by states around the world. Among the states of early modern Europe such variation reflected their diverse economies, societies, populations, religions, state structures, administrative capabilities, legal systems, political institutions, and constitutions. England, for example, relied for centuries on the taxation of trade and commerce, imposing taxes on trade as it entered and exited London and its chief coastal ports, whereas postfeudal France was largely dependent on the taxation of land, agricultural produce, and its much greater population.[5] The English state in the eighteenth and nineteenth centuries adopted a revenue strategy (i.e., taxing trade and commerce) that proved to be vastly more successful and profitable than that of France, or for that matter, any other European state—much to the enduring benefit of the English nation.

---

3. The various sources of revenue of the "royal domain" are summarized in Niall Ferguson, *The Cash Nexus: Money and Power in the Modern World, 1700–2000* (Basic Books, 2001), 53–56.

4. Russia rents seats in its spacecraft to wealthy adventurers who pay hard currency to travel into space. In April 2001, American businessman Dennis Tito paid $20 million to become the world's first "space tourist," traveling aboard a Soyuz rocket to the International Space Station. Since then, four others have paid as much as $25 million for a ride into space. The cash-starved Russian Space Agency has collected no less than $100 million to date. In the United States, NASA does not rent out seats in its spacecraft, but state governments derive considerable revenue from equally suspect sources—e.g., state-owned gambling operations (e.g., lotteries). The government of the territory of Macao, which Portugal returned to China in December 1999, relies on the receipts from thirty-one casinos for 75 percent of its public revenue. Mark McDonald, "Chinese Officials Gamble," *New York Times,* January 15, 2009, A12.

5. The differences between early modern England and France with respect to population, economy, and tax revenue are summarized in John Brewer, *The Sinews of Power: War, Money, and the English State, 1688–1783* (London: Unwin Hyman, 1989), 14–21.

   The late Charles Tilly, who contributed much to our understanding of state development, argued that those European states with specific types of economies and population centers within their territories were better situated than others to extract revenue from society to finance state building and expansion.[6] Such factors contribute to explaining the significant variations in the patterns of institutional development as well as the different revenue strategies adopted by the states of Europe. Moreover, within any given state, revenue strategies necessarily change over time as institutional development progresses. For instance, the rulers of the states of medieval Europe relied on an eclectic assortment of seigniorial fees, taxes, tribute, and other revenue sources inherent to the system of feudalism that prevailed on the continent. These feudal sources of revenue provided limited revenue that soon proved inadequate as the states of Europe began to expand in the middle of the sixteenth century in response to changes in the techniques of war making and a sharp increase in the cost of weaponry. The rapid expansion in military capacity forced rulers to scramble to secure new sources of revenue to support their larger armies, more expensive armaments, and expanded state apparatus. To the extent that rulers were able to devise new revenue strategies to secure that additional revenue, state expansion progressed. Where they could not, state development stalled.

   The vital connection between revenue and state development was recognized by such prominent social theorists of the early twentieth century as Max Weber, Joseph Schumpeter, and Otto Hintze. Their seminal insights have been refined by contemporary social theorists investigating the relationship between public finance and political development in specific case studies.[7] For example, in a comparative study of the so-called petro-states, Terry Karl associates the pattern of failed and dysfunctional politics characteristic of these states with the unique source of revenue on

---

6. The argument was most completely advanced in Charles Tilly, *Coercion, Capital, and European States: AD 990–1990* (Cambridge, MA: B. Blackwell, 1990); see also Tilly, "Reflections on the History of European State-Making," in *The Formation of National States in Western Europe,* ed. Charles Tilly (Princeton: Princeton University Press, 1975), 3–83.

7. Michael Shafer shows the linkage between "one-sector political economies" and state autonomy in Third World nations: copper mining in Zambia, coffee growing in Costa Rica, and tea production in Sri Lanka. D. Michael Shafer, *Winners and Losers: How Sectors Shape the Development Prospects of States* (Ithaca: Cornell University Press, 1994). Shafer argues that the dominant economic sector in these nations inhibits the development of state institutions by limiting the scope of decision making for political elites.

which they are dependent: "The origin of a state's revenues reveals the links among modes of economic development, the transformation of political institutions, the shaping of preferences, and, ultimately, the capacity of states to design or alter their development trajectories."[8] In this one sentence, Karl perfectly summarizes the connection between revenue and state development. Following Karl's example, my objective in this book is to elucidate the linkages between the sources of public revenue available to the American state at specific junctures of its history, the revenue strategies pursued by its political leaders in response to these factors, and the consequential impact of their revenue strategies on the development of the American state.

If revenue is vital to state development, extracting that revenue from society is extraordinarily difficult, and not every state can do it successfully. The ability of a state to sustain itself economically should never be taken for granted. As Gabriel Ardant warns: "We cannot understand the history of the state if we are not convinced of the idea that taxation is a very difficult operation, even under a good administration, and that this difficulty has always weighed heavily upon the state."[9] The burden is so great that many states fail in the endeavor and collapse under the strain. In his sweeping study of social revolution, Jack Goldstone concludes that the inability of a state to raise enough revenue to satisfy its domestic obligations (thereby triggering a "state financial crisis") is one of three prerequisites to social revolution and the collapse of state institutions.[10] Revenue scarcity attributable to an unsuccessful revenue strategy contributed to the collapse of the former Soviet Union—once a global superpower (at least, militarily) and today a retrenched national entity (Russia) largely dependent for revenue on its vast reserves of petroleum and natural gas. With the benefit of hindsight, we now realize that the amazing thing about the USSR was that it survived as long as it did—what with its anemic state-dominated economy, bloated bureaucracy, distended military apparatus, and overextended empire. In the final days of the Soviet Union, the revenue was simply not

---

8. Terry Lynn Karl, *The Paradox of Plenty: Oil Booms and Petro-States* (Berkeley: University of California Press, 1997), 222.

9. Gabriel Ardant, "Financial Policy and Economics Infrastructure of Modern Nations and States," in *The Formation of National States in Western Europe*, ed. Tilly, 164.

10. Jack A. Goldstone, *Revolution and Rebellion in the Early Modern World* (Berkeley: University of California Press, 1991), xxiii.

there, exacerbating the pressure on state officials and hastening the demise of the bankrupt communist regime.[11]

Implementing a successful revenue strategy is one of the most difficult and important challenges facing any ruler. Raising public revenue remains problematic even in those nations where a valuable commodity such as petroleum ("black gold") literally bubbles up from the ground. One would think that nations with abundant resources are blessed and destined to prosper, yet economists often refer pejoratively to this condition as the "curse of natural resources." The greater a nation's reliance on exporting natural resources (petroleum, natural gas, diamonds, gold, minerals, etc.), the slower the rate of its overall economic growth.[12] At the same time, an abundance of natural resources can corrupt the politics of a nation, inducing factions to vie for control of the state apparatus and the great wealth that comes to those who hold the reins of power.[13] This has been the sad fate of countries such as Nigeria and Sudan, where oil revenue has generated an abnormally turbulent and destructive pattern of domestic politics. Even where a stable and democratic political system is already in place before natural resources are first discovered (a condition absent in Africa and the Middle East), the state apparatus acquires an excessive and debilitating dependency on natural resources (e.g., the revenue derived from petroleum production), leading to a "boom-bust" cycle for public finance as the price of oil fluctuates on world markets.[14]

---

11. Mancur Olson made a similar observation in his last published work: "By Gorbachev's time, the center was simply unable to pay its bills without printing a lot of new money, and in the very last days of the Soviet Union virtually no resources at all were passed on to the Soviet government. The regimes that in Stalin's time took uniquely large percentages of the national output for the state had by the end devolved to such an extent that they could not finance the basic services of government. The single most important source of the collapse of communism, I believe, was that the communist governments were broke." Mancur Olson, *Power and Prosperity: Outgrowing Communist and Capitalist Dictatorships* (New York: Basic Books, 2000), 159.

12. For a summary of the argument, see Jeffrey D. Sachs and Andrew M. Warner, "The Curse of Natural Resources," *European Economic Review* 45 (2001): 827–38.

13. "The politics of the resource curse are straightforward. The surpluses constitute a large standing temptation to grab power and to hold onto it at all costs. Take over the government of a country with energy and mineral resources and you become fabulously wealthy." Mick Moore, "Rich World, Poor World," *Boston Review* (December 2004/January 2005), 43.

14. This phenomenon is evidenced in the irregular public finances of the State of Alaska, which derives most of its revenue from petroleum taxes and royalties from drilling leases, and hence, is vulnerable to swings in the price of oil. Since the completion of the Alaska Pipeline in summer 1977, oil production has been the main source of wealth in Alaska. One third of Alaska's

The strategic choices that rulers make in response to the nearly constant demand imposed on them for revenue shape the course of state development. Simultaneously, the range of options available to political elites seeking new sources of revenue is limited by a variety of factors outside their control, including the strength of the state vis-à-vis the dominant economic interests in society, exogenous pressures exerted on the state by foreign competitors, the intended uses of revenue (e.g., it is easier to raise revenue for national defense during wartime), the nature of the economy within the state's territory (agricultural, mercantile, industrial), the extent to which democratic norms have pervaded the political sphere, as well as the relative strength of representative institutions in relation to the executive. Equally important is the quality of individual leadership. The political skills of a ruler often determine the success of a revenue strategy in practice.[15] Rulers (and their functionaries) are agents of the state and act on its behalf. Some rulers are more skilled than others and accordingly, more successful in raising revenue. But no matter how successful in implementing their strategies to raise revenue, rulers never have enough of it. The ubiquitous scarcity of resources drives rulers to relentlessly seek revenue. This is the underlying premise of Margaret Levi's model of the behavior of rulers with respect to revenue, which she evocatively refers to as "revenue predation."[16]

If, as Levi persuasively argues, all rulers behave (at least, to some extent) as revenue predators, we would expect that those rulers whose territorial domain enjoys relative economic abundance will be most successful at raising revenue. Where the domestic economy is prosperous and commerce thrives (e.g., in the United States), more revenue is potentially available

---

economic base is tied to oil production and the petroleum industry. Taxes on the oil industry have generated $50 billion for the state over the last 25 years—averaging $2 billion a year. Over the last two decades 80 percent of the revenue of the state has come from taxation of the oil industry. For fiscal year 2007, about 88 percent of Alaska's revenue (or $4.3 billion) was predicted to come from oil-related taxes and royalties. Figures from *Revenue Sources Book*, Alaska Department of Revenue, Taxation Division (fall 2006).

15. As Joel Migdal puts it, "Skillful leadership must be present to take advantage of the conditions to build a strong state." Joel S. Migdal, *Strong Societies and Weak States: State-Society Relations and State Capabilities in the Third World* (Princeton: Princeton University Press, 1988), 275.

16. Levi's theory of "predatory rule," discussed further in subsequent chapters, was first published in Margaret Levi, "A Theory of Predatory Rule," *Politics and Society* 10 (1981): 431. The analysis was refined and expanded in *Of Rule and Revenue* (Berkeley: University of California Press, 1988).

to the state than where industry is deficient. Certainly, wealthy societies offer more promising sources of public revenue than poor societies. But the relationship between societal wealth and public revenue is not so simple. Getting money out of the pockets of citizens and into state coffers remains an arduous task even for the most skilled rulers of the most wealthy nations. Prosperous economies do not automatically translate into wealthy states. Indeed, rulers often confront the strongest resistance to their predatory inclinations in the wealthiest societies, where private interests are well organized and better able to resist encroachments on their property by officials of the state. In such cases, rulers must devise even more subtle revenue strategies to extract resources from society without provoking overt resistance from powerful groups and individuals, who do not give up their wealth without resistance—certainly not without demanding something in return. In democratic states, rulers must enter into "revenue coalitions" with powerful groups and interests in society, providing benefits (e.g., protection, subsidies, or favored status) in return for their revenue contributions.

How then do rulers forcibly extract revenue without upsetting the delicate balance between state and society? This is a tricky business. In modern democratic states, rulers rely on taxes as the primary source of public revenue. Taxation is but one of countless methods used to raise revenue; however, it has proven to be the most efficient and effective for extracting great quantities of revenue from prosperous economies. In particular, taxation provides a highly practical method for raising revenue in democratic states, whose political leaders are limited in their use of the most extreme and overtly coercive manifestations of state power to extract revenue from society—a less imposing constraint for the rulers of absolutist states. For this reason, taxation has surpassed and supplanted all other modes of revenue extraction in democratic states. But there are limits to the state's power of taxation—for democratic governments as well as absolutists. Recall, from the perspective of a *rational* revenue predator, the goal is to extract as much money as possible from the pockets of private businesses and citizens without provoking excessive political opposition or, in the worse-case scenario, overt rebellion. Jean-Baptiste Colbert, the French minister of finance under Louis XIV who built the fiscal foundation for the French mercantile state, allegedly once said, "The art of taxation consists in so plucking the goose as to get the most feathers with the least possible amount of hissing." The Bourbon monarchy of eighteenth-century France and the Imperial Czars of Russia provide striking examples of rulers who faced strong external pressures on their regimes and responded by greatly increasing taxes on powerful social and economic interests.[17] In these cases, Colbert's counsel was improvidently ignored, and the extra plucking provoked the "geese" to rebellion.

In contrast to Bourbon France and Czarist Russia, the English state beginning in the eighteenth century provides a compelling example of how the "plucking" can be done discreetly so as to minimize the hissing, even while maximizing the harvest. As the English economy prospered and expanded in the decades following the Glorious Revolution of 1688, sufficient wealth was generated to satisfy the needs of *both* the state and the emerging bourgeois classes. With the introduction of the first modern systems of national taxation and public borrowing, as well as the creation of a professionalized central treasury, the burgeoning English state of the late eighteenth century devised a powerful fiscal engine to support its expanding global presence. The English state provided the English nation with a worldwide empire and an unfettered domestic economy within which to conduct business and commerce, which in turn were taxed by the state. For good reason, historians and social theorists have used the model of a "fiscal-military state" to describe the powerful combination of revenue and military powers of seventeenth-century England—the most efficient European state of its time.[18]

Today, the United States provides the foremost example of how fiscal efficiency and state power can be effectively combined. Beginning in the early twentieth century, officials of the American state replaced the national government's traditional nineteenth-century system of public revenue, based as it was on a combination of "indirect" taxation (i.e., the tariff

---

17. Both regimes succumbed to "social revolution" triggered in part by tax policies that undermined support for the regime among salient groups. These cases are discussed in Theda Skocpol, *States and Social Revolutions: A Comparative Analysis of France, Russia, and China* (New York: Cambridge University Press, 1979).

18. The model of a "fiscal-military" state was developed in Brewer, *Sinews of Power;* see also Patrick K. O'Brien and Philip A. Hunt, "The Rise of the Fiscal-Military State in England, 1485–1815," *Historical Research* 66 (1993): 129–76; Richard Bonney, ed., *The Rise of the Fiscal State in Europe, c. 1200–1815* (New York: Oxford University Press, 1999); Jan Glete, *War and the State in Early Modern Europe: Spain, the Dutch Republic and Sweden as Fiscal-Military States, 1500–1660* (New York: Routledge, 2004).

and customs duties) and federal excise taxes, with a system of broad-based progressive income taxation. The revenue flows from this highly efficient system of public finance are periodically supplemented by a sophisticated system of public borrowing that gives the American state access to international capital markets. This is the fiscal engine that sustains the modern American state, which uses the vast revenue it raises to support a powerful military apparatus as well as an elaborate system of social welfare programs that cultivates support for the regime among its citizens. How this system of public finance was used by national political leaders to finance the expansion of the American state is the main subject of this book.

In considering how the modern American state raises its revenue, we must decide whether Levi's theory of predatory rule is consistent with the behavior of American political leaders. Is it a coincidence that her comparative study focuses on the rulers and revenue policies of England, France, Australia, and ancient Rome, but not the United States? Or is it because the theory of predatory rule (and public choice theory in general) is not particularly descriptive of the erratic (almost schizophrenic) revenue policies of the rulers of the American state? As we will see, the revenue policies of a broad segment of our political leadership reflects the indigenous strain of antistate and antitax ideology that has held sway over American politics since colonial times. Even with the creation of a strong American state in the twentieth century, resistance to state building and revenue predation has not dissipated. Since the enactment of the modern income tax in 1913, the foremost goal of conservatives has been to *reduce* the tax burden on business and wealthy taxpayers rather than to extract *more* revenue from society for the American state. In recent decades, the antitax faction of the Republican Party has actively and openly campaigned to cut the flow of revenue to the central state.[19] Prominent leaders of the GOP have advocated "starving the Beast"—by which they mean cutting the tax revenue that sustains the national government.[20] The incongruity is that so many

---

19. Elsewhere, I have described the antitax ideology that permeates the Republican Party. Sheldon D. Pollack, *Refinancing America: The Republican Antitax Agenda* (Albany: State University of New York Press, 2003).

20. During the 104th Congress, House Ways and Means Committee chairman Bill Archer (Republican of Texas) declared: "I personally would like to tear the income tax out by its roots and

political leaders are dedicated to reducing the supply of revenue that sustains the American state.

Notwithstanding such efforts to "starve" the national government and a pervasive antipathy toward a strong central government, the fiscal powers of the American state have been progressively strengthened over the past two centuries. During times of war, political leaders have adopted new revenue strategies to satisfy the increased revenue needs of the American state. In the chapters that follow, I explain how this was accomplished. Only a state with independent and replenishable sources of public revenue can build strong political institutions and a powerful military. The national income tax adopted in the early twentieth century provided the American state for the first time with direct access to societal resources and a share of the great wealth generated by the domestic economy. This powerful tool of revenue extraction proved critical to the development of the American state.

Toward a Comparative Theory of State Development

The rulers of the American state, like those of all states, have struggled to extract revenue from society. As we will see, the ability of the national government to extract revenue was directly connected to the development and expansion of the military powers of the American State. Because the connection between revenue and state development was not unique to North America, scholars of American political development would do well to consider the observations and conclusions of those who have already thoroughly examined the development of the states of Europe. Among such scholars, there is a consensus that warfare and military conflict played a critical role in stimulating the development of the central state over the past five hundred years. In the fifteenth and sixteenth centuries, the states of late medieval Europe developed from weak principalities into complex political organizations exerting sovereignty over expansive territories with vast populations. During periods of sustained war, the states of early modern Europe expanded as rulers built large armies and navies to

---

throw it overboard." Quoted in Barbara Kirchheimer, "Archer Addresses Contract Compromises and Reform," *Tax Notes* 66 (February 20, 1995): 1083.

pursue their military objectives. Over time, the expanded state apparatus became a permanent and prominent feature of the European state. A wide range of studies reach much the same conclusion: war and state expansion were closely linked during this formative period of institutional development. Moreover, the evidence suggests that both state building and war making in Europe were largely a function of the state's capacity to extract revenue from society.

Exactly how are war, revenue, and state building connected? To be sure, the relationship is complex, and the causal mechanisms have not yet been fully delineated. What we have learned from the study of early modern Europe is that war creates a great impetus for state building—in particular, the expansion of the military apparatus. Furthermore, because it takes enormous revenue to wage war, rulers must adopt more aggressive revenue strategies when they go to war. As Richard Bensel has observed in his authoritative study of state building during the American Civil War: "War mobilizations compel states to extract a much larger share of a society's resources than usually collected through peacetime taxation. The resulting efforts to channel resources and manpower into war force states to exploit many more sources of revenue more completely than they would during peacetime."[21] War forces rulers to expand the revenue capacity of the state—that is, to behave more like revenue predators. Although civilian populations invariably resist efforts to increase revenue extraction, they are more likely to acquiesce to demands for increased revenue during periods of wartime crisis. Likewise, expansion of the military apparatus requires the mass mobilization of men and resources, and this is most readily accomplished by skillful rulers. The ability of rulers to mobilize and extract resources from society is severely tested during wartime. Where efforts to expand the revenue base of the state during wartime prove unsuccessful, the results can be disastrous. While the debilitating consequences of revenue failure are less obvious and immediate than those of military failures on the battlefield, they are no less fatal to the survival of a state.

While we know a good deal about the connection between war, revenue, and state building in early modern Europe, the subject has not been systematically explored by historians, sociologists, and political scientists

---

21. Richard Franklin Bensel, *Yankee Leviathan: The Origins of Central State Authority in America, 1859–1877* (Cambridge: Cambridge University Press, 1990), 96.

who study the United States. In the academy, public finance has been relegated to a separate discipline, isolated from the study of domestic politics and history, rather than integrated into the study of American political development. The study of the revenue system of the United States has been left to specialists in taxation and public finance who are much less sensitive than social scientists to questions of history, politics, and institutional development. Those who study American political institutions and public policies have focused more on how the national government *spends* its revenue than on how it *raises* that revenue. Such shortsightedness is unfortunate, as much of importance about a regime is revealed by the mechanisms used by state officials to raise public revenue.[22]

In neglecting the system of public revenue of the United States, scholars overlook one of the most important manifestations of state power as well as one of the most important factors influencing the development of the American state. The ability of national political leaders to implement a new system of public finance in the twentieth century made possible the establishment of a major global military force as well as a national system of social welfare for American citizens. Both were critical to the development of the American state. At the same time, securing this new source of revenue radically altered the balance of power between the national government and the state governments, making possible a greater centralization of political power within the federal system. In short, the revenue from this new system of public finance facilitated efforts by national political leaders to build a strong American state.

In recent decades, a new and promising field has emerged within the discipline of political science, focusing on American political development. Oddly, this new subdiscipline has evolved apart from the field of comparative political analysis and has pursued its own separate scholarly agenda. As

---

22. In his masterful study of taxation in Tudor England, Roger Schofield writes: "Taxation occupies a sensitive position in the nexus of constitutional, political and social relationships, for it is through taxation that economic resources are mobilized for political ends. But societies differ not only in the ends which they deem proper to be attained by taxation, but also constrained in the kinds of tax they can levy by the nature of their economic resources, and by the level of administrative skill. Moreover, since taxes entail compulsion, the ways in which they are authorized and organized are essentially political matters. A study of taxation, therefore, should throw light not only on the social and economic characteristics, but also on its political and administrative structure and its constitutional concepts of obligation and consent." Roger Schofield, *Taxation Under the Early Tudors 1485–1547* (Oxford: Blackwell, 2004), 201.

Ira Katznelson has observed, scholars of American political development focus on how "internal processes" such as "electoral realignments, sectionalism, and the changing balance within the federal system" have affected the development of political institutions in America, while slighting the impact of war and international affairs.[23] In doing so, they miss much of importance with respect to state development. War and international affairs played a major role in shaping state development in Europe. The goal here is to consider whether a similar influence was exerted in America. In pursuit of this objective, the theories and models of European state development will be applied to the study of American political development. Such a comparative approach has already been successfully applied in studies on state development in Latin America and Asia.[24] A similar approach will similarly enrich the study of the development of the American state. At the same time, a study of the development of the American state provides an excellent opportunity to test the theories and models generated in the European context. These need to be evaluated against a wider range of historical events and settings. Ultimately, abstract theory must be consistent with, and grounded in, history. As Michael Kimmel counsels, "An ahistorical sociology is an impoverished sociology, a sociology condemned to either grand theory or abstracted empiricism."[25] A comparative study of the development of the state can add some flesh-and-blood to the abstract theories.

Is it possible to borrow a theoretical framework from the literature on the development of the European states and apply it willy-nilly to the study

---

23. Ira Katznelson, "Rewriting the Epic of America," in *Shaped by War and Trade: International Influences on American Political Development,* ed. Ira Katznelson and Martin Shefter (Princeton: Princeton University Press, 2002), 7.

24. Miguel Centeno has applied the European model of state development in his study of the states of Latin America. Miguel Angel Centeno, *Blood and Debt: War and the Nation-State in Latin America* (University Park: Pennsylvania State University Press, 2002); see also Cameron G. Thies, "War, Rivalry, and State Building in Latin America," *American Journal of Political Science* 49 (July 2005): 451. Victoria Tin-bor Hui and Bin Wong have compared state development in early modern Europe to that of China. Victoria Tin-bor Hui, *War and State Formation in Ancient China and Early Modern Europe* (New York: Cambridge University Press, 2005); R. Bin Wong, *China Transformed: Historical Change and the Limits of European Experience* (Ithaca: Cornell University Press, 1997). Bin Wong warns of the difficulties that arise in applying models based on Europe to non-European cases such as China.

25. Michael S. Kimmel, *Absolutism and Its Discontents: State and Society in Seventeenth-Century France and England* (New Brunswick, NJ: Transaction, 1987), ix.

of American political institutions? Can models of state development based on the European experience shed light on the process of state development in America? Admittedly, there is a danger in using disparate historical examples to support or verify a causal mechanism originally observed in an entirely different historical period and region of the world. In his classic book about the social welfare systems of England and Sweden, Hugh Heclo acknowledged the difficulties in such a comparative approach: "Britain is not Sweden. Each nation is planted within its own historical stream, and while the analyst may discern common patterns of movement and current, similar declivities and obstacles, the Thames is still the Thames and not the Ume. Whatever commonalities stand out do so precisely because they are imbedded within their particular national idioms of historical expression."[26] Notwithstanding the difficulties, a comparative study of *dissimilar* cases can be highly revealing to the extent that *commonalities* (in this case, common patterns of state development) are discerned. These can be used to generate a powerful explanation of the phenomenon observed. At the same time, where similar causal mechanisms play out in different historical settings (e.g., state building in early modern Europe versus late-eighteenth-century America), we would expect the final outcomes to be quite different.[27]

Just as Britain is not Sweden, America in the late eighteenth century was not early modern Europe. Social, economic, and political conditions differed dramatically across the two continents and over the span of centuries. For one thing, as political elites in late-eighteenth-century America self-consciously devised the outline of a new constitutional framework, they already had before them the example of the European nation-state, with its centralized executive power, educated civil servants, permanent bureaucracy, and professional standing army. Yet those who designed the American state expressly did not wish to emulate the European state

---

26. Hugh Heclo, *Modern Social Politics in Britain and Sweden: From Relief to Income Maintenance* (New Haven: Yale University Press, 1974), 17.

27. "The challenge of the paired comparisons of uncommon cases is to unearth how similar mechanisms of change combine differently with varying environmental conditions in distinctive trajectories of historic change." Doug McAdam, Sidney Tarrow, and Charles Tilly, *Dynamics of Contention* (New York: Cambridge University Press, 2001), 83. The authors argue for "paired comparisons of uncommon cases" to investigate radically dissimilar outcomes as opposed to the more traditional "common foundations" approach.

with respect to its organization, structure, or powers. To the contrary, they sought to steer a new course and avoid replicating the European state in North America. With few exceptions (most prominently, Alexander Hamilton), those who gathered in Philadelphia in 1787 envisioned a new central state of limited powers. It was no coincidence that political leaders adopted weak national political institutions—that was the preference of a majority of the delegates to the Constitutional Convention. Even those who championed strengthening the powers of the national government vis-à-vis the states, as well as in comparison to that of the deficient Confederacy, were not proponents of building a powerful central state in the tradition of continental Europe. Even the most ardent nationalists sought to build a state with extraordinarily limited powers by the standards of late-eighteenth-century Europe.[28] In the end, the American state that the delegates designed through a collective process of compromise and negotiation preserved an unprecedented degree of political power at the local level. This made for a very different state in America than that found in Europe. The great irony is that the American state they built eventually became more powerful than the mighty states of Europe they so feared and despised.

Another fundamental difference between state building in Europe and the United States was timing. State building commenced much later in America than in Europe. This affected how the American state was organized and the nature of the state that emerged. Representative institutions and democratic mores were already firmly established in America *before* the central state developed. This is precisely the opposite of what happened in Europe, where democracy took root *after* strong central states had already emerged. On the continent, there were strong nation-states before there were democratic institutions such as elections, universal suffrage, and party competition. As Aristide Zolberg notes, "Whereas previous great powers achieved that status before the age of liberal democracy, and by and large managed to insulate their externally oriented decision-making

---

28. The authors of *The Federalist Papers* proclaimed that they had discovered a new "science of politics." Alexander Hamilton, Paper No. 9, in Madison, Hamilton, and Jay, *Federalist Papers,* 72. This new science of politics was put to good use in devising a unique constitutional system for the American Republic—one that would check the powers of the state rather than consolidate them, as had occurred in Europe.

apparatus from the pressures of accountability, the United States rose to global leadership well after accountability was institutionalized."[29] This different sequencing of events in America (i.e., democracy preceding state development) resulted in a very different kind of state—one that is internally weak (i.e., in exerting its powers within its territories) even as it is externally strong (vis-à-vis other states).

Critical decisions made by political leaders in America at the time of the founding also affected the subsequent course of institutional development, taking America down a different path than Europe. Douglass North has argued that seemingly minor differences in "institutions" (by which he means the "rules of the game," including formal legal systems as well as informal custom and culture) can explain disparate outcomes in long-term development—for instance, the profound differences between England and Spain that emerged in the seventeenth century with respect to economic performance.[30] In recent years, social scientists have applied North's observations on economic development to a wider array of social phenomenon, including political development. Paul Pierson translates North's theory into the basic recognition that institutional development is subject to "positive feedback." This is the underlying premise of so-called path dependence theory, which holds that initial decisions can have a critical impact on subsequent development.[31] Positive feedback and path dependence are particularly useful concepts in explaining comparative state development—for instance, the differences between state building in America and Europe. As path dependence theory would predict, the initial choices made at the formative stage in the development of the American state were magnified over time, resulting in unique institutions a century

29. Aristide R. Zolberg, "International Engagement and American Democracy: A Comparative Perspective," in *Shaped by War and Trade*, 30.

30. This issue is addressed in Douglass C. North, *Institutions, Institutional Change, and Economic Performance* (New York: Cambridge University Press, 1990), 115–16.

31. Pierson suggests that path dependence explains those "patterns of institutional emergence, persistence, and change that may be of the greatest significance for the social sciences." Paul Pierson, *Politics in Time: History, Institutions, and Social Analysis* (Princeton: Princeton University Press, 2004), 27. Pierson draws connections between positive feedback and path dependence theory in "When Effect Becomes Cause: Policy Feedback and Political Change," *World Politics* 45 (July 1993): 595–628; "Increasing Returns, Path Dependence, and the Study of Politics," *American Political Science Review* 94 (June 2000): 251–67; "Not Just What, but When: Timing and Sequence in Political Processes," *Studies in American Political Development* 14 (2000): 72–92.

later. Such choices cannot be easily reversed at later stages of development, even where there is strong political will in favor of such a course of action.[32] In America, state building went down a distinct path in the late eighteenth century when the founders adopted a highly decentralized federal structure. Because of this decision, would-be state builders in the nineteenth century found it extraordinarily difficult to change direction and build a strong state. Federalism took America down a path from which it could not retreat.

Notwithstanding the significant differences between Europe and America, many of the same causal mechanisms that produced the European state can be observed in America. After all, political leaders in America in the late eighteenth century faced much the same problems as rulers in Europe—for example, the need to build a stronger army and navy, establish more effective administrative offices, maintain public order by suppressing "private violence," and secure the revenue necessary to finance all of these state activities. Over time, the same causal mechanisms produced a strong American state, just as they did in Europe. Ironically, despite the long-term trend toward state expansion, many political leaders did not want to build a strong state in America. Enjoying relative isolation from Europe and its military conflicts, the local state governments sufficed most of the time. During decades of peace and domestic tranquility, there was no need for a large standing army. But the golden age of statelessness was interrupted by the Civil War, as national political leaders were forced to build a more powerful military apparatus and the basic trappings of an administrative state to cope with the systemic crisis that faced the regime. Even then, the fiscal-military colossus built in the North during the war was dismantled soon after the conflict ended. Not until America entered the First World War more than fifty years later was a strong state needed again. And once again, the wartime apparatus was dismantled with the return of peace and prosperity in the 1920s. In short, the prevailing pattern of

---

32. As Margaret Levi puts it: "Path dependence has to mean, if it is to mean anything, that once a country or region has started down a track, the costs of reversal are very high. There will be other choice points, but the entrenchments of certain institutional arrangements obstruct an easy reversal of the initial choice." Margaret Levi, "A Model, a Method, and a Map: Rational Choice in Comparative and Historical Analysis," in *Comparative Politics: Rationality, Culture, and Structure,* ed. Mark I. Lichbach and Alan S. Zuckerman (New York: Cambridge University Press, 1997), 19–21, esp. 28.

state development in America was one of wartime expansion followed by peacetime retrenchment. It was only with America's entry into the Second World War that the centralization of fiscal and military powers became a permanent feature of the American state. This reconstituted American state possesses the capacity to make global war and extract enormous revenue from society to sustain itself.

The plan of this book is as follows. As a preliminary matter, the seminal theories of state development are surveyed in chapter 1. The starting point is Max Weber's authoritative definition of the state as that organization in society with a legitimate monopoly on violence within its territory. Weber's concept of the state as an instrument of coercion has permeated the social sciences and is central to this comparative study of state development in Europe and America. From this perspective, the state is viewed not as an "arena" in which private interest groups or social classes compete for control of the reins of government, but rather as an autonomous (or in the parlance of the state-centered theorists, "relatively autonomous") political organization that possesses coercive powers. With varying degrees of success, state officials use the coercive powers of the state ("state power") to impose policy preferences on groups, social classes, and private individuals. This includes the revenue strategies of the rulers of the state. The central argument of this book is that state autonomy ultimately depends on the state's fiscal powers—its capacity to extract revenue from society.

In chapter 2, the focus is on the development of the early modern European state. The main theories advanced by contemporary scholars to explain the development of the European state are reviewed. Their foremost conclusion is that war was the primary stimulus for state development in Europe. State development in early modern Europe was largely a response to the nearly continual geomilitary competition that engulfed the continent beginning in the late fourteenth and early fifteenth centuries. Constant warfare resulted in an expansion of the apparatus of the European states. At the same time, rulers required increased revenue to make war and build stronger states. War, revenue, and state development were intimately connected in early modern Europe.

The historic transformation of the military state into a social welfare state is recounted in chapter 3. Beginning in the late nineteenth century, the states of Western Europe assumed a function beyond their traditional military role—that of providing income-maintenance and retirement programs for industrial workers. After the First World War, the initial system of benefits for workers was expanded to cover all citizens. The modern social welfare state with its origins in Western Europe was subsequently emulated by other democratic industrial nations across the globe, including the United States. At the same time, modern states must maintain military forces in the face of persistent geomilitary competition. An enormous financial burden is imposed on those states that maintain both powerful military forces and generous social welfare programs. Where that financial burden is met, the political regime enjoys enhanced legitimacy, stability, and prosperity.

Beginning with chapter 4, the focus shifts from Europe to America. In the remaining chapters of this book, I trace the development of the American state to reveal the connection between institutional development and the sources of revenue available to the leaders of the national government at various stages in its history. The founding of the American state was instigated by political leaders who wished to establish a new political order in North America. To achieve independence from Britain, the leaders of the thirteen colonies formed a military alliance under the command of a central political authority. This was the first successful effort at state building in America. In chapter 5, the deficiencies of the regime they established are examined, especially with regard to the anemic fiscal and military powers of the national government of the Confederacy of the United States of America. The reasons behind the initial adoption of a federal constitutional structure are considered. The deficient fiscal and military powers of the early American state were attributable to the design flaws of the first constitution of the republic, the Articles of Confederation.

Chapter 6 tells the story of how political leaders reconstituted the American state in 1787 by drafting a new constitution. The national government they designed was granted additional powers by the state governments and, as a result, was better able to extract revenue from society. With a more secure fiscal foundation, the American state achieved greater state capacity, especially during periods of war. Nevertheless, it took many decades for political leaders to realize the full potential inherent in the new constitutional design. As in Europe, war played an important role in stimulating the development of the American state.

The relationship between war, revenue, and state development in America is explored in chapter 7. During the Civil War, political leaders built the first strong American state. While much of the enhanced institutional apparatus was dismantled after the Civil War, the wartime experience with state building and aggressive revenue extraction was not lost on subsequent generations of political leaders. The institutional innovations of the 1860s were resurrected during the First World War, when the income tax emerged as the primary source of revenue for the federal government. A similar pattern of state expansion prevailed during the Second World War. The tax system employed by the postwar American state can be traced to the innovations adopted during the wartime crisis of the 1940s.

The fiscal organization of the modern American state is the subject of chapter 8. Beyond its traditional military role, the national government of the United States now performs a wide variety of social welfare functions, including providing income maintenance benefits to retired workers and healthcare benefits to the poor and elderly. It takes enormous revenue to sustain these programs. To raise such revenue, the national government relies on the income tax and the Social Security wage tax. Modern democratic states such as the United States no longer engage in plundering, empire-building, colonization, or imperialism to raise revenue. The high protective tariffs that once financed the American state were abandoned in favor of free trade. The modern American state is a "tax state" that operates a benign form of a "protection racket"—collecting "tribute" in the form of income taxation and in return providing such public goods as protection from criminals and foreign invaders, free markets, a stable currency, and the "rule of law" (e.g., recourse to law courts to enforce contracts).

With an annual budget of more than $3 trillion, spending by the national government perennially exceeds its receipts. For decades, the national government state has operated at a deficit, relying on foreign investment and loans to make up its annual budget shortfalls. One result is a staggering accumulated national debt. The American state faces a massive unfunded liability arising from its long-term commitments under Social Security, Medicare, Medicaid, military pensions, and other so-called entitlement programs. New spending programs enacted to prop up the domestic economy and financial markets have added to the budget deficit. Given this unwieldy national debt, how fiscally secure is the American state? This book concludes by pondering whether this fiscal imbalance is likely to impede the future development of the American state.

1

THE STATE

Coercion and Tribute

A state is a human community that (successfully) claims the *monopoly of the legitimate use of physical force* within a given territory.

—Max Weber, *Politics as a Vocation* (1921)

The history of state revenue is the history of the evolution of the state.

—Margaret Levi, *Of Rule and Revenue* (1988)

The state is the dominant form of political organization in the world today. As Pratap Bhanu Mehta observes, "The state, for good or for ill, emerged as a decisive form of political organization in the modern world, eclipsing its rivals such as empires, federations, city states, republics."[1] How did the state come to dominate the world of nations? Over time, the state proved the most efficient form of political organization in making war and extracting wealth from society. That wealth was used to build powerful armies and navies, which in turn, were used to protect and nurture the state apparatus. The state is a powerful combination of fiscal and military organization. There are few, if any, places left on the earth where states do not exercise control over the most vital aspects of human life. Only the most primitive societies have done without some sort of state, and there are

---

1. Pratap Bhanu Mehta, *The Burden of Democracy* (New Delhi: Penguin Books India, 2003), 105–6.

few, if any, stateless societies left in the world today. Most are dominated by state organizations.

Among states themselves, there is enormous variation. Some are strong and efficient while others are weak and barely capable of carrying out the most basic functions of government. What forces account for such differences among states? What forces promote state development? These questions are of fundamental importance to those who study political and social institutions. Hence, I begin this study of the development of the American state by reviewing the academic literature on state development—in particular, that rooted in the study of the Europe state. Notwithstanding their Eurocentric focus, these theories provide a conceptual framework that can be usefully applied to a study of the development of the American state. The assumption is that, despite the significant differences between Europe and North America, the development of the American state can be understood in much the same analytical terms used to explain the development of the states of Europe. A comparative approach allows us to draw out and contrast the differences as well as the commonalities between state development in Europe and America.

The State in Political Analysis

Ironically, in the decades following the Second World War (the most monumental and deadly clash of nation-states in history), political scientists lost sight of the state in the study of politics. The tendency was less pronounced in fields such as international relations and comparative politics, where the state generally remained central. But overall, the trend was clear and pervasive. As one prominent theorist lamented in the 1960s: "The concept of the state is not much in vogue in the social sciences right now."[2] That was

---

2. J. P. Nettl, "The State as a Conceptual Variable," *World Politics* 20 (1968): 559. Nettl attributed the absence of the concept of the state in contemporary political analysis to the relative "statelessness" (i.e., weak state institutions) of the United States. According to Stephen Krasner: "From the late 1950s until the mid 1970s the term state virtually disappeared from the professional academic lexicon. Political scientists wrote about government, political development, interest groups, voting, legislative behavior, leadership, and bureaucratic politics, almost everything but 'the state.'" Stephen D. Krasner, "Approaches to the State: Alternative Conceptions and Historical Dynamics," *Comparative Politics* 16 (1984): 223.

an understatement, especially in the field of American politics. Within the confines of the domestic tranquility that prevailed in the United States in the postwar era, the state was not only "out of vogue" but nearly forgotten. What mattered most was party, policy, and the pluralist political system dominated by interest group competition. Focusing on *process,* the behavioral political science of the postwar era viewed the state as a largely irrelevant concept—a "black box" on which interest groups exert pressure and public policy emerges.

Despite past indifference, in recent decades the state has been returned to its rightful place of prominence in the study of politics and society by a new generation of political scientists, sociologists, and historians intent on "bringing the state back in."[3] The state has been brought back into contemporary political analysis with a vengeance. An expanding body of scholarship employing a state-centered model has flourished since the mid-1970s. Yet even after more than three decades of this state-centered theory, we still only dimly understand how states form and develop. We know little about the preconditions for state development as well as the factors behind institutional decline.[4] Most important from the perspective of this study, we know remarkably little about the relationship between state development and public revenue. The institutional capacity of a state ultimately depends on its ability to extract revenue from society. But exactly how are state capacity and political development related to public revenue? To answer this, we need to know more about the forces that contribute to the formation and development of states.

Notwithstanding the optimistic perspective that prevailed among political scientists in the postwar decades, most scholars today believe that there

---

3. The reference is to the title of an influential collection of essays, Peter B. Evans, Dietrich Rueschemeyer, and Theda Skocpol, eds., *Bringing the State Back In* (New York: Cambridge University Press, 1985).

4. There is a substantial literature on the decline of states. See, e.g., Paul Kennedy, *The Rise and Fall of the Great Powers: Economic Change and Military Conflict from 1500 to 2000* (New York: Random House, 1987); Mancur Olson, *The Rise and Decline of Nations* (New Haven: Yale University Press, 1981); Jean-Marie Guéhenno, *The End of the Nation-State* (Minneapolis: University of Minnesota Press, 1995); Martin van Creveld, *The Rise and Decline of the State* (New York: Cambridge University Press, 1999); Jared Diamond, *Collapse: How Societies Choose to Fail or Succeed* (New York: Viking Press, 2005). For a discussion of why some states hold together while others collapse, see Joel S. Migdal, "Why Do So Many States Stay Intact?" in *State in Society: Studying How States and Societies Transform and Constitute One Another,* ed. Joel S. Migdal (New York: Cambridge University Press, 2001), 135–69.

is no singular path to political development and no simple evolutionary progression from "backwardness" to "modernity."[5] Decades ago, Lucian Pye warned that the term *political development* was used by social scientists imprecisely and often in conflicting ways.[6] His judicious warning went largely unheeded. Today, the term remains in vogue in the academic disciplines, mainly stripped of the normative implications found in the postwar literature on political modernization. In this study, the term *political development* refers to an increased differentiation of governmental functions and the maturation of specialized institutions designed and built to carry out those functions. As such, the term goes to the level of complexity of political organizations and the degree of specialization of functions performed by state officeholders and bureaucrats. Moreover, increased state development is associated with increased institutional capacity, greater central coordination of the various administrative agencies of the administrative apparatus by some form of executive, and deeper penetration of the "periphery" (the geographic hinterlands) and "society" (which includes all modes of voluntary social life, civic organizations, as well as private economic activity) by the "center" (i.e., the apparatus of the central state). This penetration is exerted by a number of means, including resource extraction (most typically, through taxes or fees imposed by the central state), regulation of economic activity, as well as all the traditional manifestations of the "police powers" of the state. State development also refers to the capacity of officials to influence or manipulate the behavior of nonstate actors (i.e., ordinary citizens) through the promulgation of rules, regulations, and public law. Developed states perform a greater number of complex functions, and as a consequence, rely on complex legal systems to enforce the rules and regulations promulgated by state functionaries. Accordingly,

---

5. Many of the older studies on the role of the state in promoting economic development remain required reading. See, e.g., A.F.K. Organski, *The Stages of Political Development* (New York: Knopf, 1965); Daniel Lerner, *The Passing of Traditional Society: Modernizing the Middle East* (Glencoe, IL: Free Press, 1958).

6. See, e.g., Lucian W. Pye, "The Concept of Political Development," *Annuals of the American Academy of Political and Social Science* 358 (1965): 1–13. Similar sentiments were expressed by Samuel Huntington: "Definitions of political development are legion." Samuel P. Huntington, "Political Development and Political Decay," *World Politics* 17 (1965): 386. Huntington distinguished between political development and modernization, defining the former as "the institutionalization of political organizations and procedures."

complex legal systems and bureaucracies are commonly associated with advanced state development.

Such a concept of state development implies a heightened ability of state officials to carry out and perform those functions assumed by the state, whatever they may be.[7] Historically, making war has been the primary activity of states, and accordingly, a proficient military run by professional military personnel under the direction of officials of the state is one robust indicator of state development. Delivering the mail, building roads, picking up garbage, and preserving public order are but a few of the more common and mundane functions performed by modern states. Most modern democratic states, especially those with developed economies, have also assumed the obligation to provide social welfare benefits to their citizens. The specific tasks assigned to state functionaries are irrelevant to this concept of state development, just as the ideological differences among different states are not relevant.[8] What matters is the capacity and success of officials in carrying out those functions that the state chooses to perform, rather than the particular functions or policies promoted by the state. McAdam, Tarrow, and Tilly refer to this as "state capacity," which they define as "the degree of control state agents exercise over persons, activities, and resources within their government's territorial-jurisdiction."[9]

State functions are invariably delegated to specific offices and agencies, and how well the functionaries in these offices and agencies perform their assigned tasks and implement those public policies (domestic and foreign) assigned to them by state officials is one measure of state capacity and

---

7. Ken Organski and Jacek Kugler referred to political development as "the capacity of the political system to carry out tasks imposed upon it by its own political elite, or other important actors, or by the pressures of the international political environment." A.F.K. Organski and Jacek Kugler, *The War Ledger* (Chicago: University of Chicago Press, 1980), 72.

8. Recall the opening line of Huntington's classic study: "The most important political distinction among countries concerns not their form of government but their degree of government." Samuel P. Huntington, *Political Order in Changing Societies* (New Haven: Yale University Press, 1968), 1. Shocking as this sounds, Huntington was not blind to the differences between liberal democracies and authoritarian regimes; those differences were simply not relevant to his immediate concern (i.e., political stability).

9. "When state capacity increases, it does so through four often-complementary processes: the replacement of indirect by direct rule; the penetration by central states of geographic peripheries; the standardization of state practices and identities, and instrumentation—growth in the means of carrying out intended policies." Doug McAdam, Sidney Tarrow, and Charles Tilly, *Dynamics of Contention* (New York: Cambridge University Press, 2001), 78.

institutional development. The bureaucracies of developed states perform a greater number of the most complicated tasks and perform them better than those of undeveloped states. Developed states possess bureaucracies that achieve a degree of autonomy in their decision making as well as the capacity to enforce their decisions on other political actors within the state and private interest groups external to the state.[10] At the same time, the capacity of state functionaries to extract revenue within the territory under their jurisdiction is an attribute of a developed state.[11] Higher levels of taxation indicate a higher level of state activity, and by implication, a greater level of institutional development.[12]

Miguel Centeno employs similar criteria to evaluate the development of the Latin American states, which are commonly portrayed as monopolistic concentrations of power that strangle democracy and civil society.[13] To the contrary, Centeno views the states of Latin American as paper tigers. Most have difficulty asserting control and dominion beyond the major population centers within their territories (i.e., the center is unable to penetrate the periphery), and most Latin American states are capable of implementing

---

10. Daniel Carpenter argues that "bureaucratic autonomy" requires the conditions of political differentiation, organizational capacity, and political legitimacy. Bureaucratic autonomy prevails when "a politically differentiated agency takes self-consistent action that neither politicians nor organized interests prefer but that they either cannot or will not overturn or constrain in the future." Autonomy is distinguished from discretion, which is afforded agencies based on their expertise in dealing with complex technical issues. Daniel P. Carpenter, *The Forging of Bureaucratic Autonomy: Reputations, Networks, and Policy Innovation in Executive Agencies, 1862–1928* (Princeton: Princeton University Press, 2001), 14–17.

11. "Political development means capacity, and capacity is dependent on political performance in two areas: penetration of the national society by central governmental elites to control as many subject/citizens as possible within the political jurisdiction of the state; and the capacity of the government to extract resources from its society.... Taxes are exact indicators of governmental presence." Organski and Kugler, *The War Ledger*, 72.

12. Organski and Kugler, *The War Ledger*, 74. The two formulated an index to measure state development based on GNP and taxes. Elsewhere, joined by Johnson and Cohen, they argued that "taxes can indeed be used as a first step in measuring the extractive capacity of the political system.... Given a state's almost limitless demand for revenues, charting the course of taxation is a plausible way of tracing at least in outline the development of the state and the rise of central power." A.F.K. Organski, Jacek Kugler, Youssef Cohen, and J. Timothy Johnson, *Births, Deaths, and Taxes: The Demographic and Political Transitions* (Chicago: University of Chicago Press, 1984), 48. During the Second World War, Great Britain allocated an astonishing 54 percent of its gross national product to national defense, while North Vietnam extracted 45 percent during the height of war in Southeast Asia. Ibid., 68.

13. Miguel Angel Centeno, *Blood and Debt: War and the Nation-State in Latin America* (University Park: Pennsylvania State University Press, 2002).

only the most rudimentary regulatory policies.[14] They perform poorly most elemental state functions, such as building infrastructure (roads, bridges, sewage plants, electricity), providing basic healthcare to citizens, and delivering the mail. At the same time, the states of Latin America historically have extracted a much smaller share of societal wealth than richer nations—taxing their economies at roughly one-third the level of the prosperous states of Western Europe, North America, and Japan. This deficiency is telling because, as Centeno puts it, "taxation is the best measure of effective political authority and institutional development, both representing and augmenting the strength of the state as measured by the capacity to enforce centralized rule on a territory and its population."[15] With limited revenue, the states of Latin America spend relatively little on their military forces, certainly less than what is required to conduct modern warfare on a large scale. Far from a "rapacious Leviathan," the Latin American state is a fiscal dwarf.

Whether in Latin America, North America, or Europe, states come in a wide variety of shapes and forms, take varied and often unique paths as they develop, and ultimately achieve different degrees of institutional development and autonomy. Different states possess to a greater or lesser degree those features commonly associated with *stateness*—in other words, the characteristics of "strong" or developed states.[16] These include more

---

14. Michael Barnett views the Egyptian state in much the same light. Often portrayed as a powerful authoritarian state, Barnett concludes that the Egyptian state is incapable of directing or organizing Egyptian society and hence, is fundamentally a weak state: "The Egyptian state is all powerful yet unable to do anything." Michael N. Barnett, *Confronting the Costs of War: Military Power, State, and Society in Egypt and Israel* (Princeton: Princeton University Press, 1992), 14. Joel Migdal explains why so many Third World states have been so ineffective in accomplishing what their leaders have attempted, despite so much planning and effort. Like Egypt, these states simply do not "work." Joel S. Migdal, *Strong Societies and Weak States: State-Society Relations and State Capabilities in the Third World* (Princeton: Princeton University Press, 1988), 9.

15. Centeno, *Blood and Debt*, 103.

16. The notion that certain characteristics of "stateness" are associated with developed or "strong" states was pursued by J. P. Nettl in his classic essay, "The State as a Conceptual Variable," *World Politics* 20 (1968): 559. Nettl's concept of stateness is often misleadingly portrayed as a ranking of states on a scale ranging from "weak" to "strong." In fact, Nettl proposed four dimensions by which states should be evaluated. The first focuses on the "institutionalization of power"; the second is the strength of the state's internal exercise of authority vis-à-vis private groups; the third is the state's status as a cultural construct; and the fourth is the capacity of the state to project itself in the international arena. For an illuminating discussion of Nettl's typology, see Ira Katznelson, "Rewriting the Epic of America," in *Shaped by War and Trade: International Influences on American*

clearly defined boundaries from society (i.e., greater institutional autonomy), highly centralized administrative offices organized under the authority of a unified executive, more specialized and complex bureaucracies with significant penetration and control over property and persons within its geographical territory, significant internal coordination of its divisions of administration, and a strong professional military under the command of the central authority of the executive.[17] The capacity of a state to extract resources from society is one robust indicator of institutional development and, at the same time, is an important factor contributing to state development. Strong states with developed political institutions and independent sources of revenue achieve a higher degree of stability and autonomy from society, and consequently, enjoy greater prospects for long-term survival.

At the other end of the spectrum from the strong states are those weak states that achieve only minimal institutional development, insubstantial centralization of power, negligible specialization of administrative function, little penetration of the periphery by the center, inadequate capacity to extract resources from society, and little autonomy from society. Undeveloped states possess in much lesser degrees those attributes commonly associated with stateness. Prominent among such weak states are the so-called confederacies, which are little more than glorified trading or defense leagues.[18] National entities with weak federal structures tend to be short-lived and for a variety of reasons either move in the direction of more

---

Political Development, ed. Ira Katznelson and Martin Shefter (Princeton: Princeton University Press, 2002), 11–14. Krasner defines a "strong state" as one able to "remake the society and culture in which it exists—to change economic institutions, values, and patterns of interaction among private groups." Stephen D. Krasner, *Defending the National Interest* (Princeton: Princeton University Press, 1978), 56.

17. Migdal argues that the "strength" of a state is a function of its "capacities to penetrate society, regulate social relationships, extract resources, and appropriate or use resources in determined ways." Migdal, *Strong Societies,* 4. Nordlinger categorizes a state as "strong" or "weak" with respect to its degree of autonomy from society. Strong states are autonomous—i.e., capable of imposing their policy preferences on society. Eric A. Nordlinger, *On the Autonomy of the Democratic State* (Cambridge: Harvard University Press, 1981), 22.

18. The confederation of island governments loosely joined together under the banner of "Solomon Islands" is commonly cited as a definitive contemporary example of a weak state. See, e.g., Peter Dauvergne, "Weak States and the Environment in Indonesia and the Solomon Islands," in *Weak and Strong States in Asia-Pacific Societies,* ed. Peter Dauvergne (Canberra, Australia: Allen and Unwin, 1998), 135–57.

centralized state organization, merge with stronger states, or else disappear altogether from the stage of history.[19]

The United States during the period of the Articles of Confederation (1777–1788) certainly belongs in this category of weak states, as the "league of friendship" established by this first constitution of the new republic was a political organization barely worthy of designation as a nation-state. As we will see, the national government of the Confederacy had incredibly limited capacity to extract revenue from society, and hence, institutional development was minimal. The Constitution of 1787 consolidated greater powers within the apparatus of the national government; however, a substantial centralization of political power and authority in the institutions of the national government did not occur until the intense period of state building experienced during the Civil War. At that time, the United States acquired a large standing army and sufficient state capacity to extract societal resources to support the expanded apparatus of the Northern state. But most of the institutional apparatus built during the Civil War was dismantled soon after the conclusion of the military conflict. Strong institutions were not revived again until the First World War. The postbellum American state of the late nineteenth century was notoriously weak, fragmented, and uniquely decentralized—an institutional arrangement that Stephen Skowronek famously described as a state of "courts and parties."[20]

State development is neither static nor unidirectional. Even strong states with highly developed and stable institutions will experience periodic shifts in the underlying coalitions that support the regime. Over time, there will be changes to the prevailing political order. A "political order" has been defined as "a constellation of rules, institutions, practices, and ideas that hang together over time...exhibiting coherence and predictability while other things change around them."[21] A political order may be "internally

---

19. The importance of external military forces in pushing weak federal structures (confederacies) toward more strongly centralized federal structures was stressed by Riker, who viewed military threats as the crucial factor in the formation of centralized federal structures. William H. Riker, *Federalism: Origin, Operation, Significance* (Boston: Little, Brown, 1964); Riker, *The Development of American Federalism* (Boston: Kluwer Academic Publishers, 1987).

20. Stephen Skowronek, *Building a New American State: The Expansion of National Administrative Capacities, 1877–1920* (New York: Cambridge University Press, 1982), 24.

21. Stephen Skowronek and Karen Orren, *The Search for American Political Development* (New York: Cambridge University Press, 2004), 14–15. Robert Lieberman defines a political order

coherent" and stable even while undergoing change. Where there is an internal conflict within a political order, it generally will be contained and resolved by the normal political processes.[22] If the conflict is not resolved, the result may be competing political orders within the territory of a single national political organization—for example, the contending political orders (and economic systems) that prevailed in the North and South in the United States throughout the nineteenth century.[23]

With notable exceptions (most prominently, the Civil War), there has been remarkable long-term stability and consistency in the political order of the United States, even while the regime has experienced constant political change. Deciphering the impact of such change on the structure of the political order is a central concern of a loose-knit group of scholars who study American political development.[24] Two prominent theorists in this subdiscipline of political science specifically equate "political development" with fundamental political change of this nature, defining the term by reference to a "durable shift in governing authority."[25] Governing authority means the exercise of control over persons and things by the state. Durable changes persist over time. This process of political change, which defines the parameters of the "normal politics" that otherwise prevails in

as a "regular, predictable, and interconnected pattern of institutional and ideological arrangements that structures political life in a given place at a given time." Robert C. Lieberman, "Ideas, Institutions, and Political Order: Explaining Political Change," *American Political Science Review* 96 (December 2002): 702.

22. Lieberman, "Ideas, Institutions, and Political Order," 702.

23. The notion of multiple political traditions (some distinctly illiberal) coexisting in America is explored in Rogers M. Smith, "Beyond Tocqueville, Myrdal and Hartz: The Multiple Traditions in America," *American Political Science Review* 87 (1993): 549–56.

24. The formative work in American political development is Skowronek's *Building A New American State*. Other important contributions include Richard F. Bensel, *Sectionalism and American Political Development, 1880–1980* (Madison: University of Wisconsin Press, 1984); Bensel, *Yankee Leviathan: The Origins of Central State Authority in America, 1859–1877* (New York: Cambridge University Press, 1990); Karen Orren, *Belated Feudalism: Labor, the Law, and Liberal Development in the United States* (Cambridge: Cambridge University Press, 1991); Martin Shefter, *Political Parties and the State: the American Historical Experience* (Princeton, Princeton University Press, 1994); Katznelson and Shefter, eds., *Shaped by War and Trade*; Elizabeth Sanders, *Roots of Reform: Farmers, Workers, and the American State, 1877–1917* (Chicago: University of Chicago Press, 1999).

25. Skowronek and Orren, *American Political Development*, 123. Skowronek and Orren use the term development to refer to fundamental political change, as opposed to the usage herein, which focuses on the level of complexity of political organizations and the degree of specialization of functions performed by state institutions.

the United States, must be carefully distinguished from the more radical forms of political change—social and political revolution.[26]

Scholars of American political development focus on the many disruptions, transitions, departures, and sudden breaks in the temporal order of the regime. In doing so, they elucidate the politics-as-usual that otherwise prevails during periods of normalcy and stability by identifying those events that set the parameters and framework of normal politics.[27] Likewise, they concentrate on the evolution of political institutions and practices over extended periods of time.[28] For this reason, an historical approach is central to the study of American political development. The *consistency* of politics over time is important, but so are the "breakpoints," which themselves display discernable patterns and cycles.[29] These breakpoints generally occur during periods of systemic crisis and can dramatically change the nature of the political system. As Stephen Krasner notes, "Crisis situations tend to become the watersheds in a state's institutional development.…During periods of crisis politics becomes a struggle over the basic rules of the game rather than allocation within a given set of rules."[30] In the absence of disruptive crisis, institutional arrangements and processes tend to persist over time and normal politics prevails. The result is interludes of stable normal politics marked by periodic crisis breakpoints—what Walter

---

26. "Social revolutions are rapid, basic transformations of a society's state and class structures; they are accompanied and in part carried out through class-based revolts from below." Political revolutions, revolts, and rebellions "transform state structures but not social structures." Theda Skocpol, *States and Social Revolutions: A Comparative Analysis of France, Russia, and China* (New York: Cambridge University Press, 1979), 4. Social revolutions are accompanied by popular uprisings initiated from below, rather than orchestrated by political elites from above. The result is social hierarchies are swept away. Ironically, the state is often *strengthened* in the wake of social revolution—as with the French, Russian, and Chinese revolutions.

27. Skowronek defines a crisis as "a sporadic, disruptive event that suddenly challenges a state's capacity to maintain control and alters the boundaries defining the legitimate use of coercion." Skowronek, *Building A New American State,* 10; see also Skowronek, "Order and Change," *Polity* 28 (fall 1995): 91–96.

28. The importance of such an historical approach to the study of political institutions is a central concern of Paul Pierson, *Politics in Time: History, Institutions, and Social Analysis* (Princeton: Princeton University Press, 2004.

29. Skowronek and Orren refer to the cyclical patterns of "breakpoints in time, that alter aspects of politics decisively from before and with far-reaching consequences for operations elsewhere later down the road." Skowronek and Orren, *American Political Development,* 10.

30. Krasner, "Approaches to the State," 234.

Dean Burnham has referred to as "punctuated equilibria."[31] This pattern has been characteristic of the long-term development of American political institutions.[32]

While political change is important, there is another dimension to political development that often is neglected. Change is but one side of the equation; political stability (or "institutional stasis") is the other. After all, political change always takes place within the context of an existing political order. As Kimberley Johnson reminds us, "While exogenous shocks such as war or economic crisis may create critical junctures in American politics and society, each of these junctures was powerfully shaped by the preceding period of so-called stasis."[33] While it is important to understand political change, we also must consider the forces that organize a political order and preserve it over time. We need to identify the forces that initially bring together men, machinery, equipment, buildings, and all the other things that comprise a state, and discern what holds together such political organizations. The first question relates to the formation of states and the second to the preservation, legitimacy, and stability of the resultant political order. Factors such as culture, religion, and political ideology are relevant to such an inquiry. In the case of the United States, its written constitution is also highly significant.

The formalistic political science of the late nineteenth and early twentieth centuries was centered around the study of the U.S. Constitution, which was understood to express the fundamental organizing principles of American

---

31. Burnham applied the metaphor of "punctuated equilibria" (which originated in the field of evolutionary biology in the early 1970s) to the study of American political development. Walter Dean Burnham, "Constitutional Moments and Punctuated Equilibria," *Yale Law Review* 108 (1999): 2237–77. According to Burnham, American politics is characterized by periods of "long-term inertia" during which "politics as usual" prevails, regularly interrupted by "concentrated bursts of change." Krasner uses the term *punctuated equilibrium* to conjure up an image of "short bursts of institutional change followed by long periods of stasis." Krasner, "Approaches to the State," 242.

32. It is common among political scientists to divide American political history into five distinct periods, with the transition from one "party system" to another marked by so-called critical elections. V. O. Key first suggested this terminology, focusing on voter realignment during decisive elections. V. O. Key Jr., "A Theory of Critical Elections," *Journal of Politics* 17 (1955): 3–18. Burnham expanded the concept of critical elections into a theory of political realignment and institutional development in *The American Party Systems: Stages of Political Development* (New York: Oxford University Press, 1967); and *Critical Elections and the Mainsprings of American Democracy* (New York: Norton, 1970).

33. Kimberley S. Johnson, *Governing the American State: Congress and the New Federalism, 1877–1929* (Princeton: Princeton University Press, 2007), 7.

politics. For good reason, the discipline moved away from such a simplistic model, eventually recognizing that politics was more than just the formal rules and procedures prescribed by the constitutional text. But we have gone too far in abandoning the Constitution as the starting point for the study of American politics, and as a result, the analysis has been diminished. To understand the American state, we must start with its written constitution, which laid down the "rules of the game" by defining the institutions and procedures that comprised the prevailing political order, as well as the decisions of the Supreme Court, which give substance to those rules. This is not trivial. In the United States, the Constitution of 1787 (and before it, the Articles of Confederation) established an institutional legacy that continues to influence state development.[34] More so than in Europe and elsewhere, the constitutional documents have played a critical role in defining the political institutions, offices, and procedures that comprise the American state and the prevailing political order.[35]

Scholars of American political development view *all* significant political change as political development. From this perspective, institutional "retrenchment" (or contraction) is political development just as much as the expansion of the state apparatus. Likewise, the democratization of the political order originally established by the Constitution of 1787 constitutes political development. A change in the rules and procedures of politics producing a more democratic political order is political development even if state capacity is unchanged. In contrast, the main focus in this study is on political change that results in an *expansion* of state capacity and *stronger* (rather than more democratic) institutions. Moreover, expanded state capacity is specifically associated here with greater military power (i.e., large standing armies) and an enhanced capacity to extract resources from society. Admittedly, such a conception of state development is limited and

---

34. How the Constitution established an institutional legacy that informs contemporary American politics is illustrated by the decision of the founders to adopt a scheme of government in which the executive and legislative branches are separated rather than joined (as in a parliamentary system). As a result, the relationship between the president and Congress is marred by contention and disharmony at the very center of government.

35. An excellent example of how to study the interaction between the Constitution and political history is Michael Vorenberg, "Bringing the Constitution Back In: Amendment, Innovation, and Popular Democracy During the Civil War," in *The Democratic Experiment: New Directions in American Political Development,* ed. Meg Jacobs, William J. Novak, and Julian E. Zelizer (Princeton: Princeton University Press, 2003), 53–54.

ignores such important issues as representation, democratization, electoral competition, the party system, and the dynamic interplay between the separate branches of government. While critical to any comprehensive understanding of American politics, such concerns are outside the scope of this study.

Theories of State Development: Structure and Leadership

Notwithstanding the different paths to institutional development experienced in Europe and America, all states possess certain common features that lie at the heart of the concept of stateness. To the extent that states possess such common features, it is likely that they will display common patterns of development. Indeed, it would be highly unlikely that each and every state would undergo its own unique pattern of institutional development independent of all other states. For all the talk of "American exceptionalism," the American state is a political organization that displays much the same institutional attributes as all other modern states, including those of Europe.[36] For this reason, a comparative analysis is the ideal approach for revealing the basic commonalities that all states possess as large bureaucratic political organizations. These may be discerned through a careful examination of the structures and development of individual states, revealing reoccurring patterns. Focusing on a group of states situated within a single geographical area and time period (for instance, the states of early modern Europe) can increase the chance of discerning common patterns of state development. At the same time, there is no reason why states outside a particular group (e.g., non-European states) will not possess similar attributes and exhibit similar patterns of development. The development of

---

36. There is an extensive literature on the alleged exceptionalism of America. See, e.g., Ian Tyrrell, "American Exceptionalism in an Age of International History," *American Historical Review* 96 (1991): 1031–55; Byron E. Shafer, ed., *Is America Different?: A New Look at American Exceptionalism* (Oxford: Clarendon Press, 1991); Michael Kammen, "The Problem of American Exceptionalism: A Reconsideration," *American Quarterly* 45 (March 1993); Seymour Martin Lipset, *American Exceptionalism: A Double Edged Sword* (New York: W. W. Norton, 1996). For a critique of the notion of exceptionalism, see Aristide R. Zolberg, "How Many Exceptionalisms?" in *Working-Class Formation: Nineteenth-Century Patterns in Western Europe and the United States,* ed. Ira Katznelson and Aristide R. Zolberg (Princeton: Princeton University Press, 1986), 397–455.

the American state can be studied with the same analytical tools and models used to explain the states of Europe.

In pursuing a comparative approach, the goal is not to formulate a universal theory of state development, and given the wide variation among states, there is little likelihood of success if that were attempted. As Jon Elster argues, "Progress in the social sciences does not lie in the construction of general theories.... The aim of such theories—to establish general and invariable propositions—is and will always remain an illusory dream. Despite a widespread belief to the contrary, the alternative to nomological thinking is not merely descriptive or narrative ideographic method. Between the two extremes there is place and need for the study of mechanisms."[37] Thus the goal is to identify the basic attributes of states as political organizations and reveal the primary "mechanisms" of state development. Mechanisms may be defined as "frequently occurring and easily recognizable causal patterns" that are "intermediate between laws and descriptions."[38] We seek to identify frequently occurring patterns with respect to state development, recognizing that we will fall short of generating a universal law. Mechanisms fall into the middle range between universal laws and descriptive case studies.

Regarding state development, the relevant mechanisms are the processes by which states become more centralized political organizations, build more powerful bureaucracies and militaries, penetrate deeper into society via regulation, extract greater revenue from society, extend their jurisdiction and authority over territories, regulate private economic activity, and generally become more powerful organizations. Discerning such a mechanism requires an understanding of how rulers (political actors) acquire the revenue necessary to finance state activities such as maintaining public order, building roads, providing social welfare benefits, and raising armies and navies. In doing so, we seek to avoid the problems commonly

---

37. Jon Elster, *Political Psychology* (New York: Cambridge University Press, 1993), 2–3.

38. Jon Elster, "A Plea for Mechanisms," in *Social Mechanisms: An Analytical Approach to Social Theory,* ed. Peter Hedstrøm and Richard Swedberg (Cambridge: Cambridge University Press 1998), 45–73. Elsewhere, Elster suggests that a "mechanism provides a continuous and contiguous chain of causal or intentional links." Jon Elster, *Explaining Technical Change: A Case Study in the Philosophy of Science* (Cambridge: Cambridge University Press, 1983), 24. Paul Pierson convincingly argues that revealing "mechanisms" ought to be the goal of social science analysis. Paul Pierson, *Politics in Time,* 5–6, 99.

associated with a structural model of state development. Structural explanations of state development often can be reduced to an assertion that specific structural conditions produce specific political outcomes. But structures only create a set of constraints and opportunities for action; they do not lead to a single predetermined outcome or set of policy preferences. No single set of economic or social factors will consistently produce a specific type or pattern of state development.

Elster and like-minded critics lament the overly deterministic and mechanical models of causality inherent in structuralism.[39] They stress that structural models leave little room for individual leadership (i.e., human actions and intentions), which plays a critical role in determining how the mechanisms of state development work.[40] Structuralism and structural explanations ignore the *intentionality* of human behavior, which is to say, the role of humans in making their own history. Youssef Cohen, a perceptive critic of structural explanations, argues that "structural explanations assume that socio-economic and political structures determine preferences and action, which is to assume that structures can explain political outcomes directly, without reference to intentional phenomena such as values, beliefs, ideas, attitudes, intentions, and strategic thinking."[41] Following Cohen's advice, the plan here is to incorporate "intentional phenomena" into the analysis of the development of the American state by focusing on "rulers" (or more properly, political leaders) and their strategies for expanding the powers of the national government—specifically, the military and revenue-extraction powers of the American state. Political leaders manage state building, direct war making, and devise the revenue strategies that sustain the apparatus of the state. Therefore, to explain the development

---

39. For a critique of structuralism, see Margaret Levi, *Of Rule and Revenue* (Berkeley: University of California Press, 1988), 184–204; Gabriel A. Almond, "The Return to the State," *American Political Science Review* 82 (1988): 853–74; Michael Taylor, "Rationality and Revolutionary Collective Action," in *Rationality and Revolution,* ed. Michael Taylor (Cambridge: Cambridge University Press, 1988), 63–97; Youssef Cohen, *Radicals, Reformers, and Reactionaries: The Prisoner's Dilemma and the Collapse of Democracy in Latin America* (Chicago: University of Chicago Press, 1994), 9–22; Lieberman, "Ideas, Institutions, and Political Order," 697–712.

40. Barbara Geddes complains that we confront "a choice between systemic structuralist arguments that lack plausible individual-level foundations and plausible individual-level explanations that lack theoretical reach." Barbara Geddes, *Politician's Dilemma: Building State Capacity in Latin America* (Berkeley: University of California Press, 1994), 6.

41. Cohen, *Radicals, Reformers, and Reactionaries,* 3.

of the American state, we must take into account the "values, beliefs, ideas, attitudes, intentions, and strategic thinking" of its political leaders.

Weber's Concept of the State

What are the fundamental attributes of the state? According to Max Weber's seminal definition, the state is that organization defined by reference to its successful claim to a monopoly on legitimate "violence" (i.e., coercive force) exercised within the confines of its geographical territory. This claim to a legitimate monopoly on violence is the fundamental characteristic of the state, which differentiates it from all other organizations: "A compulsory political association with continuous organization will be called a 'state' if and in so far as its administrative staff successfully upholds a claim to the *monopoly* of the *legitimate* use of physical force in the enforcement of its order."[42] In so referring to the "organization" of the state, Weber meant something more than physical infrastructure, although that certainly is one important aspect of a state—the buildings, equipment, machinery, and armaments that comprise the apparatus of the state. Persons act on behalf of the state (as its agents) and organize its institutions and, thus, are also part of the state.[43] Indeed, we may define *state power* as the exercise of the coercive powers of the state by rulers, officials, and functionaries over nonstate

---

42. Max Weber, "The Fundamental Concepts of Sociology" (1913), in Max Weber, *The Theory of Social and Economic Organization* (New York: Free Press, 1947), 154. In an essay widely read in translation by American academics in the 1960s and 1970s, Weber referred to the modern state as a "compulsory association which organizes domination." Max Weber, "Politics as a Vocation," in *From Max Weber: Essays in Sociology,* ed. H. H. Gerth and C. Wright Mills (New York: Oxford University Press, 1946), 82. Questions of legitimacy were integral to Weber's analysis but are left largely unexamined in this study.

43. Peter Steinberger offers an analogy to help us grasp the nature of the state as a complex organization. Peter J. Steinberger, *The Idea of the State* (New York: Cambridge University Press, 2004), 17. Steinberger suggests that we think of an organization with which most of us are familiar—a university. A university (say, "Cornell") is comprised of buildings, libraries, equipment, etc. It includes students, faculty, administrators, and workers. Over time, buildings are torn down and replaced, and individuals leave. Despite such changes, we still refer to this organization as Cornell, even if none of the original building or persons remain. This is because Cornell is distinct from the buildings and persons that occupy it at any given moment—just as the American state is more than the sum of its buildings, political institutions, and leaders. Furthermore, as with states, it takes considerable revenue to build strong universities.

actors within the territory claimed by the state.[44] As Gianfranco Poggi puts it, the state is "best seen as a complex set of institutional arrangements for rule operating through the continuous and regulated activities of individuals acting as occupants of offices. The state, as the sum total of such offices, reserves to itself the business of rule over territorially bounded society."[45]

Social scientists have widely embraced the Weberian concept of the state, which views the state as a "complex set of institutional arrangements" for exercising coercion within a given territory. Charles Tilly defined states as "coercion-wielding organizations that are distinct from households and kinship groups and exercise clear priority in some respects over all other organizations within substantial territories."[46] According to Alfred Stepan, the state is "the continuous administrative, legal, bureaucratic and coercive system that attempts not only to manage the state apparatus but to structure many crucial relations within civil and political society."[47] Theda Skocpol views the state as a "set of administrative, policing, and military organizations" headed by an executive authority that *imposes* at least some decisions on nonstate actors.[48] Through the exercise of state power, the state *dominates* other groups and organizations in society (families, tribes, clans, churches, multinational corporations, etc.) and *pacifies* individuals living within its territory. It is not always successful in this endeavor, but the essence of the state as an organization of coercion lies in its ability to exert a monopoly on violence within its territory. States use their monopolistic powers of coercion to extract revenue from society, which is used to sustain and grow the state apparatus. Without that revenue, the state "withers."

The great English philosopher Thomas Hobbes infamously depicted the fate of societies that lack a state with a monopoly on violence, and in doing

---

44. Philip Gorski defines state power as the "capacity to defend and expand sovereign territory and govern the human and natural resources within it." Philip S. Gorski, *The Disciplinary Revolution: Calvinism and the Rise of the State in Early Europe* (Chicago: University of Chicago Press, 2003), 35.

45. Gianfranco Poggi, *The Development of the Modern State: A Sociological Introduction* (Stanford: Stanford University Press, 1978), 1. In Weber's own words, the state is a "compulsory association with a territorial basis." Weber, *Fundamental Concepts of Sociology,* 156.

46. Charles Tilly, *Coercion, Capital, and European States: AD 990–1990* (Cambridge, MA: B. Blackwell, 1990), 1. Migdal states: "Our view of the state, then, corresponds to Max Weber's notion of the state as institutional—an organization enforcing regulations, at least in part through a monopoly of violence." Migdal, *Strong Societies,* xiii.

47. Alfred Stepan, *Rethinking Military Politics* (Princeton: Princeton University Press, 1988), 4.

48. Theda Skocpol holds that "the administrative and coercive organizations" of the state constitute the basis of "state power." Skocpol, *States and Social Revolutions,* 29.

so, made the case for a strong state. In his great work, *Leviathan* (1651), Hobbes delineated the causal mechanisms by which the "state of nature" degenerates into a "state of war" in the absence of a strong state. The tragic consequences of such a failure of political institutions have been repeatedly witnessed throughout history—for instance, in Lebanon during its bloody civil war and in regions of Columbia and Mexico, where private militias and powerful criminal organizations fueled by enormous revenue generated by the illicit drug trade have effectively usurped the powers of the central state. The Italian state has long struggled to exert sovereignty (i.e., a monopoly on violence) on the island of Sicily, resulting in a virtual state of war. The central government in Islamabad does not exercise authority in the remote mountainous regions of western Pakistan. Much the same is true in Afghanistan, Somalia, and Iraq, where fledgling central governments lack the state capacity and military might to successfully exert a "monopoly on violence" throughout their territories. The authority of these states barely extends beyond the boundaries of their capital cities. In the absence of a strong state, private militiamen and bandits wreck havoc on civilian populations.

In reality, no state ever achieves a complete monopoly on violence. Everywhere, the center struggles to exert control over the periphery. Maintaining a monopoly on violence is a daunting task. At best, the state will attain status as the *primary* locus of power within its territory, even while *secondary* loci of power invariably survive the formation of the state and persist within social and economic substructures. As Anthony Giddens explains, "It is almost always the case that significant elements of actual or potential military power exist outside the control of the central state."[49] In the initial stages of its development, the state must subdue and pacify powerful organizations, interests, and individuals within society. Later, ordinary criminals must be subdued. This requires the creation of a domestic police force and the entire system of social control and punishment implemented through the prison system.[50] The process of pacification and subjugation

---

49. Anthony Giddens, *The Nation-State and Violence* (Berkeley: University of California Press, 1987), 57.

50. Domestic police forces are a relatively late innovation. The first national police force in France was not established until the 1760s and consisted of only 3,000 men in a nation of 26 million. Creveld, *Rise and Decline of the State,* 166. In the late eighteenth century, a police force of 300 men preserved public order in Vienna. In the nineteenth century, local and national police forces emerged in Europe under the authority of civilian (not military) command. Michael Mann, *The*

can take centuries, as it did in Europe. Truth be told, the process is never complete.

State formation is the process of subduing society and, at the same time, reaching accommodation with the most powerful interests and organizations in society, which must acquiesce in their own subjugation. Everywhere we find evidence of the state's continuing struggle to assert its authority over private groups through the exercise of its would-be monopoly on violence. Joel Migdal recounts how Mustafa Kemal and his supporters in Turkey in the 1920s engaged in a protracted conflict with religious authorities over the question of whether men should wear hats with brims or without. In the course of this struggle, more than seventy people were hanged for wearing the "wrong" style hat. As Migdal correctly observes: "In reality, the conflict was over who had the right and ability to make rules in that society."[51] The ability of the state to make authoritative, nonvoluntary rules (i.e., law) was at stake, and officials understood that the ability to make such rules "stick" is vital to maintaining the state's monopoly on violence. The Young Turks (or *Jöntürkler*) were unwilling to see that power compromised, not even in a confrontation over such a trivial matter.

The state's struggle to exert a monopoly on violence was evidenced in the systematic destruction of the castles and fortifications of rebel lords by Louis XIII of France during the first half of the seventeenth century and his repeated proclamations forbidding dueling among private citizens, even those legally entitled to bear arms.[52] Dueling was a form of "private warfare" that challenged the monarch's monopoly on the exercise of coercion. Likewise, when Henry VII bid the English Parliament to ban private armies of retainers pursuant to the Statute of Liveries (1504), he was asserting the monopoly on violence for the English state and attempting

---

Sources of Social Power, vol. 2, *The Rise of Classes and Nation States 1760–1914* (New York: Cambridge University Press, 1993), 404. For an account of the development of the police authorities in Europe, see David H. Bayley, "The Police and Political Development in Europe," in *The Formation of National States in Western Europe,* ed. Tilly, 328–79. The classic study of the evolution of the prison system as an instrument of social control is Michel Foucault, *Discipline and Punish: The Birth of the Prison* (New York: Pantheon Books, 1977). For an excellent discussion of Foucault's theory of law and power, see Gerald Turkel, "Michel Foucault: Law, Power, and Knowledge," *Journal of Law and Society* 17 (summer 1990): 170.

51. Migdal, *Strong Societies,* 31.

52. A. Lloyd Moore, *Louis XIII, The Just* (Berkeley: University of California Press, 1989), 118, 185–86.

to establish that military service was owed to the king, not local lords.[53] To Englishmen of the early sixteenth century, a monopoly on violence exerted by the crown was preferable to the thirty years of continual war waged between the private armies of Lancastrian and Yorkist nobles. The consolidation of power under the English crown promised an end to the "private violence" that raged during the Wars of the Roses in the absence of a strong king recognized as the legitimate sovereign of that island nation.[54]

What is the result of the consolidation of coercive powers within the apparatus of the state? For one thing, the success of a state in exerting such a monopoly indicates a general acceptance of the legitimacy of its rule. The level of "private violence" in its territory will decline as the use of armaments are denied to private citizens and reserved to state officials. This requires expansion of the police powers and the military apparatus of the state. There is evidence that domestic violence (as opposed to intrastate warfare) declined in early modern Europe as states gradually expanded and military power was centralized under the authority of the crown.[55] Private violence gradually gave way to public order with the consolidation of power in the central sovereign. In the early stages of the accumulation of power, violence may actually increase as power is consolidated within the state. Once power is consolidated, domestic violence will decline as the state maintains order by suppressing the exercise of private violence. The suggestion of a pattern of increasing and then decreasing levels of violence has been offered as an alternative to two widely held and contradictory views, one holding that strong states per se suppress violence, and the other proposing that increases in violence are associated with decaying

---

53. For an account of Henry VII's assertion of the crown's monopoly on violence, see Michael Van Cleave Alexander, *The First of the Tudors: A Study of Henry VII and His Reign* (London: Rowman and Littlefield, 1980), 132–34, 189, 201.

54. In his classic study of Tudor England, G. R. Elton argued that Henry VII merely reconsolidated the old medieval state in advance of the more radical reconstitution of the English monarchy that would follow under Henry VIII (with much assistance from Thomas Cromwell). G. R. Elton, *The Tudor Revolution in Government: Administrative Changes in the Reign of Henry VIII* (Cambridge: Cambridge University Press, 1953), 19–35. Elton argued that during the long reign of Henry VII, improvements were made to the finances of the state, the workings of the Privy Council, and the administrative functions performed by court officials such as Cromwell.

55. William H. McNeill, *The Pursuit of Power: Technology, Armed Force, and Society Since A.D. 1000* (Chicago: University of Chicago Press, 1982), 140.

state organization.[56] The phenomenon is more complex than either of those propositions alone suggests. Decaying international orders also may lead to an increase in violence. As Robert Bates has perceptively observed, the collapse of the Soviet Union and the end of the Cold War were followed by an increase in *both* democracy and rampant violence within former client-states of the two global superpowers.[57]

What results when the state lacks a monopoly on violence within its territory? The sad consequences of deficiencies in state power were experienced in Lebanon after the collapse of the state during its long civil war, which left civilian populations unprotected from the private violence inflicted by armed militias, groups of religious fanatics, and criminal gangs. Much the same story has transpired in places like Chad, the Sudan, Haiti, the Congo, and Somalia since the collapse of the central state in Mogadishu in 1991.[58] History is littered with examples of such "failed states"—that is, states that cannot maintain a monopoly on violence.[59] These serve as vivid reminders of Hobbes's warning that life is "nasty, brutish, and short" where the sovereign is weak and private violence flourishes. In the political world, anarchy is let loose where the central state does not "hold."[60]

To be sure, another entire set of problems results from the successful concentration, centralization, and monopolization of violence within the apparatus of the central state. Strong states have the capacity not only to do

---

56. Youssef Cohen, Brian R. Brown, A.F.K. Organski, "The Paradoxical Nature of State Making: The Violent Creation of Order," *American Political Science Review* 75 (1981): 901. Robert Nisbet observed that the use of force by the state increases as the traditional bonds that hold together a society weaken—a condition that he referred to as the "twilight of authority." Robert A. Nisbet, *Twilight of Authority* (New York: Oxford University Press, 1975).

57. Robert H. Bates, *Prosperity and Violence: The Political Economy of Development* (New York: W. W. Norton, 2001), 97–100.

58. Attempts to restore order to Somalia have been unsuccessful, as the central government put in place by Ethiopian troops (with the support of the United States) is on the verge of collapse in the face of persistent attacks by the Islamist insurgents. The central state has only $18 million a year to run the entire government—including the army. Without revenue, Somalia is doomed to remain a "failed state." See Jeffrey Gettleman, "In Somalia, Government Once Hailed as Best Hope Is Teetering on Collapse," *New York Times,* March 29, 2008, A6.

59. *Foreign Policy* magazine (published by the Carnegie Endowment for International Peace) ranks those states most at risk for failure in its annual Failed States Index. "The Failed States Index for 2007," *Foreign Policy* (July/August 2007), 54–63.

60. "Things fall apart; the centre cannot hold; Mere anarchy is loosed upon the world." William Butler Yeats, "The Second Coming," in *Selected Poems and Two Plays of William Butler Yeats* (New York: Macmillan, 1962), 91.

"good deeds" (such as protect their citizens, build roads, highways, schools, and hospitals) but also to inflict horrible and devastating consequences on humanity, including their own citizens. Only an efficient bureaucratic state could have implemented the complex and extensive system of mass genocide perpetrated by the Nazi regime.[61] Recent experiments in genocide in Rwanda, Bosnia, Cambodia, and Darfur were less lethal only because the state machinery was much less developed and efficient than the powerful killing machine of the Third Reich. Genocide, like war, is the handiwork of strong states.

Herein lies the quandary: human society flourishes between the extremes of "not enough" state (a deficiency in state capacity) and "too much" state (oppressive rule by a strong state), but it is difficult to find that middle ground. This was recently witnessed in Iraq when, following the toppling of the Ba'ath Party and the brutal regime of Saddam Hussein, citizens suddenly suffered an equally violent fate as the new Iraqi state proved incapable of protecting them from private violence. It is no coincidence that the very first mission of the conquerors who vanquished Saddam Hussein's army was to build a new military and a national police force. In Iraq, we see all too clearly that the ability of a state to provide its citizens with even the minimal conveniences of modern social life (things like schools, hospitals, clean drinking water, sewage treatment plants, and paved roads) is dependent on its wherewithal to first impose public order within its territory.

The solution to such problems as social instability, disorder, violence, disease and epidemics, famine, and poverty is often a stronger state—but not always. In his influential study of state development, Samuel Huntington lamented that so many governments "do not govern."[62] Like Hobbes, Huntington concluded that the worst problems confronting humankind can be traced to the weakness of government (e.g., insufficient state power to maintain social order) and that the solution lies in strengthening state institutions. That may be true in many cases, but we also confront those appalling examples of states that govern too much—states that are themselves

---

61. In painstaking detail, historian Raul Hilberg shows how an efficient state bureaucracy was crucial to the implementation of the "Final Solution." Raul Hilberg, *The Destruction of the European Jews* (Chicago: Quadrangle Books, 1961). The relationship between state power and genocide is discussed in Irving Louis Horowitz, *Taking Lives: Genocide and State Power* (New Brunswick, NJ: Transaction Publishers, 2002).

62. Huntington, *Political Order,* 2.

the greatest threat to those unfortunate enough to reside in their territories. Think of North Korea, Cuba, or Myanmar. These are nations cursed by a state that is *too* strong and unchecked by society. Discerning the right balance between the two extremes is the great challenge of statecraft. The task is to devise institutional arrangements that effectively check or limit the most brutal and deadly manifestations of state power. The state is a two-edged sword that both cuts and heals. It can bring peace and stability, but it also can be wielded to inflict great pain and suffering on mankind. In the midst of the English Civil War, Hobbes became so infatuated with the potential healing power of the sovereign's monopoly on violence (used to end private violence) that he failed to recognize that the sovereign's sword is just as lethal as the highwayman's dagger. In fact, the sovereign's sword is more dangerous because it has the potential to inflict death and destruction on a wider scale. Since the Revolution of 1688, liberal political thought has largely concerned itself with devising restrictions on the powers of the sovereign.

In this noble pursuit, Anglo-American liberal political thought has generated its own mythology of a "social contract" to sanitize the historical origins of the state. The legitimacy of the state is enhanced by the just-so story of a social contract, which masks the "original conquest." In reality, there was no social contract between kings and their subjects—only brute force and conquest as political power was consolidated within the apparatus of the state.[63] This is why David Hume cautioned against looking too closely into the historical origins of any state. Hume understood that in the genealogy of kings can be found the original crime—the usurpation of power in an act of theft and banditry: "Almost all the governments that exist at present, or of which there remains any record in story, have been founded originally on usurpation or conquest or both, without any pretence of a fair consent or voluntary subjection of the people."[64] Like ancient Rome, the modern state was founded in violence and conquest, and coercion is its most essential attribute.

---

63. Even though offered the crown by Parliament, William III and Mary II expressly rejected claims that their rule depended on the consent of that body or that they had ascended to the throne pursuant to a "contract." While they accepted the terms of the Declaration of Rights of 1689, they did so only *after* taking the crown, precisely to avoid giving credence to the idea that their reign was founded upon a contractual agreement.

64. David Hume, "Of the Original Contract," in *Hume's Moral and Political Philosophy,* ed. Henry D. Aikem (New York: Hafner, 1968), 360.

The State as a "Protection Racket"

The notion that coercion is the essential attribute of the state conflicts with the mythology of classical liberal political theory, which views the state as the product of some distant social compact entered into voluntarily for the protection of person and property. In a provocative essay, Charles Tilly once challenged that historical fiction.[65] According to Tilly, the state is more like the "protection racket" perpetuated by organized crime than a political organization created through contracting by self-interested parties. It is hard to quarrel with Tilly's basic assertion. Notwithstanding the "good works" bestowed by states on their citizens, we always must remember that the state is an organization that dominates society through force and uses its domination to fill its coffers. Even in the most democratic nations, those who fail to pay their taxes and are caught will find themselves prosecuted and perhaps imprisoned. In more repressive regimes, the consequences can be fatal. This is the very essence of a protection racket. As Frederic Lane argued, "One of the most distinctive characteristics of governments is their attempt to create law and order by using force themselves and by controlling through various means the use of force by others. The more successful a government is in monopolizing all use of force between men within a particular area, the more efficient is its maintenance of law and order."[66] A state that controls violence is able to extract "protection rent" from those living and working within its territory. Lane likened such surplus revenue to "tribute."[67]

In his last published work, Mancur Olson fleshed out the logic and rationality of the state's protection racket. Olson argued that from the perspective of the local population, military rulers (or "warlords") who behave as "stationary bandits" continuously stealing from the local population (i.e., revenue predators) are preferable to "roving bandits" who raid a territory

---

65. Tilly, "War-making and State Making as Organized Crime," in *Bringing the State Back In,* ed. Evans, Rueschemeyer, and Skocpol, 169–91.

66. Frederic C. Lane, "The Economic Meaning of War and Protection," *Journal of Social Philosophy and Jurisprudence* 7 (April 1942): 254.

67. Where the state has secured a monopoly on violence, "it can raise prices above the cost to it of producing the protection it provides," and thereby extract "surplus" revenue from those who pay protection rent. Frederic C. Lane, "The Role of Governments in Economic Growth in Early Modern Times," *The Journal of Economic History* 35 (March 1975): 8.

and then leave.[68] The roving bandit will pillage and plunder, taking away everything that he can carry, while the stationary bandit will soon realize that it is to his benefit to reduce his plunder to a "predictable tax" that takes only a "part of his victims' outputs," thereby leaving them with "an incentive to generate income"—income that he can then tax. The stationary bandit will recognize that he has an interest in protecting private property, enforcing contracts, and maintaining a stable currency to encourage commerce and long-term investment, which in turn will maximize his own tax revenue. Furthermore, the stationary bandit will eventually recognize that it is in his own interest to *exclude* other bandits from his territory, asserting a monopoly on violence within his domain. Over time, the warlord's "protection racket" evolves into a routinized system of taxation and public order. Rulers who keep their word and give protection in exchange for tribute, will have an easier time collecting revenue from their subjects.[69] The stationary bandit who provides protection is soon proclaimed "king."

Over time the king's exercise of power is routinized and institutionalized within a professional administrative bureaucracy, taking on a genuine aura of legitimacy and legality that distinguishes it from those organizations whose claim to rule is based *solely* on the possession of power and the exercise of violence—for instance, the Mafia. The chief characteristic of the modern state is that its manifestations of power are considered legitimate only to the extent they are expressed through formal rules and follow prescribed procedures (i.e., law). Weber emphasized that the coercive powers of the modern state are expressed through a legal code enacted by a legislature, administered by a bureaucracy, and subject to judicial review by an independent judiciary.[70] But if the modern state is rationalistic, legalistic, and bureaucratic, it remains in essence an organization based on coercion and tribute. Modern states demand a share of the profits of private businesses in exchange for providing protection, order, social welfare benefits, and a legal system. Taxation is but a subtle form of tribute taking.

---

68. Mancur Olson, *Power and Prosperity: Outgrowing Communist and Capitalist Dictatorships* (New York: Basic Books, 2000), 6–12.

69. As Margaret Levi observes: "Taxpayers will not voluntarily pay taxes if they expect to be duped by their rulers." Levi, *Rule and Revenue,* 60.

70. For an informative discussion of Weber's notion of "legal rational authority," see Gerald Turkel, *Dividing Public and Private: Law, Politics, and Social Theory* (Westport, CT: Praeger, 1992), 129–66.

Be that as it may, we might still side with Hobbes, concluding that rendering tribute to the king in exchange for his protection is preferable to life in the state of war. In turn, the legitimacy of the king's rule is established to the extent he provides protection—the precondition for civil society. Sir William Blackstone famously extolled this "Whig" theory of the state: "Allegiance is the tie, or *ligamen,* which binds the subject to the King, in return for that protection which the King affords his subjects."[71]

To be sure, most states evolve into something more than a glorified protection racket. They develop legal systems and political institutions that constrain the worst tendencies of rulers and deter would-be tyrants. Still, there remain those troubling cases of rulers who operate outside the rule of law, contrary to custom, and without popular support and the legitimacy that comes with it. They use the state apparatus to extract private wealth for their own benefit and purposes, leaving the economy undeveloped and the public sector starved for resources. Sadly, the metaphor of a stationary bandit operating a protection racket describes much of the troubled political history of postcolonial Africa. Catherine Boone depicts the ruling class that emerged in Senegal in the 1960s as a coalition "whose power was rooted in control over the state itself, rather than in direct control over property or production."[72] Like so many other ruling coalitions in control of African states, this one uses the state apparatus to loot the state treasury, thereby stifling the development of the domestic economy and capitalist markets as well as discouraging inflows of foreign investment. In Asia, North Korea provides another horrific example.[73] Here the state engages in

---

71. William Blackstone, *Commentaries on the Laws of England* (Oxford: Clarendon Press, 1765), vol. 1, book I, chapter 10 ("Of the People, Whether Aliens, Denizens, or Natives"), 354.

72. Catherine Boone, *Merchant Capital and the Roots of State Power in Senegal 1930–1985* (New York: Cambridge University Press, 1992), 4. For a review of the literature on state failure in Africa, see John R. Heilbrunn, "Paying the Price of Failure: Reconstructing Failed and Collapsed States in Africa and Central Asia," *Perspectives on Politics* 4 (March 2006): 135–50. Two studies on the dysfunctionality of African states are William Reno, *Warlord Politics and African States* (Boulder, CO: Lynne Rienner, 1998); Jeffrey Herbst, *States and Power in Africa: Comparative Lessons in Authority and Control* (Princeton: Princeton University Press, 2000). The classic account of agricultural policy and the failed politics that drives economic development in Africa is Robert H. Bates, *Markets and States in Tropical Africa: the Political Basis of Agricultural Policies* (Berkeley: University of California Press, 1981).

73. North Korea's protection racket is described in Jasper Becker, *Rogue Regime: Kim Jong Il and the Looming Threat of North Korea* (New York: Oxford University Press, 2005). With no private economy to tax and little revenue generated by state-owned ventures, the North Korean state

a particularly ugly form of protection racket—one in which the state plunders its own "citizens" and provides only minimal protection in return.

Fortunately, these are the extreme cases. To remain in power, most ruling coalitions must elicit support and cooperation from powerful interests and groups in society. As David Waldner points out, where there is an industrial bourgeoisie and an organized class of workers, deals must be struck that take into account *both* groups, with the state offering up benefits to both groups in the form of side payments.[74] These multilateral arrangements (i.e., revenue coalitions) enhance the legitimacy of the regime as well as moderate the polities of the state. But even democratic states are in the business of providing protection in exchange for tribute, and state power is the prerequisite for protection. At the same time, the potential for abuse of state power is always present because the state itself is the institutionalization of coercion and tribute.

Revenue and State Autonomy

As a political organization successfully exerting a monopoly on violence within a given territory, the state emerges as an entity separate and distinct from society. As such, it possesses its own unique interests. Through the exercise of its coercive powers in pursuit of those interests, the state achieves a degree of autonomy from society.[75] Thus the ability of state officials to impose their decisions on nonstate actors (the essence of state autonomy) is directly attributable to the coercive power of the state. To be sure, the precise boundaries between state and society are in flux and continually shifting: "Rather than an artifice, impartially superintending society, the state itself comes to be constituted by a network of power relations between a

---

engages in overt criminal activity (drug trafficking and counterfeiting U.S. dollars) and wields the threat of nuclear weapons in an international version of its protection racket.

74. David Waldner, *State Building and Late Development* (Ithaca: Cornell University Press, 1999), 35.

75. Skocpol delineates the possibilities for state autonomy: "States conceived as organizations claiming control over territories and people may formulate and pursue goals that are not simply reflective of the demands or interests of social groups, classes, or society." Theda Skocpol, "Bringing the State Back In: Strategies of Analysis in Current Research," in *Bringing the State Back In*, ed. Evans, Rueschemeyer, and Skocpol, 9.

wide range of constituents."[76] Furthermore, the boundaries between state and society are neither impervious nor permanent, and private interests and public authority are not always separate or distinct.

The nature of the relationship that emerges between political actors and powerful economic interests within a state strongly affects public policy outcomes. Invariably, that relationship is a two-way street—meaning, private interests influence the process through which public policy is made, but "public policy can shape private preferences" and "in many ways states organize the societies they control."[77] This is to say that states can be autonomous from society and economic interests. Contrary to the assertions of the various strains of Marxism, the state is not necessarily controlled, manipulated, or captured by the dominant economic interests in society. As Skocpol argues, the state possesses an "autonomous structure—a structure with a logic and interests of its own not necessarily equivalent to, or fused with, the interests of the dominant class in society or the full set of member groups of the polity."[78] To be sure, the state is only *potentially* autonomous from society, as the actual degree of autonomy varies from state to state, and even from one bureaucratic agency to another within the same state.[79] Moreover, the state is never fully autonomous from society, as private interests and social groups always remain connected to political elites and institutions. During periods of war and systemic crisis, the state can enhance its autonomy, as private economic interests are more likely to succumb to pressure from the state. During such times, rulers force "concessions...at

---

76. Pratap Bhanu Mehta, *Burden of Democracy,* 116.

77. Peter J. Katzenstein, ed., *Between Power and Plenty: Foreign Economic Policies of Advanced Industrial States* (Madison: University of Wisconsin Press, 1978), 18–19. Katzenstein stresses the linkage between state actors and "major interest groups and political action groups" in shaping the foreign economic policies of developed industrial states: "The governing coalitions of social forces in each of the advanced industrial states find their institutional expression in distinct policy networks which link the public and the private sector in the implementation of foreign policy."

78. Skocpol, *States and Social Revolutions,* 27.

79. Variation in the autonomy of bureaucratic agencies within the federal government is explored by Daniel Carpenter, who associates the greater skill, expertise, and problem-solving capacities of certain agencies (e.g., the Post Office, Agriculture Department) with their enhanced "bureaucratic legitimacy," which is the basis for their autonomy from politicians and private interest groups. Carpenter, *Forging of Bureaucratic Autonomy;* and "The Political Foundations of Bureaucratic Autonomy," *Studies in American Political Development* 15 (spring 2001): 113–22.

the expense of the interests of the dominant class" and in the process increase the state's autonomy from society.[80]

This is a critical point. For a state to achieve any degree of autonomy
from society, it must be capable of supporting itself financially. This requires sources of revenue that are both replenishable and within the exclusive control of officials of the state. In other words, institutional autonomy
is dependent on financial autonomy, which depends on the capacity of the
state to extract revenue from society—whether from its own citizens (as
tribute) or from those of another state (as plunder). By securing its own
revenue sources, the state can achieve independence from those private
economic interests and social classes that otherwise dominate society.
Where the state is dependent on a particular class or economic sector for
its revenue, it is unlikely to ever achieve autonomy. But contrary to the tenets of Marxist orthodoxy, a state that secures its own independent sources
of revenue can achieve a degree of autonomy from dominant economic
and social groups.[81] And contrary to the tenets of pluralist theory, a fiscally
autonomous state can impose its own preferences on nonstate actors and
private interest groups.[82]

The World of Nation-States

Weber's conception of the state as that organization in possession of a monopoly on violence is generally taken to refer to coercion and state power
exercised *within* the state's borders, but the formulation also extends to the
state's monopoly on the exercise of coercive force employed against those

---

80. Skocpol, *States and Social Revolutions,* 30.

81. Marx himself did not develop a comprehensive theory of the state, although one can be ex-
trapolated from his writings on politics and his historical studies. Neo-Marxist theorists have at-
tempted to develop such a theory. See, e.g., Immanuel Wallerstein, *The Modern World System* (New
York: Academic Press, 1974); Nicos Poulantzas, *Political Power and Social Classes* (London: New
Left Books, 1974); Ralph Miliband, *The State in Capitalist Society* (New York: Basic Books, 1969).
The classical Marxist and neo-Marxist positions are summarized in Alfred Stepan, *The State and
Society: Peru in Comparative Perspective* (Princeton: Princeton University Press, 1978), 17–26.

82. The notion that some regimes are best explained by reference to a pluralist model, some
by a neo-Marxist class analysis, and others by a statist (managerial) model is developed in Robert R.
Alford and Roger Friedland, *Powers of Theory: Capitalism, the State, and Democracy* (New York:
Cambridge University Press, 1985).

outside its borders.[83] The boundary between one state and others is no less important than the boundary between state and society, and maintaining that boundary requires the diligent exercise of state power. As Philip Bobbitt remarks, "Until the governing institutions of a society can claim for themselves the sole right to determine the legitimate use of force at home and abroad, there can be no state."[84] By maintaining its boundaries with the external world, a state achieves autonomy from other states.[85] Hence, a corollary to the classic Weberian formulation may be postulated holding that the state is that political organization that makes war with other states, and hence, stateness presupposes the capacity of such an organization to conduct warfare against (and thereby maintain independence and autonomy from) competitor states that lie beyond its borders. Geopolitical competition among self-interested states is inevitable and leads to geo-military competition. War is the most costly and deadly expression of that interstate global competition.[86]

The association of states with war is hardly unique to the new state-centered theory or the study of international relations, although previously only one side of the equation was grasped—that war is the original and formative activity of states. This was understood by Herodotus, Thucydides, Polybius, Xenophon, Josephus, whose ancient histories were fundamentally chronicles of states at war. Likewise, the importance of warfare cannot be lost on anyone who has studied the history of the world over the

---

83. As John Brewer put it, "States are Janus-faced: they look in, to the societies they rule, and out, to those states with which they are so often locked in conflict." John Brewer, *The Sinews of Power: War, Money and the English State, 1688–1783* (London: Unwin Hyman, 1989), xvii.

84. Philip Bobbitt, *The Shield of Achilles: War, Peace, and the Course of History* (New York: Knopf, 2002), 6.

85. Stephen Krasner refers to the state's assertion of authority and control within its territory as domestic sovereignty: "Domestic sovereignty refers to the formal organization of political authority within the state and the ability of public authorities to exercise effective control within the borders of their own polity." Krasner refers to the ability of the state to exclude "external actors" from its territory as "Westphalian sovereignty." Stephen D. Krasner, *Sovereignty: Organized Hypocrisy* (Princeton: Princeton University Press, 1999), 4.

86. The so-called realist movement in international relations explains the dynamics of the geopolitical competition among nation-states (whether through war or less violent forms of competition) from the perspective of self-interested actors. Realists view conflict, including war, as inevitable as regional hegemons act to protect their interests. See John J. Mearsheimer, *The Tragedy of Great Power Politics* (New York: W. W. Norton, 2001). Others realists are more optimistic, suggesting that a balance of power among states can be achieved to produce equilibrium and peaceful coexistence. See, e.g., Kenneth N. Waltz, *Man, the State, and War: A Theoretical Analysis* (New York: Columbia University Press, 1959).

last five centuries. The history of mankind is the history of states at war, and warfare has been critical in defining human civilization. As Edmund Burke so eloquently stated, "War is the Matter which fills all History."[87] This is not to say that culture, ideas, class, and economics do not matter, but only that war has been the single most important force shaping human history. This is what makes the study of the state so important. As the institutionalization of violence, states make war and thereby shape human history. Moreover, states that make war develop into stronger states and require more revenue than those at peace. In the chapters that follow, we will explore the relationship between war, revenue, and state development as it played out in early modern Europe and America.

---

87. Edmund Burke, *A Vindication of Natural Society or, A View of the Miseries and Evils Arising to Mankind From Every Species of Artificial Society: In A Letter To Lord **** By A Late Noble Writer* (1757), ed. Frank N. Pagano (Indianapolis: Liberty Fund, 1982), 20.

2

WAR AND THE DEVELOPMENT
OF THE EUROPEAN STATE

War is inherent in the very structure of the State. States historically
identify themselves by their relationship with one another, asserting
their existence and defining their boundaries by the use of force or the
immanent threat of force.

—Sir Michael E. Howard, *The Causes of Wars* (1983)

A new disease has spread across Europe; it has afflicted our princes and
made them keep an inordinate number of troops. It redoubles in strength
and necessarily becomes contagious; for as soon as one state increases
what it calls troops, the others suddenly increase theirs, so that nothing
is gained thereby but the common ruin.... The consequence of such a
situation is the permanent increase in taxes.

—Montesquieu, *The Spirit of the Laws* (1748)

As a political organization asserting a monopoly on violence within a
given territory, the state relies on armies and armaments to subjugate and
pacify its citizens as well as defend its territory against foreign competitor
states. Indeed, in its ancient origins in medieval Europe, the state was used
almost exclusively as an instrument of warfare. As the German historian
Otto Hintze once astutely observed, "All state organization was originally
military organization, organization for war."[1] To be sure, much of state

---

1. Otto Hintze, "Military Organization and the Organization of the State," in *The Historical
Essays of Otto Hintze,* ed. Felix Gilbert (New York: Oxford University Press, 1975), 181.

organization is *still* military organization—men and machinery dedicated to the deadly art of warfare.

When states actually go to war, they must marshal societal resources and organize domestic populations, directing both toward a common goal: "In order to survive conflicts between them, states need...to squeeze the resources of the population and mobilize the people for war."[2] During times of war, the apparatus of the state invariably expands as rulers build more powerful armies, navies, and the administrative offices necessary to carry out their military operations. Thus states at war undergo more rapid development than those at peace, and war leads to stronger states that are increasingly adept at making war. As Charles Tilly famously put it: "War made the state, and the state made war."[3]

If war is associated with increased state development, not all warfare has the same impact on state institutions. Arguably, certain kinds of war stimulate development more than others. In their study of war and state making in Europe from the sixteenth century to the Second World War, Karen Rasler and William Thompson emphasize the impact of "global war" on institutional development. Global wars are those "decisive contests fought over the issue of succession to world leadership.... Although global wars are not defined in terms of scope, participation, or costs, they tend to be unusually extensive in terms of geography encompassed and the number of actors involved. Global wars tend also to among the most costly wars in terms of both lives lost and resources expended."[4] Others suggest that the critical distinction is between "limited war" and "total war." Total war is warfare that involves the "complete mobilization of a society's resources

2. Uri Ben-Eliezer, "From Military Role-Expansion to Difficulties in Peace-Making: The Israel Defense Forces 50 Years Later," in *Military, State, and Society in Israel*, ed. Daniel Maman, Eyal Ben-Ari, and Zeev Rosenhek (New Brunswick, NJ: Transaction, 2001), 142.

3. Charles Tilly, "Reflections on the History of European State-Making," in *The Formation of National States in Western Europe*, ed. Charles Tilly (Princeton: Princeton University Press, 1975), 42.

4. Karen A. Rasler and William R. Thompson, "War Making and State Making: Governmental Expenditures, Tax Revenues, and Global Wars," *American Political Science Review* 79 (1985): 494; see also Rasler and Thompson, *War and State Making: The Shaping of Global Powers* (Boston: Unwin Hyman, 1989). For a discussion of Rasler and Thompson's theory of global war, see Meyer Kestnbaum and Theda Skocpol, "War and the Development of Modern National States," *Sociological Forum* 8 (December 1993): 665.

to achieve the absolute destruction of an enemy, with all distinction erased between combatants and noncombatants."[5] Miguel Centeno contends that Latin America was largely spared the destructiveness of total war. The many limited wars fought in the region failed to stimulate the development of strong states such as those that emerged in Europe, where war was more extreme and comprehensive in scope, intensity, and duration.[6]

In contrast with Latin America, five centuries of nearly continuous warfare in Europe beginning in the fifteenth century resulted in the steady expansion and centralization of state power in the apparatus of the state. But the relationship between war and state development is not so simple or direct. After all, states across the globe made war for thousands of years without undergoing the kind of institutional development experienced in early modern Europe. Today, states in economically undeveloped regions of Africa constantly make war among themselves without undergoing comparable political change. Something more is required for state development. That essential ingredient is revenue.

States at war require significantly more revenue than those at peace. Armies and armaments do not come cheap, and building a powerful military requires enormous revenue. While all rulers are subject to constant pressure for revenue, rulers of states at war are subject to a heightened revenue imperative. Their ability to acquire that revenue is critical to the state's success in geomilitary competition and, hence, its survival. The prerequisite for *both* war making and state development is a stable and replenishable source of revenue under the control of state officials. Without reliable revenue streams, prolonged war making and state development are impossible. As Cicero observed two thousand years ago, "infinite

---

5. David A. Bell, *The First Total War: Napoleon's Europe and the Birth of Warfare as We Know It* (Boston: Houghton Mifflin, 2007), 7. According to Bell, the first "total war" was the Napoleonic campaign that began in the late eighteenth century. He suggests that while the term is useful, no war actually involves the complete or "total" mobilization of a society's resources.

6. Miguel Angel Centeno, *Blood and Debt: War and the Nation-State in Latin America* (University Park: Pennsylvania State University Press, 2002), 24, 47. Centeno argues that because Latin American nations emerged out of the collapse of the Spanish Empire in the early nineteenth century, they never acquired "centralized authority and certainly could not enforce a monopoly on the use of violence" within their territories. In Latin America, violence typically has been experienced *within* states, rather than as warfare *between* states.

treasure" is "the sinews of War."[7] It may be added that infinite treasure is
the sinews of state development.

The Military Revolution and the State

The modern nation-state has its origins in early modern Europe. State development commenced in Europe in the middle of the sixteenth century
when, in the words of Philip Bobbitt, the "princely state" of the fourteenth
and fifteenth centuries gave way to the "kingly state" of the sixteenth and
seventeenth centuries, which in the eighteenth century evolved into the
"territorial state"—an institutionalized political organization exerting jurisdiction over a specific geographic territory.[8] The territorial state of the
eighteenth century was the forerunner of the great nation-states of the nineteenth century exemplified by Napoleonic France and Germany under the
Kaiser.[9] The nation-state is a territorial state that governs its geographical territories as the embodiment of a distinct "people" or nation.[10] Not all
states will necessarily assume this form, but eventually all the states of early
modern Europe did.

How did the princely states of the fourteenth and fifteenth centuries
differ from the kingly states of the sixteenth and seventeenth centuries?
How did they differ from their precursors of medieval Europe? To begin

---

7. The Latin phrase is *nervos belli, pecuniam infinitam* ("the sinews of war, infinite treasure").
Marcus Tullius Cicero, "Philippic V," in *Cicero: Philippics* (Cambridge: Harvard University Press,
1926), 15:261.

8. The terminology is from Bobbitt's extraordinary inquiry into the state's origins in war and
the evolution of its constitutional order. Philip Bobbitt, *The Shield of Achilles: War, Peace, and the
Course of History* (New York: Knopf, 2002), 334.

9. David Bell argues that while the roots of French nationalism can be traced to a wider European movement that began earlier in the eighteenth century, French nationalism emerged as a
new phenomenon during the Revolution when "the nation" came to represent "the source of all
legitimate authority" for a significant portion of the French population. David A. Bell, *The Cult
of the Nation in France: Inventing Nationalism, 1680–1800* (Cambridge: Harvard University Press,
2001), 8. Others identify Germany, unified by Prussia under the leadership of Bismarck in the late
nineteenth century, as the first great European nation-state.

10. "With the French Revolution and its Napoleonic aftermath, state building received re-
newed emphasis while the concept of the nation and the nation-state became full blown both in the
sense of a shared community of purposes, privileges, and benefits, and in the sense of a 'peculiar people,' exercising its rights of self-determination." Samuel E. Finer, "State- and Nation-Building in
Europe: The Role of the Military," in *Formation of National States in Western Europe,* ed. Tilly, 144.

with, the princely state was "institutionalized coercion" on a much lesser scale than that of the kingly state. At the same time, the princely state of the fourteenth century was more powerful and centralized than the states of medieval Europe, wherein considerable power remained vested in local elites. The states of medieval Europe did not possess or even claim a monopoly on violence, as local elites commonly used violence to settle disputes among themselves. Medieval states did not have substantial capacity to extract revenue from society. Like feudal lords, the medieval king paid for his households and retainers out of his own revenue sources: rents of land, feudal fees, and other customary payments due from tenants.[11] The medieval king was expected to "live of his own" (*vivre du sien*)—that is, live off the royal lands and feudal fees.[12] Even in times of war, local power holders did not cede control over their retainers and armaments to a central authority; these were merely loaned to the ruler on a temporary basis. The medieval ruler functioned as a "coordinator" of infantry, cavalry, and artillery contributed by local feudal lords.[13] War in medieval Europe was not yet a national enterprise of one people against another but rather remained a "vocation of the upper classes whose members, representing little but their own interests and sense of justice, donned armor and fought each other as the occasion demanded."[14] While the rulers of medieval states adopted military strategies, directed campaigns, and negotiated peace, their armies did not belong to them and were not permanent organizations. When a war ended, their armies melted away, returning to the local communities from whence they came.[15]

---

11. For a discussion of the limited resources available to medieval rulers, see Richard Bean, "War and the Birth of the Nation State," *Journal of Economic History* 33 (March 1973): 2013.

12. Margaret Levi, *Of Rule and Revenue* (Berkeley: University of California Press, 1988), 99. The difficulty of the European monarchies in living off the "royal domain" is discussed in Niall Ferguson, *The Cash Nexus: Money and Power in the Modern World, 1700–2000* (Basic Books, 2001), 53–57.

13. For an account of the structure of the medieval military command, see Jan Glete, *War and the State in Early Modern Europe: Spain, the Dutch Republic, and Sweden as Fiscal-Military States, 1500–1660* (New York: Routledge, 2004), 10–11.

14. Martin Van Creveld, *The Rise and Decline of the State* (Cambridge: Cambridge University Press, 1999), 155–56.

15. Glete summarizes the tenuous relationship between the medieval ruler and local elites during wartime as follows: "The ability to use armed force operationally was vested with local power: land-owners, cities, local militias, and even various parts of the Church. Without the

Compared to the medieval state, the princely state of the fourteenth and fifteenth centuries exhibited a notable increase in the centralization of power. Even so, this was a state with much weaker institutions than those of modern states. The princely state was little more than a loose alliance of "powerful individuals and their group of followers and associates, with uncertain or varying spatial boundaries."[16] The princes were rulers "without nations and without states" who "governed realms," not countries or nations.[17] These were political organizations with only the most rudimentary of administrative apparatuses. The principality was an extension of the royal household (characterized by patrimonial rule) asserting its authority over an ill-defined geographical territory.[18] These rulers did not govern in the modern sense, nor were their provinces clearly defined territories. As Anthony Giddens puts it, their domains had "frontiers, not borders."[19] The princely state "mainly expressed and extended the particular powers and interests of individual rulers and dynasties" and was one in which "political prerogatives were undifferentiated components of privileged social standing."[20] As an extension of the household of the ruling elite, the princely state was firmly rooted in society and not autonomous from it.

In contrast, the kingly state that emerged in Europe in the sixteenth century possessed state power on a grand scale and exerted authority over a larger and more clearly defined territory. Its powers were vested in offices separate from those of the household of the individual ruler. The powers of the kingly state were institutionalized in the offices of a bona fide state apparatus, albeit not yet on the scale or magnitude of the monarchies of the eighteenth century or the powerful nation-states of the nineteenth century.

---

active co-operation of the elites that controlled the power structure in local societies, states lacked operational military capability." Glete, *War and the State,* 12.

16. Gianfranco Poggi, *The State: Its Nature, Development and Prospects* (Cambridge, England: Polity Press, 1990), 25.

17. Bobbitt, *Shield of Achilles,* 78.

18. One reason that there were no formal and fixed borders between states is that maps were highly inaccurate. Not until 1472 was there a map showing the entirety of France, and even then it was riddled with errors and lacking in scale. As late as the 1690s, Louis XIV lacked dependable maps of his kingdom. For an interesting discussion of the inaccuracy of maps and surveys in Europe, see Creveld, *Rise and Decline of the State,* 143–45.

19. Anthony Giddens, *The Nation-State and Violence* (Berkeley: University of California Press, 1987), 4.

20. Poggi, *The State,* 25.

The state apparatus was no longer a mere extension of the ruler's personal household.[21] Citizens owed their allegiance to the state as a political organization, not just to the individual ruler who happened to be sitting on the throne. The kingly state began to compete with the Church for revenue and eventually succeeded in securing its own independent sources of revenue at the expense of the Church. With its own revenue sources under the control of state officials, the sixteenth-century kingly state developed into an institution separate and autonomous from society. For example, France under Cardinal Richelieu was transformed from a medieval kingdom into a centralized monarchy separate from French society once the monarchy acquired its own independent sources of royal revenue. Even still, state powers remained limited by contemporary standards. There was little "penetration" of society, as the kingly rulers generally left their subjects alone so long as they paid their taxes. Resistance persisted against efforts by the state to dominate local society, as evidenced in France by the eruption of the Fronde in 1648. While the center held, the periphery was obviously still not pacified.

What factors were responsible for the evolution of the princely state into the kingly state and the subsequent development of the kingly state into the territorial nation-state? When did this institutional transformation begin? Among scholars, there is considerable disagreement. Different historians locate the birth of the modern European state in different regions and times. Furthermore, the changes were not uniform throughout Europe; the princely state survived in Italy and Germany well into the nineteenth century. Nevertheless, there is a consensus that a new international order of states was established in Europe with the Peace of Westphalia in 1648. A system of international diplomacy emerged among the states of Europe by the 1660s, with virtually all the kingly states of Europe sending representatives, or "ambassadors," to foreign courts.[22] This international order prevailed for the next three hundred fifty years. What forces created this new order of states? The answer is, war. Beginning in the fifteenth century

---

21. According to Bobbitt, the kingly state that emerged in the sixteenth century had six distinct institutional structures: a standing army (or navy); a centralized bureaucracy; a system of national taxation; permanent diplomatic representation abroad; systematic state policies to promote commerce and the national economy; and the elevation of the king to the head of a national church. Bobbitt, *Shield of Achilles,* 118.

22. Creveld, *Rise and Decline of the State,* 134.

and continuing throughout the sixteenth and seventeenth centuries, nearly constant warfare plagued Europe. On the continent, there were fewer than ten years of peace in the sixteenth century and only four in the seventeenth century.[23] The unremitting warfare transformed social and political institutions, including the structure and development of the states of early modern Europe.

How did warfare affect state structure and development in Europe? As the rulers of the principalities of the late fifteenth century sought to extend and enlarge their territories through military conquest within the context of this geomilitary competition, they made use of new innovations and techniques for making war. Most important among these were dramatic improvements in armaments and weaponry. The lance and the pike were gradually replaced by the arrow and musket, with devastating effect on the mounted feudal knight and cavalry. By the middle of the sixteenth century, the use of small arms by infantry was common. The use of gunpowder for military purposes, particularly in conjunction with the use of artillery, proved a decisive innovation during this period.[24] Arms allowed infantry to overcome large masses of pikemen and cavalry as "*fire* replaced *shock* as the decisive element on the battlefield."[25] The introduction of artillery capable of breaching the walls of old feudal castles led to innovations in the design of fortifications. In response, cities (particularly in Italy) adopted new "bastion defenses" for protection. These fortifications were effective against conventional forms of military assault but were still vulnerable to full-scale siege.[26] The bastion defenses relied on improvements in architectural design (known as the *trace italienne*) and the construction of significantly thicker walls for defensive fortifications. These new fortifications were extremely expensive to erect; only the wealthiest rulers could

---

23. Calculations of the periods of war versus peace are reviewed and assessed in Geoffrey Parker, *The Military Revolution: Military Innovation and the Rise of the West, 1500–1800* (Cambridge: Cambridge University Press, 1988), 1–2, 176 fn 2.

24. "The principal revolution was in the increasingly successful use of gunpowder in siege and field artillery." Bruce D. Porter, *War and the Rise of the State: The Military Foundations of Modern Politics* (New York: Free Press, 1994), 31. Gunpowder was probably invented in China and then brought to Europe. The earliest references to gunpowder in Europe date to the second half of the thirteenth century. Creveld, *Rise and Decline of the State*, 156.

25. Bobbitt, *Shield of Achilles*, 69.

26. Thomas Ertman, *Birth of the Leviathan: Building States and Regimes in Medieval and Early Modern Europe* (New York: Cambridge University Press, 1997), 95.

afford them. Geoffrey Parker, the esteemed military historian, argues that the improved fortifications led to dramatic and substantial changes in the composition of armed military forces as armies needed significantly more men to overcome the new defensive fortifications and cities needed many more men to defend against the larger equipped armies.[27] This trend favored states with centralized administration and the capacity to mobilize greater numbers of men.

The greater number of men required to defend and overcome the new defensive fortifications reflected a broader trend in early modern Europe. Innovations in military organization made it possible for rulers to organize and maintain large standing armies.[28] A standing army is an extraordinarily powerful weapon of war and, hence, constitutes a powerful instrument of state power. The old feudal military organizations were no match for the new larger armies, which were better organized, equipped, drilled, and disciplined. Relying on such improvements to military organization, the Swiss military defeated the feudal armies of Austria and Burgundy in the fourteenth and fifteenth centuries through their superior organization and strategic skills as well as their ability to use an army "tactically"—that is, the ability "to move and deploy a large mass of troops according to a unified plan and for specific war aims."[29]

The rulers of feudal Europe were unable to muster standing armies anywhere near as large (based on population) as those of Ancient Rome or the early Byzantine empires.[30] That changed between 1500 and 1700, as the armies of Europe expanded appreciably, with some increasing tenfold.[31] Comparable changes occurred at sea, as monarchs built large and well-armed royal navies that extended their military presence beyond

---

27. Parker, *Military Revolution*, 156.

28. William H. McNeill, *The Pursuit of Power: Technology, Armed Force, and Society since AD 1000* (Chicago: University of Chicago Press, 1982), 133–39.

29. Hintze, "Military Organization," 197.

30. Bean, "War and the Birth of the Nation State," 211. Bean estimates that up to 6 percent of national income was spent on the military by the Roman Empire, less than 1 percent in medieval Europe, more than 2 percent in the sixteenth century, and 6 to 12 percent in the eighteenth century. This contrasts with about 10 percent for the United States in the postwar era.

31. Parker, *Military Revolution*, 1, 24, 162–63. Parker believes that there was a natural limit to the size of the armies the medieval European states could support. He calculates that a force of 150,000 men was the maximum in the sixteenth and seventeenth centuries. Not until 1670 did the entire armed forces of France exceed 200,000. By 1695, the army of Louis XIV was twice that size. With the enemies of France building up their armed forces, the total number of troops in Europe

their own borders.[32] By the last decades of the seventeenth century, France had 120,000 troops in its army, Spain had 70,000, the Dutch had 120,000, Sweden had 63,000, and Russia had 130,000 men. One notable exception was the standing army of England, which was comprised of only 15,000 men.[33] The great armies on the continent included significant numbers of foreign troops for hire, as entire armies comprised of infantry and cavalry could be hired for specific military campaigns.[34] Foreign mercenaries were preferred where rulers were afraid to arm and train the local peasantry. They also displayed a higher level of training and superior tactical skills. It was more practical to train professional soldiers in the new and more complicated techniques of military organization than local conscripts organized into militias. In the late sixteenth and early seventeenth centuries, new techniques employing infantry drills, cavalry and platoon systems, and unitary vertical command were introduced by the Dutch and Swedish armies. The Swedish Army was infamous for defeating much larger forces through its highly organized infantry and superior battlefield tactics.[35] Significantly, the Swedish Army mastered advanced military techniques that proved decisive on the battlefield. Prior to the seventeenth century, Sweden was a relatively weak Baltic state. Under the reign of Gustavus Adolphus (1611–1632), Sweden emerged as a major military force and the dominant power in the region based upon its mastery of these new techniques of military organization.[36]

Collectively, the new techniques and tools of warfare constituted what historian Michael Roberts famously referred to as the "military revolution"

---

reached an estimated 1.3 million by 1710. Estimates of troop strength are found in ibid., 45–46; and Glete, *War and the State,* 30–36.

32. The expansion of navies is recounted in Paul Kennedy, *The Rise and Fall of the Great Powers: Economic Change and Military Conflict from 1500 to 2000* (New York: Random House, 1987), 46.

33. Figures from Geoffrey Parker, "The 'Military Revolution,' 1560–1660—a Myth?" *Journal of Modern History* 48 (1976): 206.

34. The use of foreign mercenaries was not new to the sixteenth century but dates back to medieval Europe. The army of William the Conqueror included a contingent of mercenaries.

35. Parker, *Military Revolution,* 23–25. The Swedish army was a conscript militia, as opposed to the mercenary armies that had become the norm on the European Continent.

36. Gustavus Adolphus implemented important reforms that centralized of the tax system, the national treasury, and the education system. His army had more than 175,000 men under arms. Bobbitt, *Shield of Achilles,* 70, 112.

of early modern Europe.[37] Pursuant to this military revolution, small de-centralized armies of feudal lords were gradually replaced by much larger "centrally financed and supplied armies" that were equipped with "ever more sophisticated and expensive weaponry."[38] Roberts suggested that the military revolution that made possible large-scale organized military power in Europe was responsible for the terrible devastation and horrors of the Thirty Years' War (1618–1648), when between 100,000 and 200,000 men were under arms.[39] Not that there had not been great devastation and horror on the battlefields of medieval Europe, such as was experienced at Agincourt in 1415 during the Hundred Years' War (1337–1453), but the death and destruction inflicted there was on a much lesser scale.[40] Signifi-cantly, these revolutionary changes in the organization of warfare led to changes in the development of the states of premodern Europe.

What was it about these changes in the nature of warfare in the fifteenth and sixteenth centuries that had such a momentous impact on state devel-opment? The answer is that the new armaments, navies, and large stand-ing armies (along with the defensive fortifications built to resist them) were

---

37. The notion of a "military revolution" in early modern Europe was first suggested by Rob-erts in his well-known 1956 lecture, "The Military Revolution 1560–1660," delivered in Belfast, Ireland. The lecture was expanded in Michael Roberts, "The Military Revolution, 1560–1660," in *Essays in Swedish History,* ed. Michael Roberts (Minneapolis: University of Minnesota Press, 1967), 195–225. Many of Roberts's claims have been subjected to criticism by a later generation of mili-tary historians, including his former student Sir Geoffrey Parker. Criticisms range from question-ing the use of the term *revolution* when changes occurred over more than a century, to quibbling over the specific time and place of the so-called military revolution. Parker himself emphasized the importance of the development of more powerful defensive fortifications designed to resist ar-tillery attack. Despite such criticisms, Roberts's basic premise remains incontrovertible: there were relatively sudden changes in military techniques, tactics, strategies, army size, organization, and weaponry that dramatically altered the nature of warfare in early modern Europe. In turn, this had a major impact on state development.

38. Brian M. Downing, *The Military Revolution and Political Change: Origins of Democracy and Autocracy in Early Modern Europe* (Princeton: Princeton University Press, 1991), 10.

39. Roberts, "Military Revolution," 215.

40. English historian Anne Curry concludes that Shakespeare and other historians, whether for dramatic or patriotic reasons, overstated the size of the French forces at Agincourt. Curry her-self estimates that an army of about 12,000 Frenchmen faced a force of about 9,000 English and Welsh soldiers on the battlefield. Anne Curry, *Agincourt: A New History* (Stroud, UK: Tempus, 2005), 187. Prior estimates put those on the battlefield at anywhere from 6,000 to 7,000 English-men to a French force of 10,000 to as many as 200,000 (with 25,000 considered the most reliable). John Keegan, *The Face of Battle: A Study of Agincourt, Waterloo, and the Somme* (New York: Pen-guin, 1978), 88.

significantly more expensive than the older instruments of war. This led to an enormous increase in the cost of warfare, which in turn, stimulated state expansion and the centralization of authority and power under the crown. The high cost of the new instruments of war greatly disadvantaged the local gentry, who could no longer easily afford state-of-the-art armaments, let alone large standing armies. Greater centralized authority was needed to manage the larger armies as well as raise the enormous revenue needed to sustain them. Consequently, the military function once shared by the local nobility of medieval Europe was gradually consolidated under the crown, and local power elites became less important. Larger states with greater populations and more centralized administration gained an advantage in the new forms of warfare.[41] In the memorable words of Sir Michael Howard, war in Europe brought the "bureaucratic and fiscal mechanisms that transformed loose coagulations of territorial authority into highly structured centralized states whose armed forces, though not necessarily large, were permanent, disciplined and paid."[42]

The centralization and consolidation of power and authority translated into fundamental changes in the nature of the European state. More than anywhere else, this was true in France, where the state developed and political power was centralized through centuries of continuous and costly warfare. This was a long process rather than a dramatic overnight "revolution." At times, the military struggle in France was between the crown and the local gentry, and at times with the local civilian populations. But mostly, it consisted of prolonged warfare with other European states—most often, England. As Rasler and Thompson put it: "France was essentially created through several hundred years of warfare, primarily but not exclusively with the English."[43] The states of Italy and Spain were similarly hardened

41. Porter summaries the relationship between war and the state as follows: "Changes in military technology and tactics from 1350 to 1500 greatly increased the cost of fielding armies. Rising costs, in turn, favored larger countries and more centralized governments, which alone could afford and manage the new warfare." Porter, *War and the Rise of the State,* 31; see also McNeill, *Pursuit of Power,* 117–43.

42. Howard, *Causes of Wars and Other Essays,* 16–17.

43. Rasler and Thompson, *War and State Making,* 64. The conflict from 1648 to 1653 (during the minority of Louis XIV) known as the Fronde was the last major resistance to the royal crown by the nobility of Paris. It resulted in the defeat of the nobles and the strengthening of royal authority. In 1667, a permanent police force was created in Paris to maintain order and

and political power centralized by centuries of warfare within the European community of kingly states.

Financing the Military State

The formation of large standing armies, technical innovations in the art of warfare, and the rising cost of new armaments imposed significant revenue demands on those rulers who sought to expand their territorial domains or defend their kingdoms against foreign invasion. Those states that could raise enough revenue to pay for standing armies and the new armaments, did so. Those states that could not raise the necessary revenue struggled and fell behind in the geomilitary competition that engulfed early modern Europe. By virtue of this nearly continuous competition over the course of centuries, many of the princely states did not survive into the modern era. Over the course of four centuries, the number of independent states in Europe dramatically declined. In 1500, there were some five hundred principalities, independent city states, and uncontested territories in Europe; by 1900, the number of European states had fallen to approximately twenty-five.[44] The "fittest" of the European states adapted to the new military and fiscal reality and thereby survived in this Darwinian struggle. The rest either disappeared or were swallowed up by more powerful neighbors. These were "the losers in a protracted war of all against all."[45]

The ability of a state to survive and prosper in the new geomilitary competition depended in large measure on its ability to mobilize economic and human resources within its domain and then deploy those resources for military purposes. This was facilitated by the centralization of power within the state and an expansion of the state apparatus—specifically, that component devoted to the military and its logistic support. Because centralization and the expansion of administrative capacity itself required

suppress riots. During the reign of Louis the XIV, the army increased from 50,000 to 500,000. Perry Anderson, *Lineages of the Absolutist State* (London: Verso, 1974), 102.

44. Bobbitt, *Shield of Achilles,* 96; Poggi, *The State,* 22.

45. Youssef Cohen, Brian R. Brown, and A.F.K. Organski, "The Paradoxical Nature of State Making: The Violent Creation of Order," *American Political Science Review* 75 (1981): 902.

additional revenue, rulers faced even greater pressure to secure new sources of revenue. Medieval rulers could live lightly off the land, collecting feudal fees and taxes owed them by virtue of their status in the feudal system. But princely rulers required more revenue than they could collect under the seigneurial regime, and the kingly states needed even more. How then did the states of the sixteenth and seventeenth centuries obtain the enormous revenue necessary to acquire the new and expensive armaments and standing armies? Because the states of early modern Europe were not themselves economic entities capable of generating their own revenue, rulers needed to appropriate revenue from individuals and social organizations located within their own territories or else from conquered territory and colonies. The variations in state development experienced among the states of Europe can be attributed to differences with respect to their capacity for revenue extraction, the societal wealth potentially subject to extraction, and the different revenue strategies employed by rulers to marshal societal resources for military purposes.

The methods used by the kingly states to extract revenue from society were quite different from those of the states of medieval Europe. Medieval rulers financed their limited military organizations through the feudal system of revenue extraction. The feudal prince, like the manorial lords beneath him, was owed tribute, service of arms from those living within his realm, and a wide variety of fees by virtue of the social organization and hierarchy that comprised the feudal system. Feudal fees remained an important source of revenue to the English crown as late as the Tudor period. G. R. Elton referred to such fees as the "ancient revenue of the crown," in contrast with the much greater revenue granted to kings by Parliament.[46] The collection of revenue by medieval rulers depended on the feudal system of hierarchy and loyalty, but the states of early modern Europe possessed larger armies that could be used to seize resources. Often, this force was deployed beyond the ruler's own territories and used to plunder foreign lands. Beyond supply lines, even relatively large armies could live off the booty they might seize. This was true of the Swedish Army deployed by Gustavus Adolphus on the continent during the Thirty Years' War.

---

46. G. R. Elton, *The Tudor Revolution in Government: Administrative Changes in the Reign of Henry VIII* (Cambridge: Cambridge University Press, 1953), 161.

That seventeenth-century army lived off the resources it seized in conquered territories—mostly that of the weak princely states in Germany.[47]

But there were limits to the system of state finance based on feudal fees and foreign plunder. Armies eventually returned home, and except in extreme emergencies, plunder is not an effective method of extracting revenue from within a state's own territory. For one thing, the use of coercion by rulers within their own territories invariably produced opposition from the landed gentry, manorial lords, nobility, as well as the clergy. The wealthy commercial classes in urban areas likewise resisted seizure of their property, and urban populations invariably resisted conscription. More subtle means of acquiring revenue were required. In those states with urban populations and significant commercial activity within their territories, rulers gradually moved toward regularized systems of extraction: laying imposts on wealthy individuals, land, and commercial activities, and using the revenue to support their armies. French kings initially responded to the increased cost of warfare by imposing a wide variety of temporary levies on their feudal vassals and subjects (including the peasantry). These levies were imposed on top of whatever ordinary dues or obligations were owed the crown based on the ancient principles, relationships, and obligations that were the lasting legacy of feudalism. The sale of venal offices, tax farming, customs farming, the sale of *rentes,* and "inside" credit (borrowing from office holders) were also important sources of revenue for the early modern French state.[48] But as the size of armies continued to grow, the feudal levies and these ad hoc fees and miscellaneous revenue sources proved insufficient to support those rulers who embraced the military revolution and engaged in substantial state building. With foreign troops serving in their armies, the cost of warfare increased further. The patchwork system of feudal levies could not support large standing armies of professional soldiers.[49]

---

47. Downing, *Military Revolution and Political Change,* 196. Downing reminds us that Gustavus Adolphus's first principle of war was that the venture "ought to pay for itself" (*bellum se ipsum alit*).

48. Ertman, *Birth of the Leviathan,* 76, 91–105, 140–42. The French crown repeatedly attempted to outlaw the practice of trafficking in offices but was unsuccessful during this period.

49. "What amounted to a gradual commercialization of the military sector thus put greater pressure on the crown's ability to extract the resources necessary to pay its troops." Rasler and Thompson, *War and State Making,* 64.

Rulers were forced to secure entirely new sources of revenue to support their expensive new militaries. Sometimes rulers devised successful financial innovations, but not always. Henry VIII (who inherited a small surplus of funds from his father) was constantly under pressure to find additional revenue. He acquired sizeable proceeds from the dissolution of the monasteries and friaries in the 1530s, just as many princes on the continent seized papal properties in the wake of the Reformation.[50] But the monastic estate was a one-time nonreplenishable source of revenue, and most of that revenue was squandered on Henry's numerous military ventures against France in the 1540s. The treasury of the English state was depleted as the cost of supporting its army in France greatly exceeded the plunder derived from the venture. The Tudor state ended up deeply in debt and weakened by the constant and significant revenue shortfalls it experienced. On her death, Elizabeth bequeathed a stronger administrative state to the Stuarts but also left a huge debt. It has been observed that "financial difficulties are no more than symptoms of deeper causes."[51] In this case, the deeper cause was the inability of the Tudor state to secure permanent and renewable sources of revenue for its expanded military activities. As a result, England, like other European monarchies, turned to debt financing and constantly ran into trouble meeting its debt obligations.[52] Similar financial problems were faced by the Spanish crown, which repeatedly defaulted on its private loans from financiers throughout the sixteenth and seventeenth centuries. (The Spanish crown declared itself bankrupt in 1557, causing a number of prominent private banking houses to go under with it.) When Spain again defaulted on its loans in 1575, the army of Philip II in the Low Countries went into mutiny, effectively ending Spanish control of the Netherlands.[53] Because of shortages of revenue necessary to pay wages to soldiers, the Dutch Army was periodically struck by mutinies during the 1680s, and units of the Swedish Army stationed in Germany mutinied in 1633 for the same reason.[54]

---

50. The seizure of the church's land by the elector Joachim II of Brandenburg is described in Diarmaid MacCulloch, *The Reformation: A History* (New York: Viking, 2004), 220. Napoleon seized what was left of the Papal States and imprisoned Pius VI when he protested.

51. Barrington Moore, Jr., *Social Origins of Dictatorship and Democracy: Lord and Peasant in the Making of the Modern World* (Boston: Beacon Press, 1966), 244.

52. Bean, "War and the Birth of the Nation State," 216.

53. Parker, *Military Revolution,* 153; see also Kennedy, *Rise and Fall of the Great Powers,* 47.

54. Parker, "The 'Military Revolution,'" 212.

The kingly rulers needed more productive sources of revenue capable of supporting the mobilization of the greater share of domestic resources demanded by their larger armies and virtually continuous military campaigns. But what they needed most was *replenishable* sources of revenue. This dictated in favor of a system of regularized taxation pursuant to which local populations pay tribute in exchange for protection. This arrangement (a protection racket, if ever there was one) first emerged in the cities of northern Italy where regular taxes were collected from merchants and citizens to pay armed men for protection, simultaneously ending the plunder of the cities and providing a regular profession for the armed men. As William McNeill summarizes, "Enough citizens concluded that taxes were preferable to being plundered to make the commercialization of organized violence feasible in the richer and better-governed cities of northern Italy. Professionalized fighting men had precisely parallel motives for preferring a fixed rate of pay to the risks of living wholly on plunder."[55]

The integrated system of commercialized "organized violence" that emerged was one of professional soldiers (often foreign mercenaries) defending citizens in exchange for tribute collected through taxes and other imposts. This was the system of military organization that Niccolò Machiavelli praised, for it offered citizens stability and peace in exchange for tribute.[56] The arrangement worked quite efficiently and spread to larger states. In France, the *taille royale* was imposed in 1439 during the Hundred Years' War as the first regular national tax (on land) and initially was used to support a unit of Scottish mercenaries employed by Charles VII.[57] Such new forms of taxation financed the gradual transformation of the feudal state into the nation-states that would dominate the European continent for centuries to come. In the second half of the fifteenth century, the revenue of the state greatly increased, representing no less than a doubling of the per capita burden on the citizenry.[58] By the late sixteenth century, the *taille* was the source of roughly half the income of the French crown.

---

55. McNeill, *Pursuit of Power,* 74.

56. "Although I have elsewhere maintained that the foundation of states is a good military organization, yet it seems to me not superfluous to report here that, without such a military organization, there can neither be good laws nor anything else good." Niccolò Machiavelli, *The Prince and The Discourses,* trans. Luigi Ricci (New York: Random House, 1940), 503.

57. Anderson, *Lineages of the Absolutist State,* 32. The total tax was set by the king and then apportioned among the various provinces. Clergy, nobles, officers of the crown, military personnel, magistrates, and certain cities (such as Paris) were generally exempt.

58. Bean, "War and the Birth of the Nation State," 217.

This was a direct tax consisting of the *taille réelle* (levied on the estimated value of land) and the *taille personnelle* (levied on the estimated wealth of an individual). From 1523 to 1600, the royal income of the French crown increased fourfold as the *taille* and other taxes proved extremely effective in raising revenue. In England during the reign of Henry VIII, the royal income of the crown tripled.[59] The creation of a permanent, fruitful, and replenishable system of taxation was integral to the development of the feudal state into the kingly territorial state of the sixteenth and seventeenth centuries.[60] The new "authority and power" was that of the kingly state, which used its national taxes to finance its expanded military capabilities.

To raise the national tariffs used to support the new professional armies, rulers relied on corporate participatory assemblies (estates, parliaments, *états generaux,* and *landtage*) to cultivate consensus and gather support for the new taxes and to facilitate the extraction process. This had the further effect of centralizing political authority, although not necessarily under the crown. Rulers called such assemblies mainly for the purpose of securing revenue (usually in the form of temporary taxes on wealth and land) for new military ventures. For centuries, this was the most important function performed by the English Parliament. By the fifteenth century, the king was dependant on parliamentary authorization to impose taxes. It has been said that the main reason the early Tudors summoned Parliaments in England was to acquire special grants for taxation. These grants of authority were required for direct taxation by the king of his subjects; generally, they were only granted during times of military conflict and emergency. In his authoritative account of taxation under the Tudors, Roger Schofield found that during the years from 1485 to 1547, with only three exceptions, grants from Parliament to the king for taxation "were made during times

---

59. Figures on royal income are reported in Michael S. Kimmel, *Absolutism and Its Discontents: State and Society in Seventeenth Century France and England* (New Brunswick, NJ: Transaction, 1987), 58–59.

60. "The right to impose and collect—that is, to administer—taxes became one of the means by which seigneurial or patrimonial authority over people was transformed into authority over territory, and by which authority and power of a feudal character, with all its mutual rights and obligations, was converted into authority and power of a quite different nature." Rudolf Braun, "Taxation, Sociopolitical Structure, and State-Building: Great Britain and Brandenburg-Prussia," in *Formation of National States in Western Europe,* ed. Tilly, 244.

of war or of imminent war."[61] Later, rejection of Stuart encroachments on Parliament's prerogative to approve such levies was a contributing factor leading to the English Civil War.

On the continent, where the corporative participatory assemblies never controlled the purse strings, the connection between the state's military power and the power to tax was even more direct and obvious. There the crown routinely used the national assemblies to legitimize the new systems of taxation. By the mid fifteenth century, French monarchs began to assert the right to increase levels of taxation themselves without consultation or approval of the Estates General, which in any event was only called sporadically during this period.[62] Similarly, the Spanish crown gained control over the power of taxation. But if the rulers of the powerful kingly states of continental Europe in the sixteenth and seventeenth centuries were better equipped than their princely predecessors to raise revenue independent of parliaments or estates, they were not absolutists. Society was not theirs to plunder at will.

To collect the new revenues required to support their more powerful standing armies, rulers needed to build a stronger administrative apparatus. As Brian Downing has suggested, "The means of destruction changed from relatively small feudal levies and militia to large mercenary and standing armies, which required a new superstructural apparatus to guarantee inputs of capital and labor. A more centralized and coercive state was needed to extract these inputs from an unwilling population."[63] This transformation did not occur everywhere in Europe at the same time. There

---

61. "National taxes were expected to be episodic rather than permanent. They could be levied only with the consent of parliament, though parliament could not withhold consent if the crown's claim that a state of emergency existed was correct. In practice and with few exceptions, both crown and parliament in the Tudor period respected these reciprocal obligations." Roger Schofield, *Taxation under the Early Tudors 1485–1547* (Oxford: Blackwell, 2004), 202. Schofield concludes that during this period, "there was a close relationship between war and parliamentary lay taxation." Ibid., 4–5.

62. Philip the Fair (1285–1314) was the first to convene the Estates General in France in 1302 for the purpose of gaining support in a struggle with the pope. Thereafter, he called the Estates General to obtain support for increased and new taxes. This support was not given during times of peace, although it was forthcoming during the Hundred Years War. After the defeat at Agincourt, the Estates General was revived and permanent taxation was imposed. The French monarchy generally dispensed with the Estates after the late 1400s and asserted the right to impose taxes on its own. Ertman, *Birth of the Leviathan,* 72–74, 91–110.

63. Downing, *Military Revolution and Political Change,* 57.

were differences in the timing and sequencing, and the impact of war on state development was not uniform throughout Europe.[64] Once again, the experience in England was distinct from that of the states on the continent. England was spared the burden and significant expense of maintaining a large standing army because of its relative isolation and distance from the European continent and the constant geopolitical competition that held sway there. England did not maintain a significant standing army until the formation of the New Model Army of 1645. At the time of the Restoration in 1660, the standing army was reduced to fewer than 6,000 men. The situation changed dramatically after the Revolution of 1688 as England became enmeshed in the geopolitical competition that absorbed European states on the continent. Thereafter, England maintained a significantly larger navy than before.[65] By the end of the War of the Spanish Succession in 1714, England had an army of more than 144,000 men—a force nearly as large as the army of France, which had a population almost twice that of England.[66] Arguably, because England did not need to maintain a large standing army prior to the seventeenth century, it did not experience the same effects on its state structure and was spared the absolutism that permeated the continent. The authority of Parliament checked that of the crown. This allowed England to maintain its ancient constitutional structure, which was subsequently infused with liberal and democratic political values.[67] Internally, England was a weak state even while it was a strong state vis-à-vis its competitors in the international order.

---

64. Ertman argues that differences in the organization of local government at the critical time of state formation and the timing of sustained "geomilitary competition" explain the variation in the nature of the political regimes and the institutional structures of the states of Europe. Ertman, *Birth of the Leviathan.*

65. Glete, *War and the State,* 40. Geography allowed England to go for so long without a standing army. As Sir Lewis Namier put it: "A great deal of what is peculiar in English history is due to the obvious fact that Great Britain is an island." Lewis Namier, *England in the Age of the American Revolution* (New York: St. Martin's Press, 1961), 7. The notion that England's security was attributable to her isolation has been challenged in recent years. See, e.g., John Brewer, *The Sinews of Power: War, Money and the English State, 1688–1783* (London: Unwin Hyman, 1989), 10–11.

66. Brewer, *Sinews of Power,* 7–8.

67. "Between 1600 and 1688, England was never exposed to heavy, protracted warfare requiring large, modern armies. It remained effectively removed from the continental wars; constitutional government prevailed." Downing, *Military Revolution and Political Change,* 179. Pursuant to the Declaration of Rights (1689), William and Mary agreed that consent of Parliament was required to raise a standing army.

During the reign of Queen Anne, the English state emerged as a constitutional monarchy financed in large measure by taxing the great wealth generated by the prosperous commercial economy that was already emerging by the beginning of the eighteenth century. This was a conscious decision, as affirmed by Queen Anne herself in a revealing speech delivered in 1714 to the opening session of Parliament: "This made us really formidable abroad, and brought riches home, and is what God and nature by our situation has pointed out to be our true interest; . . . I have [made] this maxim the aim of my government. . . . It is this nation's interest to aggrandize itself by trade."[68] In the long-run, this arrangement whereby the state linked its fortunes to the success of the commercial classes worked extraordinarily well, generating incredible wealth for both state and society. The English state emerged as the most significant power in Europe, even while consuming a lesser share of societal wealth than the states on the continent. Conversely, the French state floundered in the eighteenth century as the national economy experienced a steep decline.[69] Spain experienced a similar fate.[70]

Even before the reign of Queen Anne, England had already begun implementing numerous reform measures following the Glorious Revolution that provided the English state with the administrative capacity to tap the great wealth of the domestic economy. The state created its own apparatus to collect tax revenues, abolishing the old system of tax farming.[71] The new administrative apparatus included collection agencies, as well as a central treasury that exercised budgetary control over state spending—particularly

---

68. Quoted in Geoffrey S. Holmes and William A. Speck, eds., *The Divided Society: Parties and Politics in England, 1694–1716* (New York: St. Martin's Press, 1968), 96. These sentiments were echoed by the great proponent of trade and commerce, Daniel Defoe: "The rising greatness of the British nation is not owing to war and conquests, to enlarging its dominions by the sword, or subjecting the people of other countries to our power; but it is allowing to trade, to the increase of our commerce at home, and the extending it abroad." Daniel Defoe, *The Complete English Tradesman* (London, 1724), chap. 25; reprinted in Eugen Weber, ed., *The Western Tradition: From the Ancient World to Louis XIV* (Lexington, MA: D.C. Heath, 1995), 476–81.

69. Between 1688 and 1685, state expenditures in France and England accounted for roughly 7 percent of national product. In France, government spending rose to 13 or 14 percent during the wars of Louis XIV and settled at 12 percent by 1774. In England, the figure was only 4 percent. Figures cited in Frederic C. Lane, "The Role of Governments in Economic Growth in Early Modern Times," *The Journal of Economic History* 35 (March 1975): 8–17.

70. The decline of Spain under Charles V and the Habsburgs is recounted in Kennedy, *Rise and Fall of the Great Powers,* 50–55.

71. Brewer, *Sinews of Power,* 92.

with regard to military expenditures. Perhaps the most important reform was restructuring the system of public finance. This involved direct borrowing from the general public rather than from a small group of wealthy financiers.[72] Prior to the Financial Revolution of the eighteenth century, the English state borrowed from a "hotchpotch" of individuals and small groups of lenders, mostly located in London. In the 1700s, public finance moved to a longer-term basis with the creation of the joint-stock company and larger pools of capital, including foreign investors willing to lend to the English state. No longer beholden to a small group of wealthy individuals and bankers, the state could raise vast amounts of money in the new public markets. This was a critical event in the history of the development of the English fiscal-military state.[73] Of course, the ability of the English state to create a modern system of public borrowing was dependent on its ability to impose and collect taxes to repay its debt obligations. As John Brewer put it, "An effective tax system, providing the government with a substantial and *regular* income, was a necessary condition of the new credit mechanisms which...revolutionized eighteenth-century public finance."[74] In other words, the financial revolution of the eighteenth

---

72. Victoria Tin-bor Hui, *War and State Formation in Ancient China and Early Modern Europe* (New York: Cambridge University Press, 2005), 124.

73. The classic account of the creation of a market for government securities in eighteenth-century England is P.G.M. Dickson, *The Financial Revolution in England: A Study in the Development of Public Credit, 1688–1756* (New York: St. Martin's Press, 1967). As Dickson put it: "The provision of long-term capital to finance the state's war expenses was the most novel feature of the Financial Revolution." Ibid., 341.

74. Brewer, *Sinews of Power,* 89. In Brewer's account of the development of a "peculiarly British" version of the fiscal-military state, the creation of an effective tax administration is seen as the pivotal event: "The effectiveness with which the British state taxed its subjects was in large part a direct consequence of a major transformation in the British fiscal system that occurred gradually between the Restoration and the mid-eighteenth century, as England moved from a fiscal system marked by heterogeneity and amateurism to a tax administration characterized by the orderly collection of public moneys by a predominantly professional body of state officials." Ibid., 91.

Similar sentiments are expressed by O'Brien and Hunt: "The rise of a powerful and economically functional state in Britain waited upon two interrelated developments in its fiscal system: firstly, the establishment of a permanent public debt and, secondly, the provision of increasing flows of revenue (derived mainly from indirect taxes) required to service the regular interest payments which constituted the precondition for the debt's erratic but rapid accumulation in wartime." Patrick K. O'Brien and Philip A. Hunt, "England, 1485–1815," in *The Rise of the Fiscal State in Europe, c. 1200–1815,* ed. Richard Bonney (New York: Oxford University Press, 1999), 65.

century was possible only after the English state secured a replenishable stream of tax revenue.

Expenditures related to military activities (war, war preparation, and debt service on loans incurred to finance past wars) added up to more than the total expenditures devoted to all other purposes.[75] Most of the resources of the European state were devoted to military concerns. As Michael Mann observes, "Simply from an analysis of state finances, the functions of the [English] state appear overwhelmingly military and overwhelmingly geopolitical rather than economic and domestic. For more than seven centuries, somewhere between 70 and 90 percent of its financial resources were almost continuously deployed in the acquisition and use of military force."[76] From its inception, the military and taxing powers of the European state were closely linked. Taxes were used to support the military apparatus, and the military was used to collect taxes.

This is not surprising. The state's claim to an exclusive right to the use of coercion within the state's territory goes hand in hand with its power to extract resources from society through taxation.[77] The military apparatus of the state is dependent on the revenue of the state, and the revenue-raising powers of the state are dependent on the state's coercive powers. The state is a political organization that uses its coercive powers to extract revenue from society, which revenue is used to sustain the increasingly expensive military apparatus of the state. This proved the perfect formula for state building in early modern Europe. With stable sources of replenishable revenue, the rulers of the European states could deploy the new and more expensive methods of warfare. This in turn led to the expansion of

---

75. Bean, "War and the Birth of the Nation State," 216. Bean estimates that during the fourteenth, fifteenth, and sixteenth centuries, England spent from 60 to 75 percent of its budget on expenditures related to the military.

76. Michael Mann, *The Sources of Social Power,* vol. 1, *A History of Power from the Beginning to A.D. 1760* (New York: Cambridge University Press, 1986), 511.

77. Norbert Elias once observed: "Free use of military weapons is denied the individual and reserved to a central authority of whatever kind, and likewise the taxation of the property or income of individuals is concentrated in the hands of a central social authority. The financial means thus flowing into this central authority maintains its monopoly of military force, while this in turn maintains the monopoly of taxation. Neither has in any sense precedence over the other; they are two sides of the same monopoly." Norbert Elias, *Power and Civility* (New York: Pantheon, 1982), "The Civilizing Process," 2:104.

administrative capacities as more state officials were needed to collect the additional revenue raised through the tax systems.

The earliest examples of developed states in Europe in the middle of the sixteenth century (e.g., France, England, Spain, and Sweden) all created permanent bureaucracies and adopted centralized taxation in response to the need to finance increasingly expensive military operations. The new forms of warfare stimulated the development of the early modern state, and the early modern state required more revenue. The demand for greater revenue continued into the nineteenth century as the great nation-states of Europe emerged. Under Napoleon, the revenue derived from property taxes increased two and a half times, plus he added a whole new series of taxes to the arsenal of the French state.[78] On the other side of the English Channel, William Pitt the Younger implemented the world's first national income tax (5 percent on incomes over £200) in 1799 to finance England's ongoing war with France.[79] During the Napoleonic Wars, more than 30 percent of national income was extracted by the English state.[80] Most was collected through regressive "indirect" taxes (e.g., excise taxes and customs duties), which in the nineteenth century became the favored means for extracting revenue from society. Throughout Europe, taxation financed the development of the state. Where the economy was prosperous, as in England, this was an ideal mechanism for extracting societal wealth.

Thus far the analysis has focused on why certain states undergo the kind of development that results in stronger, more centralized political institutions with expanded state capacity, while other states do not. Equally significant and problematic is why some states of Europe achieved a democratic and liberal politics while others remained autocratic and illiberal. One response to the latter question comes from Brian Downing, who argues that where rulers were able to resist the militarization of the state during the crucial period of the military revolution of the sixteenth century, constitutional arrangements survived and provided the basis for liberal, constitutional rule in subsequent centuries—most notably, in England.[81]

---

78. Credveld, *Rise and Decline of the State,* 151.

79. This first income tax (known as the "war income tax") was enacted by Parliament in 1799 and repealed in 1816. For an account of this tax, see, Levi, *Of Rule and Revenue,* 122–44.

80. Michael Mann, *The Sources of Social Power,* vol. 2, *The Rise of Classes and Nation States 1760–1914* (Cambridge: Cambridge University Press, 1993), 115.

81. Downing, *Military Revolution and Political Change.*

According to Downing, where the military revolution overwhelmed the state, the result was "military-bureaucratic absolutism" and illiberal politics. This echoes the sentiment of Alexis de Tocqueville, who argued in his classic study of the destruction of the ancien régime that the centralizing force of the French monarchy shattered the remnants of the feudal system, the aristocracy, and the structures of local medieval society, and in doing so paved the way for the sweeping abuses of the Revolution.[82] For his part, Thomas Ertman attempts to explain both the variation among government or regime types ("absolutist" versus "constitutional") as well as differences in the "character" of the state apparatus ("patrimonial" versus "bureaucratic").[83] He suggests that the "timing" or "sequence" of key historical factors in the development of the militaries and industrial economies of the European states explains a good deal of the variation in the development among them—specifically, with regard to differentiating those states that we commonly regard as constitutional regimes from the autocratic or absolutist. As Ertman puts it, "Differences in the timing of the onset of sustained geopolitical competition go a long way towards explaining the character of the state infrastructures found across the Continent at the end of the 18th century."[84] The degree of independence of local representative assemblies explains some of the variations among the states of Europe. Those that experienced significant institutional development after the middle of the fifteenth century were more likely to build a modern, rational-legal bureaucracy within the framework of their constitutional regime than those that built a state apparatus prior to that period.[85]

---

82. Alexis de Tocqueville, *The Old Regime and the Revolution* (New York: Harper and Brothers, 1856), chap. 5 ("How Centralization Crept in Among the Old Authorities, and Supplanted Without Destroying Them"), and chap. 11 ("Of the Kind of Liberty Enjoyed Under the Old Regime").

83. Ertman classifies regimes into four categories: patrimonial absolutism (France, Spain, the Italian states), bureaucratic absolutism (Prussia), patrimonial constitutionalism (Poland, Hungary), and bureaucratic constitutionalism (England, Sweden).

84. Ertman, *Birth of the Leviathan*, 26. John Brewer argued that the timing of the emergence of a fiscal-military state in England affected the nature and structure of that state. Because England did not build a large standing army and stayed out of military conflicts on the continent during the sixteenth and early seventeenth centuries, a fiscal-military state developed in England that was quite distinct from the French state. Brewer, *Sinews of Power*, 24.

85. States that built bureaucracies after 1450 were better able to utilize new models and take advantage in hiring newly trained jurists who themselves were the product of a nascent system of university education in Europe. Those states built before 1450 generally adopted feudal patrimonial structures and were locked into those choices for centuries to come. Ibid., 27–28.

Whether the character of a regime affects its capacity to extract revenue from society is far from clear. Arguably, where the legitimacy of a constitutional regime is buttressed by representative assemblies, it will be easier for the executive to impose taxes. In this sense, representation may facilitate revenue extraction, while conversely, efforts to impose taxation without representation are liable to generate resistance from powerful interests. But this is far from the only possible outcome. After all, representative assemblies also provide the opportunity for discrete social and economic interests to organize, and thereby resist, the imposition of taxes that adversely affect them. Absolutist regimes are relatively unconstrained by the need to take into account such interests. This allows them to behave like predatory revenue extractors. Accordingly, we must consider further whether representative assemblies advance or constrain revenue extraction. Our study of American political development will shed light on this question. For now, we must side with Niall Ferguson, who rightly concludes that "the correlation between representation and taxation has not been universal."[86]

War, Revenue, and State Development

Not all rulers responded in the same way to the financial demands attributable to the expansion of the military apparatus. According to Tilly's theory of "coercion, capital, and state development," those European states with access to large numbers of men and "volumes of capital" had the clear advantage and built more stable state structures based on more durable patterns of extraction (i.e., revenue-raising techniques).[87] The interplay between geomilitary competition *and* economic conditions was critical. The nature and level of economic development in a particular state limits the war mobilization strategies available to its rulers. States with capital concentrated in cities followed a "capital intensive" path toward state development. Among these were the commercial states of Genoa, Switzerland, and Holland. States that lacked access to capital and population centers could not secure such sources of revenue. In large agrarian territories, landed gentry mobilized peasant populations into their armies through

86. Ferguson, *The Cash Nexus,* 83.
87. Tilly, *Coercion, Capital, and European States,* 65.

conscription. These became the great "tribute-taking" empires of Russia, Poland, Hungary, Sweden, and Prussia.

The most successful states of Europe followed the capital-intensive path. These were able to tap the wealth of cities and commercial activities conducted within their realms and raise armies from agrarian populations, thus emerging as the most developed and dominant states of Europe after the seventeenth century. Later, these states emerged as the great nation-states of the nineteenth century. They became the dominant political organizations in Europe precisely because of their relative advantages (financial and military) over competitors. These states had "access to a combination of large rural populations, capitalists, and relatively commercialized economies" that gave them military advantages. The nation-state of Europe became the model for states everywhere to emulate precisely because of its powerful combination of "coercion and capital."[88]

Extracting revenue from territories outside the state's own formal jurisdiction (whether through wartime plundering, colonization, or imperialism) has also been an important source of revenue throughout history. In the second half of the sixteenth century, Spain derived some 20 to 25 percent of its revenue inflows from precious metal transferred from its empire in the New World.[89] But plunder and colonization contribute little to state coffers in the postcolonial world, as foreign territories and "protectorates" typically impose a financial drain on the mother country.[90]

If the initial stimulant to state development in Europe in the fifteenth and sixteenth centuries was the increased cost of armaments and standing

---

88. Ibid., 30.

89. Anderson, *Lineages of the Absolutist State,* 71.

90. Maintaining its overseas "possessions" was costly to England. See E. James Ferguson, *The Power of the Purse: A History of American Public Finance, 1776–1790* (Chapel Hill: University of North Carolina Press, 1961), 19–20. Despite the psychological damage suffered by its defeat, England benefited economically from the loss of its American colonies, as it was relieved of a great financial burden. After the war, England enjoyed trade with its former colonies without the expense. Recall that Adam Smith urged England to abandon the American colonies on the grounds that the arrangement was expensive in peacetime and prohibitive during war: "The expense of the peace establishment of the colonies was, before the commencement of the present disturbances, very considerable, and is an expense which may, and if no revenue can be drawn from them ought certainly to be saved altogether. This constant expense in time of peace, though very great, is insignificant in comparison with what the defence of the colonies has cost us in time of war." Adam Smith, *The Wealth of Nations* (New York: The Modern Library, 1937), book 5, chap. 3 ("On Public Debts"), 899.

armies, financing their new military forces remained a continuing problem. The problem that arises in such situations lies in *maintaining* the expanded and permanent state apparatus and military organization. The small, temporary military organizations of feudal rulers, as well as princely rulers of the fourteenth and fifteenth centuries, could be sustained through a combination of feudal fees and plunder—what Tilly refers to as the "coercive-intensive" modes of revenue-raising.[91] However, the larger and more permanent military organizations of the kingly states required more regular and institutionalized modes of revenue extraction—most prominently, taxation of private wealth, land, and commercial activity. Where revenue demands cannot be satisfied, states experience systemic crisis and, even worse, "state breakdown." This is Skocpol's powerful argument with respect to the French monarchy in the eighteenth century. The inability of Louis XIV to raise sufficient revenue to maintain his armies, engaged in protracted war with England and on the continent, forced the Bourbon monarchy to increase domestic taxation on agriculture, consumption, and the wealthy and privileged nobility. This in turn stimulated the alienation and opposition of powerful groups (e.g., the landed nobility), which triggered social revolution.[92]

States with direct access to credit and a developed commercial economy have always had an advantage over those states that lack such resources—for example, states with agrarian economies.[93] Rasler and Thompson argue

---

91. Tilly, *Coercion, Capital, and European States,* 30.

92. Skocpol, *States and Social Revolutions,* 61. Goldstone traces the fiscal crisis of 1787–1789 to the system of taxation implemented by the French crown—overly dependent on land and agriculture (a declining sector), while discouraging of manufacturing and commerce. Jack A. Goldstone, *Revolution and Rebellion in the Early Modern World* (Berkeley: University of California Press, 1991), 198–228. Paul Kennedy attributes the decline of powerful states to diverting too large a portion of societal resources to military purposes, overextending the state strategically, and thereby weakening national power in the long-term. Kennedy, *Rise and Fall of the Great Powers,* xvi.

93. Brewer summarizes the advantages of states with developed commercial economies (e.g., England) over agrarian economies (e.g., France): "All tax collectors face three major problems: those of measurement—assessing liability on the basis of wealth or output; of collection—persuading or coercing subjects and citizens to pay their taxes; and of remittance—getting money from the point of collection into the coffers of the state. All three are exceptionally difficult to accomplish not only in a poor economy but in one characterized by subsistence agriculture, by scattered, small-scale production, by local markets, poor communications and by exchange in kind rather than through cash or credit. Conversely, an economy with commercialized farming, concentrated or large-scale production, inter-regional and national markets and a well-developed monetary or credit system will be much easier to tax." Brewer, *Sinews of Power,* 182.

that the maritime and commercial powers of Europe that flourished from 1500 to 1800 (Portugal, England, and the Netherlands) had the edge over the territorial states of the continent, such as France and Spain. The maritime and commercial powers had more developed financial systems and accordingly, were better able to borrow money. They built navies rather than large standing armies, which cost more to maintain. Overall, they were in a superior position to finance state activities. Public finance played an important role in furthering the success of the maritime and commercial powers in global warfare: "The earliest winners in the struggle for world leadership owed a significant proportion of their success to their ability to obtain credit inexpensively, to sustain relatively large debts, and generally to leverage the initially limited base of their wealth to meet their staggering military expenses."[94] Those maritime states able to create an efficient administrative apparatus to extract revenue from their commercial economies prospered—for example, eighteenth-century England, the first great fiscal-military state.

Even after the rise of the modern state in Europe, warfare continued to be a powerful stimulant to state development. At the same time, the European states assumed new functions beyond military protection. The "protection racket" was expanded. Beginning in the late nineteenth century, the states of Europe began to provide social welfare benefits to their citizens in addition to military protection. As a result, political leaders came under even greater pressure to raise revenue. The emergence of the modern nation-state, with its expensive armies and social welfare programs, is the subject of chapter 3.

---

94. Rasler and Thompson, *War and State Making*, 89. Tilly argued that "as the scale and expense of war expanded rulers who had access to credit and commercialized, easily taxable, economy gained great advantages in the conduct of war." Tilly, *Coercion, Capital, and European States*, 189.

3

The Rise of the Social Welfare State in Europe

The cure of social ills must not be sought exclusively in the repression of Social Democrats but simultaneously in the positive advancement of the welfare of the working classes.

—Kaiser Wilhelm I, "Address to the Reichstag" (1881)

Organization of social insurance should be treated as one part only of a comprehensive policy of social progress....Social security must be achieved by co-operation between the State and the individual. The State should offer security for service and contribution.

—Sir William H. Beveridge, *"Social Insurance and Allied Services"* (1942)

War making is the original and enduring activity of the state. In the pursuit of this ancient endeavor, rulers have dedicated vast resources over the centuries toward acquiring the expensive armaments of warfare for their armies and navies. Military spending has imposed a constant and nearly overwhelming financial burden on those states that make war, forcing their rulers to devise new and more aggressive revenue strategies. In the modern world, rulers now confront a second, and in many cases, even stronger pressure for revenue. Beginning in the late nineteenth century, the states of Western Europe gradually assumed the obligation to provide social welfare and retirement benefits to workers, and these programs expanded over the decades to cover all citizens. Following their lead, democratic states across the globe have adopted similar programs. Australia, New Zealand,

and the nations of Scandinavia have been especially generous in the benefits offered to their citizens, providing "cradle-to-grave" coverage. While the United States was relatively late in adopting its own programs, it too eventually made a comparable commitment. If social welfare programs in the United States are structured differently and somewhat less generously than their European and Scandinavian counterparts, they are nearly as expensive.

With the social welfare function overtaking war making as the primary activity of modern states (especially, those whose claim to legitimacy is based on consent), the financial burden imposed on public treasuries has increased dramatically. Indeed, the high cost of operating social welfare programs coupled with the great expenses associated with maintaining a modern military force is driving even the most prosperous democratic states of Western Europe and North America toward long-term financial insolvency. These states must now raise enough revenue not only to support their armies, which rely on expensive new technologies and weaponry, but also to pay for the wide array of social welfare benefits promised to their citizens. How rulers respond to these extraordinary financial demands is of critical importance to future state development. New revenue strategies are required to fund trillion dollar budgets. Before we consider these revenue strategies, we must ascertain how the state, a political organization originally and almost exclusively devoted to making war and defending its territories, evolved into the modern social welfare state.

The Great Transformation of the State

The first modern social welfare programs in Europe were adopted in the late nineteenth century, marking the beginning of what has been referred to, without exaggeration, as "a basic transformation of the state itself, of its structure, its functions, and legitimacy."[1] This fundamental reconstitution of the state is evidenced in dramatic changes in the long-term patterns of public spending and resource allocation. Public spending is one

---

1. Peter Flora and Arnold J. Heidenheiner, "Historical Core and Changing Boundaries of the Welfare State," in *The Development of Welfare States in Europe and America,* ed. Peter Flora and Arnold J. Heidenheiner (New Brunswick, NJ: Transaction Books, 1981), 23.

powerful indicator of a state's commitments. How a state allocates and distributes resources under its budget reveals much about the regime, and much is learned about the essential nature of a state by examining its finances.[2] As Rudolf Goldscheid once observed, "The budget is the skeleton of the state stripped of all misleading ideologies."[3] By the middle of the twentieth century, an examination of the budgets of the states of Western Europe would have revealed that, other than during periods of war, these states were spending more on social welfare and retirement programs than for armaments, armies, and national defense. A political organization that historically was the institutionalization of "violence" was transformed in a remarkably short time into an organization devoted primarily to the distribution of social welfare benefits to its citizens.

Was Leviathan tamed? To some extent, but not defanged. Modern states still maintain large, powerful, and expensive military forces. Even the democratic states of Western Europe, which have enjoyed relative peace and prosperity for more than a half century, maintain small armies (presumably, for protection from foreign invaders) and domestic police forces that exercise the state's monopoly on violence within their own borders. But make no mistake about it, the budget commitments and allocation of resources in the states of Western Europe indicate that their *primary* activity these days is distributing social welfare benefits, not making war. This dramatic shift in commitment represents a truly monumental event in the history of mankind—the "great transformation" of the state.[4] To the cynical, this fundamental shift in commitment is just one more manifestation

---

2. "Simply stated, the revenues a state collects, how it collects them, and the uses to which it puts them defines its nature." Terry Lynn Karl, *The Paradox of Plenty: Oil Booms and Petro-States* (Berkeley: University of California Press, 1997), 13.

3. Goldscheid's adage became known to an English-speaking audience when quoted in the translation of Joseph A. Schumpeter, "The Crisis of the Tax State" (1918), reprinted in *International Economic Papers* 4 (1954): 5–38.

4. Philip Bobbitt describes this transformation as a shift from the constitutional order of the nineteenth-century "state nation" (which put "the people in the service of the State") to that of the "nation state" (which derives its legitimacy from "putting the State in the service of its people"). Philip Bobbitt, *Terror and Consent: The Wars for the Twenty-First Century* (New York: Knopf, 2008), 193. The notion of a "great transformation" of the state is borrowed from Karl Polanyi, who argued that a transformative moment occurred in Europe in the nineteenth century with the breakdown of the old economic order and the rise of a modern market economy. Karl Polanyi, *The Great Transformation: The Political and Economic Origins of Our Time* (New York: Rinehart, 1944).

of the state's "protection racket." Rulers now provide protection *and* social welfare benefits in exchange for tribute. But this is no minor change. In little more than a century, the protection racket has evolved into an arrangement that bears a striking resemblance to a "social contract." Needless to say, there remain those states whose rulers are little more than stationary bandits who use the powers of the state to line their own pockets, providing little protection and few benefits in exchange for the tribute they command. But these are now generally seen as rogue states headed by illegitimate rulers who are outcasts among the nations of the world. Among modern democratic states, there is a genuine commitment to providing social welfare and retirement benefits to all citizens, and expansive systems of public finance have been enacted to pay for these income transfer programs. To paraphrase Justice Holmes, taxes are what we moderns pay in exchange for comprehensive retirement and social welfare coverage.[5]

What forces led to this great transformation of the state? We can trace this important institutional development to key events in European history—in particular, the French Revolution and its Napoleonic aftermath, as well as the democratization of European politics following the First World War. In retrospect, we can see that the French Revolution signaled the death knell of the ancien régime not only in France, but throughout Europe, and that the upheaval set in motion ultimately led to the mass democracies that emerged in Western Europe after the First World War. How did the revolution in France lead to the European social welfare state? Following the Treaty of Paris (1814) and the Congress of Vienna (1814–1815), with the time-honored institutions of Europe still racked by the repercussions of the French Revolution, the rulers of the great states on the continent became increasingly concerned with preserving the stability and legitimacy of their own regimes. During the revolution in France, citizenship was extended to those previously excluded under the "estate societies" of the eighteenth century (including French Jewry), and the notion of universal citizenship began to spread across the continent. After the defeat of Napoleon and his armies, the rulers of the nation-states of nineteenth-century Europe found themselves appealing openly for support

---

5. Oliver Wendell Holmes, Jr., certainly no Pollyanna, once wrote that: "Taxes are what we pay for civilized society." *Compania General de Tabacos v. Internal Revenue Service,* 275 U.S. 88, at 100 (Holmes, J., dissenting).

to a wider spectrum of persons and groups within their territories, not just the representatives of the estates that traditionally had been dominant. These included the rising bourgeoisie and the new industrial class. The expansion of citizenship in Europe necessitated a new style of governance, one that recognized interest groups and political parties that mobilized the lower classes. The new political order was heralded by Charles Maurice de Talleyrand, who judiciously warned the newly restored French monarch Louis XVIII of the perils of governing in the nascent Age of Democracy: "However legitimate a power may be, its exercise nevertheless must vary according to the objects to which it is applied.... Now, the spirit of the present Age in great civilized states demands that supreme authority shall not be exercised except with the concurrence of representatives chosen by the people subject to it."[6]

As the rulers of the states of nineteenth-century Europe were forced to cultivate popular support to enhance the legitimacy of their regimes, there was a gradual transformation of the raison d'être of the state. No longer exclusively commanders of military organizations (although they certainly remained that as well), the rulers of Europe found themselves presiding over nation-states in which citizenship was widely held. These rulers needed to forge durable relations with a wider range of social classes, providing a quid pro quo to the newly enfranchised classes to preserve what was left of the old order. Henceforth, the legitimacy of their regimes would need to be secured (at least in part) through an expression of "consent" by the people—if not through formal elections, which would not come to Europe until later, in the twentieth century following the First World War, then at least through popular acceptance of the legitimacy of the regime. In furtherance of this goal, sovereign rulers would need to pursue a broader conception of the general welfare of the nation, one encompassing more than just military protection.

The notion that the legitimacy of a regime depends on the consent of its citizens only arrived on the continent as a serious proposition in the early nineteenth century—much later than in the United States. Nevertheless, by the end of the century the principle was established throughout

---

6. "Report Presented to the King During His Journey From Ghent to Paris, June 1815," in *The Correspondence of Prince Talleyrand and Louis XVIII During the Congress of Vienna*, ed. M. G. Pallain (New York: Charles Scribner's Sons, 1881), 540.

Western Europe. The individual citizen, rather than the old estates, gradually emerged as the "basic unit" of the national political community. With an expanded citizenry and the subsequent intrusion of radical socialist parties into the political process, greater political pressure was exerted on the rulers of Europe. The enactment of the first social welfare programs in the late nineteenth century can be seen as a strategic response to the political pressures exerted on rulers from below.

Building a Social Welfare State

Scholars trace the origins of the modern social welfare state to events that transpired in the new German state, unified in the late nineteenth century through the efforts of Otto von Bismarck following Prussia's victory in the Franco-Prussian War of 1870.[7] Under the governance of Kaiser Wilhelm I and Chancellor Bismarck, the German state began to enact a comprehensive package of social welfare benefits for workers. This commenced in 1883 with the adoption of a system of compulsory sickness insurance for workers. Under the program, employers paid two-thirds of the cost of the insurance, with workers paying the balance. In 1884 and 1885, an accident insurance plan was added (funded entirely by employers), and the Old Age and Disability Insurance Law providing comprehensive pensions for the aged and disabled was added in 1889. In addition, an extensive code of factory regulations was put in place to regulate the conditions of labor.[8] While there was no national unemployment insurance until 1920, many municipal governments in Germany provided some measure of relief for the unemployed.[9] These programs had as their immediate goal the stabilization of income flows and the provision of basic services to workers at risk from the vagaries of the new industrial economy. In Germany, the state-mandated social insurance programs represent one more aspect of the penetration of society by the state. During this same period, the railroads were nationalized and a mass conscript army was organized.

---

7. The story of German unification is told in Christopher Clark, *Iron Kingdom: The Rise and Downfall of Prussia, 1600–1947* (Cambridge: Belknap Press, 2006), 556–67.

8. Thomas Katsaro, *The Development of the Welfare State in the Western World* (New York: University Press of America, 1995), 210–11.

9. Ibid., 211.

Limited as they were by today's standards, these programs were the first step in the critical process of linking state legitimacy to the distribution of social welfare benefits to the citizenry at large. The new social welfare programs were distinct from the old programs previously established in Europe for the indigent, such as poor laws, Catholic charity, and the sporadic distribution of monetary benefits to military veterans.[10] Gaston Rimlinger contrasts the first phase of European poor laws that emerged in some cases as early as the sixteenth century and lasted until the late nineteenth century with the "Liberal" phase that began in the late nineteenth century and continued until the First World War:

> The old relief system, the poor laws, applied mainly to those at the bottom of the socioeconomic ladder. It was never just relief; it started from the assumption that people were in need because of some character deficiency; relief, therefore, was provided under conditions that were intended partly as retribution for past failings and partly as a check against future failures. Social security implies an entirely different conception of social protection.... Its benefits are normally unrelated to the needs of the recipient....Generally, social security programs tend to redistribute income...among individuals, which involves issues of equity and justice.[11]

The chief characteristic of the new social welfare programs in Western Europe was that benefits would be distributed by the state to individuals by virtue of their being within defined legal categories. As Reinhard Bendix emphasized, in Western Europe "public goods" such as social welfare benefits henceforth would be due to individuals by virtue of their status as "citizens," unrelated to social position or inherited privilege.[12]

Bismarck's motives for initiating these social welfare and insurance programs were ambiguous and have generated considerable debate among

---

10. A detailed account of efforts in Europe to care for the poor and infirm prior to the creation of the modern social welfare state is found in Abram de Swaan, *In Care of the State: Health Care, Education, and Welfare in Europe and the USA in the Modern Era* (New York: Oxford University Press, 1988), 13–51; see also Anton C. Zijderveld, *The Waning of the Welfare State* (New Brunswick, NJ: Transaction Publishers, 1999), 15–36; Hugh Heclo, *Modern Social Politics in Britain and Sweden: From Relief to Income Maintenance* (New Haven: Yale University Press, 1974), 46–64.

11. Gaston V. Rimlinger, *Welfare Policy and Industrialization in Europe, America, and Russia* (New York: John Wiley, 1971), 3–4.

12. Reinhard Bendix, *Nation-Building and Citizenship: Studies of Our Changing Social Order* (New York: John Wiley, 1964), 106.

scholars ever since. The dominant view is that Bismarck, working in conjunction with the kaiser, engineered these initiatives to diffuse "socialist challenges to traditional, patriarchal rule."[13] According to this interpretation, the social legislation was enacted as part of a conservative, patriarchal effort to co-opt the working classes, undermine the growing strength of Social Democrats, the General German Workingmen's Union, and the radical socialist parties, and at the same time stabilize and unify the new German state.[14] There is considerable support for this view. Bismarck had witnessed the Paris Commune in 1871 and feared similar developments in Germany. After pursuing a harsh campaign to crush the budding socialist and unionist movements following the election of 1877, Bismarck suddenly and dramatically changed course—likely because the effort was failing. Thereafter, he began to promote the idea of distributing social welfare insurance to workers, providing them with the most prominent benefits on the socialist agenda, thereby satisfying workers' demands within the confines of the given social order while undercutting the appeal of the radical parties. Bismarck's program has been appropriately characterized as "a strategic response of a patriarchal state to the growing strength of the socialist workers' movements."[15] According to Rimlinger, Bismarck's "central political consideration was not the creation of new rights, consistent with a new interpretation of the rights of citizenship, but the preservation of the traditional relationship of the individual to the state.... The whole thrust of his measures was to preserve the traditional system of political inequality."[16]

Be that as it may, Bismarck wanted not just to appease and silence workers, but actually to *align* their interests with those of the patriarchal German state, effectively vitiating the appeal of the socialist parties and radical unionists. In 1881, the kaiser himself revealed the logic underlying this pursuit in his address to the opening session of the Reichstag: "The cure of social ills must not be sought exclusively in the repression of Social

---

13. Edward Crankshaw, *Bismarck* (London: Macmillan, 1981), 378; Alexander Hicks, *Social Democracy and Welfare Capitalism: A Century of Income Security Politics* (Ithaca: Cornell University Press, 1999), 19.

14. "Bismarck made a bid for unification of the Second Reich through the introduction of an epochal scheme of social legislation." Polanyi, *Great Transformation,* 175.

15. Hicks, *Social Democracy and Welfare Capitalism,* 43.

16. Rimlinger, *Welfare Policy and Industrialization,* 112.

Democrats, but simultaneously in the positive advancement of the welfare of the working classes.... Those who are disabled in consequence of old age or invalidity possess a well-founded claim to a more ample relief on the part of the State than they have hitherto enjoyed."[17] Notice that the kaiser did not renounce the repression of Social Democrats. He merely declared that henceforth such repression would be pursued in conjunction with a second prong in the assault on Social Democrats—namely, the establishment of social welfare programs for the working classes to bind their allegiance to the German state.

In actuality, the system of social insurance instituted in Germany in the 1880s served multiple interests (the state, political elites, workers, socialist parties) and could have been appropriated and used by whatever political interest happened to be in power. As Alexander Hicks suggests, "The principle of public insurance readily catered both to liberal interests in the subordination of public income to earlier labor market activity and to state-bureaucratic interests in an easily legitimated and administered mode of financing."[18] From a statist perspective, the social welfare and retirement insurance programs can be seen as furthering the interests of the state and entrenched political elites by quelling political discontent and enhancing institutional stability. These kinds of programs (especially retirement programs with contributions made over a long period and coverage vesting only at the *end* of the worker's life) create a strong attachment to the existing regime. After all, a change in regime could result in the loss of a worker's vested interest in retirement benefits. (This was the case with the fall of the Soviet Union, as the benefits paid to retirees and pensioners were cut severely under the postcommunist regime.) There was no comparable financial arrangement that bound citizens to the states of medieval or early modern Europe (although there were strong kinship ties that held these states together), as the collapse of a state or the ousting of the ruling clique had no direct impact on the financial status of a peasant or worker under those regimes. In premodern Europe, citizens and workers were not dependent on the survival and continuity of any particular regime as they are in the modern social welfare state. This was the conservative impact of Bismarck's programs. At the same time, it cannot be denied that these

---

17. Kaiser Wilhelm I, quoted in ibid., 114.
18. Hicks, *Social Democracy and Welfare Capitalism,* 13.

early social welfare programs provided valuable benefits to workers, easing the strains and discontinuities in income flows experienced in the new industrial economy. From a class-based perspective, the mobilization of the working class through unions and leftist parties can be credited with prodding the political system to distribute these benefits.[19] It is no coincidence that the social welfare programs were considered successful from the perspective of *both* state officials and the beneficiaries. This explains the longevity and broad appeal of such programs wherever they have been adopted.

The initial success in Germany was replicated elsewhere as social welfare programs were soon adopted by other states in Europe. For example, after some initial public haggling, political accommodation was reached between the Liberal and Labour parties in England following the election of 1906. Thereafter, the new Liberal government of Anthony Asquith enacted England's first national Old Age Pensions Act in 1908.[20] By 1913, a million persons were receiving old age pensions in England from public funds.[21] In 1911, health and unemployment insurance was instituted by the Liberal government. A minimum wage was established for industrial workers, and workmen's compensation was enacted, requiring employers to insure their workers against injuries from most industrial and workplace accidents.[22] The new social welfare system spread to other countries in Europe. The initial participants included Denmark, Sweden, Belgium, France, Switzerland, and Italy.[23] By the 1920s, all of the states of Western Europe had adopted programs providing some minimal degree of protection or income support in one or more of the following categories: income maintenance programs for old age, disability, survivors,

---

19. For a detailed discussion of the various theoretical approaches to explaining the welfare state, see Hicks, *Social Democracy and Welfare Capitalism,* 13–34.

20. For a comprehensive comparison of the social welfare programs in England and Germany, see E. P. Hennock, *The Origin of the Welfare State in England and Germany, 1850–1914: Social Policies Compared* (New York: Cambridge University Press, 2007).

21. Katsaro, *Development of the Welfare State in the Western World,* 229.

22. For an account of the enactment of these measures by the Liberal Government, see Katsaro, *Development of the Welfare State in the Western World,* 228–29; Hicks, *Social Democracy and Welfare Capitalism,* 43–44.

23. For an account of the development of social insurance programs in these countries, see Peter Flora and Jens Alber, "Modernization, Democratization, and the Development of Welfare States in Western Europe," in *Development of Welfare States in Europe and America,* ed. Flora and Heidenheiner, 37–80.

and unemployment; health insurance; and workman's compensation for those injured in the workplace. Aid to working mothers with children came later—in the 1930s in Italy and France, and in the 1940s in Britain, Sweden, and Canada.[24] Alexander Hicks describes the initial programs enacted from 1880 to the 1920s as characteristic of a period of "extensive industrial expansion, mass enfranchisement, and social reform."[25] Furthermore, much of the initiative behind these programs came from state actors, rather than unions or political parties on the left. As Hugh Heclo describes the enactment of unemployment insurance in Britain in 1911, it was not the unions or political parties that petitioned the government for these programs, instead "it was a question of the government departments lobbying to persuade them [the interest groups] rather than vice versa."[26] This is an important point. Making a similar argument, Peter Swenson observes that "private interests were simply overwhelmed by state officials and policy experts with their autonomous problems, ideals, ambitions, and powers."[27]

A second phase of social welfare policymaking followed in the wake of the First World War, which destroyed what little remained of the hierarchical structures and social institutions of the ancien régime in Europe. Beginning in the early 1920s, the initial social welfare programs were consolidated and institutionalized as permanent functions of the state. There

---

24. See Robert T. Kudrle and Theodore R. Marmor, "The Development of the Welfare State in North America," in *Development of Welfare States in Europe and America,* 83; Margaret S. Gordon, *Social Security Policies in Industrial Countries: A Comparative Analysis* (New York: Cambridge University Press, 1988), 6–7.

25. Hicks, *Social Democracy and Welfare Capitalism,* 45. Hugh Heclo describes this initial period from the 1880s to the 1920s as an "era of experimentation." Hugh Heclo, "Toward a New Welfare State?" in *Development of Welfare States in Europe and America,* 383–85.

26. Hugh Heclo, *Modern Social Politics in Britain and Sweden: From Relief to Income Maintenance* (New Haven: Yale University Press, 1974), 84.

27. Peter A. Swenson, *Capitalists against Markets: The Making of Labor Markets and Welfare States in the United States and Sweden* (New York: Oxford University Press, 2002), 294. Swenson is critical of the notion that the scope and generosity of a nation's social welfare programs is determined by the strength of its leftist prolabor parties as well as the simplistic assumption that business interests are uniformly opposed to such programs. He stresses the important role of capitalists and political elites in both countries in shaping labor markets and structuring social welfare policies—admittedly to suit their own interests, but nonetheless, generous and to the benefit of workers as well. "In Sweden, as in the United States, employers quietly endorsed the main components of the welfare state, not out of resignation but out of self-interest." Ibid., 293.

are several of reasons why this consolidation occurred following the global war. As Bruce Porter explains:

> The experience of total war on the 'home fronts' of Europe greatly facilitated the emergence of welfare states all across the continent; that experience was both an important contributing factor in its own right and a *catalyst* of other underlying causes.... The welfare impetus of industrialized warfare stems not only from the implicit bargain of social discipline in exchange for welfare concessions but also from the intense social *cooperation* that this kind of war demands and brings about.[28]

The price for the support of the citizenry during the First World War was that the European state would provide increased public goods during the peace that followed. Was this arrangement a protection racket or social contract? It is hard to say. In any event, by the early 1930s, the states of Europe were spending more on social welfare and the distribution of public goods than on their military forces. That would change with the buildup in spending for armaments during the period immediately prior to the Second World War. But even following that global war, when overall state spending decreased with peacetime budgets, spending on social welfare programs exceeded prewar levels.[29]

As previously discussed, government spending significantly increases during sustained periods of war—whether defined as "global war" or "total war." With regard to the two world wars of the twentieth century, the higher levels of wartime military spending translated into higher levels of postwar spending on social welfare programs. As Alan Peacock and Jack Wiseman concluded, increased wartime spending permanently raises the level of public expenditures in general. Their thesis is a variation and refinement of Wagner's Law of expanding state expenditures—attributed to Adolf Wagner (1835–1917), the German economist who claimed that

---

28. Bruce D. Porter, *War and the Rise of the State: The Military Foundations of Modern Politics* (New York: Free Press, 1994), 180–81.

29. In England, the commitment by the Labour government to expand social welfare benefits following the Second World War was first publicly articulated by Sir William H. Beveridge, a British economist and social reformer. The so-called Beveridge Report (1942) outlined the major programs of what would become the English "Welfare State," providing cradle to grave coverage for all citizens. William H. Beveridge, *Social Insurance and Allied Services* (London: H. M. Stationery Office, 1942).

government spending in industrial nations tends to rise at a faster pace than the expansion of their national economies.[30] Refining Wagner's logic, Peacock and Wiseman argued that during wartime crisis, normal civilian resistance to taxation weakens, permitting state officials to significantly increase tax rates and broaden tax bases to support increased spending on the military: "People will accept, in times of crisis, methods of raising revenue formerly thought intolerable, and the acceptance of new tax levels remains when the disturbance has disappeared."[31] In their analysis of governmental expenditures in twentieth-century England, Peacock and Wiseman found that postcrisis spending (including nonmilitary expenditures) declined from wartime highs, but nevertheless remained higher than prewar levels. This permanent "displacement effect" (often referred to as a "ratchet effect") explains the widespread trend among the democratic nation-states in the twentieth century pursuant to which government spending has consistently outpaced economic growth.

If this displacement effect resulted in higher overall public spending in Europe following the global wars of the twentieth century, much of that spending was earmarked for social welfare and retirement insurance programs. By mid-century, most of the states of Western Europe were spending no less than 10 percent of gross domestic product (GDP) on social welfare and retirement insurance programs—far more than the United States. By the mid-1970s, Western Europe states were allocating an average of almost 25 percent of their national resources to social welfare and retirement insurance, compared to less than 2 percent for military programs.[32] The postwar spending spree on social welfare was fueled largely by expanding

---

30. In 1863, Adolf Wagner formulated his law of an expanding state. He referred to a "law of increasing expansion of public, and particularly state, activities," which translates into "the increasing expansion of fiscal requirements." See, e.g., Adolf Wagner, "Three Extracts on Public Finance," in *Classics in the Theory of Public Finance,* ed. Richard A. Musgrave and Alan T. Peacock (New York: MacMillan, 1958), 8.

31. Alan T. Peacock and Jack Wiseman, *The Growth of Public Expenditure in the United Kingdom* (Princeton: Princeton University Press, 1961), xxiv. The two subsequently refined their methodology in Alan T. Peacock and Jack Wiseman, "Approaches to the Analysis of Government Expenditure Growth," *Public Finance Quarterly* 7 (1979): 3–23.

32. A comparison of national spending on social security in 1980 as a percentage of GDP reveals considerable variation among 26 nations, ranging from 24–28 percent at the upper end (e.g., Scandinavia and Western Europe), 14–17 percent in the middle range, and 10 percent at the lower end. See Gordon, *Social Security Policies in Industrial Countries,* 21; B. Guy Peters, *The Politics of Taxation: A Comparative Perspective* (Cambridge: Basil Blackwell, 1991), 75–81.

economies, inflation, and the general prosperity enjoyed in the postwar decades.[33] Among the most "generous" states (Austria, Denmark, Sweden, Norway, Ireland, and Great Britain), spending on social welfare averaged 23 percent of GDP. From 1960 to 1990, expenditures for social welfare and retirement insurance programs as a percentage of GDP had increased among the Western democracies by as much as 96 percent in some cases, but in no event by less than 84 percent.[34] The trend ended in the mid-1990s, when states implemented significant cutbacks in services and pursued a general policy of "programmatic retrenchment." Even the states of Western Europe most committed to providing comprehensive social welfare coverage for their populations were forced to rethink, and in some cases cut back, their programs during periods of economic stagnation. Notwithstanding such periods of retrenchment, social welfare and retirement insurance programs remain deeply ingrained and well established in the traditions and budgets of the democratic states of Western Europe, Scandinavia, Australia, and New Zealand.[35]

If social welfare spending has increased in the postwar period, the states of Western Europe have spent less on their military forces. In 2005, Great Britain allocated only $49 billion and France $40 billion toward military spending in their budgets. In recent years, spending on defense as compared to total expenditures for these countries has been approximately 7 percent and 14 percent, respectively. In 2005, Germany spent less than $30 billion on defense, while Italy spent $17.5 billion, Spain $9.9 billion, and Belgium $3.3 billion. These figures represent even lower percentages of total expenditures than those for France and England. In contrast,

---

33. The period of expansion for social welfare programs from the mid-1950s to 1990 is discussed in Hugh Heclo, "Toward a New Welfare State?" in *The Development of Welfare States in Europe and America*, 393–98; see also Neil Gilbert, *Transformation of the Welfare State* (New York: Oxford University Press, 2002), 23–24.

34. Figures are from Hicks, *Social Democracy and Welfare Capitalism*, 153. A good summary of spending trends (as a percentage of GDP) for eleven Western European states, Great Britain, four Eastern European states, and the United States is found in Gordon, *Social Security Policies in Industrial Countries*, 12–19.

35. "Programmatic retrenchment" is discussed in Hicks, *Social Democracy and Welfare Capitalism*, 194–229; see also Paul Pierson, "Post-Industrial Pressures on the Mature Welfare State," in *The New Politics of the Welfare State*, ed. Paul Pierson (New York: Oxford University Press 2001), 80–104; Peter Starke, *Radical State Welfare Retrenchment: A Comparative Analysis* (New York: Palgrave Macmillan, 2008). After 1993, there was a general slowdown and then reversal of the growth rate for spending on social welfare. Gilbert, *Transformation of the Welfare State*, 23.

the United States dedicated $419 billion to its military in fiscal year 2006 out of total expenditures of $2.58 trillion.[36] The modern state is a social welfare state that maintains a small army on the side for emergencies—with the notable exception of the United States, which maintains social welfare programs and a very large and expensive army on the side.

A detailed analysis of the various programs in all the different states is beyond the scope of this study. What is germane is that the deep commitment of the modern nation-states to social welfare and retirement insurance programs has translated into an extraordinary demand for revenue that is exacerbated by even greater pressures attributable to maintaining military forces addicted to expensive, high-technology weaponry. The twin pressures for revenue (social welfare and military) were felt most strongly during the Cold War by the United States and the former Soviet Union, nations that greatly increased their military spending throughout the period even while the democracies of Western Europe reduced theirs. In the Soviet Union, the state relied on central planning to control the production and distribution of military goods, as well as most social welfare benefits and most necessities of life.[37] The results were disastrous. In the end, distributing and financing these social welfare benefits, while at the same time attempting to maintain a large modern techno-military apparatus in competition with the United States, proved beyond the economic capacity of the Soviet state. The result was a classic case of state breakdown followed by regime collapse, all in an amazingly short time. How a state goes about solving the critical problem of raising revenue to finance its social welfare programs is of utmost importance to the development and survival of that regime. The Soviet Union failed in this endeavor,

---

36. International Institute for Strategic Studies, U.S. Department of Defense; Center for Arms Control and Non-Proliferation; Office of Management and Budget, *The Budget for Fiscal Year 2007,* historical table 3.2 ("Outlays by Function and Subfunction: 1962–2011"); *The Europa World Year Book 2005* (London: Routledge, 2005). The attitudinal differences between Europe and the United States with respect to the use of military force (i.e., state power) in international diplomacy are emphasized by Robert Kagan in his provocative essay, "Power and Weakness: Why the United States and Europe See the World Differently," *Policy Review* 113 (June/July 2002): 3–28.

37. According to the assessment of one prominent scholar of the former Soviet Union: "The [Soviet] state is, effectively, the sole distributor of social welfare benefits in the realm of health, education, housing, culture and recreation." Neil Harding, "Conclusion," in *The State in Socialist Society,* ed. Neil Harding (Albany: SUNY Press, 1984), 309.

and the separate states of the old federation gladly departed following the collapse of the center.[38]

In the United States, where social welfare programs were introduced relatively late, the demand for revenue has mounted steadily since the 1960s. In recent decades, the rising cost of the social welfare programs of the American state has even outstripped spending for the military. At the same time, changing demographics has undermined the financial integrity of Social Security, the national income-maintenance program for the elderly. The financial position of the American state has been strained by the so-called entitlement programs (especially, Social Security and Medicare). Entitlement spending is outside the control of the normal congressional budget and appropriation process. Whether state officials can continue to raise enough revenue through taxes and borrowing to finance *both* the expensive military and social welfare programs of the United States remains to be seen. The continued development of the American state depends on it. Accordingly, we will return to this important subject in chapter 8 after we examine the historical origins of the American state and the development of its fiscal and military powers in the eighteenth and nineteenth centuries.

---

38. Fueled by revenue from its vast gas and oil resources, Russia has recently adopted a more aggressive posture toward its former satellite states—as witnessed most vividly in the Republic of Georgia in August 2008.

4

Origins of the American State

It is proposed that humble application be made for an act of Parliament of Great Britain, by virtue of which one general government may be formed in America, including all the said colonies, within and under which government each colony may retain its present constitution, except in the particulars wherein a change may be directed by the said act.

—*Preamble,* Albany Plan of Union (1754)

America is therefore the land of the future, where, in the ages that lie before us, the burden of the World's History shall reveal itself.

—Georg Wilhelm Friedrich Hegel, *The Philosophy of History* (1837)

In the chapters that follow, we turn from Europe to the New World to trace the development of the American state from its initial formation in the late eighteenth century as a weak, highly decentralized confederacy to the emergence of a strong fiscal-military state in the twentieth century. This institutional transformation is all the more remarkable given that the American state at its founding possessed neither a significant military nor any effective means for revenue extraction. Nor did the American state perform any social welfare or regulatory functions in the late eighteenth century. Indeed, the national government of the American state originally functioned as little more than the executive committee for the mutual defense league created by the thirteen separate states to fight the British. Even as the political order underwent significant political changes during the first half of the nineteenth century (in particular, the emergence of democratic political norms and a competitive party system), the national government remained extraordinarily weak within the confines of the federal structure established by the Constitution of 1787. Yet today the American state possesses both the most powerful military in the world and an extraordinarily efficient system of revenue extraction, engages in extensive regulation of its domestic economy, and provides its citizens with social welfare benefits nearly as generous as those of the social democracies of Western Europe.

While the familiar story of the founding of the United States is one of the great successes of our political leaders in waging the Revolution and founding the republic, the focus here is on the *deficiencies* of the state apparatus they built, especially with regard to the traditional indices of stateness: administrative capacity, military power, social and economic regulation, and revenue extraction. From this perspective, the early American state must be viewed as a notable *failure,* incapable of developing beyond this embryonic stage on account of its overly decentralized constitutional structure and perennial shortages of resources. The inability of officials of the national government to raise sufficient revenue reflected the peculiar constitutional design of the early American state in which political power was preserved at the local level to a degree unknown in Europe. This extreme decentralization of political power remains the distinguishing structural feature of the American state.

The decision to adopt a federal constitutional structure had a profound impact on the subsequent development of the American state. It has been observed that the distinctive features of the American state are "incoherence and fragmentation in governmental operations" and the "absence of clear lines of authoritative control."[1] Such structural defects can be largely attributed to its archaic eighteenth-century constitutional design.[2] Yet in

---

1. Stephen Skowronek, *Building A New American State: The Expansion of National Administrative Capacities, 1877–1920* (New York: Cambridge University Press, 1982), viii. Kimberley Johnson identifies two fundamental problems of the modern American state: "the jarring mix of institutional incoherence and strength, and the fragmented and disjointed nature of public policy." Kimberley S. Johnson, *Governing the American State: Congress and the New Federalism, 1877–1929* (Princeton: Princeton University Press, 2007), 5.

2. Samuel Huntington wryly observed that the founders adopted sixteenth-century political institutions precisely at the time England was abandoning them: "The principal elements of the English sixteenth-century constitution were exported to the new world, took root there, and were given new life precisely at the time that they were being abandoned in the home country. They

spite of the grave shortcomings of the constitutional design of the early American state, political leaders eventually succeeded in expanding the powers and capacity of the national government. New revenue strategies were adopted, and a powerful military was built. How this remarkable reconstitution of the American state was accomplished is the subject of the chapters that follow.

America: The Nonstate State

Notwithstanding the prosperity it now enjoys, the American state was not always grounded on a secure financial foundation. At its inception in the late eighteenth century, the American state possessed fiscal powers that were weak and precarious at best. Indeed, *all* of the powers of the national government were extraordinarily limited under the nation's first constitution, the Articles of Confederation (1781–1788). Although the new political order conceived in Philadelphia during the summer of 1787 effected genuine improvements, fundamental problems remained. The national government still performed relatively few and exceedingly limited functions, possessed a minimal military force and administrative apparatus, asserted negligible control over social and economic activity within its territory, and most important, lacked the capacity to extract resources from society to sustain even its insignificant state apparatus. Over the next two centuries, political elites struggled to expand the powers of the national government and establish a more coherent political order. This proved a daunting task.

A preliminary question arises at the onset of any study of the development of the American state: Why did political leaders adopt such a weak, fragmented, and decentralized constitutional structure in the first place? There had been no feudalism in North America, and those political leaders who sought to build a centralized nation-state in the late eighteenth century did not face the same kind of resistance to the consolidation of political power found in medieval Europe, where it took centuries for the princely rulers to pacify and overcome the local centers of power and the system

were essentially Tudor and hence significantly medieval in character." Samuel P. Huntington, *Political Order in Changing Societies* (New Haven: Yale University Press, 1968), 96.

of feudal hierarchy that dominated medieval society. Given the absence of feudalism, one might have expected a swift consolidation of political power within a new central state once independence from England was achieved. That did not happen. Instead, nationalists confronted powerful resistance from entrenched interests in the states hostile to the institution-alization of political power and authority in the offices of the national gov-ernment. These local interests and factions were rooted in the economic and social fabric of the states, whose political leaders perceived (correctly) that any reconstitution of existing political arrangements would be at their expense. Their opposition to the centralization of political power and au-thority under a national banner was reinforced by the longstanding and deeply ingrained sense of loyalty and attachment that citizens felt for their local state governments. As Merrill Jensen once observed: "The belief in the 'nationality' of the states was...a strong force against centralization. The state was a nation in the minds of its citizenry."[3] As long as citizens owed their primary allegiance to their local state governments, it was im-possible to build a strong nation-state in the European sense.[4]

Deep-rooted resistance to the centralization of political power and au-thority persisted for decades following the founding of the republic and erupted into outright rebellion in the middle of the nineteenth century. While a strong central state was built in the North during the Civil War and Unionists ultimately prevailed in that military conflict, the underly-ing issues concerning the division of power were never fully resolved and continued to fester into the twentieth century. Indeed, the resistance of the periphery to the center has never been fully overcome. To this day, an extra-ordinary degree of political power in the United States remains entrenched at the local level, even as the overall balance of power within the federal structure has shifted in favor of the national government since the 1930s. The enduring conflict and institutional incoherence of the political order is attributable to the decision in the late eighteenth century to constitu-tionalize, and hence preserve, the extant division of sovereignty between the national government and the states, a constitutional arrangement once

---

3. Merrill Jensen, *The Articles of Confederation: An Interpretation of the Social-Constitutional History of the American Revolution, 1774–1781* (Madison: University of Wisconsin Press, 1940), 12.

4. Similarly, contemporary efforts to create a unified pan-European political organization are doomed to failure so long as citizens retain their primary loyalty to the ancient states of Europe.

commonly referred to as "dual sovereignty."[5] Pragmatic and strategic as this decision may have been, it sent America down a particular path toward state building and established a peculiar institutional legacy that had a profound and lasting influence on the development of our national political institutions.

The peculiar constitutional structure adopted in the late eighteenth century for the newborn American state was the product of a bargain and compromise struck by the political leaders of the thirteen former British colonies pursuant to which only minimal power was conceded to a new national government, while the local state governments were largely preserved as autonomous political organizations, each retaining most of its traditional powers and authority within its own territory. Most important, the state governments retained jurisdiction over their historic military organizations and tax systems. At the same time, extraordinarily little power of any kind was delegated to the national government under the decentralized federal system established by the Articles of Confederation, thereby threatening the survival of the political union itself. Lacking revenue and arms, the center struggled to hold. Under the successor regime designed in Philadelphia in 1787, greater (enumerated) powers were surrendered to the central government by the local state governments, including greater military and revenue-extraction powers. But the powers delegated to the center under the Constitution were still relatively modest, and national political institutions remained weak, especially compared to those of contemporary European states of the late eighteenth century.

By preserving the autonomy of the state governments within the decentralized federal system, the United States was left with a notoriously weak national government. In the early nineteenth century, the United States was widely regarded in Europe as a "nonstate" state—a political organi-

---

5. "The idea of divided sovereignty, however illogical, it may or may not be, has, in one form or another, characterized American thought from the beginning of the constitutional period up to the present day." M.J.C. Vile, *The Structure of American Federalism* (London: Oxford University Press, 1961), 25. The idea of divided sovereignty was not without its critics even in the early years of the republic. John Randolph of Roanoke expressed amazement at the idea of dividing sovereignty between the states and a national government: "Asking one of the States to surrender part of her sovereignty, is like asking a lady to surrender part of her chastity." Quoted in William Cabell Bruce, *John Randolph of Roanoke, 1773–1833* (New York: G. P. Putnam's Sons, 1922), 2:203–4. The implication of Randolph's comment is that *none* of the sovereignty of the states should be surrendered to the national government.

zation with extraordinarily weak institutions. Based on the European experience, it was presumed that a strong state required an insulated bureaucratic class, centralized administration, and a large standing army, all under the control of an executive.[6] These attributes were generally absent in America, reflecting the purported lack of stateness in the New World.[7] But that designation missed the mark. In America, the local state governments were minicenters of political power within the federal structure. If most political power remained at the local level, that did not mean that America was "stateless"—only that it possessed a very different kind of state than found in Europe.[8]

There have been benefits and detriments attributable to the absence of a strong central government in America. Preserving so much political power at the local level had the beneficial effect of preventing the consolidation of excessive power (e.g., potentially tyrannical power) within the offices of the executive. In America, there would be no Caesar or Napoleon. This was Alexis de Tocqueville's famous prediction in *Democracy in America* (1835), wherein he argued that the state governments would check

---

6. Hegel identified the bureaucracy with the "universal" interest of the entire nation, rather than the particular interests of the estates: "The universal class, or, more precisely, the class of civil servants, must purely in virtue of its character as universal, have the universal as the end of its essential activity." Georg Wilhelm Friedrich Hegel, *Hegel's Philosophy of Right,* trans. T. M. Knox (Oxford: Oxford University Press, 1952), § 303. For a discussion of Hegel's theory of the universality of the state bureaucracy, see Shlomo Avineri, *Hegel's Theory of the Modern State* (Cambridge: Cambridge University Press, 1972), 155–61.

7. In typical fashion, Marx turned Hegel on his head, declaring that the *absence* of European-style state institutions signaled that the bourgeoisie had devised and institutionalized a form of state organization most conducive to protecting its class interests in private property and commerce: "Through the emancipation of private property from the community, the state has become a separate entity, beside and outside civil society; but it is nothing more than the form of organization which the bourgeois necessarily adopt both for internal and external purposes, for the mutual guarantee of the property and interests.... The most perfect example of the modern State is North America." Karl Marx, "The German Ideology," in *The Marx-Engels Reader,* ed. Robert C. Tucker (New York: W. W. Norton, 1972), 151.

8. The notion that America has had a "weak" state is challenged in William J. Novak, "The Myth of the 'Weak' American State," *The American Historical Review* 113 (June 2008): 752–72. Contrary to Novak's assertion, the notion of a strong state with a centralized bureaucratic administration and a large standing army is not just a relative construct based on the European experience. It is an objective basis for measuring state power. That the United States was able to exercise authority and state power through alternate means (i.e., decentralized modes of public administration) does not alter the fact that in the late eighteenth and early nineteenth centuries, the apparatus of the American state was notoriously weak, with incoherent lines of authority.

the concentration of power in the national government, thereby avoiding the tyranny known in Europe.[9] Arguably, the extreme decentralization has checked potential abuses of political power. But grandiose claims that federalism is somehow inexorably linked to democracy or liberal politics are suspect and unsubstantiated by either historical example or persuasive argument.[10] In fact, federalism is a *neutral* constitutional structure that preserves the powers and autonomy of entrenched local elites and interests—whether liberal or illiberal.

Why did the forces of localism prevail for so long within the confines of the decentralized American state, while Europe experienced a more definitive consolidation of political power at the center? For one thing, in America in the late eighteenth century, would-be state builders confronted an unrelenting hostility toward centralized government that can be traced to an indigenous strain of political thought that first emerged in British North America in the 1750s and 1760s. The virulent antistatism of colonial political thought was the product of the radical Calvinism that suffused religious dogma in the British colonies during the seventeenth and eighteenth centuries.[11] The antistatism of colonial political thought, fueled by "New Light" antinomian Protestant religious doctrine, provided the theoretical underpinning and driving force behind the radical political

---

9. Alexis de Tocqueville, *Democracy in America,* ed. J. P. Mayer (Garden City, NY: Anchor Books, 1969), 87–98 ("Political Effects of Administrative Decentralization in the United States"). As previously discussed, Ertman argues that the presence of local representative assemblies led to the development of liberal constitutionalism in Europe. Thomas Ertman, *Birth of the Leviathan: Building States and Regimes in Medieval and Early Modern Europe* (New York: Cambridge University Press, 1997).

10. Unsubstantiated claims that the emergence of federations is related to the movement for democracy or individual freedom can be found in Carl J. Friedrich, *Trends of Federalism in Theory and Practice* (New York: Praeger Press, 1968); Karl W. Deutsch, *Political Community in the North Atlantic Area: International Organization in the Light of Historical Experience* (Princeton: Princeton University Press, 1957). Such claims were subject to harsh criticism in William H. Riker, "Federalism," in *The Handbook of Political Science, Volume V: Government Institutions and Processes,* ed. Fred I. Greenstein and Nelson Polsby (Reading, MA: Addison Wesley, 1975), 131.

11. The origins of colonial political thought are diverse and bound up with colonial religious doctrine. Among the best discussions of the interconnection between eighteenth-century American religious dogma and democratic political thought are Perry Miller, *Life in the Mind in America: From the Revolution to the Civil War* (New York: Harcourt, Brace and World, 1965); Perry Miller, *Errand into the Wilderness* (Cambridge: Harvard University Press, 1956); Alan Heimert, *Religion and the American Mind: From the Great Awakening to the Revolution* (Cambridge: Harvard University Press, 1966).

equalitarianism of the pre-Revolutionary period as well as the most significant and dramatic historical event of all—the severing of constitutional
ties with the English monarchy.[12] The radical antistatism that pervaded
Revolutionary political thought carried over to the initial period of state
formation and had a profound influence on political institutions during
the 1770s and 1780s. This antistate sentiment was expressed in the design
of the Articles of Confederation and incorporated into the new political
order established by the Constitution of 1787. Hostility to the national government and centralized political authority persisted for decades as a tenet
of Jeffersonian Republicanism and permeated the states' rights theory
heard throughout the South during the nineteenth century. Antistatism
still resonates in contemporary American politics in the political ideology
of the libertarian movement, the far right, and the conservative wing of the
Republican Party.[13]

It has been aptly observed that "opposition to power, and suspicion of
government as the most dangerous embodiment of power, are the central
themes of American political thought."[14] Given such a political culture,
one that spawned a unique and peculiar vision of constitutionalism founded
on the dubious principle that tyrannical political power can be checked by
denying the central government all the fundamental powers and attributes
of stateness, how did the United States emerge in the twentieth century
as the most powerful nation-state in the world with a robust revenue system capable of supporting a global military force as well as the panoply
of expensive social welfare programs adopted since the 1930s? How did
national political elites build a strong central state and raise the enormous
revenue necessary to finance such an expansion of the state apparatus?

---

12. Among the best accounts of American political thought prior to and during the Revolution are Bernard Bailyn, *Ideological Origins of the American Revolution* (Cambridge: Harvard University Press, 1967); Gordon S. Wood, *The Creation of the American Republic, 1776–1787* (New
York: W. W. Norton, 1972); and Wood, *The Radicalism of the American Revolution* (New York:
Knopf, 1992).

13. In the twentieth century, antistatism survived in the works of such popular writers as Ayn
Rand, the author of the best-selling novel *The Fountainhead* (1943), and Alfred Jay Nock, author
of the popular antistate manifesto *Our Enemy, the State* (1935). Similar sentiments can be found in
Murray Rothbard, *Man, Economy, and State* (1962) and Robert Nozick, *Anarchy, State, and Utopia*
(1974) and Milton Friedman, *Capitalism and Freedom* (1962).

14. Samuel P. Huntington, *American Politics: The Promise of Disharmony* (Cambridge: Belknap
Press, 1981), 33.

In addressing these critical questions, we must bear in mind that the thirteen British colonies were already "relatively autonomous" political organizations, if not actual sovereign states, at the time the Revolutionary War broke out. The initial task is to identify the forces that first led the political leaders of the thirteen separate states to join together in a political union, weak though it was, after political ties with Britain were severed. Thereafter, we must identify the structural deficiencies of the American state in the late eighteenth century (specifically with regard to its military and revenue-extraction capacities) as well as those factors that influenced its subsequent development—for example, the preservation of the states as semiautonomous political organizations within the federal arrangement. The starting point of this investigation is the preliminary attempt to build an American state pursuant to the Articles of Confederation, the nation's first constitution. Following the abrupt abandonment of this constitution, political leaders adopted a constitutional blueprint for a reconstituted American state, one with a stronger national government. Over the next two centuries, the American state developed through a series of sporadic episodes in state building (i.e., periods of "punctuated equilibria"), each a distinct moment in political development during which national institutions were fundamentally reconstituted. At the same time, the flaws of the original constitutional design were replicated within the architecture of the successor regime, thereby thwarting efforts to forge a more coherent structure for the American state. Rather than defeated, the forces of localism were accommodated and incorporated into the constitutional structure of the new federal state.

The expansion of the national government of the American state required that political elites confront and overcome the structural flaws inherent in its original constitutional design. In practical terms, this meant overcoming the institutional legacy inherited from the Articles of Confederation and carried over into the Constitution of 1787. But altering an entrenched political order is always extremely difficult. This much is predicted by path dependence theory. How then did political leaders change course and reconstitute the American state? As we will see, the most dramatic and fundamental changes to our national political institutions were implemented during periods of war. From what we know of the European experience, we recognize that this was no coincidence. War made the early modern European state. The systemic crisis that accompanies war leads to the centralization of political power, enhanced state capacity, expanded authority of the national government, increased complexity in the tasks or functions performed by the apparatus of the central state, and an overall increase in the level of "penetration" of society by the central state, especially with regard to revenue extraction. In America no less than in Europe, war made the state.

To be sure, the development of the American state did not follow a linear path toward the centralization and consolidation of political power in the national government. To the contrary, periods of wartime expansion were invariably followed by periods of institutional retrenchment during which the capacity of the American state was reduced to prewar levels. The creation of a strong state in America was never inevitable. At critical junctures in the history of the United States, political leaders struggled to expand the military and secure new sources of public revenue. The ability of political leaders to achieve their goals was always in doubt. Raising the necessary revenue was contingent on an expansion of administrative capacities and a deeper penetration of society by the national government. But state expansion generates resistance from powerful local economic interests. Only through a long series of "negotiations" and compromises with important societal interests did political leaders solve the problem of revenue scarcity for the American state. Political elites eventually negotiated and implemented a more efficient and productive revenue strategy, one capable of supporting successive stages in the development of the American state. But state building is never easy and always is expensive. To this day, political leaders struggle to raise the enormous revenue required to sustain the modern American state.

Discerning the Origins of the American State

This study of the development of the American state is premised on the notion that political elites are the agents of political change (i.e., political development), and hence, understanding political development requires that we comprehend the motives of those political leaders who "built" the American state—not in the literal sense of laying the bricks and foundation for the Capitol building, but rather in the figurative sense of first visualizing the constitutional blueprint for the new republic and then organizing the political institutions, offices, rules, and procedures that comprise the American state. Accordingly, this study is at odds with much contemporary historiography on the American Revolution and the founding of the nation. In recent decades, academic historians have embraced willy-nilly the so-called new history and its related methodology, aptly described as writing "history from below."[15] When approaching these seminal historical events, practitioners of the new history typically examine the lives and conditions of the "ordinary" people (including workers, immigrants, women, and Negro slaves), the structure and hierarchy of colonial society, and the social forces underlying the conflict. Their notion of what is most important and distinct about America (inequality, class, racism, sexism) is in stark contrast with that of prior generations of scholars who celebrated (too often uncritically) the lives and achievements of the "founders."[16]

One basic premise of the new history is now largely uncontested: any comprehensive history of the United States must take into account the lives of the ordinary people—those men and women (free and enslaved) who labored to build America, performing such vital tasks as constructing the nation's Capitol in Washington, serving in the army, delivering the mail, and otherwise keeping the federal government running. But this study is *not* a comprehensive history of the United States, and the methodology of the new history is distinctly unsuited to an analysis of the development of political institutions and the reconstitution of a political order. The new history slights the role of political leaders and political ideology in favor of social and cultural factors and, thus, is at odds with a study of political institutions premised on the notion that ideas "matter" and political elites are the agents of political change (i.e., political development). If culture, religion, class, and social hierarchy are legitimate concerns of a comprehensive history of America, they matter here only to the extent they supported or undermined the political order or influenced the motives of the founders as they built the American state.

---

15. See, e.g., Jim Sharpe, "History From Below," in *New Perspectives on Historical Writing,* ed. Peter Burke (University Park: Pennsylvania State University Press, 2001), 25–42.

16. Scholars today use the term *founders* to refer to those who were known to prior generations as the Founding Fathers. I will conform herein with current usage, but under protest. I concur with Harvey Mansfield, who objects that this change in nomenclature casts a "taint of undeserved privilege" on our political leaders. Harvey C. Mansfield Jr., *America's Constitutional Soul* (Baltimore: Johns Hopkins University Press, 1991), 3.

Like it or not, those who built the American state (again, in the figurative sense) were the most prominent political leaders in their communities. To grasp the underlying logic of state building in America, we need to understand the motives, intentions, and ideology of the nation's founders. At the same time, we must bear in mind that the founders were practical politicians, not just nation builders. This is often difficult to accept because we are so easily distracted by their genuine greatness. As Gordon Wood has perceptively observed, succeeding generations of Americans have been "unable to look back at the Revolutionary leaders and constitution makers without being overawed by the brilliance of their thought, the creativity of their politics, and the sheer magnitude of their achievements."[17] Notwithstanding their brilliance, the founders were political elites whose actions were rational, purposeful, and explicable in terms of the objectives they pursued—that is, building a new American state. No doubt, external geomilitary forces influenced their actions and defined the basic framework for decision making, but in the end, the course of action they took and the political institutions they built reflected their personal objectives and preferences, as well as their broader understanding of the political world.[18] In this way, the authoritative political vision of the founding generation established an institutional legacy that continues to inform American politics to the present day.

To be sure, it is never easy to discern the motives of political elites. Adding to the confusion, the motives and intentions of political leaders throughout the colonies were decidedly mixed during the critical period leading up to the Revolutionary War. As much as a third of the population opposed the war—a significant portion of these being Tories who openly supported the British. Among those who emerged as "mainstream" revolutionaries after 1774, few had the express intention of undermining, let alone destroying, the social hierarchy that prevailed in late-eighteenth-century

---

17. Gordon S. Wood, *Revolutionary Characters: What Made the Founders Different* (New York: Penguin Press, 2006), 4.

18. A discussion of how intent and purpose are reflected in institutional design is found in the essays by John Ferejohn ("Practical Institutionalism") and Rogers M. Smith ("Which Comes First, the Ideas or the Institutions?") in *Rethinking Political Institutions: The Art of the State,* ed. Ian Shapiro, Stephen Skowronek, and Daniel Galvin (New York: New York University Press, 2006), 72–90, 91–113. Once established, political institutions take on a life, logic, and interests of their own.

America. But with the outbreak of hostilities, events quickly spiraled out of control. Enthusiasm for republicanism spread, and its most resolute proponents aspired to much more than severing ties with a corrupt European empire. Widespread popular sentiment in favor of equality and a pervasive rejection of monarchy and social hierarchy emerged in all the former colonies. Democratic inclinations were most openly and strongly expressed in political practices in those states where radicals took control of the state legislatures—for instance, in Pennsylvania, where in 1776 a State Convention adopted what has been called "the most egalitarian constitution produced anywhere in Revolutionary America."[19] In that same year, no less an enthusiast for democracy than Thomas Jefferson expressed genuine amazement at how far and fast those events and sentiments that he had helped set in motion had progressed in only a matter of two years. Jefferson mused that so many Americans had rejected all that was "monarchical" and "taken up the republican government with as much ease as would have attended their throwing off an old and putting on a new suit of clothes."[20]

As sudden and dramatic as the American Revolution was, it was a *political* revolution, not a *social* revolution—certainly not in the same category as the upheavals that would later engulf France and Russia. In America, there was no class-based revolt from below, and in most of the thirteen states, the social hierarchy that had characterized colonial life remained largely intact and untouched by the Revolution. As Bernard Bailyn once put it, "The primary goal of the American Revolution, which transformed American life and introduced a new era in human history, was not the overthrow or even the alteration of the existing social order but the preservation of political life threatened by the apparent corruption of the [English] constitution, and the establishment in principle of the existing conditions of liberty."[21] In this respect, the break with England that severed political

---

19. Sean Wilentz, *The Rise of American Democracy: Jefferson to Lincoln* (New York: W. W. Norton, 2005), 14. The radical Pennsylvania constitution of 1776 provided for a unicameral legislature, whose members were elected annually, and a Council of Censors, intended to evaluate the activities of the government and "censure" alleged constitutional violations. This constitution was replaced in 1790. For an account of the radical politics that took hold in Pennsylvania during the Revolution, see Wood, *Creation of the American Republic,* 83–90.

20. Quoted in Wood, *Creation of the American Republic,* 92.

21. Bailyn, *Ideological Origins of the American Revolution,* 19.

ties with the crown was a conservative restoration of the rights and freedoms of English citizens living in British North America suppressed by a corrupt king. In the "loyalist" colonies (such as Virginia, which had supported the royalist cause during the English Civil War), the military conflict produced "remarkably little change in the state's social structure and even less in its government."[22] Even in Pennsylvania, with its radical constitution, there was no social revolution, only a reconstitution of politics and restructuring of political institutions in the state capital—which itself was reversed and undone in a matter of fourteen years. This is important because social revolutions displace and destroy traditional social hierarchies, customs, institutions, and entrenched interests, paving the way for a greater centralization and consolidation of political power once Thermidor has run its course. While that occurred in both Russia and France, resulting in strongly centralized nation-states, no equivalent destruction of the existing social hierarchy occurred in the United States. There was no comparable centralization and consolidation of political power in America following its revolution.

That said, significant changes, which involved more than just the displacement of a European monarch and his court with a coterie of homegrown rulers, resulted from this political revolution. There were radical dimensions to the American Revolution. If this was a political revolution, rather than a social revolution, it imposed a radically democratic imprint on political practices and social norms in the United States, as well as the subsequent development of political institutions. Nevertheless, scholars still disagree in their characterization of these historic events.[23] This is because "the American Revolution was actually many revolutions at once, the product of a complicated culmination of many diverse personal grievances

---

22. Robin L. Einhorn, *American Taxation, American Slavery* (Chicago: University of Chicago Press, 2006), 52.

23. Merrill Jensen once suggested a plausible reason for the dissension among historians. Because there was no consensus among the founders themselves regarding the nature and purpose of the revolution they made, it is possible today to make "arguments to support almost any interpretation one chooses." Merrill Jensen, *The New Nation: A History of the United States During the Confederation, 1781–1789* (Boston: Northeastern University Press, 1950), viii. For a summary of the various explanations offered to explain the American Revolution (e.g., economic, social, ideological), see Charles A. Kromkowski, *Recreating the American Republic: Rules of Apportionment, Constitutional Change, and American Political Development, 1700–1870* (New York: Cambridge University Press, 2002), 40–47.

and social strains."[24] While the overall shift in public sentiment was from accommodation to rebellion and then to independence, a wide spectrum of political views was openly expressed throughout the period, thereby complicating the work of future generations of historians. World-historical events defy easy explanations and categorization, and the American Revolution was, if anything, a complicated world-historical event.

The founding of the American state is most commonly associated with the dramatic events that transpired in Philadelphia during the summer of 1787. Obviously, the adoption of the Constitution of 1787 was of profound significance to the establishment of a new political order as well as the subsequent development of the American state. Yet this occurred more than eleven years after independence had been declared by the former colonies and four years after independence had been formally recognized by Parliament in the Treaty of Paris of 1783.[25] Any explanation of the formation of the American state must take into account the interim governing body organized to direct the war effort during the Revolution—the Continental Congress. There also is the troubling matter of the first constitution of the new republic, the short-lived Articles of Confederation, which is so often conveniently forgotten or ignored. This flawed constitution and the political institutions established under it created an institutional legacy that strongly influenced the subsequent development of the American state.

The political leaders who drafted the Constitution of 1787 were keenly aware that they were not writing on a clean slate. A strong and deeply rooted institutional legacy carried over from the period of the Confederacy, to say nothing of the legacy of the colonial governments that in many cases were in place for more than a century and a half before the drafting of the Constitution. We need to consider how this institutional legacy influenced decision making at the Constitutional Convention in 1787. We also need

---

24. Wood, *Creation of the American Republic,* 75. The great complexity of these political events was not lost on the participants themselves. John Adams observed that "the principles of the American Revolution may be said to have been as various as the thirteen states that went through it, and in some sense almost as diversified as the individuals who acted in it." Letter, "John Adams to Mercy Warren, Quincy" (July 20, 1807), in *Massachusetts Historical Collection* (Boston, 5th series 1878), 4:338.

25. By March 1782, Parliament had already declared its intention to cease the use of military force against the colonies. This followed in the wake of Washington's victory at Yorktown in October 1781. The Treaty of Paris, ratified by the Congress of the Confederacy on January 14, 1784, formally ended the state of war between the colonies and Great Britain.

to understand why the Articles of Confederation was abandoned so soon in favor of a new constitutional arrangement that furthered the development of stronger national political institutions. What forces were aligned behind this decisive stage in the reconstitution of the American state? Why were political leaders moved to build a stronger state—in particular, to strengthen the apparatus of the central government, even while retaining a federal structure for the new political order they created? Most important, how did political leaders obtain the revenue necessary to finance the founding of the republic and each successive stage in the expansion of the American state?

Rarely if ever do states emerge full blown from society. As Margaret Levi reminds us, state formation typically commences with the "consolidation or takeover of an organization that already performs at least some of the functions of a state."[26] Some initial force or triggering event must set in motion the process of "consolidation" or lead to a "takeover" of a weak state by another more powerful political organization. This was the pattern of state development experienced in Europe as medieval states were gradually consolidated into larger political organizations by the armies of ambitious rulers and as small principalities were conquered and incorporated by larger territorial states. In early modern Europe, nearly constant war and revolutionary changes in weaponry and the conduct of warfare spurred the consolidation of political power under the crown, gradually transforming the medieval states of the fourteenth century into the powerful nation-states of the nineteenth century. We must consider whether there were equivalent forces behind the formation of the American state during the Revolutionary period as well as subsequent efforts to consolidate greater power in the new national government established by the Constitution of 1787.

Warfare played a critical role in the formation of the American state. At the same time, state development in America was dependent on the ability of political leaders to devise and implement a successful revenue strategy. By the late eighteenth century, weaponry and armaments had become so expensive that only nation-states with access to significant sources of revenue could ever hope to succeed in warfare. Without that revenue, the

---

26. Margaret Levi, *Of Rule and Revenue* (Berkeley: University of California Press, 1988), 41.

expansion and development of the American state beyond its original archaic constitutional design would not have been possible. The goal here is to identify and delineate the mechanisms employed by American political leaders to extract from society the enormous revenue required to sustain their periodic endeavors in state building, war making, and institutional expansion.

5

State Formation in the
Early Republic

The said States hereby severally enter into a firm league of friendship
with each other, for their common defense, the security of their liberties,
and their mutual and general welfare.

—Articles of Confederation, art. III (1781)

This Confederation had none of the attributes of sovereignty in
legislative, executive, or judicial power. It was little more than a congress
of ambassadors, authorized to represent separate nations, in matters in
which they had a common concern.

—Roger B. Taney, *Dred Scott v. John F. A. Sandford* (1857)

Those political leaders who designed and built the American state in the
late eighteenth century were not writing on a clean slate. Long before the
outbreak of the American Revolution and the formal severing of ties with
the English Crown, there were functioning governments in the colonies.
Indeed, the thirteen colonial governments functioned more or less as "relatively autonomous" political organizations, each with its own unique history, traditions, and political institutions. By the time of the American
Revolution, the institutional legacy of several of the colonies already dated
back more than a century and a half. Moreover, colonial history included
a strong tradition of representative legislative bodies and self-governance.
These factors influenced the *nature* of the national government that emerged
in North America in the late eighteenth century. The American state created by the founders included many important institutional innovations,

especially with respect to enhanced fiscal and military powers for the national government. But at the same time, the reconstituted state was the product of, and hence limited by, nearly 150 years of political development in North America.

The Colonial Legacy: Legislatures and Taxes

The colonies of British North America enjoyed a great deal of control over their local affairs under the dominion of the English Crown. Each colony had its own political institutions, legal system, constitution (or charter), military force, and tax system. The colonies also had considerable experience with representative government prior to achieving independence from England. For instance, the colonial government of the Virginia colony provided for a representative body, later known as the Virginia House of Burgesses, which was first convened in Jamestown in July 1619.[1] This legislature played an important role in the governance of the colony. As Elkins and McKitrick put it, "As with the other colonial assemblies in the period prior to about 1760, the House of Burgesses had steadily acquired and assumed a range of prerogatives and powers having to do with finance, military policy, appointments, elections, districting, and public works. Concurrently, it had built up an enormous sense of its own dignity and privileges."[2] So it was with the proprietary colony of Maryland, where a representative assembly first convened in 1637. The Massachusetts colony had its own long history of local control over its affairs and enjoyed widespread participation of the citizenry through its established representative bodies, which can be traced back to 1634 when the General Court was transformed into an elective body comprised of some twenty deputies and the governor and his lieutenant. While the other royal colonies (Georgia, New Jersey, New York, the Carolinas, and New Hampshire) were ostensibly under the direct authority of the Crown, they too enjoyed a good

---

1. Initially, all free men could vote for their representatives in the House of Burgesses. Subsequently, land ownership requirements were imposed, although the franchise was still widely held in the Virginia colony because land-ownership was widespread and common.

2. Stanley Elkins and Eric McKitrick, *The Age of Federalism: The Early American Republic, 1788–1800* (New York: Oxford University Press, 1993), 39.

deal of independence, with legislative bodies that exerted a significant degree of authority and control over their territories. Over time, governmental functions in the colonies were usurped from the Crown's governors by
the local assemblies. As this occurred, the colonies emerged as semisover-
eign political organizations subject only to sporadic oversight by the king's
ministers.

The degree of independence enjoyed by the colonial legislatures varied
enormously from colony to colony during the seventeenth and eighteenth
centuries.[3] Notwithstanding such differences, by the middle of the eighteenth century all thirteen colonies possessed to varying degrees the basic
attributes of sovereign states. Each possessed the authority to make its own
laws, which were adjudicated and enforced by indigenous courts comprised
of local judges who themselves enjoyed a great deal of independence from
the Crown.[4] Colonial legislatures exerted control over their own internal
affairs, including their militias and courts.[5] Separated from the king's ministers by thousands of miles of ocean, the colonial governments also exercised considerable authority over the taxes and duties imposed within their
territories. Not surprisingly, with their own distinct political systems, histories, and traditions, as well as the disparities in regional economies, the
colonies had very different systems of taxation. Notwithstanding such differences, we can readily discern a strong relationship between public revenue and political development throughout the colonies of British North
America.

We know a good deal about the colonial systems of government. Historians have compiled a fairly comprehensive portrait of the colonial tax

---

3. The rules and procedures followed in the colonial legislatures are outlined in Calvin C. Jill-
son and Rick K. Wilson, *Congressional Dynamics: Structure, Coordination, and Choice in the First
American Congress, 1774–1789* (Stanford: Stanford University Press, 1994), 24–38. The authorita-
tive study of the origins of representative political assemblies in the North American colonies is
Michael G. Kammen, *Deputyes & Libertyes: The Origins of Representative Government in Colonial
America* (New York: Knopf, 1969).

4. For an account of colonial law and courts, see Lawrence M. Friedman, *A History of American Law* (New York: Simon & Schuster, 1973), 29–90. The independence of colonial judges is
described in Bernard Bailyn, *The Ideological Origins of the American Revolution* (Cambridge: Harvard University Press, 1967), 105–8.

5. The organization and proceedings of the colonial legislatures are discussed in Donald S.
Lutz, "The Colonial and Early State Legislative Process," in Kenneth R. Bowling and Donald R.
Kenyon, eds., *Inventing America: Origins and Establishment of the First Federal Congress* (Athens:
Ohio State University Press, 1999), 49–75.

systems and how they functioned within the broader context of the co-lonial governments.[6] There was no uniform system of taxation, as each colony relied on its own system of fees, duties, and taxes imposed on dif-ferent tax bases in the various colonies. Each colonial tax system was the product of a unique history shaped by decades of bargaining and negotiat-ing among the competing social and economic interests in that particu-lar territory (e.g., farmers versus merchants, seaport towns versus inland towns, new towns versus old towns, slaveholders versus nonslaveholders). Interests were accommodated in different ways as each colonial govern-ment adopted a revenue strategy suited to local conditions.

Notwithstanding the disparities among the colonies, the administrative systems employed to extract societal resources shared common characteris-tics within the various geographic regions. For instance, the southern colo-nies as a whole had relatively simple systems of taxation. Notwithstanding Virginia's great wealth, population, and long history of self-government, it possessed what was arguably the most primitive tax system among the col-onies, raising the bulk of its revenue from an annual poll tax on "tithables" (free men plus enslaved men and women). Virginia imposed other taxes on exported tobacco as well as imported slaves (based on their purchase price). A carriage tax was instituted during the French and Indian War. The taxes imposed by Virginia were typical of those used in other southern colonies. The distinctive feature of the southern tax systems was that local admin-istrators did not attempt to value the objects that were taxed. That would have required a degree of administrative capability and sophistication lacking in the southern colonies. Furthermore, corruption in enforcement

---

6. A new comprehensive history of the colonial tax systems is Alvin Rabushka, *Taxation in Colonial America* (Princeton: Princeton University Press, 2008). This study will prove an invaluable resource on the subject. Another recent contribution of merit is Robin L. Einhorn, *American Taxa-tion, American Slavery* (Chicago: University of Chicago Press, 2006). The standard histories of tax-ation in the colonies and the Confederacy are Robert A. Becker, *Revolution, Reform, and the Politics of American Taxation, 1763–1783* (Baton Rouge: Louisiana State University Press, 1980); Roger H. Brown, *Redeeming the Republic: Federalists, Taxation, and the Origins of the Constitution* (Baltimore: Johns Hopkins University Press, 1993); Edwin R. A. Seligman, *The Income Tax: A Study of the His-tory, Theory, and Practice of Income Taxation at Home and Abroad* (New York: Macmillan, 1911), pt. 2, chap. 1, 367–87. The definitive history of public finance during the revolutionary period is E. James Ferguson, *The Power of the Purse: A History of American Public Finance, 1776–1790* (Cha-pel Hill, NC: University of North Carolina Press, 1961). A comprehensive account of economic conditions in the colonies is John J. McCusker and Russell R. Menard, *The Economy of British America, 1607–1789* (Chapel Hill: University of North Carolina Press, 1985).

was rampant at the local level in the South, where tax collectors were appointed rather than elected through an open political process providing participation and input from local interests, as was generally the case in the North—most particularly, in Massachusetts. Overall, the tax systems in the South were weaker than their counterparts in the North.

In her account of colonial taxation, Robin Einhorn attributes the superiority of the revenue systems in the North to their more developed and democratic political institutions: "By the outbreak of the Revolution, northern colonies had sophisticated tax systems, competent and experienced (and annually elected) local officials, and long traditions of democratic struggle between groups who had competing interests, including interests in who bore the tax burden. In the southern colonies, however, tax systems were primitive and local officials (elites who were appointed rather than elected) were far less capable of performing complex administrative tasks."[7] The northern colonies possessed more developed political systems and greater administrative capacity that enabled them to operate more sophisticated tax systems, thereby permitting local authorities in the North to raise more revenue—despite the fact that the South was more prosperous economically than the North. The greater revenue generated by their more sophisticated tax systems reinforced the more advanced level of development of the colonial governments in the North. In colonial America, as in early modern Europe, revenue extraction and state development were mutually dependent and reinforcing.

Economic conditions were generally conducive to revenue extraction by the colonial tax authorities. During the eighteenth century, the colonies enjoyed greater overall economic growth than England itself.[8] Increased spending by Britain during the French and Indian Wars (1754–1763) brought sudden economic prosperity to the New England colonies. During this global military campaign, known in Europe as the Seven Years'

---

7. Einhorn, *American Taxation, American Slavery,* 27. The account that follows of Virginia's colonial tax system as well as that of Massachusetts relies on the scholarship of Einhorn and Rabushka.

8. Estimates are that the colonial economy grew twice as fast as England's between 1690 and 1785. McCusker and Menard, *Economy of British America,* 55; see also Charles A. Kromkowski, *Recreating the American Republic: Rules of Apportionment, Constitutional Change, and American Political Development, 1700–1870* (New York: Cambridge University Press, 2002), 47: "By the 1770s the material standard of living for the average white colonial family surpassed the British average and likely was the highest in the world."

War, England accumulated a staggering national debt.[9] While the New England colonial governments incurred substantial debt of their own during the conflict, tax collections increased as the local economy boomed. This allowed the colonial authorities to retire their obligations by 1775, even while England struggled to cope with its war debt. This pushed Parliament to increase domestic taxes in England and impose a host of new and onerous taxes and restrictions on the colonies in North America. These included the Stamp Act of 1765, the Townshend Act of 1767, and the Intolerable Acts of 1774. These intrusive acts of Parliament directly threatened the revenue sources of the colonial legislatures, and in doing so, provoked rebellion against the British monarch.[10] Ironically, notwithstanding these provocative royal taxes, the period from 1763 to 1774 was actually one of an overall decline in taxation in the colonies, which were hardly overtaxed.[11]

By the 1770s, all the New England colonies had adopted various forms of "faculty" taxes, which were levies imposed on a man's skill or profession (such as taxes on lawyers, physicians, merchants, and mechanics).[12] The goal was to reach the wealth of those citizens who were not farmers (whose land and produce was easier to measure and value, and hence, tax). Because faculty taxes were based on the perceived "profits" of these professional men, the northern tax systems were considerably more progressive than those in the South. Conversely, because the southern colonies relied almost exclusively on "flat" poll taxes (such as the Virginia system of tithables), their tax systems were regressive in their incidence. Issues of equity aside, progressive tax systems have the potential to raise greater revenue for the state because they reach greater societal assets. There is a natural limit to what can be raised from a flat (regressive) tax such as a poll tax or a capitation (head) tax.[13] When rates for such taxes become too high,

---

9. Becker, *Revolution, Reform,* 19, 33–35.

10. For a discussion of the impact of these acts of Parliament on the colonies, see Dall W. Forsythe, *Taxation and Political Change in the Young Nation, 1781–1833* (New York: Columbia University Press, 1977), 10–13.

11. Becker, *Revolution, Reform,* 34, 37–38. Becker attributes the low taxes to the low cost of running the colonial governments. Government salaries were minimal or nonexistent, as officials customarily derived their incomes from fees and kickbacks.

12. The concept of a faculty tax is discussed in Seligman, *The Income Tax,* pt. 2, chap. 1, 367–87; see also Becker, *Revolution, Reform,* 11.

13. Niall Ferguson points out that regressive poll taxes provoked numerous tax revolts in England over the centuries—most recently in 1990 when an ill-conceived capitation tax contributed

they become especially burdensome on the poor, often triggering popular discontent and defiance of local tax collectors. Conversely, a regressive capitation tax that is bearable to the poor and working classes will hardly be felt by wealthy citizens and hence, will fail to produce an optimal revenue yield for the treasury.

The colonial governments in both the North and South suffered from a lack of hard specie. Because of this, it was difficult to pay bills and keep the local governments running. The common practice was to emit bills of credit and other forms of paper money to provide local governments with currency.[14] Bills of credit were used as a form of deficit spending, allowing the local authorities to spend in excess of current tax revenues. But the practice resulted in the devaluation of the official currency, which in turn provoked Parliament to issue the Currency Acts of 1751 and 1764. These statutes restricted the colonies in issuing their own paper money.[15] The colonial governments were permitted to issue paper money only if it was not made legal tender and sufficient taxes were collected to redeem each issue in a reasonable time.[16] Colonial governments accepted bills of credit for payment of taxes at face value, which helped maintain the value of the official currency.

This financial system worked reasonably well for the colonial governments until the extraordinary costs incurred during the Revolutionary War strained local treasuries. With the outbreak of war, the differences between the tax systems in the North and the South were magnified as the revenue needs of the states increased. The state legislatures suddenly found it necessary to raise new monies to support their expanded military

---

to the fall of the government of Prime Minister Margaret Thatcher. Niall Ferguson, *The Cash Nexus: Money and Power in the Modern World, 1700–2000* (New York: Basic Books, 2001), 64.

14. A comprehensive account of coins, paper money, and other currency in the colonies is John J. McCusker, *Money and Exchange in Europe and America, 1600–1775: A Handbook* (Chapel Hill: University of South Carolina Press, 1978); see also Margaret G. Myers, *A Financial History of the United States* (New York: Columbia University Press, 1970), 6–12.

15. In enacting such prohibitions, the British Parliament and the Crown intended to "safeguard their overseas investments and economic arrangements from currencies that were ever subject to rapid devaluations." James D. Savage, *Balanced Budgets and American Politics* (Ithaca: Cornell University Press, 1988), 61.

16. Notwithstanding Parliament's prohibition against printing paper money, the Massachusetts colony had declared its paper bills as legal tender for public and private debts in December 1692. An account of this important "monetary innovation" is found in Rabushka, *Taxation in Colonial America,* 364.

forces. All the states struggled to raise revenue for the war effort, but the negative effects were strongest in the South. Because the governments in the southern states were weaker, their tax systems were less productive than those in the North. This stalled political development. In the end, the northern states were better equipped for the vital task of revenue extraction because they possessed more developed political institutions than the southern states, and they had more developed political institutions because they could raise greater public revenue. These differences persisted even after the first political union was formed by the former colonies.

State Formation and Federalism

The origins of the first political union in America can be traced to endeavors undertaken by colonial leaders even prior to the Revolutionary War. With the outbreak of hostilities, local colonial leaders organized their own independent state governments and adopted new constitutions and political institutions. At first, the goal was to coordinate the resistance to England. Only later did local leaders envision a political organization separate and apart from the governments of the thirteen sovereign states. Because the colonies enjoyed relative autonomy and financial independence even before severing ties with the English Crown, we must consider why their leaders agreed to form a political union, transferring some of their own political power and authority to a new national government. Strong incentives must be present for rational, self-interested political actors to adopt a course of action so obviously at their own expense.[17] Thus we must consider what factors led the states to join together in a political union, a

---

17. The notion of the state as an organization comprised of rationally self-interested "political actors" pursuing individual and collective goals is developed in Barbara Geddes, *Politician's Dilemma: Building State Capacity in Latin America* (Berkeley: University of California Press, 1994), 7–11. This perspective pervades the work of rational choice and public choice theorists. For example, Harsanyi argues that in explaining political change, we must ask why "some people have decided that their interests would be better served by a new type of institutional arrangement." John Harsanyi, "Rational-Choice Models of Political Behavior vs. Functionalist and Conformist Theories," *World Politics* 21 (July 1969): 532. Dougherty employs a rational choice model of collective action to analyze decision-making under the Articles of Confederation. Keith L. Dougherty, *Collective Action under the Articles of Confederation* (New York: Cambridge University Press, 2001).

decision that had an enormous impact on the subsequent development of the America state.

Beginning in 1774, with the conflict with Britain growing more intense, governing committees were organized in the thirteen colonies. These committees emerged as de facto political authorities as they replaced the old colonial governments that were collapsing in the face of widespread public opposition. Shortly thereafter, the newly established political authorities moved to adopt their own written constitutions, an overt act asserting sovereignty over their territories. In Massachusetts, this process began earlier than in the other colonies with the rapid collapse of the colonial government there. In the political vacuum, leaders rushed to build new political institutions. At the same time, it soon became apparent that there was little agreement on how to replace the defunct colonial governments. For many citizens of Massachusetts, adopting a new state constitution was too extreme an act, signifying as it did a formal repudiation of the authority of the British Crown over the colony. Not all were ready for such an act of defiance and rebellion—certainly not the inherently cautious John Adams, who still believed there was time to reach accommodation with England.[18] By the fall of 1774, a consensus emerged in favor of reviving the old colonial Charter of 1691 as a compromise and alternative to adopting a new constitution. This course of action was perceived as less radical and threatening than drafting a new constitution and thus, quickly gained support within the colony.[19] Soon after, a revised version of the Charter of 1691 was adopted as the "new" constitution of the Massachusetts colony.

Throughout the spring and summer of 1776, with the outbreak of hostilities between the colonial militias and English troops, other colonies

---

18. Adams defended the English constitution right up to the outbreak of military hostilities and even then only reluctantly took the great leap of faith from republicanism to revolution. As late as July 3, 1776 (the day on which he and all the other representatives voted to declare independence), Adams proclaimed that he was genuinely surprised by the "Suddenness, as well as the Greatness of this Revolution." "John Adams to Abigail Adams" (July 3, 1776), in *The Book of Abigail and John Adams: Selected Letters of the Adams Family,* ed. L. H. Butterfield, Marc Friedlaender, and Mary-Jo Kline (Cambridge: Harvard University Press, 1975), 139.

19. The notion of reviving the old colonial charter originated in the western regions of the colony and spread to the east. The issue was then raised with the Continental Congress, which balked at the idea. In June 1775, after the battles at Lexington and Concord, the Congress relented and approved the plan. The story is recounted in Jerrilyn Greene Marston, *King and Congress: The Transfer of Political Legitimacy, 1774–1776* (Princeton: Princeton University Press, 1987), 254–61.

followed the lead of Massachusetts in drafting a new state constitution.[20] Because Connecticut and Rhode Island already possessed republican governments dating from the issuance of their colonial charters in the mid seventeenth century, they needed only to adopt minor amendments to their constitutions and legal documents—minor changes such as eliminating references to the king and the colonial governor. The governors of these colonies had always been elected. Pennsylvania, Delaware, and Maryland were hereditary proprietorships, and thus it was necessary for them to adopt entirely new republican state constitutions. This was done by special conventions whose sole responsibility was to draft a new state constitution.[21] The remaining colonies were viceroyalties with their governors appointed by the Crown—except for New York, which elected its governor. With the outbreak of armed conflict within their territories, several of the royal colonies were forced to wait until 1777 to adopt new constitutions.

With their own constitutions, legislative bodies, legal systems, militias, and systems of taxation, the former colonies now possessed all the basic attributes of sovereign nation-states.[22] True, they were *weak* states by

---

20. On May 10, 1776, the Continental Congress passed a resolution approving the actions of Massachusetts and authorizing "the respective assemblies and conventions of the united colonies where no government adequate to the exigencies of their affairs have been hitherto established, to adopt such government as shall, in the opinion of the representatives of the people, best conduce to the happiness and safety of their constituents in particular, and America in general." Worthington C. Ford et al., eds., *Journals of the Continental Congress, 1774–1789* (Washington, DC: Government Printing Office: 1904–37), 4:342.

21. The definitive account of the adoption of new state constitutions between 1775 and 1777 is Marc W. Kruman, *Between Authority and Liberty: State Constitution Making in Revolutionary America* (Chapel Hill: University of North Carolina Press, 1997); cf. Gordon S. Wood, *The Creation of the American Republic, 1776–1787* (New York: W. W. Norton, 1972), 127–43. Kruman emphasizes the role of conventions in drafting constitutions in the states and is critical of Gordon Wood, who (according to Kruman) overemphasizes the role of legislatures. Kruman summarizes the role of those who drafted the state constitutions as follows: "The authors of the first state constitutions believed that they were writing documents that would influence future generations.... Viewing the constitutions as fundamental law, they wrote declarations of rights and plans of government that defined and restrained rulers, in legislatures and elsewhere; they also protected the constitutions by restricting the amending process." Kruman, *Between Authority and Liberty,* 59.

22. Distain for European institutions was so strong that in the wake of their declaration of independence from England, many state legislatures banned all references to English cases in their common law courts. In practice, the English common law remained in force, as there was a dearth of local authorities and precedents on which to rely. Principles were followed without citing the English cases. For an account of how the state courts jettisoned English law, see Lawrence M. Friedman, *A History of American Law* (New York: Simon and Schuster, 1973), 93–100.

contemporary standards, but they were sovereign within their borders—except, of course, in those areas occupied by British troops. During this brief period, the thirteen former colonies were for all practical purposes independent. Contrary to ideologically motivated claims advanced decades later by Whigs and Republicans during the calamitous events leading up to the American Civil War, authority did not pass directly from the Crown in London to the Continental Congress on the adoption of the Declaration of Independence.[23] Notwithstanding their suspect claims for secession, nineteenth-century advocates of states' rights were correct in asserting that there had been a brief period during which the thirteen former colonies functioned as independent nation-states prior to the formation of the federal union. To be sure, this period of sovereignty did not last very long, ending as it did with the formation of the Confederacy. Even then, the state governments retained most of their traditional prerogatives and powers.

There had been several notable attempts to form a union prior to the 1770s, some more serious than others. All of them failed. In 1643, the leaders of the New England colonies (Massachusetts, Plymouth, Connecticut, and New Haven) entered into a "firm and perpetual league of friendship and amity for offence and defence" against the Indian tribes and the Dutch. The official name of the union was the United Colonies of New England, or more commonly, the New England Confederation.[24] Contrary to the

---

23. Abraham Lincoln repeatedly made this dubious claim in response to assertions by the southern states that they had the right to withdraw from the Union on the grounds that they had been independent states prior to the formation of the Union into which they had voluntarily entered. Lincoln raised this point in his First Inaugural Address and repeated it in his address to Congress on July 4, 1861: "Our states have neither more, nor less power, than that reserved to them, in the Union, by the Constitution—no one of them ever having been a State out of the Union. The original ones passed into the Union even before they cast off their British colonial dependence." President Abraham Lincoln, "Message to Congress in Special Session" (July 4, 1861), in Abraham Lincoln, *Speeches and Writings 1859–1865* (New York: Library of America, 1989), 254. Jackson had made a similar argument in his "Proclamation" against South Carolina's assertion of a right to nullify federal legislation. There he argued that the American "nation" was not created by sovereign states, but rather predated the adoption of the Constitution of 1787. President Andrew Jackson, "Proclamation Regarding Nullification, December 10, 1832," in *A Compilation of the Messages and Papers of the Presidents, 1789–1897,* ed. James D. Richardson (Washington, DC: Government Printing Office, 1896), 2:640–56.

24. Article 2 of the Articles of Confederation of the United Colonies of New England proclaimed: "The said United Colonies for themselves and their posterities do jointly and severally hereby enter into a firm and perpetual league of friendship and amity for offence and defence,

intentions of its founders, this "perpetual" union soon dissolved after Massachusetts refused to join in military action against the Netherlands in 1684. Another attempt to form a political union came out of a conference held in 1754 in Albany by representatives of seven of the northern English colonies. Meeting to discuss a common response to the French threat in the northwest and deteriorating relations with the Indian tribes, the assembled representatives did not stop there. Acting beyond the scope of their delegated authority, the body approved a proposal for union drafted by Benjamin Franklin and subsequently modified by Thomas Hutchinson, governor of the Massachusetts colony. This was the so-called Albany Plan of Union.[25] Under the plan, the president of the union was given the sole power to declare war and make peace with the Indians, negotiate treaties, and govern western territories, while the union itself would possess the power to raise armies and levy taxes for the benefit of the common treasury. Although approved by the representatives, the Albany Plan of Union was rejected by the English government as well as all seven of the participating colonial legislatures, which strenuously objected to this encroachment on their political autonomy—in particular, the power of taxation.[26]

The most successful attempt to form a collective organization among the colonies was the Stamp Act Congress of 1765. This Congress was called

---

mutual advice and succor upon all just occasions both for preserving and propagating the truth and liberties of the Gospel and for their own mutual safety and welfare."

25. The Preamble to the Albany Plan of Union states: "It is proposed that humble application be made for an act of Parliament of Great Britain, by virtue of which one general government may be formed in America, including all the said colonies, within and under which government each colony may retain its present constitution, except in the particulars wherein a change may be directed by the said act." For a discussion of the importance of the Albany Plan of Union, see Samuel Eliot Morison, Henry Steele Commager, and William E. Leuchtenburg, *The Growth of the American Republic* (New York: Oxford University Press, Seventh Edition, 1980), 1:114–15.

26. Had the attempt to create this union succeeded, subsequent events might have unfolded differently. Reflecting on these events in 1789, Franklin himself suggested that had the Albany Plan of Union been successful, "the subsequent Separation of the Colonies from the Mother Country might not so soon have happened, nor the Mischiefs suffered on both sides have occurred, perhaps during another Century. For the Colonies, if so united, would have really been, as they then thought themselves, sufficient to their own Defence, and being trusted with it, as by the Plan, an Army from Britain, for that purpose would have been unnecessary: The Pretences for framing the Stamp-Act would not then have existed, nor the other Projects for drawing a Revenue from America to Britain by Acts of Parliament, which were the Cause of the Breach, and attended with such terrible Expence of Blood and Treasure: so that the different Parts of the Empire might still have remained in Peace and Union." "Benjamin Franklin to Matthew Carey" (February 9, 1789), in *Papers of Benjamin Franklin* (Philadelphia: American Philosophical Society, unpublished), 5:368.

in response to British tax policies that threatened the revenue sources of the colonial authorities and provoked widespread popular opposition. After Parliament passed the Stamp Act in 1765, the Massachusetts Assembly unanimously agreed to a resolution authorizing a meeting of representatives of the colonies. The meeting (the so-called Stamp Act Congress) convened October 7 to 25 in Federal Hall in New York City, with delegates from nine colonies in attendance. The meeting produced three petitions for redress of grievances and a statement of colonial rights (the so-called Declaration of Rights and Grievances) asserting that taxes imposed on the colonies without their consent were unconstitutional. With that the Congress permanently adjourned, as there was never any intent to form a permanent political organization. Following protests against the Stamp Act in both the colonies and among merchants in England, Parliament relented and repealed the act in March 1766.[27]

Keeping in mind these prior events, we return to the salient question in any inquiry into the formation of the American state in the late eighteenth century: Why did the political leaders of the thirteen former English colonies, each with its own constitution, representative assembly, militia, and tax system, agree to permanently transfer a portion of their power and authority to a new central government? In addressing this question, we should like to know what factors were present in the 1770s that were missing when prior attempts to form a political union had failed. Additionally, we must consider the motives and interests of local political leaders. After all, this was a voluntary act on their part. There was no "conquest" of the states by a foreign power that forced them to do this, nor did one powerful state compel the weaker states to merge into a political union, as was the case with the unification of the German principalities under Prussian rule in 1871. In America, political leaders in the states made the strategic decision to create a new national government within a new confederation. Strong incentives must be present for rational, self-interested political actors to adopt a course of action so obviously at their own expense.[28]

---

27. For an account of the proceedings of the Stamp Act Congress, see Jillson and Wilson, *Congressional Dynamics*, 38–42.

28. The decision by local leaders to cede some of their power and authority to a new central political authority was motivated by individual or collective goals that overcame personal self-interest in preserving their status in the entrenched political order. A rational choice model of collective action with regard to the decision to form a federation among the separate states provides a potentially fruitful starting point for the analysis. It also provides a useful perspective to

The most convincing response to this line of inquiry was advanced by William Riker, who identified those conditions under which independent states will join together into federations and "weak" federations will adopt stronger, more centralized federal arrangements.[29] While no longer a topic in the forefront of contemporary political science, a substantial literature on federalism was produced by an earlier generation of scholars.[30] Riker himself was drawn to a critical question left unanswered in those studies—namely, why do the rulers of small states join together to form coalitions or federations? He vigorously rejected the many unsubstantiated claims in the literature on federalism, wherein one finds assertions that federations form among states that share a common language, culture, or race.[31] A cursory review of the many federations and unitary states found in the modern world will dispel such a simplistic generalization. If it is not race, religion, or common culture, what then motivates the leaders of separate sovereign states to form federations? What is the historical origin of federalism as a constitutional arrangement that brings together previously independent and autonomous states?

Federalism is a constitutional arrangement pursuant to which a central political organization exercises a degree of authority over the territory that comprises the federation, while separate constituent units (whether

---

explain subsequent measures approved by the state legislatures to strengthen the national government following the Revolution as well as the decision-making behind the adoption of the Constitution of 1787.

29. Perhaps Riker's most important academic contribution in his long and distinguished academic career was in the application of game theory and rational choice theory to the study of politics. He used game theory to explain the formation of political coalitions. William H. Riker, *The Theory of Political Coalitions* (New Haven: Yale University Press, 1962). Riker applied the logic of game theory and coalition formation to analyze the decision of separate states to join together in federations. William H. Riker, *Federalism: Origin, Operation, Significance* (Boston: Little, Brown, 1964); and *The Development of American Federalism* (Boston: Kluwer, 1987).

30. See, e.g., Kenneth C. Wheare, *Federal Government* (New York: Oxford University Press, 1947); William Livingston, *Federalism and Constitutional Change* (London: Oxford University Press, 1956); A. H. Birch, *Federalism, Finance, and Social Legislation in Canada, Australia, and the United States* (London: Oxford University Press, 1955); A. H. Birch, "Approaches to the Study of Federalism," *Political Studies* 14 (1966); M.J.C. Vile, *The Structure of American Federalism* (London: Oxford University Press, 1961); Daniel J. Elazar, *Exploring Federalism* (Tuscaloosa: University of Alabama Press, 1987).

31. See, e.g., Wheare, *Federal Government,* 38–39. Oddly, Wheare himself went on to list Canada and Switzerland as examples of federal systems that were formed "in spite of differences of language and race."

called states, provinces, *Länder,* etc.) simultaneously exercise authority within their respective localities.[32] In a "weak" federal arrangement (often referred to as a confederation or confederacy), the central political organization possesses the authority to make decisions only on limited issues. This would be typical of a partnership among trading states or a military alliance among separate states formed to wage a military campaign under a unified command, but denied the authority to perform governmental functions beyond that. In such a decentralized federation, most decision making is reserved to the local constituent units.[33] Conversely, in a "strong" federation, virtually all power and authority is consolidated in the central government, with only minimal decision making and authority reserved to the local constituent units. In many respects, a highly centralized constitutional arrangement (e.g., the former Soviet Union) resembles unitary states such as France and Italy, wherein all political power and authority is consolidated within the national state, and local authorities function merely as administrative units of the central government.

What forces and interests drive the political leaders of independent states to join together in a federation? What forces and interests hold together such federations once they form? According to Riker, it is the threat of war or foreign conquest that induces the leaders of independent states (with their own military and tax powers) to transfer a significant amount of their powers to a new central political organization.[34] At the same time, the threat of military attack or foreign conquest is generally insufficient to induce the constituent states to dissolve and merge into a single unitary state with absolute jurisdiction over all the territories and citizens, with a single military force and centralized power of taxation. That kind of extreme consolidation of state power generally requires brute force and military conquest. Riker himself portrayed federalism is an "alternative to empire" where no single state possesses the power to conquer

---

32. Riker, *Federalism,* 11.

33. This is the current status of the European Union. A central administration and representative bodies meet in Brussels (considered the de facto capital of the EU) to manage a unified economy as well as coordinate public policy on the environment, trade, agriculture, and other issues, among the 25 constituent states. While there has been some integration of domestic security forces as well as the introduction of a common currency, the individual states generally remain sovereign in the critical areas of national defense and foreign relations.

34. Federations formed in response to external military threats include Switzerland, Canada, and the former Yugoslavia. Riker, *Development of American Federalism,* 3–16.

neighboring states, but where there are strong incentives for some degree of cooperation and consolidation. Federalism is the product of a rational bargain struck between prospective national leaders and the rulers of the constituent states "for the purpose of aggregating territory, the better to lay taxes and raise armies."[35] Political leaders from separate states form unions when they perceive that a larger political organization will be more efficient in performing the most essential function of a state—for instance, making war.[36] The potential economic benefits from increased trade and commerce may be sufficient to bring separate states together into a trading league, but more powerful incentives are required to motivate the rulers of independent states to cede power and authority to a new central state. That kind of motivation comes from the threat of war or conquest by a common foreign enemy. The threat of invasion and conquest will induce rational self-interested political leaders to give up power and authority to a central political organization *if* they conclude that the formation of a unified military organization is the only way to resist an external military threat.[37]

In surveying those states with federal forms of government, Riker identified a significant number whose origins can be traced to such external military threats. One of those is Canada—a nation-state on the same North American continent as the United States and populated by people of similar ethnic background who similarly adopted a federal constitutional structure. As such, Canada provides the ideal subject for transnational comparisons with the United States.[38] Pursuant to the British North America

---

35. Ibid., 12.

36. This was the case with the unification of the German principalities in 1871 under pressure from Prussia. See Otto Pflanze, *Bismarck and the Development of Germany: The Period of Unification, 1815–1871* (Princeton: Princeton University Press, 1963).

37. Others have argued that in addition to the threat of war, additional conditions are required for the formation of federations by independent states. These include joint economic interests and ideological sympathy among the constituent political units. See, e.g., Wheare, *Federal Government,* 35–44; Birch, "Approaches to the Study of Federalism," 15–33.

38. Many have drawn comparisons between Canada and the United States. See, e.g., Seymour Martin Lipset, *Agrarian Socialism; the Coöperative Commonwealth Federation in Saskatchewan, a Study in Political Sociology* (Berkeley: University of California Press, 1950); and *Continental Divide: the Values and Institutions of the United States and Canada* (New York: Routledge, 1990). Canadian jurisprudence is compared with that of the United States in the essays in Stephen L. Newman, ed., *Liberal Constitutionalism in Canada and the United States* (Albany: State University of New York Press, 2004).

Act of 1867 (subsequently renamed the "Constitution Act, 1867" in 1982), a governmental superstructure (the "Dominion of Canada") was created by Nova Scotia, New Brunswick, and the Province of Canada—three of the remaining English colonies in North America.[39] What induced these independent colonies to join together in a federation? The representatives of the colonies of British North America who first met in September 1864 at the Charlottetown Conference on Prince Edward Island to discuss federation did so for the singular purpose of creating a stronger political organization to resist the external military threat from the United States. The threat of invasion by the United States (which possessed the largest standing army in the world during the Civil War) provoked the leaders of these independent British colonies to form the Canadian federation in 1867.

In the late eighteenth century, it was the threat of military confrontation with England and its powerful navy and professional army that motivated local political leaders in the thirteen colonies to the south to join in a unified coalition against the English Crown. With their common cultural backgrounds, language, and affinity for republican government, a union among the thirteen former colonies was all the more feasible. If factors such as shared culture, religion, political persuasion, and language, as well as geographic proximity, are insufficient by themselves to induce separate states to join together in a federation, they can make the formation of a political coalition more likely and practicable. These factors can also play an important role in holding together a federation once it has been formed and after the external military threat has subsided. This is what happened in America, when religious dogma, ideological fervor, and philosophic discourse cultivated support for the movement for independence that commenced in the 1760s. But these factors do not explain the strategic decision to form a political union among the several states in 1776. Keep in mind that the movement for independence was separate from the strategic decision to form a union among the independent states. There was a distinct political ideology behind the movement for independence. Historians have

---

39. There were four original provinces in the Dominion of Canada: Nova Scotia, New Brunswick, Ontario, and Quebec. Other colonies and the Northwest Territories eventually joined the Canadian federation as well, although under different circumstances. In 1949, Newfoundland joined the union as the tenth province of Canada. For a brief history and description of Canadian federalism, see Peter W. Hogg, *Constitutional Law of Canada* (Toronto: Carswell, 1985), 79–105.

worked diligently to discern the "ideological origins" of the American Revolution. But the local leaders who formed the confederation were driven less by ideology and more by practical concerns—that is, responding to the British military force sent to North America to suppress the rebellion. The origins of the American state can be traced to the strategic response of political leaders to the imminent threat of war with Britain.

No single event clearly defines or marks the date on which the leaders of the thirteen states first decided to join together in a political union.[40] To say the least, the decision-making process was informal and fluid, and the first steps toward union were taken even before the outbreak of armed conflict with the English Crown on April 19, 1775. Nevertheless, the unionist movement was directly related to the impending military conflict with Britain. Beginning in 1773, the leaders of the provincial assemblies initiated preliminary contacts among themselves conducted through so-called Committees of Correspondence. Communication among these committees with regard to the military crisis increased with the onset of hostilities in 1774. Fueled by widespread indignation at the so-called Intolerable Acts, a series of laws enacted by Parliament in 1774 that provoked strong and widespread discontent in the colonies, the Committees of Correspondence of twelve of the colonies agreed to a formal meeting of representatives of the individual colonies to discuss common concerns. These twelve colonies sent seventy representatives to meet at a conference officially known as the First Continental Congress.[41] Although this political organization was not itself a sovereign state, it was the historical precursor of the modern American state.[42]

---

40. Nor was there a definitive moment that marks the beginning of the movement for independence. It is mostly by custom that the date is fixed as July 4, 1776. In actuality, nothing of great consequence occurred on that date, as it was on July 2 that Richard Henry Lee's resolution proclaiming independence was adopted by the Second Continental Congress. The official copy of the declaration was published in Philadelphia on July 4, but signatures were not affixed until later, beginning in August. The confusion and arbitrariness surrounding the dating of this historic event is discussed in Gary Wills, *Inventing America: Jefferson's Declaration of Independence* (New York: Vintage Books, 1978), 334–44; Pauline Maier, *American Scripture: Making the Declaration of Independence* (New York: Knopf, 1997), 44–45; 160–70.

41. Georgia did not send a representative to the First Continental Congress, but eventually sent a single representative to the Second Continental Congress in July 1775.

42. Jerrilyn Greene Marston explains how the allegiance of colonists shifted from the king to the First Continental Congress after 1774. Once the legitimacy of the Crown was undermined, the colonists came to view the Continental Congress as the legitimate government. This transfer

The First Continental Congress convened in Philadelphia from September 5 to October 26, 1774.[43] Although lacking in the basic attributes of a nation-state, this body of delegates laid the foundation for what would eventually become the national government of the United States. Soon after its first meeting, the Congress organized two committees to assist in its workload: a Committee on Grievances to prepare a statement of grievances and to seek redress from George III and a Committee on Trade and Manufactures. The major accomplishments of the First Continental Congress consisted of organizing a boycott against British goods and proposing for the following spring a gathering of its own successor organization. This would be known as the Second Continental Congress. Even while the First Continental Congress sat in session, the threat of military conflict was already in the air. By the time the Second Continental Congress convened in May 1775, bloody military skirmishes had been fought the prior month in Massachusetts at Lexington and Concord. Reflecting the looming military threat, George Washington, who had been elected as a delegate from Virginia, attended sessions of the Second Continental Congress in full military uniform even prior to his appointment as commander-in-chief. The impending threat of military engagement pushed political leaders in the separate states to form a political union that would serve their mutual interests in defense.

Like its predecessor, the Second Continental Congress was never intended to be a permanent political organization, let alone the central government for a strong nation-state. The leaders of the American resistance had time to contemplate only the issues immediately before them—the struggle for independence and the military campaign itself. They gave little thought to the question of what kind of national government would be formed by the former colonies after independence was achieved. The Second Continental Congress served mainly as the central command center

---

of loyalty was hastened by the king's unequivocal rejection of petitions from the Congress for accommodation. Marston, *King and Congress.*

43. An informative account of the role of the Continental Congress in directing the revolution is Jack N. Rakove, *The Beginnings of National Politics: An Interpretive History of the Continental Congress* (New York: Knopf, 1979). The proceedings and organization of the Continental Congress are analyzed in Jillson and Wilson, *Congressional Dynamics;* see also Marston, *King and Congress,* 75–99. The standard history of the period remains Merrill Jensen, *The Founding of a Nation: A History of the American Revolution, 1763–1776* (New York: Oxford University Press, 1968).

for the military alliance created by the thirteen independent state governments. Political leaders in the states recognized that thirteen separate armies would never be as effective in mounting armed resistance against the British as a single army under a unified command. The Second Continental Congress provided a unified military command following the proclamation of the Declaration of Independence and performed a few basic governmental functions beyond that. For example, the Congress established a Continental Post Office, regulated trade, directed Indian affairs, and occasionally heard disputes among the states.[44]

The gathering of the Second Continental Congress perfectly illustrates Riker's contention that separate sovereign states will come together to create a federation in response to an external military threat, even while the pressures for consolidation are too weak to compel the formation of a unitary state. In this case, the threat of war with England led to the formation of an umbrella organization for the limited purpose of directing the war effort. While there remained political leaders who opposed any form of union, the overall sentiment in the states was for collective action to achieve independence. Of course, the *degree* of authority that would be transferred to a central government remained a matter of intense controversy. In the end, very little power or authority was transferred to the Continental Congress by the states. Truth be told, the Second Continental Congress was little more than a committee comprised of representatives of the several states. There was virtually no institutional apparatus created. The Congress did not possess any permanent bureaucracy or support staff. The national government had few officials, functionaries, and agents to do its bidding. Most significantly, it did not possess a standing army of any significance and lacked the capacity to extract resources from society. If this was a national government, it lacked all of the basic attributes of stateness.

It is telling that the Congress, which constituted the entire apparatus of the national government (as there was no executive or judiciary), did not even possess its own building in which to convene—one more indicator of the weakness of this political organization.[45] From May 10, 1775, to

---

44. For a description of the few governmental functions performed by the Continental Congress, see Maier, *American Scripture,* 13.

45. Many private clubs and social organizations (e.g., chapters of the Elks Club or Rotary International) own their own buildings in which they meet and conduct business. Countless

September 1777, the Second Continental Congress borrowed space in Philadelphia in the Pennsylvania State House, today known as Independence Hall. At one point, the Congress shared this building with both the newly elected Pennsylvania Provincial Conference (which replaced the disbanded colonial assembly) and the delegates to the Pennsylvania Convention who had assembled to draft the new Pennsylvania state constitution. Things progressively got worse, as the Congress was forced to flee to nearby York to escape the advance of British troops on Philadelphia. Subsequently, the Congress relocated to Baltimore and then Lancaster, returning to Philadelphia only after the British departed.[46] Lacking a permanent capital city or even its own building in which to convene, and possessing only the most minimal authority and political power, the Second Continental Congress was hardly what we would think of as a sovereign state. By all the aforementioned criteria commonly used to evaluate stateness and political development, we must conclude that the Continental Congress was an extraordinarily weak political organization—one barely capable of sustaining its own existence, let alone penetrating society to extract revenue or regulate the private economy. Given these severe institutional limitations, it is all the more remarkable that the Continental Congress managed the war effort was well as it did.

Beginning in the fall of 1775, the Continental Congress established a number of committees (ad hoc and standing) to assist with its workload.[47] These included committees to manage the military campaign, foreign affairs, as well as the national treasury. The first financial committee had been appointed in June 1775 to prepare an estimate of the expenses of the Congress itself. This was a standing committee for supervising the treasury function and continued until a more permanent institution was established in February 1776. At that time, the size of the committee was

---

churches own their own buildings. Yet the Continental Congress, the national government of the American state, did not possess even this minimal infrastructure.

46. After the war, the Congress sat in Philadelphia, Princeton, Annapolis, and Trenton. During this period of itinerancy, it was difficult to get a quorum. In late December 1784, the Congress moved to New York where it remained for the duration of the Confederacy. See James Sterling Young, *The Washington Community, 1800–1828* (New York: Columbia University Press, 1966), 13; Rakove, *The Beginnings of National Politics,* 334–36; Richard B. Morris, *The Forging of the Union, 1780–1789* (New York: Harper and Row, 1987), 90–95.

47. The best account of the committee system and procedures of the Second Continental Congress is Jillson and Wilson, *Congressional Dynamics,* 59–67, 91–131.

expanded from five members to ten, and its powers were enlarged.[48] Such institutional reforms reflected the continuing efforts of national political leaders to strengthen the powers of the Continental Congress. In essence, the committees functioned in lieu of bureaucratic organization, of which there was none. They enabled the Congress to perform the limited functions for which it was created. This was a relatively minor example of political development compared with what would come in the nineteenth century, but it was a beginning.

During this period of institutional weakness and geographic itinerancy, the Continental Congress constantly struggled to carry out its two intended functions: coordinating the military campaign (to be fought almost exclusively by state militiamen) and marshalling societal resources for the war effort. The problem was that the Continental Congress did not possess sufficient power or authority to carry out even these minimal functions.[49] The Continental Congress lacked its own standing army as well as sufficient institutional capacity to extract revenue from society. Because the states remained sovereign, the Continental Congress only could pass nonbinding resolutions requesting the state governments meet their respective quotas of revenue, armaments, and troops. As the states were under no compulsion to obey these requests, they were routinely and flagrantly ignored, resulting in persistent shortages of resources (men, equipment, and money) for the war effort. The Continental Congress was forced to borrow from foreign sources and print its own paper currency to pay for firearms and powder for troops under its command.[50] This currency greatly depreciated in value during the course of the Revolutionary War and sparked persistent

---

48. For an account of the finance committee of the Continental Congress, see Albert S. Bolles, *The Financial History of the United States, from 1774 to 1789* (New York: D. Appleton, 1879), 10–18. Although dated, Bolles's history remains an invaluable source of information on the workings of the treasury committee and the financial affairs of the Continental Congress.

49. From the perspective of the so-called new institutionalism, Jillson and Wilson argue that the "norms, rules, and institutional structures of the Continental Congress... were as much to blame for the institution's eventual failure" as its lack of power vis-à-vis the states. Jillson and Wilson, *Congressional Dynamics,* 3, 162.

50. The Congress issued the first bills of credit in June 1775—totaling 2 million Spanish dollars, which coinage was the standard currency of the period. Bolles, *Financial History of the United States,* 31–33. From 1776 to 1780, the Congress printed $241,550 in paper currency. Foreign borrowing was limited until the victory of the Continental Army at Saratoga in 1778. After that, the French lent more than $4.5 million in specie between 1778 and 1783. Dougherty, *Collective Action,* 56.

inflation throughout the period.[51] The Congress had little choice, as it did not possess the authority to impose its own taxes. It had no tax collectors, customs officers, or capacity to extract resources from society, even for the limited purpose of providing for the common defense of the states that comprised the union. Revenue predation was simply not an option.

Without a power of taxation, the leaders of the Continental Congress had no viable revenue strategy. Without an independent source of revenue, the Congress was forced to borrow funds and print paper money for the war effort. From the onset of the military conflict through the spring of 1781, the Congress raised revenue through three methods: the emission of bills of credit (mostly printing paper money known as Continental dollars), loans from domestic sources (wealthy Americans willing to buy certificates of indebtedness at interest rates initially set at 4 percent and later raised to 6 percent), and borrowing from foreign sources (mostly located in France and Holland). In February 1780, the Congress adopted a general system of requisitions of goods (beef, pork, rum, flour) from the states for the war effort.[52] This was an indirect form of taxation that worked remarkably well; however, hard specie was still needed to keep the government functioning and the army supplied. While the domestic economy fared well during the war, generating significant profits for merchants, traders, and profiteers, the national government lacked any effective means of appropriating a share of that wealth for itself.

The military force under the command of the Continental Congress was nearly as anemic as the system of public finance used to bankroll the war effort. As we have seen from our study of early modern Europe, public revenue and military power are closely related, each dependent on the other. In the case of the Continental Congress, the weakness of its system of revenue extraction rendered it incapable of organizing and adequately equipping the military force under its command. In June 1775, the Congress had authorized the formation of the Continental Army under the command of George Washington for the purpose of promoting the

---

51. With the depreciation of the currency, Congress imposed price controls beginning in 1777. These were largely ineffective. For a comprehensive account of how the Continental Congress maintained this currency during the Revolutionary War, see Ferguson, *Power of the Purse,* 25–105; see also Curtis P. Nettles, *The Emergence of a National Economy, 1775–1815* (New York: Holt, Reinhart and Winston, 1962), 23–34.

52. The system of requisitions is discussed in Ferguson, *Power of the Purse,* 48.

common defense and waging a unified military campaign.[53] In 1776, the Congress put 89,600 men in uniform—the largest number of troops raised in any single year of the war. Of these, 42,700 were state militiamen contributed by the state governments, and the rest were "regulars" serving directly in the Continental Army. In 1777, when the Continental Congress was at the peak of its power and authority, it requested another 80,000 men from the states to serve in the Continental Army. Only 34,820 were ever provided, making for a total of 68,720 men (state militiamen and regulars) in the military force under Washington's command. The acute shortage of money made it difficult for the Congress to raise and supply troops.[54] By 1781, with the war at its height, fewer than 30,000 men were available to face the British on the field of battle. Of these, fewer than 13,300 were regulars, with the balance consisting of irregular state militiamen organized in battalions under the command of officers of the Continental Army.[55] The majority of the troops that fought in the Revolutionary War were under the control of the state legislatures.

An estimated 232,000 troops (regulars and militia combined) in total served under the command of the Continental Congress during the course of the Revolutionary War.[56] This was out of a population of 2.5 million persons then living in the former colonies.[57] An estimated 10.4 percent of the population participated in the Revolutionary War.[58] At any given time, however, the size of the army was never very great. As leader of the Continental Army, General Washington never commanded more than 17,000

53. The definitive account of the organization of the Continental Army is Robert K. Wright, *The Continental Army* (Washington, DC: Center of Military History, 1986).

54. As Washington lamented in 1778: "Can *we* carry on the War much longer? certainly NO, unless some measure can be devised and speedily to restore the credit of the currency.... Without these can be effected, what funds can stand the present expences of the Army?" "Letter to Gouverneur Morris" (October 4, 1778), in *The Writings of George Washington From the Original Manuscript Sources, 1745–1799,* ed. John C. Fitzpatrick (Washington, DC: U.S. Government Printing Office, 1931–44), 13:21.

55. Figures from Mark Mayo Boatner III, *Encyclopedia of the American Revolution* (New York: David McKay, 1966), 262–64. The deficiencies of the Regular Army and Washington's reluctance to rely upon the state militia is recounted in Marston, *King and Congress,* 145–69.

56. Christopher Duffy, *The Military Experience in the Age of Reason, 1715–1789* (New York: Routledge and Kegan Paul, 1987), 17.

57. Population statistics from U.S. Bureau of the Census, *Historical Statistics of the United States: Colonial Times to 1970* (Washington, DC: U.S. Department of Commerce, 1975), series A 6–8 ("Annual Population Estimates of the United States: 1790 to 1970"), part 1, 8.

58. Hugh Rockoff, "Veterans," in *Historical Statistics of the United States,* ed. Carter et al., 5–342.

men on the field of battle at any one time.[59] The military conflict was waged with armies that were tiny compared with those engaged on the battlefields of Europe during the eighteenth century. The British themselves never had more than 80,000 troops stationed on the entire North American continent—this to exert the authority of the Crown over a vast territory ranging from Canada to Florida.[60] To the British, the conflict in North America was but one theater of war in a much larger geomilitary struggle in which England found itself engaged (mostly against France) for nearly two centuries.[61] Much to the advantage of the colonies, Britain dedicated the bulk of its resources to the unrelenting military conflict with France, the most powerful nation-state on the continent, rather than the campaign to suppress the rebellion in North America.

A Constitution for the Confederacy

Recognizing the limitations of their authority and power, the leaders of the Second Continental Congress moved to establish a stronger government and more permanent political institutions. On June 7, 1776, Richard Henry Lee of Virginia introduced his celebrated motion for independence from England.[62] History has afforded the ensuing campaign for independence a central place in our national lore. No less significant, later that same day

---

59. Boatner, *Encyclopedia of the American Revolution,* 264. Others estimate that the maximum number under Washington's command was never more than 13,000 troops. See, e.g., Duffy, *The Military Experience in the Age of Reason, 1715–1789,* 17: "The largest body which Washington commanded in the field probably reached only about 13,000 troops."

60. This number included some 30,000 "Hessian" foreign mercenaries. Of course, England had other large armies and its navy was already quite significant. But the bulk of these forces were deployed outside of North America.

61. The succession of wars fought in the eighteenth century in North America by England and France (and their proxies) were extensions of the broader struggle between the powers of Europe, rather than separate events (as they are commonly perceived on this side of the Atlantic Ocean). William M. Fowler, Jr., *Empires at War: The French and Indian War and the Struggle for North America, 1754–1763* (New York: Walker, 2005).

62. The king's refusal to offer any concessions convinced the delegates of the Continental Congress to issue a formal declaration of independence. According to Jack Rakove: "The delegates had to decide what useful purposes a formal declaration would actually serve....For most intents and purposes, the Americans were already acting as if they were an independent nation: waging war, creating new governments, issuing money, and enacting other expedient measures....In the end, independence emerged as a logical conclusion flowing from principles and

Lee moved that "a plan of confederation be prepared and transmitted to the respective Colonies for their consideration and approbation."[63] This second motion proposing a constitution for the political union already in existence was immediately adopted by the Congress, which appointed a drafting committee comprised of one delegate from each colony to prepare a written plan of confederation.[64] John Dickinson, a wealthy Philadelphia lawyer and political moderate who later represented Delaware (formerly known as the "Lower Counties on the Delaware," a territory of Pennsylvania) in the Continental Congress, was selected to chair the drafting committee.

Dickinson was a curious and influential figure in the middle colonies.[65] Elected to the Pennsylvania General Assembly at age thirty in 1762, Dickinson was appointed as a delegate to the Stamp Act Congress of 1765 held in New York. Still not convinced of the need for independence, Dickinson was finally swayed by Parliament's clumsy attempt to reorganize the colonial customs pursuant to the Townshend Acts of 1767. In response to this unwanted intrusion into a realm traditionally reserved to the colonial tax authorities, Dickinson wrote the hugely popular *Letters from a Farmer in Pennsylvania to the Inhabitants of the British Colonies* (1767) in which he acknowledged the constitutional right of Parliament to legislate and regulate commerce between the colonies and the mother country, but denounced it for levying onerous taxes solely for the purpose of raising revenue for the mother country.[66] Later, Dickinson emerged as the leader of a group of

---

opinions that most delegates commonly shared and as a response to events they could neither control nor evade." Rakove, *Beginnings of National Politics,* 89, 102.

63. Ford et al., eds., *Journals of the Continental Congress,* 5:425.

64. The members of the committee were John Dickinson (chairman), Samuel Adams, Josiah Bartlett, Button Gwinnett, Joseph Hewes, Stephen Hopkins, Robert R. Livingston, Thomas McKean, Thomas Nelson, Edward Rutledge, Roger Sherman, and Thomas Stone. Francis Hopkinson subsequently joined the committee in June.

65. There is a vast literature on Dickinson, who served in the Continental Congress originally representing Pennsylvania and then Delaware. An introduction to his life and political thought is David Louis Jacobson, *John Dickinson and the Revolution in Pennsylvania, 1764–1776* (Berkeley: University of California Press, 1965).

66. John Dickinson, *Letters from a Farmer in Pennsylvania to the Inhabitants of the British Colonies* (Philadelphia: David Hall and William Sellers, 1768). The *Letters* appeared in 1767 and 1768 in the *Pennsylvania Chronicle* and were later published as a pamphlet widely read in the colonies and England. Dickinson argued that duties that regulated trade were consistent with longstanding principles of the English constitution, but those imposed to raise revenue for the Crown were not. This flatly contradicted Parliament's assertion in the Declaratory Act of 1766 that it had

moderates in the Continental Congress who counseled on the dangers of *not* forming a stronger federal union, pointing for justification at the "political turmoil" generated in the states (in particular, Pennsylvania) by the adoption of radical state constitutions and governments.[67]

In June 1776, Dickinson and the drafting committee took up the daunting task of writing a new constitution for the confederation. Because the committee met in secret, we know precious little about the politics or logic behind the drafting of the text. The document that emerged, referred to therein as the "Articles of confederation and perpetual union," was presented to the Congress on July 12 in the handwriting of Dickinson, who is generally presumed to have authored most of the text.[68] Its contents were then debated by the Committee of the Whole during the summer of 1776, with particularly heated discussion on how representation in the national legislature would be apportioned among the states, the boundaries of western land, and the apportionment of taxes. The thrust of Dickinson's draft was to strengthen the powers of the Congress. His plan forbade the states from conducting foreign affairs, discriminating against citizens of other states, and prohibited discrimination based on religious grounds. With the approval of nine states, the Congress could declare war. Ironically, the Dickinson plan did not include a power of taxation, other than to support the Post Office. The states would supply revenue to the Congress through assessments based on population (excepting Indians). The Dickinson draft survived several amendments by the Committee of the Whole and Congress, but in the final version the powers of the Congress were greatly muted.[69] The opposition, led by Thomas Burke of North Carolina, was committed to preserving the traditional powers of the sovereign states. The debate and political haggling dragged on for another sixteen

---

"full power and authority to make laws and statutes of sufficient force and validity to bind the colonies and people of America...in all cases whatsoever."

67. Rakove, *Beginnings of National Politics,* 157.

68. Six other drafts of a written constitution for a federation were produced between 1775 and 1776. There are no copies of three of these. One was drafted and presented to Congress by Benjamin Franklin, but it was never formally considered. These earlier drafts are discussed in Rakove, *Beginnings of National Politics,* 136–37.

69. The political battle over Dickinson's plan for a strong central government is recounted in David Brian Robertson, *The Constitution and America's Destiny* (New York: Cambridge University Press, 2005), 47–48; Morris, *Forging of the Union,* 84–90; Forrest McDonald, *E Pluribus Unum: The Formation of the American Republic, 1776–1790* (Boston: Houghton Mifflin, 1965), 8–9.

months, with a diluted version of Dickinson's plan finally approved by the Congress on November 17, 1777. The text was then sent to the states for ratification accompanied by a blunt message warning of the difficulties the states would face in attempting to form a "permanent union."[70]

As the unanimous consent of all thirteen states was required for ratification, the cumbersome process dragged on for another three years. Given that the ratification process took place during some of the most intense fighting of the American Revolution, delay was inevitable. On February 5, 1778, South Carolina became the first state to approve the Articles of Confederation, voting for union in light of the "imminent dangers" the states faced. Thereafter, the ratification process stalled on account of recurring disputes between Maryland and Virginia over borders and rights to western land—a perennial issue among those states with land claims.[71] Official ratification was not achieved for three more years as the disputes continued. On March 1, 1781, the last holdout state, Maryland, finally approved the Articles of Confederation after finally reaching accommodation with Virginia over the unresolved land dispute.[72] Later that day, the Congress proclaimed the Articles of Confederation in effect.

In many respects, the adoption of this first constitution, rather than the signing of the Declaration of Independence, the first meeting of the Continental Congress, or the ratification of the Constitution of 1787, marks the founding of the American state. For more than seven years, the Articles of

---

70. The Congress sent the text to the states with the recommendation that it "be candidly reviewed under a sense of the difficulty of combining in one general system the various sentiments and interests of a continent divided into so many sovereign and independent communities, under a conviction of the absolute necessity of uniting all our councils and all our strength, to maintain and defend our common liberties: let them be examined with a liberality becoming brethren and fellow-citizens surrounded by the same imminent dangers, contending for the same illustrious prize, and deeply interested in being forever bound and connected together by ties the most intimate and indissoluble; and finally, let them be adjusted with the temper and magnanimity of wise and patriotic legislators, who, while they are concerned for the prosperity of their own more immediate circle, are capable of rising superior to local attachments, when they may be incompatible with the safety, happiness, and glory of the general Confederacy." Ford et al., eds., *Journals of the Continental Congress,* 9:933.

71. The dispute between Virginia and Maryland (as well as other states) over western lands is described in Rakove, *Beginnings of National Politics,* 285–87. How representation would be apportioned among the various states was the other perennial subject of dispute.

72. Late in 1780, Virginia suddenly reversed its position and ceded all of its lands north of the Ohio River to the Congress. This was enough to satisfy Maryland. The incident is recounted in McDonald, *E Pluribus Unum,* 15–16.

Confederation served as the official constitution of the Confederacy of the United States of America. Moreover, during the long delay in the ratification process, the Continental Congress generally followed the rules and procedures prescribed under the Articles of Confederation. Thus, for all intents and purposes, the Articles of Confederation functioned as the constitution of the Confederacy from November 17, 1777 (the date the text was approved by the Congress), until June 21, 1788 (the date the Constitution of 1787 was officially declared effective). Most important, it was a constitution intentionally designed to create a weak and decentralized federation—a decision of lasting importance and influence on the subsequent development of the American state.

The Confederacy of the United States

The political order (i.e., the political institutions, rules, and procedures) established by the Articles of Confederation was quite different than that found today in the nation's capital.[73] Any comprehensive account of the development of the American state must take into account the curious political organization established by the Articles of Confederation. The weaknesses of the nineteenth-century American state ultimately can be traced back to the decisions and preferences constitutionalized during this early period of state formation. The institutional legacy that shaped American politics and decision making for the next two centuries was cast during the Confederacy, when the path to federalism was first taken.

What factors account for the weak national political institutions established by the Articles of Confederation? Recall that in the late eighteenth century, the states of Europe were already quite advanced in terms of institutional development, and those who drafted the Articles of Confederation were familiar with their design and structure. Instead, they designed a constitutional structure that integrated the state governments with a new national government of extraordinarily limited powers. Admittedly, it is

---

73. Theodore Lowi aptly refers to the political order established by the Articles of Confederation as the "First Republic" and that by the Constitution of 1787 as the "Second Republic." Theodore J. Lowi, *American Government: Incomplete Conquest* (New York: Holt, Rinehart and Winston, 1976), 90 fn10.

unclear whether building a strong "consolidated" state in the European sense would have been possible in North America in the late eighteenth century. But most assuredly, that was not the goal of the founders of the Confederacy.

The state designed and built by the drafters of the Articles of Confederation has been judged harshly by history. That is understandable. As the blueprint for the Confederacy, the Articles of Confederation failed to include a central government with even the most basic powers and authority. By its own terms, this founding document did not establish a nation-state so much as a "firm league of friendship" among the several states.[74] The drafters of the Articles of Confederation simply codified the existing relationship between the national government and the state governments as it had emerged during the days of the Continental Congress. Rather than shift the locus of power from the periphery to the center within the federal structure, they left most political power exactly where it was—with the state governments.

From the perspective of statecraft and constitutional design, this initial attempt to construct a political order must be judged a failure. The weaknesses of the Confederacy were notorious. In the waning days of the Confederacy, John Adams lamented that the Congress was "not a legislative assembly, not a representative assembly, but only a diplomatic assembly."[75] The weaknesses of the political institutions of the Confederacy were apparent to those who served in the Continental Congress and voted to adopt the Articles of Confederation. Most were willing to accept the obvious deficiencies in order to secure ratification, which was accomplished through a strategic decision to reject all amendments offered by the states as a precondition for ratification.[76] Many in the Continental Congress who voted to approve this first constitution expected that the national government would be strengthened *after* ratification through amendments. That

---

74. "The said States hereby severally enter into a firm league of friendship with each other, for their common defense, the security of their liberties, and their mutual and general welfare...." Articles of Confederation, art. III.

75. John Adams, "A Defence of the Constitution of Government of the United States of America," in *The Political Writings of John Adams* (Indianapolis: Bobbs-Merrill, 1954), 143.

76. The many amendments proposed and rejected by the delegates charged with drafting and approving the Articles of Confederation are discussed in Rakove, *Beginnings of National Politics*, 186–90.

never happened because amendments required approval by the Congress and the unanimous consent of the states, something virtually impossible to secure. Legislation concerning most of the important things that states do (declaring war, raising an army or navy, entering into treaties, borrowing and appropriating money, etc.) required the assent of nine states.[77] That was difficult enough to obtain; unanimous consent of the states proved impossible.

Lacking support from the state legislatures, the Congress took actions of its own to enhance its administrative capacity, including the creation in 1781 of four executive departments: Foreign Affairs, Finance, War, and Marine. The establishment of these administrative offices, primitive as they were, marked an important first step in the development of the apparatus of the American state. The military campaign was placed under the direction of the War office. The Finance department was created to deal with the persistent revenue shortages that handicapped the war effort. Public finance was a major challenge to the national government of the Confederacy as the Congress was unable to service the massive debt it was accumulating. James Savage has summarized the situation as follows: "The Revolutionary War left the states and the national government with a massive public debt, and the Articles of Confederation left the nation with an unworkable institutional arrangement for retiring that debt."[78]

Even the rulers of the strongest states must "negotiate" a revenue coalition with the dominant political organizations and economic interests in society, offering benefits such as protection in exchange for tribute. In America, such negotiations have been particularly arduous, as the constitutional structure of the regime was expressly designed to *deny* state officials direct access to revenue. The founders of the Confederacy wished to avoid creating a native American Leviathan to replace the English monarch they had just cast aside. In furtherance of this goal, representatives of powerful local interests in the states opposed the consolidation of the most basic governmental powers (most particularly, military powers and the power of taxation) in the national government. This opposition was expressed in the constitutional design of the Confederacy. Taxation and standing armies, after all, are among the most obvious manifestations of the coercive powers

---

77. Articles of Confederation, art. IX.
78. Savage, *Balanced Budgets and American Politics,* 72.

of the state, and one of the principal goals of American constitutionalism has been to impose limits and checks on the exercise of these coercive powers. In this regard, the original constitutional design worked all too well, crippling the national government of the Confederacy. Extreme decentralization became part of the institutional legacy with which officials of the American state were forced to contend for the next two hundred years.

From its inception, the national government of the Confederacy faced serious revenue deficiencies. On February 3, 1781, in an effort to alleviate the unrelenting revenue crisis, the Congress adopted a motion advanced by Robert R. Livingston of New York (who later that year would be elected secretary of foreign affairs) requesting that the states impose a duty of 5 percent on imports, such tax to be collected by officers of the United States and used to pay down the massive debt (and accumulated interest) amassed by the Congress for the war effort.[79] This proposal reflected the realization among the delegates of the Congress that on account of the deteriorating financial position of the national government, it would be impossible to finance the war solely by printing paper money—the only means the national government then had to "raise" revenue. While twelve states ratified the amendment granting a new taxing power to the Congress, the legislature of Rhode Island voted unanimously (53–0) against the impost in November 1782. Rhode Island had few natural resources but considerable commerce passed through its ports. Most of the imported goods that entered Rhode Island were reexported to buyers in other states. The state legislature objected to what it viewed as an encroachment by the national government on the state's traditional power to tax such imported goods. Whatever the merits of this position, under the inflexible and unrealistic

---

79. The full text of the motion reads: "Resolved, That it be recommended to the several states, as indispensably necessary, that they vest a power in Congress, to levy for the use of the United States, a duty of five per cent. ad valorem, at the time and place of importation, upon all goods, wares and merchandises of foreign growth and manufactures, which may be imported into any of the said states from any foreign port, island or plantation, after the first day of May, 1781; except arms, ammunition, cloathing and other articles imported on account of the United States, or any of them; and except wool-cards and cotton-cards, and wire for making them; and also, except salt, during the war.... That the monies arising from the said duties be appropriated to the discharge of the principal and interest of the debts already contracted, or which may be contracted, on the faith of the United States, for supporting the present war: That the said be continued until the said debts shall be fully and finally discharged." Ford et al., eds., *Journals of the Continental Congress*, 19:112–13.

procedure established for amending the Articles of Confederation, Rhode Island's veto was enough to sink the campaign to grant this expanded power of taxation to the Congress.

The impost of 1781 was supported by Robert Morris of Philadelphia, who had been appointed in February by a nearly unanimous Congress as superintendent of finance in the newly established executive department. Morris is commonly but inaccurately portrayed as the "financier of the Revolution"—inaccurate because Morris did not accept the post until May 1781 and did not actually take office until September, only a month before the American victory at the Battle of Yorktown, which effectively ended the military phase of the conflict.[80] That said, the military situation that Morris confronted when he took office was genuinely grave, and he played a critical role in provisioning the Continental Army during the final years of the Revolutionary War and then in organizing the finances of the Confederacy. For these reasons, Morris deserves much credit for his tireless efforts in strengthening the institutions (military and fiscal) of the early American state.

Prior to taking national office, Morris was an experienced and respected figure in Pennsylvania colonial politics, having served on the Committee of Correspondence, in the state legislature, and as a representative to the Second Continental Congress from 1775 to 1778. In the latter capacity, he had voted against the Declaration of Independence on July 1, 1776, although he subsequently signed the document.[81] In his new post at the Office of Finance, Morris emerged as the leading proponent of enhanced fiscal powers for the young republic. Only three days after accepting his commission, in the face of the worsening fiscal crisis, Morris submitted his "Plan for Establishing A National Bank," which envisioned a national bank to be

---

80. The myth of Morris as "financier of the Revolution" can be traced to late-nineteenth-century biographers. See, e.g., William Graham Sumner, *Robert Morris* (New York: Dodd, Mead, 1892); Charles Henry Hart, *Robert Morris: The Financier of the American Revolution* (Philadelphia: Collins, 1877); see also Ellis Paxson Oberholtzer, *Robert Morris, Patriot and Financier* (New York: Macmillan, 1903). There are no recent biographies of Morris, nor are his letters and papers available in a single published series. An informative account of his career as Superintendent of Finance of the Confederacy is Clarence L. Ver Steeg, *Robert Morris: Revolutionary Financier* (Philadelphia: University of Pennsylvania, 1954).

81. Morris and Roger Sherman of Connecticut were the only two individuals who signed all three of the founding documents of the United States: the Declaration of Independence, the Articles of Confederation, and the Constitution of 1787.

charted by Congress and funded by private subscriptions.[82] The proposal led to the chartering of the Bank of North America, the predecessor of the First Bank of the United States and the first commercial bank in the country. Through the bank, Morris rendered vital financial services to the nation during the final years of the military campaign, when he was directly involved in supplying goods to Washington's exhausted army, and later during the short-lived Confederacy.[83]

The national bank was part of Morris's broader plan to resolve the financial crisis that gripped the national government in 1781. The main elements of that plan included the consolidation of all fiscal powers within his office, stabilization of the deteriorating currency by replacing the worthless bills of credit and continental currency then in circulation with new notes under his own signature as superintendent (so-called Morris notes), improvement of provisioning for the Continental Army, establishment of a national mint, and the consolidation of the war debt—calculated by Morris as $25 million.[84] The consolidated debt would be serviced out of a national treasury funded by a host of new national taxes and excise duties. Morris and the Congress faced a major crisis in 1781 with the near collapse of public credit, which was largely attributable to the continued deterioration of the creditworthiness of the national government rather than to any serious decline in the health of the economy itself.[85] During the first five years of the war, some $226 million in Continental dollars were put into circulation. By April 1781, the value of the Continental dollar had depreciated to near zero and ceased to circulate.[86] In an attempt to ease

---

82. The plan called for an initial capitalization of $400,000 to be raised by selling stock for $400 per share. With twelve private directors, the bank was in essence a private bank "under governmental auspices" that would serve the financial needs of the government. The workings of the bank are discussed in detail in Ver Steeg, *Robert Morris,* 66, 84–88, 115–17.

83. The bank's capitalization was too small for making significant loans and was mostly used to finance ordinary operations through short-term lending. Ferguson, *Power of the Purse,* 136–38.

84. Ver Steeg, *Robert Morris,* 126.

85. Ibid., 57.

86. Farley Grubb, "The U.S. Constitution and Monetary Powers: An Analysis of the 1787 Constitutional Convention and the Constitutional Transformation of the U.S. Monetary System," *Financial History Review* 13 (April 2006): 46; see also Grubb, "The Continental Dollar: What Happened to It after 1779?" NBER Working Paper No. 13770 (Cambridge, MA: National Bureau of Economic Research, February 2008). According to Grubb, the likely cause of the collapse of the continental dollar was the inability of the national government to issue taxes to redeem its currency, which was never backed by specie. States also issued paper money during the Revolutionary

the national government's immediate financial deficiency, the Congress issued a new revenue assessment to the states in November 1781, requesting $8 million in specie to support the military campaign in the coming year. To speed up collection of the revenue for the national treasury, Morris appointed a "receiver" (an employee of the national government) in each state to assist in collecting the revenue assessments on behalf of the Congress. Collections from the states increased markedly during Morris's tenure as superintendent of finance.[87] Later, Morris would reorganize the treasury office (known then as the Treasury Board) and introduce the first system of budgeting for the national government under the supervision of the Office of Finance. These administrative reforms enhanced the state's fiscal capabilities, thereby furthering the ability of the national government to carry out its delegated functions. Morris pursed an aggressive revenue strategy in an attempt to bolster the weak and ineffective national government of the Confederacy.

As Morris consolidated more and more governmental functions within his office, his power came to rival that of the Congress itself, especially given that he was the official who provided money and provisions to the Congress and its army.[88] Contrary to the accusations of his most virulent detractors, Morris did not seek personal gain through the powers of his office, although he did amass a great fortune during the war as a merchant and profiteer.[89] Morris continued to conduct private business even while serving as superintendent of finance, but this was with the full knowledge and consent of the Congress. Indeed, this was a precondition for his acceptance of the post in the first place. Beyond the relentless pursuit of his own private financial interests, Morris had a clear vision of a stronger Confederacy, and his primary goal in office was to fortify the fiscal

---

War, but these currencies did not depreciate nearly as much—perhaps because the states had the power to impose taxes.

87. Dougherty, *Collective Action,* 63.

88. A summary of Morris's role in the new government is Rakove, *Beginnings of National Politics,* chap. 13 ("The Administration of Robert Morris"), 297–329.

89. Despite the great fortune Morris amassed during the Revolutionary War as a privateer and international merchant, and after the war in numerous business ventures (including land investments in New York), he ended up one of the largest individual debtors in the Confederacy. After leaving office, his highly leveraged land company collapsed, and Morris served time in debtor's prison from February 1798 to August 1801. He died penniless in Philadelphia in May 1806. See, Oberholtzer, *Robert Morris, Patriot and Financier,* 349–55.

powers of the national government within the parameters established by the Articles of Confederation. In this respect, his vision of nationalism fell short of that of Gouverneur Morris (his close friend and assistant in the Office of Finance), Robert Livingston (another friend and business associate), James Wilson, James Madison, and Alexander Hamilton, all of whom came to regard the Articles of Confederation as hopelessly inadequate and beyond reform. Among these, Hamilton was the strongest critic of the Confederacy. As early as 1780, he complained vociferously that under the Articles of Confederation, the Congress lacked adequate control over the military forces and a defective power of the purse, while conversely, the states retained too much control over these vital functions of the central state.[90] From the perspective of ardent nationalists such as Hamilton, improvements to the system of state requisitions amounted to little more than "patchwork" reform of what he regarded as fatal defects in the constitutional design of the Confederacy. Madison eventually came to much the same conclusion.

Many of the deficiencies of the Confederacy were attributable to the drafters' lack of a clear idea of how a federal system would work in practice.[91] Given the lack of historical precedent for a large centralized federation, this short-sightedness was understandable. What was the right balance between national and state powers? The answer was not obvious to state builders in the late eighteenth century, nor is there a consensus today. To designate the Articles of Confederation a failure presumes that its drafters were attempting to form a strongly centralized state in the first place, rather than the weak confederacy they created. In fact, the first American

---

90. "The confederation itself is defective and requires to be altered; it is neither fit for war nor peace. The idea of an uncontrolable sovereignty in each state, over its internal police, will defeat the powers given to Congress, and make our union feeble and precarious.... The confederation gives the states individually too much influence in the affairs of the army; they should have nothing to do with it.... The confederation too gives the power of the purse too intirely to the state legislatures. It should provide perpetual funds in the disposal of Congress—by a land tax, poll tax, or the like." Alexander Hamilton, "Letter to James Duane" (September 3, 1780), in *The Papers of Alexander Hamilton,* ed. Harold C. Syrett et al. (New York: Columbia University Press, 1961), 2:402–4.

91. Benjamin Rush admitted as much: "Although we understood perfectly the principles of liberty, most of us were ignorant of the forms and combinations of power in republics." Benjamin Rush, "Address to the People of the United States" (January 1787), in *The Documentary History of the Ratification of the Constitution,* ed. Merrill Jensen (Madison: State Historical Society of Wisconsin, 1976), 13:46; quoted in Dougherty, *Collective Action,* 131.

state was *intended* to be strong enough to accomplish only one goal: coordinate the war effort against the English. The scant powers delegated to the national government by the state legislatures under the Articles of Confederation reflected the prevailing consensus among political elites that it was *undesirable* to create strong national political institutions. The founders of the Confederacy were not looking to create a strong American state or a national government with powers independent of the states—only a central authority to coordinate the war effort.

With the achievement of independence and peace in 1783, the only apparent reason for a union among the states ceased to exist. Rather than looking to expand the powers of the central state, political leaders such as George Mason, Richard Henry Lee, and Patrick Henry were perfectly content to retain the Confederacy as the weak political organization it was or see it disbanded altogether. To these Virginians, a strong central state with a standing army and the power of taxation threatened a return of the tyranny of the English Crown they had just cast off.[92] In their view, the Articles of Confederation did just what it was intended to do: it strengthened the hand of the Continental Congress during wartime by providing the Congress with a stronger mandate from the states to lead the resistance against British rule. For them, nothing beyond that was required—certainly not in peacetime. From this limited perspective, the national government established by the Articles of Confederation might be deemed a success if only it had actually functioned efficiently in coordinating the war effort. But the minimal powers delegated to the national government made it difficult for the national political leadership to accomplish even this one important goal.

---

92. The fear of standing armies among the colonists was derived from a longstanding tradition dating to the English Civil War. In his *Letters,* Dickinson associated standing armies with the collection of the despised taxes of the Crown. In the Declaration of Independence, Jefferson complained that George III had "kept among us, in times of peace, Standing Armies without the Consent of our legislatures," quartered troops in civilian homes, and in various other ways misused his military force in the colonies. For an informed discussion of the ideological meaning of standing armies to the British colonists, see Bailyn, *Ideological Origins of the American Revolution,* 62–63; Richard H. Kohn, *Eagle and Sword: The Federalists and the Creation of the Military Establishment in America, 1783–1802* (New York: Free Press, 1975), 2–6. The Antifederalists' principled opposition to a large standing army for the new republic is discussed in Max M. Edling, *A Revolution in Favor of Government: Origins of the U.S. Constitution and the Making of the American State* (New York: Oxford University Press, 2003), 89–115.

The problem was, to perform even the minimal functions assigned to the national government, significantly greater state capacity was needed than what had been provided for under the Articles of Confederation. Under its flawed constitutional design, there was no judiciary or executive for the Confederacy.[93] Because there was no judiciary, there were no federal prisons or courts. Because there was no executive, there were no administrative agencies or institutional mechanisms to enforce the scant federal law that was enacted. For instance, under the Treaty of Paris of 1783, England had agreed to withdraw its forces from frontier outposts that were now within the territory of the United States. The British failed to carry out this obligation, yet the national government of the Confederacy lacked the means to force the issue. This was a state that could barely maintain its own territorial integrity.

Under the express terms of the Articles of Confederation, the states retained their sovereignty and all powers not otherwise granted to the Congress.[94] Since very little power was actually delegated to the Congress, virtually everything of significance was left to the states. Most important, the states possessed their own sources of revenue, which, not surprisingly, local political leaders retained exclusively for themselves, even as they struck the political bargain for the federation.[95] It is no coincidence that under the Articles of Confederation, the national government lacked the authority to impose its own taxes. The state legislatures were unwilling to concede any portion of this essential power to the Congress. At the same time, proponents of a strong national state were too weak to force any significant change to the status quo. In negotiating with local authorities for greater revenue for the national government, they proved too weak to impose a more favorable revenue strategy (from their perspective) on the states.

---

93. While there was no executive, there was a president of the Congress beginning with the First Continental Congress. In all, fourteen different presidents presided over the Congress between 1774 and 1789. The weaknesses of the institution of the presidency of the Congress are discussed in Jillson and Wilson, *Congressional Dynamics,* 71–90.

94. "Each state retains its sovereignty, freedom, and independence, and every power, jurisdiction, and right, which is not by this Confederation expressly delegated to the United States, in Congress assembled." Articles of Confederation, art. II.

95. This limitation on the tax power of the new government was intentional. In his study of public finance during this period, Ferguson argued that "after independence [eighteenth-century Americans] tried to safeguard the sovereignty of their new states under the Articles of Confederation by denying Congress the right to tax." Ferguson, *Power of the Purse,* xv.

What revenue powers were granted the national government under the Articles of Confederation? The Congress relied entirely on the state legislatures for revenue. The Congress was authorized to "assess" the states, subject to a requirement that such revenue assessments be apportioned to the several states in proportion to the value of all land and improvements within each state.[96] This apportionment requirement was cumbersome and restrictive but might have worked *if* the national government had only possessed the authority and power to *enforce* its revenue assessments. But the Congress was forced to rely on the state legislatures to collect and remit its assessments to the national treasury. For revenue, the national government was dependent on the voluntary compliance of the state legislatures, something that was seldom forthcoming.

The first revenue assessment by the Congress was made in November 1777, requesting that the state governments deliver a total of $5 million during the next year. Since it proved difficult, if not impossible, to base assessments on land value during the war, quotas were based on estimated population.[97] Between 1781 and 1786, the Congress assessed the states a total of $15.7 million, but only $2.4 million was paid.[98] This was not out of malice; the states themselves were burdened with paying their own war debts and had difficulty raising additional money for the national government. The result of the failure of the states to pay their assessments was that the national government was constantly starved for revenue and forever teetering on the brink of financial ruin. Although contributions picked up in 1787, the financial position of the national government was critical. Between October 1, 1786, and March 31, 1787, the treasury took in only $633, leaving the national government unable to pay its debts.[99] Madison specifically mentioned the failure of the requisition system as one of the main causes for the "gloom" that pervaded the "public mind" in the

---

96. "All charges of war, and all other expenses that shall be incurred for the common defense or general welfare, and allowed by the United States in Congress assembled, shall be defrayed out of a common treasury, which shall be supplied by the several States in proportion to the value of all land within each State, granted or surveyed for any person, as such land and the buildings and improvements thereon shall be estimated according to such mode as the United States in Congress assembled, shall from time to time direct and appoint." Articles of Confederation, art. VIII.

97. Ferguson, *Power of the Purse,* 33.

98. Figures cited in Savage, *Balanced Budgets and American Politics,* 73.

99. Brown, *Redeeming the Republic,* 24.

spring of 1787 as the delegates gathered in Philadelphia at the Constitutional Convention.[100]

Figures compiled by Roger Brown confirm the failure of the requisition system of the Confederacy, showing that the states were uniformly noncompliant in collecting and remitting the revenue requested by the Congress. According to Brown, the states collectively paid an average of only 37 percent of the six federal revenue assessments between October 1781 and August 1786. New York and Pennsylvania contributed the most (67 and 57 percent, respectively), while North Carolina contributed a mere 3 percent and Georgia nothing.[101] This created the sorry state of affairs that plagued the Confederacy, which has been aptly summarized as follows: "Under the Articles of Confederation, extractive capacity was severely limited, and neither legal authority nor bureaucratic machinery existed to enforce the demands of the Continental Congress for revenues."[102] Rather than a revenue predator or the perpetrator of some protection racket, the national government of the Confederacy was a pauper and beggar that relied on contributions from the states for virtually all its funds.[103] The medieval princes of twelfth-century Europe were better equipped to raise revenue for their armies than was the debt-ridden Congress of the Confederacy of the United States of America.

---

100. "The reiterated and elaborate efforts of Con[gress] to procure from the states a more adequate power to raise the means of payment had failed. The effect of the ordinary requisitions of Congress had only displayed the inefficiency of the auth[ority] making them; none of the States having duly complied with them, some having failed altogether or nearly so; and in one instance, that of New Jersey a compliance was expressly refused." James Madison, "Preface," *Notes of Debates in the Federal Convention of 1787 Reported by James Madison* (New York: W. W. Norton, 1966), 13.

101. Brown, *Redeeming the Republic,* table 1 ("Congressional Requisitions"), 14.

102. Forsythe, *Taxation and Political Change,* 14.

103. One might reasonably ask, why did the states *ever* voluntarily contribute to the national government? This interesting question is addressed in Dougherty, *Collective Action.* A theory of public goods would suggest a total lack of compliance, yet the states did contribute *some* revenue to the national government. Dougherty argues that this partial compliance was not based on civic duty. Rather, the states contributed to the national treasury when it "advanced local interests" (i.e., when there were excludable aspects of public goods produced by Congress that directly benefited local interests). Alexander Hamilton himself made much the same point: "The states near the seat of war, influenced by motives of self-preservation, made efforts to furnish their quotas, which even exceeded their abilities; while those at a distance from the danger were for the most part as remiss as the others were diligent in their exertions." Alexander Hamilton, Federalist No. 22, in James Madison, Alexander Hamilton, and John Jay, *The Federalist Papers* (New York: New American Library, 1961), 145–46.

On April 18, 1783, the Congress once again pursued measures to improve its financial position. On the recommendation of Robert Morris,
the Congress adopted a package of revenue reform provisions, the most
controversial of which was an impost on commerce intended to give the
Congress its own independent source of revenue specifically dedicated to
repayment of the consolidated war debt. This tax was substantially similar
to that requested by the Congress in 1781—a 5 percent ad valorem tax
on imported goods, scheduled to expire in twenty-five years. The revenue
package of 1783 also provided for excise duties imposed on commodities
such as salt, sugar, rum, wine, liquor, and tea. Morris recommended his
own favored taxes (a land tax and a poll tax), but these were rejected by
the Congress. In addition, the package requested additional revenue assessments from the states for the next twenty-five years and proposed an
amendment to the Articles of Confederation that would have deleted the
aforementioned requirement that revenue assessments be allocated among
the states based on the value of land. The real estate valuation system was
always highly impractical and never could be implemented during the
war; for this reason, the amendment substituted population as the basis
for the allocation. This modification was supported by both Hamilton and
Madison. Of course, apportionment based on population opened another
highly divisive political issue: slavery. Would slaves be counted for purposes of the apportionment? Pursuant to a compromise reached in closed
session between representatives from the South and New England, the
Congress finally adopted a "three-fifths" rule for purposes of determining
population, counting five African slaves as three persons.[104] This was an
early version of the infamous three-fifths rule subsequently adopted by the
drafters of the Constitution of 1787 as a compromise to resolve intractable
disputes between the northern and southern states over representation and
taxation.[105]

---

104. The proposed amendment reads as follows: "all charges of war and all other expences
that have been or shall be incurred for the common defence or general welfare ... shall be defrayed
out of a common treasury, which shall be supplied by the several states in proportion to the whole
number of white and other free citizens and inhabitants, of every age, sex and condition, including those bound to servitude for a term of years, and three-fifths of all other persons not comprehended in the foregoing description, except Indians, not paying taxes, in each State." Ford et al.,
eds., *Journals of the Continental Congress,* 24:260.

105. The political compromise behind the adoption of the three-fifths clause in the Constitution, which applied to both representation and taxation, is analyzed in Bruce Ackerman,

Once the Congress approved the package of revenue measures, it was transmitted to the state legislatures with a letter of support from James Madison of Virginia. General Washington came out in favor of the finance plan of 1783, predicting a "National Bankruptcy, with all its deplorable consequences" if the plan was not adopted and the fiscal powers of the central government were not strengthened.[106] Despite backing from such esteemed leaders, opposition to the proposed impost ran deep, with the strongest opposition concentrated in Virginia, New York, and Rhode Island. In Virginia, George Mason, Richard Henry Lee, and Patrick Henry spoke out against granting *any* new powers of taxation to the Congress. Their argument, which subsequently would be raised by opponents of the Constitution of 1787, was that to prevent tyranny by the national government, the states had to maintain exclusive control over the power of the purse. As James Ferguson puts it in his definitive study of the finances of the period, "Conscious of pursuing the traditions of Parliament in its struggle against the Crown, the Americans as colonists manipulated their control of taxation to wrest authority from British governors. After independence was achieved, they tried to safeguard the sovereignty of their new states under the Articles of Confederation by denying Congress the right to tax."[107]

The legislatures of New Jersey, Delaware, Connecticut, and North Carolina moved quickly to approve the finance plan of 1783 and other states soon joined them. Even Rhode Island, which had blocked ratification of the 1781 impost, passed this measure in February 1785. By July 1786, twelve of the thirteen states had approved the new federal impost of 5 percent. But the legislature of New York repeatedly rejected the measure, and this proved fatal to the campaign for fiscal reform. Ironically, Hamilton withheld his personal support for the measure, having already decided that a more radical course of action was necessary to overcome the deficiencies of the Confederacy. Because the unanimous consent of the states was required to amend the powers of the Congress under the Articles of Confederation, this second campaign for revenue reform was again thwarted

"Taxation and the Constitution," *Columbia Law Review* 99 (January 1999): 1–58; see also Einhorn, *American Taxation, American Slavery*, 138–45, 173.

106. "Circular to the States," (June 8, 1783), in Fitzpatrick, ed., *Writings of George Washington*, 26:489–91.

107. Ferguson, *Power of the Purse*, xv.

by the objections of a single state.[108] In the end, the Congress received no new powers of taxation, and Morris subsequently resigned his position in despair, departing office in November of 1784. Hamilton vacated his seat in the Congress in July 1783, while Madison quit the national legislature later that fall and returned to Virginia.

The lack of an independent source of revenue for the national government severely inhibited the institutional development of the early American state. As Madison himself put it, "No money is paid into the public Treasury; no respect is paid to the federal authority. Not a single State complies with the requisitions; several pass over them in silence, and some positively reject them.... It is not possible that a Government can last long under these circumstances."[109] Even if the constitution of the Confederacy had authorized stronger national political institutions and provided for a greater role for the central state within the federation, and even if there had been the desire and political will to build a more powerful central state, the Congress still lacked the revenue necessary to carry out such an endeavor. In the end, this was a state charged with one limited function: organizing and directing an army in the war against the British.[110] Yet performing even this was extremely difficult given the inability of the central government to forcibly extract revenue from society. Without adequate funding, the military force under the command of the Congress faced persistent and debilitating shortages of goods and supplies. The failure to pay soldiers their back pay was the direct cause of the discontent that nearly led to open rebellion at Newburgh in the spring of 1783. As the Congress lacked the funds to pay what had been promised to the soldiers, the troops grew restless. A group of officers waited in Philadelphia to approach the Congress with their financial grievances. Open mutiny was averted only because of the intervention of the revered General Washington.[111]

---

108. For a detailed account of the political maneuvering behind the revenue reform proposal of 1783, see Merrill Jensen, *The New Nation: A History of the United States During the Confederation, 1781–1789* (Boston: Northeastern University Press, 1950), 407–17; Rakove, *Beginnings of National Politics,* 317–24; Brown, *Redeeming the Republic,* 22–24.

109. "Letter from James Madison to Edmund Pendleton" (February 24, 1787), in *The Papers of James Madison,* ed. Robert A. Rutland (Chicago: University of Chicago Press, 1975), 9:294–95.

110. Keith Dougherty estimates that the Congress spent 95 percent of its expenditures on the Continental Army during the war. Dougherty, *Collective Action,* 10.

111. In March 1783, Washington intervened, using his influence to dissuade the officers of the discontented troops, who had threatened to march on the Congress in protest. A comprehensive

The lack of funds was not the only problem facing those who supported a strong national military. With the cessation of hostilities following the signing of the Peace Treaty of 1783, the British evacuated New York in November. At that time, virtually all regiments of the Continental Army stood down and disbanded. Washington himself dutifully resigned his command on December 23, 1783, and retreated to his beloved home at Mount Vernon. This left the national government without any significant military force. On April 4, 1783, the Congress appointed Hamilton to chair a committee (which included Oliver Ellsworth, James Madison, James Wilson, and other nationalists) to determine the appropriate size of a peacetime military for the republic. Hamilton proposed an overhaul of the state militias and a national army of three thousand men, but the Congress failed to act on his recommendation.[112] At the beginning of 1784, with a population of nearly 4 million persons, the United States was left with an army of only seven hundred soldiers.[113] On June 2, 1784, the last remaining regiment of the Continental Army was discharged. The next day, the Congress voted to establish the U.S. Army; however, that consisted of only a single regiment stationed at West Point and a handful of troops stationed in isolated frontier fortifications to guard against hostile Indians in northern New York and Ohio. This minuscule army was barely functional.[114]

With the end of the military conflict with England, the forces that originally brought together the separate states in the federation began to dissipate. With the stand-down of the national military force, the Confederacy found itself without a purpose or reason to exist. The national government now lacked both of the two basic attributes of a sovereign state: revenue and a standing army. Like the Continental Congress, the Confederacy did not have a permanent physical location, as no capital city was provided for under the Articles of Confederation.[115] The government still did not own its

---

account of the Newburgh affair is found in Kohn, *Eagle and Sword*, 17–39; see also Jensen, *The New Nation*, 69–72, 76–77. In June 1783, the Congress was forced to flee from Philadelphia to Princeton in the face of another mutiny, this time by Pennsylvania militiamen.

112. The recommendation of the committee is discussed in Edling, *Revolution in Favor of Government*, 121–22; Kohn, *Eagle and Sword*, 42–45.

113. Boatner, *Encyclopedia of the American Revolution*, 264

114. The shortcomings of the federal army are discussed in Kohn, *Eagle and Sword*, 68–72.

115. During the First Republic under the Articles of Confederation, the Congress met in Philadelphia, Princeton, Annapolis, Trenton, and New York. Not until 1790 did Congress delegate to President Washington the authority to select a location for a permanent capital city for

own buildings or infrastructure of any kind. Admittedly, given the limited functions delegated to the national government by the state legislatures, not much of a state apparatus was needed. The American state did not perform many nonmilitary functions in the late eighteenth century. It did not build roads or schools, was not responsible for public safety or the health and welfare of the citizenry, and the national government played no role in cultivating or managing the national economy. Until 1785, the Congress lacked the authority to issue national coinage, and none was actually issued until 1793.[116] Penetration of society by the national government was virtually nonexistent during the Confederacy. After 1783, the Congress possessed even less power, prestige, and legitimacy than it had during the Revolutionary War. With the war over, the forces that had compelled the states to band together into a national political union waned. State and regional conflicts surfaced. Maintaining a quorum to conduct business in the Congress became increasingly difficult as attendance among delegates declined precipitously. This was a government distant from the hearts and minds of its citizens.

These severe deficiencies in state capacity were responsible for the fiscal crisis that the national government confronted throughout the 1780s.[117] During the period from 1781 to 1786, the federal treasury collected on average only about $500,000 a year—barely enough to keep the government running.[118] During the Revolutionary War, the Congress had attempted to finance the war effort mainly by issuing unsecured bills of credit. This resulted in inflation that slowly increased from 1776 to 1778, and then exploded in 1779. After the war, the national government was

---

the new republic. In 1800, the federal government finally moved into its new quarters on the Potomac River. Unfortunately, the construction of the City of Washington went uncompleted for another half century. The fascinating history of the creation of the nation's capital city is told in James Sterling Young, *The Washington Community, 1800–1828* (New York: Columbia University Press, 1966).

116. National coinage was not issued until after the Constitution of 1787 was adopted and following the creation of the United States Mint in 1792. Until then, English, French, and Spanish coins were in regular circulation in the states.

117. For an account of the fiscal weaknesses of the national government during the period of the Articles of Confederation, see Savage, *Balanced Budgets and American Politics*, 54–84.

118. In 1784, the total debt of the national government (foreign and domestic) reached more than $39 million. Yearly interest on this debt amounted to $1.875 million, exceeding the annual income of the national government in 1785 and 1786 by about $1.32 million a year. This explains why the national debt soared to more than $52.78 million by 1790. Figures cited in Nettles, *Emergence of a National Economy*, 94.

unable to finance even the minimal activity it was constitutionally authorized to conduct, let alone retire the $54 million debt that the Congress had
amassed during the Revolutionary War.[119] The national government's lack
of an independent power of taxation left the Confederacy forever teeter-
ing on the brink of fiscal collapse. The fiscal and military deficiencies of
the national government of the Confederacy precipitated what an earlier
generation of American historians, following John Fiske, referred to as the
"Critical Period."[120]

Undoubtedly, Fiske exaggerated the weaknesses of the Confederacy
under the Articles of Confederation and the overall instability experienced
in the states during the 1780s.[121] But if there was no economic or social crisis, there surely was a *political* crisis at the center of the Confederacy.[122] The
nationalists were particularly concerned with the inability of the national
government to respond to internal military crises and domestic violence.
Their fears were not without foundation. When a small group of Pennsylvania soldiers mutinied in June 1883 and surrounded the building where
the Congress was meeting in Philadelphia, the Pennsylvania state council refused to call out the militia to protect the members of the Congress.
The Congress departed Philadelphia for Princeton, leaving proponents of
a stronger central government severely shaken. Confidence in the national
government was further undermined when a rebellion broke out in Western Massachusetts in August 1786. A group of farmers protesting high
debt and an odious capitation tax and other fiscal policies of the legislature

---

119. The war debts of the Continental Congress (but not those of the states) were assumed by
the new "United States in Congress" established under Article XII of the Articles of Confederation. Because the Continental Congress had agreed to reimburse militia expenses that it had expressly authorized, some state war debts were assumed as well.

120. John Fiske, *The Critical Period of American History, 1783–1789* (Boston: Houghton, Mifflin, 1888). Gordon Wood notes that the term *critical period* was not coined by Fiske but was
commonly used during the 1780s to refer to the uncertainties and perceived dangers in the post-
Revolution era. Speaking at his commencement address at Harvard in 1787, John Quincy Adams
referred to "this critical period" when the nation was "groaning under the intolerable burden
of . . . accumulated evils." Quoted in Wood, *Creation of the American Republic,* 393.

121. Fiske's infamous characterization of this period was criticized by Merrill Jensen in *The
New Nation,* xi–xiii; see also Rakove, *Beginnings of National Politics,* 333.

122. Despite its obvious weaknesses, the Congress of the Confederacy did resolve one major
issue: what to do with the territories acquired after independence. The Northwest Ordinance was
unanimously passed on August 7, 1789, providing for the admission of new states carved out of the
territories and establishing a boundary between free and slave regions.

rampaged throughout the state for months. Led by Daniel Shays, a veteran officer of the Revolutionary War, the rebels came close to seizing the nation's second largest armory in Springfield. Henry Knox, secretary of war, requested federal troops to respond to the rebellion. But without a standing army of its own, the Congress was forced to rely on the states to provide both funds and militiamen. While the state delegations in the Congress voted unanimously to raise troops and authorized requisitions from the states to support the troops, only Virginia paid its requisition.[123] The Massachusetts legislature was unwilling to contribute funds for a state militia to suppress the rebellion. Eventually, the governor of Massachusetts, James Bowdoin, and a group of wealthy bankers from Boston raised the revenue and organized a militia themselves. After a decisive battle at the Springfield Armory, the militia finally subdued the rebellion in February 1787.[124] Their victory was achieved without any assistance from the national government.

Shays' Rebellion had a chilling effect on the thinking of prominent political leaders throughout the states. It confirmed the widespread suspicion that the Confederacy was dangerously weak. During this period, Washington repeatedly wrote letters to friends and colleagues (including the Marquis de Lafayette, James Madison, and Henry Knox) expressing his great alarm that the national government was unable to respond to the rebellion in Massachusetts because it lacked its own military force.[125] His apprehension over the rebellion in Massachusetts was likely what provoked him to come out of retirement to campaign publicly for a stronger national government.[126] Washington and other nationalists were concerned with a

---

123. Dougherty argues that Virginia was willing to provide funds for federal troops because it wanted the federal army to be used after the suppression of the rebellion to fight the Wabash and Shawnee Indians along the Ohio River who were threatening settlers. Shays' Rebellion is offered as an example of the inability of the Congress to take collective action and provide public goods under the Confederacy. See Dougherty, *Collective Action,* 103–28.

124. A comprehensive account of the rebellion in Massachusetts is Leonard L. Richards, *Shays' Rebellion: The American Revolution's Final Battle* (Philadelphia: University of Pennsylvania Press, 2002).

125. See, e.g., "Letter to James Madison" (November 5, 1786), "Letter to Henry Knox" (December 26, 1786), and "Letter to Henry Knox" (February 25, 1787), in *Writings of George Washington,* 29:50–53, 121–25, 169–70. Hamilton warned of the danger of foreign invasion and "domestic insurrection" (Shays' Rebellion) and foresaw the need for a "military force in time of peace." Alexander Hamilton, Paper No. 25, in Madison, Hamilton, and Jay, *The Federalist Papers,* 162–67.

126. Richards, *Shays' Rebellion,* 1–4, 129–30.

number of other strategic military issues. First, there was the continuing presence of British forces garrisoned in the Northwest Territories along the border with British Canada after the peace treaty had been signed. They also feared the very real possibility that the growing Kentucky territory would ally with Spain rather than join the United States. Virginians in general were alarmed about the inability of the regular army of the Confederacy to maintain peace between settlers and Indians in western Georgia, Virginia, and western Pennsylvania. Finally, nationalists lamented the failure of Congress to stop the so-called Barbary states that freely engaged in hostage taking and seizures of American merchant ships in the Mediterranean along the North African coast. All their fears were based on the recognition that the national government lacked the financial means and the military capacity to cope with such imminent threats to national security.

In pondering the serious deficiencies of the national government under the Articles of Confederation, Alexander Hamilton summed up the situation when he wrote, "A nation, without a national government, is, in my view, an awful spectacle."[127] The awful spectacle that Hamilton witnessed and feared was the direct consequence of the failure to establish a strong American state. This failure of government (rather than economic self-interest) prompted nationalists such as Hamilton and Madison to propose that an assembly of state representatives meet in Annapolis, Maryland, in the fall of 1786 to discuss the problems plaguing the Confederacy and devise remedies for the pervasive and potentially fatal defects in the government established by the Articles of Confederation. Their goal was nothing less than a fundamental reconstitution of the American state.

---

127. Alexander Hamilton, Paper No. 85, in Madison, Hamilton, and Jay, *The Federalist Papers,* 527.

6

Reconstituting the American State

The confederation itself is defective and requires to be altered; it is neither fit for war nor peace. The idea of an uncontrolable sovereignty in each state, over its internal police, will defeat the powers given to Congress, and make our union feeble and precarious.

—Alexander Hamilton, "Letter to James Duane" (1780)

Either the several states must continue separate, totally independent of each other, and liable to all the evils of jealous dispute and civil dissention...or they must constitute a general head, composed of representatives from all the states, and vested with the power of the whole continent to enforce their decisions. There is no other alternative.

—Noah Webster, *Sketches of American Policy* (1785)

While there was widespread recognition by 1786 that the political order established by the Articles of Confederation was deficient (especially, with regard to the fiscal and military powers of the national government), there was no prevailing consensus with regard to solutions. Nationalists wanted a stronger national government than that provided for under the Confederacy. Alexander Hamilton had raised the idea of a convention to debate the merits of a new constitution as early as 1780 and 1782, and the New York legislature approved resolutions embracing the idea, but the other states ignored these proposals.[1] Sentiment for restructuring the political

---

1. Jack N. Rakove, *The Beginnings of National Politics: An Interpretive History of the Continental Congress* (New York: Knopf, 1979), 325.

order emerged only gradually after repeated efforts to reform the worst features of the Confederacy failed. In pursuit of this goal, numerous regional conferences were proposed to discuss matters such as interstate relations, jurisdiction on navigable waterways, regulation of foreign trade, and the facilitation of trade between the states.

One such meeting was held in March 1785 at the Mount Vernon estate of George Washington. Here representatives of four states (Delaware, Maryland, Virginia, and Pennsylvania) met at the instigation of James Madison to address long-standing disputes over navigation and the harvesting of oysters and crabs in the Chesapeake Bay and Potomac River. The Mount Vernon conference failed to produce a treaty or resolution, but a group of state legislators in Virginia, frustrated by barriers to trade between the states, followed up by inviting all thirteen of the states to send delegates to yet another meeting to be held at Annapolis, Maryland, in September 1786 to address broader issues relating to trade and commerce. The ostensible purpose of the meeting was to "take into consideration the trade of the states" and draft a "uniform system in their commercial regulations."

If prior reform efforts lacked widespread support and ultimately failed, conditions were arguably different this time. Recent events such as Shays' Rebellion and the deteriorating financial position of the national government created increasing interest among political elites in restructuring the political order established by the Articles of Confederation.[2] Significantly, the legislature of Virginia, the wealthiest and most populated state in the Confederacy, threw its support behind the proposal. The endorsement of Virginia induced other states to participate. Even still, delegates from only five states (New York, Pennsylvania, Delaware, New Jersey, and Virginia) made the trip to Annapolis that autumn. Alexander Hamilton was the only representative from the New York delegation who actually showed up. The host state of Maryland failed to send delegates on the grounds that the meeting exceeded the authority of the Congress.[3] Facing imminent failure, those delegates in attendance made a fateful decision, one that

---

2. Madison considered the "insurrection of Shays in Massachusetts" as the primary motivation for calling the Annapolis convention and the Constitutional Convention in Philadelphia. See Madison's Preface, *Notes of Debates in the Federal Convention of 1787 Reported by James Madison* (New York: W. W. Norton, 1966), 13.

3. Richard B. Morris, *The Forging of the Union, 1780–1789* (New York: Harper and Row, 1987), 254–55. While seven states did not send delegates, those sent by Pennsylvania and New Jersey

turned out to be of greater significance than they ever could have imagined at the time. The delegates feared that returning home empty handed would only further weaken the prestige of the Congress, already suffering a serious decline in popular support. To avoid that, they took up a suggestion from Hamilton and James Madison of Virginia to summon delegates to yet another meeting to discuss ways to amend the glaring defects of the Articles of Confederation.

It is unclear why the delegates thought that a second convention would succeed where the Annapolis assembly had obviously failed. As Jack Rakove puts it, "The decision to call a second convention was recognizably a gamble, justified not by any change in the odds against such a measure actually succeeding but rather by the need to salvage something from the potentially harmful consequences of adjourning without reaching any decision at all."[4] Gamble or not, the Annapolis delegates approved a resolution calling for a convention to be held in Philadelphia on the second Monday in May of the following year. This would prove an historic event in the history of the development of the American state.

The Philadelphia Gamble

On September 20, 1786, the report of the Annapolis delegates was presented to the Congress of the Confederacy. Authored by John Dickinson, chairman of the Annapolis conference, the report recommended convening a new convention to formulate reform measures sufficient "to render the constitution of the Federal Government adequate to the exigencies of the Union."[5] Initially, the Congress ignored the recommendation of the Annapolis delegates and referred the matter to a committee. A number of representatives suspected that the Annapolis delegates intended to discard the Articles of Confederation, rather than merely consider reform measures. But later that autumn, the Virginia legislature voted unanimously

---

were granted broad authority to resolve disputes among the states. That may have encouraged Hamilton and Madison to initiate another conference.

4. Rakove, *Beginnings of National Politics,* 375.

5. The report of the Annapolis delegates is found in Worthington C. Ford et al., eds., *Journals of the Continental Congress, 1774–1789* (Washington, DC: Government Printing Office: 1904–37), 31:678–80.

to send a delegation to Philadelphia. After some initial hesitation, General Washington was persuaded to join the Virginia delegation, thereby putting his considerable prestige behind the idea of a national constitutional convention. New Jersey, Pennsylvania, Delaware, and North Carolina appointed delegates without waiting for a response from the Congress. The Massachusetts legislature, which was initially reluctant to participate, finally acquiesced. (Only Rhode Island remained opposed to the plan and refused to send a delegation.) This forced the hand of the Congress, which voted to accept the recommendation of the Annapolis delegates to convene a second conference. On February 21, 1787, the Congress approved a resolution calling on the states to send representatives to a convention to be held in Philadelphia to consider ways to reform the Confederacy and report back to the Congress with their recommendations.[6]

The states followed through with their pledge and the next spring sent their representatives—these the "most experienced & highest standing Citizens," as Madison would later describe them.[7] Madison's description was accurate given the many distinguished luminaries who joined him in attendance at the convention: Alexander Hamilton, George Washington, Benjamin Franklin, John Dickinson, James Wilson, George Mason, Oliver Ellsworth, Robert Morris, and Gouverneur Morris. (Among those not present were John Adams, John Jay, and Thomas Jefferson.) Some historians have properly noted that not all of the delegates were of such elevated stature, and truth be told, many were entirely undistinguished.[8] Be that as it may, there was no shortage of brilliant minds, political skill, and firm determination among those in attendance at the Constitutional Convention. With memories of the turbulent events of the prior year fresh in mind,

---

6. The full text of the resolution reads as follows: "That it be recommended to the States composing the Union that a convention of representatives from the said states respectively be held for the purpose of revising the Articles of Confederation and perpetual Union between the United States of America and reporting to the United States in Congress assembled and to the States respectively such alterations and amendments of the said Articles of Confederation as the representatives met in such convention shall judge proper and necessary to render them adequate to the preservation and support of the Union." Ford et al., eds., *Journals of the Continental Congress,* 32:72.

7. Madison's Preface, *Notes of Debates,* 12.

8. See, e.g., Forrest McDonald, *E Pluribus Unum: The Formation of the American Republic, 1776–1790* (Boston: Houghton Mifflin, 1965), 162; Rakove, *Beginnings of National Politics,* 377.

fifty-five delegates assembled in Philadelphia in May 1787 to ponder ways to rectify the worst deficiencies of the Articles of Confederation.

Reflecting their enthusiasm, the delegation from Virginia arrived early in Philadelphia, even as several state delegations were delayed. While awaiting the other representatives, the nationalists from Virginia devised a bargaining strategy, adopting as their opening position a model for a new constitution based on concepts recently enunciated by James Madison.[9] Under the plan as originally conceived by Madison, the national government would be strengthened almost to the point of creating a unitary (or as late eighteenth-century theorists would have put it, "consolidated") government. The national government would be comprised of three branches. Significantly, the Congress of the national government would be granted the power to veto state legislation. Oddly, there was no provision for a power of taxation for the national government. Proportional representation would be used to apportion seats in the national legislature based on population, and the lower house would elect the upper house of the Congress, thereby providing even greater independence from the state legislatures.

Governor Edmund Randolph, the most prominent member of the Virginia delegation, opened the business of the Constitutional Convention on May 29 by offering his solemn assessment of the weaknesses of the Confederacy and proposing fifteen resolutions (the so-called Virginia Plan) to amend the Articles of Confederation, which according to Randolph needed to be "corrected" and "enlarged" to provide for the common welfare and defense and to secure the liberty of the people.[10] As is well known, the Virginia Plan was fervently opposed by the delegations from the smaller states—in particular, Connecticut and New Jersey. Nevertheless, by introducing their plan at the opening of the convention, the

---

9. In a paper drafted in the spring of 1787, Madison set forth his views on the deficiencies of the Confederacy and the need to strengthen the national government and subordinate the states. This document is critical to understanding Madison's thinking at the convention. James Madison, "Vices of the Political System of the United States," in *The Papers of James Madison,* ed. Robert A. Rutland (Chicago: University of Chicago Press, 1975), 9:345–58.

10. *Notes of Debates,* 28–33. Robertson presents a novel interpretation of how Madison's opponents from the small states, led by Roger Sherman of Connecticut, forced changes to Madison's original vision. David Brian Robertson, "Madison's Opponents and Constitutional Design," *American Political Science Review* 99 (2005): 225–43.

Virginian nationalists set the agenda and defined the parameters for the debates that followed, thereby influencing the final outcome.[11]

While the delegates ostensibly came to Philadelphia to reform the Articles of Confederation, after only a few days of debate their attention shifted to drafting an entirely new constitution. It is evident from Madison's account of the proceedings that by May 30 the focus of the discussion had already shifted to the formation of a national government with powers far beyond those of the Congress under the Articles of Confederation.[12] The new constitutional design provided for a stronger national legislature as well as an executive and judiciary, both of which were conspicuously missing from the national government of the Confederacy. Thereafter, nary a word was again spoken about reforming the Articles of Confederation, other than a stern lecture on June 9 from William Paterson of New Jersey warning the delegates that they were exceeding their authority by moving to abandon the Confederacy and replace it with a strong "national government." The warning was duly ignored, and the issue of limiting the scope of the convention to reforming the Articles of Confederation was not raised again.

Diplomatically chaired by the General Washington, the delegates debated a wide range of options and perspectives, with a variety of positions advanced. The question of representation for the several states would be a particularly divisive issue. But there was general agreement on several important issues. Notably, the delegates abandoned a fundamental principle underlying the organization of the Confederacy—namely, that the states would remain sovereign and retain all of their traditional powers. Under the plan devised at the convention, the national government would be delegated specific (enumerated) powers and authority of its own, thereby establishing a greater degree of autonomy from the states. Political space would be carved out

---

11. Robertson suggests that to understand the text of the Constitution, the appropriate question is, what policy problems were the delegates at the convention trying to solve? Madison and the Virginians had a coherent plan to solve certain policy issues, but others had a different view of what they were trying to accomplish. David Brian Robertson, *The Constitution and America's Destiny* (New York: Cambridge University Press, 2005), xi, 116.

12. *Notes of Debates,* 34–38. According to Roger Brown, there was support for radical reform of the Confederacy even before the convention: "Many of the several state's top echelon of elite political leaders were already...friends if not advocates of the central government's radical reform." Roger H. Brown, *Redeeming the Republic: Federalists, Taxation, and the Origins of the Constitution* (Baltimore: Johns Hopkins University Press, 1993), 30.

within which the national government would be sovereign, while certain of the traditional powers of the state governments would be curtailed. Despite the emerging consensus that the national government needed to be stronger, little support was voiced at the Constitutional Convention for abolishing the states or replacing the federal structure with a unitary government.[13]

To be sure, a few voices outside the convention on the political fringes advocated the adoption of a unitary state. The anonymous author of a political pamphlet, *The Political Establishments of the United States of America* (1784), called for the "abolition of our state governments and the forming of a constitution whereby the whole nation can be united in one government."[14] This simply was not an option for the delegates to the Constitutional Convention, who after all had to report back to the state legislatures at the end of the day. The state legislatures ultimately had to approve any document they drafted. Neither Madison nor any of the other nationalists from Virginia spoke of the abolition of the states; they sought only the supremacy of the national government within the limited sphere of its enumerated powers.[15]

George Read of Delaware was one of the few delegates at the Constitutional Convention who seriously contemplated a unified national government without state governments competing for the loyalty of the citizenry. A member of the Delaware General Assembly and a delegate to the Annapolis Convention, Read advocated replacing the Articles of Confederation with a new constitution altogether—arguing that "to amend the Articles was simply putting old cloth on a new garment."[16] In Philadelphia, Read urged the delegates from the small states to accept the idea that the "whole States must be incorporated." He cautioned that if "the States remain, the representatives of the large ones will stick together, and carry everything before them." To avoid this domination by the large states, all the states "must be done away with."[17]

---

13. Debate at the convention over dividing sovereignty between the states and the national government is recounted in Robertson, *Constitution and America's Destiny,* 166–77.

14. Quoted in Rakove, *Beginnings of National Politics,* 382.

15. The political objectives of Madison and those who argued for a strong central government as well as those who opposed such a reconstitution of the existing political order are discussed in Robertson, *Constitution and America's Destiny,* 18–25, 64–99.

16. Quoted in Robert K. Wright Jr. and Morris J. MacGregor Jr., *Soldier-Statesmen of the Constitution* (Washington, DC: Center of Military History, U.S. Army, G.P.O., 2007), 168.

17. *Notes of Debates,* 213.

Alexander Hamilton was the other prominent delegate at the convention who advocated abandoning the states in favor of a unitary government. Born in the British West Indies and schooled in New York City (at King's College, known today as Columbia University), Hamilton had joined the military staff of General Washington in the second year of the Revolutionary War and later secured a field command in the Continental Army, serving ably at Yorktown.[18] While he represented New York in the Congress of the Confederacy, Hamilton was more cosmopolitan and less beholden to state affiliation and loyalties than most native-born Americans.[19] As such, he was favorably inclined toward a unitary national government. During the first days of the convention, Hamilton kept a self-imposed silence, yielding to his more senior colleagues out of respect. On June 18, he broke his silence and lectured the delegates at considerable length on the dangers and failings of weak confederacies throughout history. In his learned speech, Hamilton came close to arguing that general sovereignty should be vested in one national government, with the states retained merely as administrative units thereof. He warned of the danger of dividing sovereignty: "The general power whatever be its form if it preserves itself, must swallow up the State powers.... Two sovereignties can not co-exist within the same limits." For good measure, Hamilton emphasized that there would be a great "diminution of expenses" realized by "extinguishing" the states and "substituting a general Gov[ernment]."[20] While the other delegates listened politely to Hamilton's oration and responded with mild applause, they rejected virtually everything he proposed. Hamilton surely must have

---

18. Ron Chernow's best-selling biography provides a comprehensive history of Hamilton's life and political career. Ron Chernow, *Alexander Hamilton* (New York: Penguin Books, 2004).

19. In the words of Gary Wills, Hamilton "never felt the divided loyalty—to state as well as nation—that stalled men such as Samuel Adams in the backwaters of mere resistance once independence had been won." Gary Wills, *Explaining America: The Federalist* (Garden City, NY: Doubleday, 1981), 58.

20. *Notes of Debates,* 133–34. In Robert Yates's transcription of the proceedings, Hamilton declares that "all federal governments are weak and distracted" and that to avoid "the evils deductible from these observations, we must establish a general and national government, completely sovereign, and annihilate the state distinctions and state operations." Max Farrand, ed., *The Records of the Federal Convention of 1787* (New Haven: Yale University, 1966), 1:297. Hamilton later adopted a more conciliatory approach, arguing against that proposition on the grounds that "an entire consolidation of the States into one complete national sovereignty would imply an entire subordination of the parts." Alexander Hamilton, Paper No. 32, in James Madison, Alexander Hamilton, and John Jay, *The Federalist Papers* (New York: New American Library, 1961), 198.

anticipated that reaction, as he himself candidly acknowledged that his plan would "shock the public opinion."[21] But Hamilton was practical and willing to settle for the mere *subordination* of the states to the national government. This had been one of the chief failings of the Articles of Confederation, and if anything was to be achieved, Hamilton knew that problem must be rectified under the new constitution the delegates were drafting. He understood all too well that the delegates would never approve a plan providing for the outright abolition of the states as sovereign political organizations.

Was it preordained that the states would be retained as semiautonomous political organizations within the new federal structure? Even at this early juncture in the nation's history, political power was too deeply entrenched in local state governments and America was too far down the path of federalism to make such a radical change as abolishing the state governments in favor of a consolidated government.[22] The long sequence of events that had culminated in independence for the states in 1776 and a weak federal structure for the Confederacy dictated that the states would not be abolished in 1787. After all, the delegates were not writing on a clean slate. Political institutions, traditions, and culture dating back to the colonial period were deeply rooted in the individual histories of the states, and these were not so easily cast aside. Furthermore, the Articles of Confederation had already established its own institutional legacy of federalism that limited the range of options open to the delegates in Philadelphia. A unified government was simply not part of that legacy. Nevertheless, most of those in attendance at the Constitutional Convention agreed that the political institutions of the national government needed to be stronger in the new American state they were designing. For this reason, Max Edling rightly suggests that deliberation at the convention "is best seen as a debate about state formation" rather than as a struggle between the forces of democracy and aristocracy.[23]

---

21. Farrand, ed., *Records of the Federal Convention,* 1:287.

22. This remains true, contrary to perennial predictions that the states will soon wither away. In a cover story of *The New Republic* magazine, the editor advocated abolishing the states and federalism—something as unlikely to happen today as in 1787. Michael Kinsley, "The Withering Away of the States," *The New Republic* (March 28, 1981), 17–21.

23. Max M. Edling, *A Revolution in Favor of Government: Origins of the U.S. Constitution and the Making of the American State* (New York: Oxford University Press, 2003), 11. Along similar

Be that as it may, the question of *how* to strengthen the national government divided the delegations and generated intense and protracted debate.
There were disputes over such critical issues as the internal structure of the
new national government, the method of selecting an executive, the basis
for the representation of the states within the federal government (i.e., equal
representation or representation based on population or size), the necessity
of a bill of rights, the nature of relations among the three branches, and the
reasons for having three branches of government in the first place. What
is important is that at the end of the day, after all the debate and compromise, the delegates produced a blueprint for a more strongly centralized
federal system, an innovation in constitutional design without historical
precedent. Admittedly, the range of opinions at the Constitutional Convention had already been limited by self-selection of the delegates. Those
who flatly rejected the notion of a strong national government were not
present.[24] Those in attendance were committed to no less.

But commitment does not automatically translate into concrete results. This was an ad hoc decision-making process, one lacking a coherent perspective, and the fruits of their labor were uncertain and uneven at
best.[25] The constitutional design that was ultimately drafted and adopted
included peculiar institutions and procedures and was replete with internal inconsistencies.[26] Many of the procedures and structural features of the

---

lines, Hannah Arendt famously observed that "the true objective of the American Constitution
was not to limit power but to create more power, actually to establish and duly constitute an entirely new power center." Hannah Arendt, *On Revolution* (New York: Viking Press, 1965), 152.

24. Estimates are that no more than six of the fifty-five delegates attending the convention
were ardent Antifederalists, and of these, several departed once they realized the other delegates
planned to jettison the Articles of Confederation altogether. Keith L. Dougherty, *Collective Action under the Articles of Confederation* (New York: Cambridge University Press, 2001), 146; William H. Riker, "The Lessons of 1787," *Public Choice* 55 (1987): 12–15. Patrick Henry of Virginia
declined to attend, declaring he "smelt a rat." As Richard Morris concludes: "In absenting themselves or quitting the Convention, the Antifederalists permitted that body to achieve a consensus
by avoidance of certain controversial issues and the settlement of others by compromise." Morris,
Forging of the Union, 269.

25. "The Constitution was largely an unanticipated by-product of politically expedient compromises rather than the product of a single plan. With pragmatic imprecision, the delegates constructed an unfinished national policy workplace and stocked it with a limited range of policy
tools, expecting future politicians to use and add to these tools in pursuit of their own political
agendas." Robertson, "Madison's Opponents and Constitutional Design," 225.

26. The many internal inconsistencies in the design of the Constitution were the product of compromises. For example, there is no logical reason why, having separated the national

new national institutions were jerry-built and lacked a coherent vision. After all, this was constitution-making by committee. Furthermore, the final draft established a national government that was considerably weaker than what the nationalists on the Virginian delegation had initially proposed, while the states retained most of their traditional powers. Nevertheless, the nationalists realized that the final draft was the best deal that they could negotiate. They could return home secure in the knowledge that the design of the national government under the new constitution was a marked improvement over that of the deficient Articles of Confederation.

From the perspective of strengthening the national government, what were the most salient features of the new constitutional design? Most notably, the military powers of the national government were enhanced within the reconstituted federal structure. The national government was expressly granted the authority to raise its own army and navy, ending its debilitating dependency on the state militias. Under the new federal arrangement, the national government would have its own standing army.[27] Furthermore, the national government was authorized to take control of the state militias in times of emergency: "The Congress shall have Power To...provide for calling forth the Militia to execute the Laws of the Union, suppress Insurrections and repel Invasions."[28] To be sure, the states retained their own militias, which were deemed a crucial element of their traditional prerogatives. Under the federal arrangement, a form of joint administration was provided for the military power. Not surprisingly, numerous problems

---

government into three supposedly independent branches, the vice president should preside over the Senate or cast the deciding vote in the event of a tie in the chamber (thereby mixing the functions of the executive and legislature), or why the chief justice of the Supreme Court should preside over a trial in the Senate to remove the president. For a discussion of such defects in the constitutional design, see Sanford Levinson, *Our Undemocratic Constitution: Where the Constitution Goes Wrong (And How We the People Can Correct It)* (New York: Oxford University Press, 2006).

27. Madison defended this power in *The Federalist Papers* on purely pragmatic grounds: "Is the power of equipping armies and fleets necessary?...Was it necessary to give an INDEFINITE POWER of raising TROOPS, as well as providing fleets; and of maintaining both in PEACE as well as in WAR?...If one nation maintains constantly a disciplined army ready for the service of ambition or revenge, it obliges the most pacific nations, who may be within the reach of its enterprises, to take corresponding precautions." James Madison, Paper No. 41, in Madison, Hamilton, and Jay, *The Federalist Papers,* 256–57.

28. U.S. Constitution, art. 1, sec. 8. Under the Articles of Confederation, the states had the authority to appoint officers under the rank of colonel in any "land forces" raised by that state for the "common defense." Articles of Confederation, art. VII.

have arisen over the years in delineating the boundaries between the military powers of the national government and those of the states. From a strategic military perspective, such a division of military command and authority defies all logic and experience. Nevertheless, it was necessitated by the bargain struck for the new federal constitution, which dictated that the states be retained as semiautonomous political entities. Over time, the balance of power between the state militias and the national military shifted toward the center. The Revolutionary War was mostly fought with state militias, but these went into a steep decline between 1792 to 1860.[29] Today, the state militias function as reserve units of the national army, receiving training and financial support from the national government, remaining under the command of state officials until such time as they are called up for federal service in a national emergency.[30]

Just as the military power of the national government was enhanced in the new constitutional design, its fiscal powers were strengthened by granting the national legislature the express authority to impose and collect taxes from the citizenry at large, ending its dependency on the states for its revenue. In granting a broad power of taxation, the new constitutional charter simply stated: "The Congress shall have Power To lay and collect Taxes, Duties, Imposts and Excises."[31] Such a power of taxation was exactly what the national government lacked under the Articles of Confederation and

---

29. In January 1790, Secretary of War Henry Knox presented a plan to Congress for reform of the state militia system by granting the national government greater control over the training and supplying of the state forces. But that plan was ignored by Congress. The situation changed with the decisive defeat in November 1791 of federal troops under the command of Arthur St. Clair (senior general of the U.S. Army) by the hostile Indian tribes encamped along the Wabash River. After the disastrous Battle of the Wabash (also known as St. Clair's Defeat), Congress reorganized the national military into the "Legion of the United States" (essentially, four small armies with about 1,200 men each), voted funds for the regular army, and enacted legislation providing federal aid to the state militias. This legislation (the Militia Act of May 8, 1792) was less than what Knox had proposed. The Knox plan and the 1792 legislation are discussed in Richard H. Kohn, *Eagle and Sword: The Federalists and the Creation of the Military Establishment in America, 1783–1802* (New York: Free Press, 1975), 128–38.

30. The peculiar role of the state militias within the federal arrangement is the subject of William H. Riker, *Soldiers of the States: the Role of the National Guard in American Democracy* (Washington, DC: Public Affairs Press, 1957). The militias were largely abandoned after their poor performance during the War of 1812, but they were revived by the states after the great railroad strike of 1877 and used as an internal police force to suppress labor unrest.

31. U.S. Constitution, art. 1, sec. 8. At the Constitutional Convention, there was relatively little debate over this important clause (on August 16) and only one dissenting vote—from Elbridge Gerry of Massachusetts, who thought that the legislature "could not be trusted with such a power," which might be used to "ruin the Country." *Notes of Debates*, 466–69.

just what nationalists sought for the reconstituted American state. Despite this seemingly broad grant of fiscal authority to the national government, the power of taxation was seriously compromised by two enigmatic requirements, the exact meaning and intent of which remained unknown to all those outside the Constitutional Convention and apparently many of those in attendance as well. First, the final draft of the text prescribes that all duties, imposts, and excise taxes imposed by Congress be "uniform" throughout the United States.[32] Taken by itself, this requirement would not constitute a particularly burdensome limit on the taxing power of the national government. Certainly, land taxes, capitation taxes, income taxes, import duties, and excise taxes could be imposed at a uniform rate throughout the United States—assuming it is the *rate* of taxation that is supposed to be uniform under this provision. But the Constitution further demands that all "direct taxes" (but by implication, not "indirect taxes") be "apportioned among the several states" based on population.[33] This creates an obvious difficulty. How can a direct tax (e.g., a capitation tax, slave tax, or a land tax) both be "uniform" and "apportioned" among the states based on population? The two provisions are in direct conflict with each other. The text creates an artificial (and untenable) distinction between indirect taxes that must be uniformly imposed and direct taxes that must be apportioned among the states based on population. As a result of apportionment, direct taxes *cannot* be uniform. These cryptic and incoherent clauses in the Constitution were little understood at the time of drafting and ratification and would prove an invitation to more than a century of controversy played out in the federal courts over the national government's power of taxation.[34]

---

32. "All Duties, Imposts and Excises shall be uniform throughout the United States." U.S. Constitution, art. 1, sec. 8.

33. "Direct Taxes shall be apportioned among the several States which may be included within this Union, according to their respective Numbers." U.S. Constitution, art. 1, sec. 2. At the convention, the delegates apparently did not know the precise meaning of "direct taxation," but nonetheless, approved the clause. *Notes of Debates,* 494. Ackerman offers a plausible explanation of the bargain struck between the populated northern states and the slave-owning southern states over how to count slaves for purposes of determining representation in Congress and apportioning direct taxes. Bruce Ackerman, "Taxation and the Constitution," *Columbia Law Review* 99 (1999): 1–58.

34. In *Hylton v. United States* (1796), the Supreme Court judiciously skirted the issue. Recognizing from the outset the confusion inherent in the constitutional language, the Court held that because the two provisions could not be reconciled, the tax at issue (a carriage tax enacted by the Federalists in 1794) could not be a "direct" tax, and hence, was not unconstitutional. Despite this

Notwithstanding these dubious requirements for apportionment and uniformity, the important thing from the perspective of future state development is that the national government finally obtained a general power of taxation. Under the new constitution, the national government was granted the authority to extract resources directly from society, bypassing the state legislatures and thereby gaining a significant degree of autonomy from the states.[35] At the same time, there was no express prohibition against borrowing by the national government. As a result, a combination of federal taxes and loans could be used to finance a standing army and navy, creating the possibility that over time national political leaders could build a strong American state within the framework of the new political order.

The independence of the national government from the states was further enhanced by the authorization for the direct election of the members of the House of Representatives by the citizenry at large, rather than by the state legislatures.[36] For the first time, this established a direct linkage between the national government and civil society. In the original text, the linkage was only partial, as the Senate, the "upper" chamber of the national legislature, was comprised of members selected by the state legislatures, seemingly ensuring a measure of control of the national government by the states.[37] But efforts to control the voting habits of appointed senators proved notoriously unsuccessful in the early decades of the nineteenth century, and by the end of the century a number of states were already experimenting with different methods for the direct election of senators by the enfranchised citizenry.[38] The practice of direct election of Senators

---

sensible decision to ignore the ambiguity in the text, the issue resurfaced at the close of the nineteenth century. In *Springer v. United States,* 102 U.S. 586 (1881), the Supreme Court held that the Civil War income tax of 1862 was not a "direct" tax requiring apportionment, but rather an "excise." In dictum, the Court indicated that only taxes on real property and slaves were direct taxes. The Supreme Court muddied the waters in the infamous case of *Pollock v. Farmer's Loan and Trust Co.,* 157 U.S. 429c (1895); 158 U.S. 601 (1895) (rehearing). For a review of the evolution of the case law, see Alan O. Dixler, "Direct Taxes under the Constitution: A Review of the Precedents," *Tax Notes* 113 (Dec. 25, 2006): 1177–91.

35. It is worth noting that the Constitution banned the national government from taxing exports: "No Tax or Duty shall be laid on Articles exported from any State." U.S. Constitution, art. 1, sec. 9.

36. Ibid., art. 1, sec. 2.

37. Ibid., art. 1, sec. 3.

38. For a discussion of the inability of state legislatures to maintain control over the voting habits of their delegates to the Senate and the subsequent rise of the movement for popular

was formalized with the ratification of the Seventeenth Amendment in 1913.[39] Furthermore, political parties emerged early in the nineteenth century, creating an even stronger linkage between the new national political institutions and its citizenry, thereby establishing a more coherent and democratic political order.

Finally, considerable effort was expended by the delegates at the Constitutional Convention establishing the basic framework for a national economy in lieu of the thirteen separate local economies that traded among themselves as foreign nations. It was agreed that the national government would be expressly authorized to regulate foreign and interstate "commerce," although that authority apparently did not extend to the regulation of "manufacturing" in the state economies.[40] Simultaneously, the states were prohibited from imposing duties on imports or exports.[41] This eliminated the barriers to free trade and commerce that had been erected by the states themselves, even while cutting off one of the most important sources of revenue of the state governments. In addition, the national government alone was authorized to strike coinage.[42] The states, which since colonial times had issued bills of credit that were commonly used to pay debts, fees, and taxes to the state governments themselves, were expressly prohibited from coining money, emitting bills of credit, or denominating anything other than gold or silver coins as legal tender.[43] Following heated debate, the delegates decided not to provide the national government with

---

election of senators, see William H. Riker, "The Senate and American Federalism," *American Political Science Review* 49 (June 1955): 452–69.

39. "The Senate of the United States shall be composed of two Senators from each State, elected by the people thereof." U.S. Constitution, 17th Amendment.

40. "The Congress shall have Power To...regulate Commerce with foreign Nations, and among the several States, and with the Indian Tribes." Ibid., art. 1, sec. 8. The Supreme Court maintained the distinction between the regulation of commerce and manufacturing until 1941, when it sanctioned national regulation of the local economy under the authority of the interstate commerce clause, thereby overturning settled law. *United States v. Darby,* 312 U.S. 100 (1941), rev'g *Hammer v. Dagenhart,* 247 U.S. 251.

41. "No State shall, without the Consent of the Congress, lay any Imposts or Duties on Imports or Exports." U.S. Constitution, art. 2, sec 10.

42. Even still, a national mint was not established by Congress until passage of the Coinage Act of 1792, and foreign coins (mostly Spanish) circulated as legal currency during the first decades of the nineteenth century.

43. U.S. Constitution, art. 1, sec. 10. Opponents of the Constitution would object to this prohibition on the authority of the states to issue bills of credit as legal tender.

specific authority to issue bills of credit.[44] This meant that the national government lacked express authority to determine legal tender. By declaring what is legal tender, a government requires that a creditor accept the official paper currency at face value in satisfaction of a debt and thereby potentially receive less than the market value of the debt as measured in specie or exchange property—at least where the currency has been inflated. This was a highly controversial matter during the colonial period and remained so at the Constitutional Convention.[45] In the end, the issue was left unresolved by the delegates.

Another issue left unsettled was whether the national government had the authority to charter a national bank. The states traditionally possessed the power to charter corporations, including state banks, and nothing in the new constitution expressly barred them from continuing with that practice.[46] At the same time, there was no express authorization for the national government to charter a national bank—an important component in the fiscal organization of a modern state. Arguably, the national government possessed that authority as an "implied power," but the matter was not directly addressed in the text. In 1791, on the recommendation of Treasury Secretary Alexander Hamilton, Washington requested that Congress grant a charter to the First Bank of the United States, such bank to be capitalized at $10 million. Whether the federal government actually possessed such a power remained a matter of contention. Contrary to Madison and Jefferson, Hamilton argued that incorporating a national bank was an implied power of Congress, "necessary and proper" for the execution of other enumerated powers of Congress, such as imposing taxes and maintaining a national treasury.[47] When the issue finally came before the Supreme Court

---

44. On August 16, 1787, by a vote of 9 to 2 (and reflecting a variety of reasons), the delegates to the convention deleted a provision in the original draft of the Constitution that would have provided such authority to the national government to emit bills of credit. *Notes of Debates,* 470–71.

45. For a discussion of how the delegates to the Constitutional Convention of 1787 viewed legal tender laws, see Farley Grubb, "The U.S. Constitution and Monetary Powers: An Analysis of the 1787 Constitutional Convention and the Constitutional Transformation of the U.S. Monetary System," *Financial History Review* 13 (April 2006): 47–50.

46. The Marshall court had held that states may not charter banks, but that ruling was subsequently overturned by the Taney court.

47. "Opinion on the Constitutionality of the Bank," (1791) in *Reports of Alexander Hamilton,* ed. Jacob E. Cooke (New York: Harper and Row, 1964), 83–114.

in 1819, Chief Justice John Marshall (himself a High Federalist) concurred with Hamilton's prior assertion of national authority.[48]

Incongruously, the new constitution did not impose a single currency on the nation or ban the state-chartered banks from issuing the paper notes that traditionally functioned as a form of local currency in the states. This too created an obstacle to nationalists who envisioned a strong role for the federal government in promoting a national economy. Even still, the essential preconditions were established for the subsequent emergence of a common monetary unit—the U.S. dollar.[49] In his comprehensive study of the issue, Farley Grubb concludes that "the Constitution established the legal framework that allowed for the ascendance in the U.S. of the modern bank-based financial system."[50] In this way, the drafters established the basic structural framework for a national economy, even if they left blank many of the most important details.

The abandonment of the Confederacy and the adoption of entirely new political institutions at the convention represented the culmination of a decade of dissatisfaction with the Articles of Confederation. But drafting a new constitution was only the first step. Thereafter, the approval of nine states was required for ratification. The campaign for ratification in the states was led by political elites with nationalist aspirations and a shared vision of a strong central state. These nationalists, ironically known as Federalists, favored a radical restructuring of the regime to enhance the military and fiscal powers of the central state. "The delegates wished to create a new, more perfect union that would promote an enlightened class of

---

48. *McCulloch v. Maryland,* 17 U.S. 316 (1819). The political controversy over the Second Bank of the United States is discussed in Margaret G. Myers, *A Financial History of the United States* (New York: Columbia University Press, 1970), 84–94.

49. On July 6, 1785, Congress declared the silver dollar as the money unit of the United States, thereby replacing the Spanish dollar as the official currency (although Spanish dollars still circulated for decades). Albert S. Bolles, *The Financial History of the United States, from 1774 to 1789* (New York: D. Appleton, 1879), 341–42. For a review of the various instruments and securities used to pay debts and taxes during the 1780s, see Max M. Edling and Mark D. Kaplanoff, "Alexander Hamilton's Fiscal Reform: Transforming the Structure of Taxation in the Early Republic," *William and Mary Quarterly* 61 (October 2004): 713–44.

50. Grubb, "The U.S. Constitution and Monetary Powers," 43. Grubb provides an overview of the debate at the convention over decisions affecting such matters as currency and banking. See also Curtis P. Nettles, *The Emergence of a National Economy, 1775–1815* (New York: Holt, Reinhart and Winston, 1962), 98–101.

rulers who would think continentally instead of in straitened, self-interested terms."[51] Conversely, local political elites were less favorably inclined toward an expansion of the powers of the national government—an innovation that they recognized would be at their own expense. But most state leaders understood that the national government created under the Articles of Confederation was too weak. This was especially true in the border states, which were vulnerable to attack by the British from Canada and by hostile Indian forces in Florida and the Southwest. In the border states, external military threats compelled local political leaders to support the campaign to strengthen the national government and its military power.

Most of those who opposed the expansion of national powers, pejoratively labeled Antifederalists by their opponents, did not attend the Constitutional Convention in Philadelphia. Those who remained at home in the states were unlikely to be persuaded to change their minds by anything that came out of that meeting. The ideology of the Antifederalists was imbued with a passionate hostility to the centralization of power in the national government, which they believed would "subvert popularly controlled local institutions, the primary function of which were to preserve liberty against the encroachments of the power of the rulers."[52] To the Antifederalists, standing armies and centralized taxation (powers granted to the reconstituted national government under the new constitution) were associated with the corrupt English monarchy that they had just discarded and clearly did not wish to resurrect. This concern was central to their opposition to the reconstituted federal structure.[53]

51. Sean Wilentz, *The Rise of American Democracy: Jefferson to Lincoln* (New York: W. W. Norton, 2005), 32.

52. Edling, *Revolution in Favor of Government,* 41. The classic studies of the ideology of the Antifederalists are Jackson Turner Main, *The Antifederalists: Critics of the Constitution, 1781–1788* (Chicago: Quadrangle Books, 1961); Cecelia M. Kenyon, "Men of Little Faith: The Anti-Federalists on the Nature of Representative Government," *William and Mary Quarterly* 3d ser., 12 (January 1955); 3–43; Herbert J. Storing, ed., *The Anti-Federalist* (Chicago: University of Chicago Press, 1985). Much of the important writings of the period can be found in David Wootton, ed., *The Essential Federalist and Anti-Federalist Papers* (Indianapolis: Hackett, 2003). The positions of the Federalists and the Antifederalists during the campaign for ratification are summarized in Dougherty, *Collective Action,* 164–73; Brown, *Redeeming the Republic,* 200–218.

53. Such concerns were held even by supporters of the Constitution. Madison himself warned, "War is the parent of armies; from these proceed debts and taxes; and armies, and debts, and taxes are the known instruments for bringing the many under the domination of the few. In war, too, the discretionary power of the Executive is extended; its influence in dealing out offices, honors,

While the opposition was strong in key states, the Antifederalists ultimately lost the political battle over ratification. On December 7, 1787, Delaware became the first state to vote for ratification when the state legislature there unanimously approved the new charter. Pennsylvania followed suit only six days later, albeit by a split vote, and the next week New Jersey voted for the new constitution by a vote of 38 to 0. Georgia ratified on December 31 by a vote of 26 to 0. This generated critical momentum for the campaign for ratification. On June 21, 1788, New Hampshire became the ninth state to approve the text, thereby ensuring formal ratification. Nevertheless, it remained critical that the key states of New York and Virginia join the union for it to succeed. Hamilton and Madison, who along with John Jay of New York penned *The Federalist Papers* as a spirited defense of the new constitutional design, were instrumental in garnering support for ratification in New York. In the summer of 1788, the legislatures of both Virginia and New York approved the document in extremely close contests. In Virginia, the vote was 89 to 79, with the Federalists narrowly carrying the day. Their success in Virginia helped sway the New York legislature, where the margin of victory of the nationalists was only three votes. North Carolina withheld approval for a brief while longer, but finally ratified the text in November of the following year. But by that time, the issue was moot, as the forces behind the adoption of the Constitution of 1787 had already prevailed. The decision became unanimous on May 29, 1790, when Rhode Island relented and finally approved the Constitution—this after the other twelve states threatened to impose duties on imports from Rhode Island as if it were a foreign nation. The threat of financial retribution was enough to bring Rhode Island back into the fold of the reconstituted federal union. Even still, the situation was ominous. On October 10, 1788, the Continental Congress closed shop before the new national government was in place.[54] A new American state would have to be built virtually from scratch.

---

and emoluments is multiplied; and all the means of seducing the minds, are added to those of subduing the force, of the people." James Madison, "Political Observations, April 20, 1795," in *The Papers of James Madison,* ed. Thomas A. Mason, Robert A. Rutland, and Jeanne K. Sisson (Charlottesville: University of Virginia Press, 1985), 15:518.

54. October 10, 1788, was the last date there was a quorum in the Congress. Thereafter, attendance was sporadic (with one or two delegates present each day), and no business was again conducted. Ford et al., eds., *Journals of the Continental Congress,* 34:599–601. During the final days of

Notwithstanding that the Antifederalists lost the political battle over ratification to the nationalists, the fortified national government remained confined within an extremely narrow political space under the Constitution of 1787. This would still be a national government of limited (enumerated) powers. Furthermore, the local state governments survived the Constitutional Convention virtually intact as sovereign political organizations. In the new political order, the local state governments retained most of their military powers as well as unfettered access to their traditional sources of revenue. Indeed, during the first decades of the republic, the militias, financial resources, and tax systems of the states remained superior to those of the national government. The adoption of the Constitution did not immediately solve the problem of weakness at the center. For decades, the triumph of the nationalists was more potential than actual. Under the new federal structure, the national government still possessed what can only be characterized as extremely limited administrative capacity. There is no mention at all in the Constitution of an administrative branch or even of executive offices. It took decades for political leaders to flesh out the powers of the national government. Those nationalists who favored a strong American state understood that the newly ratified Constitution was only the architectural blueprint for a political order that did not exist yet. The plan had been adopted by political leaders, but it was now necessary to cultivate support for the regime among the citizens. Considerable effort was required to enhance the legitimacy of the new national government, assert political powers beyond those of the previous regime, and build real flesh-and-bones political institutions. This would take time—especially with respect to fortifying the fiscal powers and military apparatus of the national government.

The widespread respect for General Washington was critical in aligning the people behind the new regime. Washington played his role well, both as the president and commander in chief of the military forces of the central government. But more than anyone else, it was Alexander Hamilton

---

the Confederacy, the entire national government consisted of a "foreign office with John Jay and a couple of clerks to deal with correspondence from John Adams in London and Thomas Jefferson in Paris;...a Treasury Board with an empty treasury;...a 'Secretary at War' with an authorized army of 840 men;...a dozen clerks whose pay was in arrears, and an unknown but fearful burden of debt, almost no revenue, and a prostrate credit." Leonard D. White, *The Federalists: A Study in Administrative History* (New York: Macmillan, 1948), 1.

who comprehended the immensity of the task that confronted the leaders of the national government. As chief financial officer, he would play a crucial role in instructing and guiding his colleagues, including his fellow Federalists, in how to establish a national government that could actually govern. Hamilton would provide the initiative, inspiration, and strategic plan for those nationalists who would build a strong American state.

Hamilton's Vision of an American Fiscal-Military State

A thirty-two-year-old delegate from New York, Alexander Hamilton went to the Constitutional Convention in 1787 as one of the chief proponents of a strong national government. In his speech of June 18, Hamilton spoke eloquently in favor of a national government with an executive possessed of almost monarchical powers. That executive (undoubtedly, Hamilton's beloved General Washington) would be chosen by electors, who themselves would be elected in local districts to serve an unlimited term on the condition of "good behavior." Hamilton boldly proposed that the executive be granted the authority to veto any law passed by the bicameral legislature, negotiate treaties, and appoint all executive officers of the government.[55] He proclaimed the British government "the best in the world" and recommended it to the delegates as the model for the new American state they were designing.[56]

The delegates were uniformly unmoved by Hamilton's appeal for an executive with regal powers. Washington, the heir apparent to the throne, flatly rejected monarchy for America. Even Hamilton's ally at the convention, James Madison, opposed such expansive powers for the executive and eventually would part ways with Hamilton over his monarchical predilections and English sympathies. Despite his disappointment over the rejection by the delegates of his plan for a strong executive, Hamilton would vigorously defend the text drafted at the Constitutional Convention in the critical debate over ratification in New York—proclaiming support even

---

55. *Notes of Debates,* 138–39. Such a veto power granted to a governor or the executive of the national government invariably raised the specter of the royal veto of the Crown and hence, was suspect to many.

56. Max Farrand, ed., *Records of the Federal Convention,* 1:282–93; *Notes of Debates,* 134.

for provisions that he had openly opposed in the debates in Philadelphia. This reflected his calculated assessment that all in all, the design of the national government in the final constitutional design was a significant improvement over that of the Confederacy, even if it amounted to less than what he desired. As a pragmatist, he was willing to accept the Constitution with all its imperfections as the best possible outcome under the circumstances. Hamilton understood that resolute statesmen later could build on and enhance the political institutions initially established by the Constitution.

The process began on September 2, 1789, when Congress enacted enabling legislation that created the Treasury Department. Nine days later, President Washington appointed (and the Senate immediately confirmed) Hamilton as the nation's first secretary of the treasury. This was most fitting, as Hamilton possessed a clear and cogent plan for strengthening the fiscal powers of the national government. He set out to accomplish this by simultaneously bolstering the office of the executive and the military powers of the new American state. In doing so, Hamilton sought to emulate the English state. By the middle of the eighteenth century England already possessed a developed administrative capacity, an organized treasury office, effective taxes, a central banking system, and the capacity to borrow in wartime large sums of money against future tax revenues through a sophisticated system of public finance. At the same time, Hanoverian England possessed a formidable military apparatus capable of projecting its power globally to protect the interests of the English nation and its vast colonial empire. This was the English fiscal-military state that Hamilton wished to replicate in America.[57] As chief financial officer of the republic and a leader of the Federalist Party, Hamilton was in the ideal position to build a fiscal-military state for America.[58]

---

57. As Gordon Wood observes: "As the new secretary of treasury Hamilton aimed to copy Britain's success and turn the United States into a great power that would eventually rival Britain and the other European states on their own war-making terms." Gordon S. Wood, *Revolutionary Characters: What Made the Founders Different* (New York: Penguin Press, 2006), 132.

58. So trusted was Hamilton's advice during his tenure as secretary of the treasury that Congress decided in September 1789 to dispense with the Committee on Ways and Means that it had previously formed. For the remainder of his term, Congress took direction on financial matters directly from Hamilton. The committee was reconstituted after Hamilton left office. Wood, *Revolutionary Characters*, 129.

Hamilton understood that Britain's great wealth was the ultimate source of the power of the English state. For this reason, he proposed that officials of the national government actively promote domestic manufacturing in America and build the infrastructure that would facilitate commerce: "The prosperity of commerce is now perceived and acknowledged by all enlightened statesmen to be useful as well as the most productive source of national wealth, and has accordingly become a primary object of their political actions."[59] Critical of both the French physiocrats who believed that the wealth of nations was derived exclusively from agriculture and those laissez-faire economists who wished to exclude government from a role in directing the national economy (most prominently, Adam Smith), Hamilton prescribed an active role for government and encouraged enlightened statesmen in America to cultivate a national economy. It was no coincidence that one of Hamilton's most cherished heroes was the "great Colbert," minister of finance for Louis XIV who built the French mercantile state. Hamilton shared with Colbert his mercantile philosophy and a belief that the government should play an active role in nurturing industry and commerce—a view vigorously rejected by Jefferson and his followers as well as many Federalists. To Hamilton, an active government was the precondition for a prosperous commercial economy, which in turn would support a strong nation-state armed with the power of taxation.

Although an advocate of commerce and manufacture, Hamilton was no lackey for the "moneyed men" and landed property-owners. Nor was his aim to make the upper classes wealthier.[60] Rather he envisioned a commercial republic wherein the interests of the rising commercial classes would be aligned and allied with those of the nation as a whole, providing greater stability and legitimacy for the national government.[61] As a side benefit, by encouraging domestic manufacturing and commerce, the nation would

---

59. Alexander Hamilton, Paper No. 12, in Madison, Hamilton, and Jay, *The Federalist Papers,* 91.

60. The common misperception that the Federalists were an aristocratic party has been traced to the writings of Charles Beard and Merrill Jensen's simplistic portrait of the American Revolution as a struggle between democratic radicals and conservatives in control of the postrevolutionary government under the Federalist party. See, e.g., Kenyon, "Men of Little Faith," *William and Mary Quarterly,* 5; Edling, *A Revolution in Favor of Government,* 33–35.

61. Hamilton's understanding of how manufacturing and commerce promote a strong state is examined in Michael D. Chan, *Aristotle and Hamilton on Commerce and Statesmanship* (Columbia: University of Missouri Press, 2006).

never again be cut off from supplies, as it had been during the Revolutionary War. In the opening lines of his famous "Report on Manufactures," Hamilton argued that the main purpose of promoting manufacturing in America is "to render the United States independent on [sic] foreign nations for military and other essential supplies."[62] Later, the national government itself would benefit from the increased revenue collected from the prospering commercial and manufacturing classes through taxes.

Hamilton's vision of a commercial republic was in direct opposition to the ideals of Jefferson and Madison. "The Virginians preferred to pursue a policy of free trade: America would remain an agricultural nation and export its surpluses in exchange for manufactured goods from Europe."[63] In particular, the Republican vision of an agrarian republic of virtue contrasts sharply with Hamilton's intention to create a commercial and manufacturing society. In his famous *Notes on the State of Virginia* (1781), Jefferson extolled the virtues of the noble yeomen: "Those who labour in the earth are the chosen people of God, if ever he had a chosen people, whose breasts he has made his particular deposit for substantial and genuine virtue."[64] Jefferson's extended praise for farmers and those who till the earth has become what Drew McCoy refers to as the "centerpiece of the republic's cultural heritage, a quintessential expression of the impassioned concern for the natural, earthbound virtue of a simple and uncorrupted people."[65] Jefferson associated the "corruption of morals" and a host of other social problems with manufacture. Wanting no part of that in the New World, he recommended to his fellow Americans that the "workshops remain in Europe." In contrast with Jefferson's vision of an agrarian republic, Hamilton was intent on cultivating a thriving commercial society that would support a national government with all the essential features of the fiscal-military state of Britain that had brought prosperity and global domination to the English nation. In this respect, Hamilton was profoundly influenced by David Hume's defense of commercial society and

---

62. "Report on Manufactures" (1791), in *Reports of Alexander Hamilton,* 115.

63. Chan, *Aristotle and Hamilton on Commerce and Statesmanship,* 104.

64. Thomas Jefferson, *Notes on the State of Virginia* (Chapel Hill: University of North Carolina Press, 1955), 164–65.

65. Drew R. McCoy, *The Elusive Republic: Political Economy in Jeffersonian America* (Chapel Hill: University of North Carolina Press, 1980), 13. McCoy's study provides a comprehensive discussion of Jefferson's vision of America as an agrarian republic of virtue.

English "court" philosophy, which has been contrasted with the republican "country" doctrine that animated Jefferson's thinking.[66]

Beyond its fundamental role in promoting manufacturing and commerce, the national government should, according to Hamilton, use the executive's power of appointment and patronage (what Hume referred to as "corruption") to cultivate a strata of men loyal to the regime, planting "in the interior of each State, a mass of influence in favor of the Federal Government."[67] This would encompass the appointment of an army of bureaucrats: customs officials, tax collectors, postmasters, and military officers. As the head of a large executive office, Hamilton was in a position to make many of these appointments, thereby cultivating support for the national government in the hinterlands. "Since these appointees were located in every large town and section of the United States and touched every aspect of economic life in America, they were important for building support for the new government, even among former opponents of the Constitution."[68]

Like Robert Morris, his predecessor in charge of the Treasury of the Confederacy, Hamilton recognized that strengthening the financial resources of the national government was critical to its success and longevity. In particular, this required a viable system of public credit. To this end, Hamilton tirelessly argued that the creditworthiness of the central state depended on its ability to assume, consolidate, and eventually pay off the war debt.[69] To achieve this, he proposed a broad program of institutional innovations intended to end the endemic revenue crisis that still plagued the national government. When the Federalists took office in 1789, the nation was, in the words of Robert Goodloe Harper of South Carolina, "without

---

66. The classic account of how republican theory penetrated American political thought is J.G.A. Pocock, *The Machiavellian Moment: Florentine Political Thought and the Atlantic Republican Tradition* (Princeton: Princeton University Press, 1975).

67. Alexander Hamilton, "The Continentalist No. VI" (July 4, 1782), *The Papers of Alexander Hamilton*, ed. Harold C. Syrett et al. (New York: Columbia University Press, 1962), 3:105.

68. Wood, *Revolutionary Characters*, 131.

69. Hamilton advocated the assumption of the war debts of the states, notwithstanding the absence of authorization in the Constitution. He warned of the dangers and inequities that would arise if the debts of the states were left unpaid. Alexander Hamilton, Paper No. 7, in Madison, Hamilton, and Jay, *The Federalist Papers*, 60–66. Eventually, Congress enacted legislation for the assumption of much of the state war debts. E. James Ferguson, *The Power of the Purse: A History of American Public Finance, 1776–1790* (Chapel Hill: University of North Carolina Press, 1961), 330.

a shilling of permanent revenue; without a system of finance; burdened with a debt arising from the war,... and without money in the treasury sufficient for the ordinary expences of government." As a consequence, "public credit was... completely annihilated."[70] Hamilton's proposals for rectifying this sorry financial condition included the consolidation and repayment at face value of the national government's war debt (including securities purchased at a discount by speculators during the war from the original holders), the assumption of the war debts of the states, the establishment of a strong national banking system and a national mint, and the adoption of the U.S. dollar as the national currency.[71] Objecting to the emission of paper by both the states and the national government, the treasury secretary preferred that the national bank issue paper money backed by specie.[72] He also viewed the national bank as an important mechanism to facilitate lending and borrowing by the national government.[73] Finally, Hamilton proposed in his "Report on Manufactures" a program of public projects (building public roads and canals to "assist the manufacturers" and to facilitate the "transportation of commodities"), internal development, and the use of "pecuniary bounties" and tariffs on imports for the purpose of stimulating and protecting emerging domestic industries.[74]

While many elements of Hamilton's nationalist plan met with resolute opposition from the nascent Jeffersonian faction, most items on his agenda were adopted in some form or another during the course of Washington's two terms as president, as Federalists controlled both houses of the national

---

70. "A Letter From Robert Goodloe Harper, of South Carolina, to his Constituents" (Providence: John Carter, 1801), 11. Harper, a Federalist from South Carolina, was elected to Congress in 1795 and served as the chairman of the Committee on Ways and Means during the Fifth and Sixth Congresses.

71. Alexander Hamilton, "Report Relative to a Provision for the Support of Public Credit" (1790) and "Second Report on the Further Provision Necessary for Establishing Public Credit (Report on a National Bank)" (1790), in *Reports of Alexander Hamilton*. In his "Report on the Establishment of a Mint," Hamilton proposed the free coinage of gold and silver, the establishment of the U.S. dollar as the national currency and the banning of foreign coins, and the use of coins in small denominations to divide the dollar. "Final Version of Report on the Establishment of a Mint" (1791), in *Papers of Alexander Hamilton*, ed. Syrett et al., 7:570–607.

72. "Second Report on the Further Provision Necessary for Establishing Public Credit (Report on a National Bank)" (1790), in *Reports of Alexander Hamilton*, 62–63.

73. In Michael Chan's words, "Hamilton saw the national bank as a powerful mechanism to extend and vivify America's fledgling capital market, which was the key to the nation's economic growth." Chan, *Aristotle and Hamilton on Commerce and Statesmanship*, 166.

74. Alexander Hamilton, "Report on Manufactures" (1791), in *Reports of Alexander Hamilton*.

legislature.[75] The First Bank of the United States was chartered in 1791.[76] The war debt of the Congress of the Confederacy was consolidated and assumed by the new national government, which finally possessed a power of taxation capable of generating revenues to service that debt. More controversial was the matter of the assumption of the states' war debt by the national government, as this pitted the states that had already paid off their own war debts (Virginia, Maryland, North Carolina, and Georgia) against those that still had significant debt outstanding (Massachusetts and South Carolina). The assumption of state debt by the national government raised basic questions about the economic organization of the federation and the nature of the relationship between the national government and the states within the federal structure. Over and over, Hamilton argued that by assuming the war debt of the states, the national government would be strengthened and animus against the national government would be deflated. He even argued that a national debt would be a "national blessing" and a "powerful cement" of the union.[77] The goal was to link "the interest of the State in an intimate connection with those rich individuals belonging to it."[78] In this way, the allegiance of the wealthy men who were owed the money would be transferred to the national government on its assumption of the debt from the state governments. Madison was equally adamant in his objections.

In 1790, Jefferson brokered a compromise pursuant to which the state war debt would be assumed by the national government and, to appease the Virginians, the nation's new permanent capital city would be located

---

75. The Federalist legislative program is summarized in Nettles, *Emergence of a National Economy, 1775–1815,* 109–26.

76. Subscriptions for stock in the bank opened on July 4, 1791, and sold out in one hour. Of the $400 per share purchase price, only $25 was required as a down payment in exchange for scrip— essentially an option for the stock. Furious speculation in the script followed. See Stanley Elkins and Eric McKitrick, *The Age of Federalism: The Early American Republic, 1788–1800* (New York: Oxford University Press, 1993), 242–44.

77. "A national debt, if it is not excessive, will be to us a national blessing; it will be a powerful cement of our union." "Letter to Robert Morris from Alexander Hamilton" (April 30, 1781), in *Papers of Alexander Hamilton,* ed. Syrett et al., 2:635. Morris himself had written: "A public debt supported by public revenue, will prove the strongest cement to keep our confederacy together." Quoted in Clarence L. Ver Steeg, *Robert Morris: Revolutionary Financier* (Philadelphia: University of Pennsylvania, 1954), 124.

78. "Letter to Robert Morris" (1780), in *The Works of Alexander Hamilton,* ed. John C. Hamilton (New York: John F. Trow, 1850), 1:125.

along the Potomac River at a site to be determined later.[79] Under the compromise, $21.5 million in war debts of the states was assumed by the na-
tional government—only slightly less than what Hamilton had originally
proposed. With the assumption of the state debt, the total obligations of
the national government swelled to more than $70 million. In his exhaus-
tive study of the struggle over the assumption of the state war debts, James
Ferguson concludes that:

> Because of the integral relation between debts, the power of taxation, and
> sovereignty, Congress's ownership of the debt implied a basic reorganiza-
> tion of the federal system and produced a tendency in that direction. In the
> years following the war, the task of paying the debt was the chief func-
> tion of a central government which otherwise lacked compelling reasons
> for existence.[80]

Following the assumption of the state debt, Congress established an
agency to supervise the process of paying off the national debt.[81] Congress
dedicated surplus revenue generated from customs duties to this agency,
which in 1795 was designated the Commission of the Sinking Fund.[82]

Notwithstanding that the financial resources available to the national
government had been significantly expanded under the Constitution, they
remained inadequate to service the enormous public debt amassed by the
Congress during the Revolutionary War. Once it was organized in April
1789, the first order of business of the House of Representative was to consider a proposal by Madison.[83] This was an ad valorem duty of 5 percent
on most imported products—an impost almost identical to what had been
pursued unsuccessfully in 1783. After passing the House, the tax proposal

---

79. The compromise was worked out between Madison and Hamilton over the dinner table
in June 1790 at a meeting arranged by Jefferson in his home in New York City. Jefferson left several unpublished versions of the event, each one slightly different. The assumption issue and the
compromise are discussed in Elkins and McKitrick, *The Age of Federalism,* 146–61.

80. Ferguson, *Power of the Purse,* 335.

81. 1 Stat. 186 (August 12, 1790).

82. The activities of the Commission of the Sinking Fund, which was dominated by Hamilton, are described in White, *The Federalists,* 350–52.

83. The organization of the 1st Congress is explained in Charlene Bangs Bickford, "The First
Federal Congress Organizes Itself," in *Inventing America: Origins and Establishment of the First
Federal Congress,* ed. Kenneth R. Bowling and Donald R. Kenyon (Athens: Ohio State Univer-
sity Press, 1999), 138–65.

became bogged down in debates in the Senate over amendments intended to benefit regional interests. The cleavages that emerged in the debate over the impost were similar to those that would prevail for the next hundred years over tariff policy: northern manufacturing interests supported the impost, southerners objected, while New Englanders weighed the competing claims of import merchants and manufacturers. Nevertheless, a compromise measure was adopted by the 1st Congress on July 4 providing for a 5 percent duty and various excise taxes on such commodities as sugar, coffee, and tea.[84] These taxes raised approximately $2 million in 1789, a sum sufficient to operate the minimalist American state of the late eighteenth century but dwarfed by the national debt, which climbed to more than $70 million with the assumption of the state war debts the next year. By the conclusion of Washington's second term in office, federal receipts had risen to approximately $8 million annually, generating annual budget surpluses in the range of $2 million—a considerable improvement, but still insufficient to retire the war debt.[85] To strengthen the fiscal position of the national government, Federalists in Congress enacted at Hamilton's behest an elaborate system of internal taxes, including a carriage tax in 1794 as well as excise taxes on distilled alcohol (including whiskey), the manufacture of snuff, and the refining of sugar and sale of salt. An excise tax was imposed on investments and bonds, and high tariffs were levied on the importation of such luxuries as tea and coffee.[86] In 1797, Congress adopted a federal stamp tax—a highly ironic and revealing decision in light of the heated opposition by the colonists to the Stamp Act of 1765 enacted by Parliament.[87] The next year, in response to declining revenue from the tariff, Congress

---

84. For a description of this first tariff act, see Myers, *A Financial History of the United States,* 56–60; Dall W. Forsythe, *Taxation and Political Change in the Young Nation, 1781–1833* (New York: Columbia University Press, 1977), 63–64.

85. James D. Savage, *Balanced Budgets and American Politics* (Ithaca: Cornell University Press, 1988), 86–87.

86. Hamilton believed that government should avoid taxing the necessities of life and instead impose stiff taxes on such items as alcohol, tea, and coffee, which he viewed as "pernicious luxuries." Chan, *Aristotle and Hamilton on Commerce and Statesmanship,* 178–79.

87. The stamp tax was enacted pursuant to the Act of July 6, 1797, 1 Stat. 527 (5th Cong. 1st sess.). It was signed by President Adams on July 6, but was not effective until July 1, 1798. In 1799, the first full year of collection, the stamp tax raised $241,000, almost 25 percent of all internal revenue collected that year. See Charlotte Crane, "Some Possible Images of Federalism: The 1797 Stamp Act," unpublished paper delivered at conference on "Historical Perspectives on Tax Law and Policy," UCLA School of Law, UCLA, Los Angeles, California, July 16, 2007.

enacted the first direct tax imposed by the national government—an impost on land (including dwellings) and slaves.[88] Even with this direct tax, more than 90 percent of the revenue of the national government was derived from customs duties.

To collect the new Federalist internal taxes, the office of the Commissioner of Revenue had been created in 1792. The land tax enacted in 1797 required additional bureaucracy, as every house and all real estate in the nation needed to be assessed.[89] Under Hamilton's direction, the federal customs service was also organized. This agency was highly successful in carrying out its duties and served as an "impressive model of administrative efficiency."[90] Enforcement of both direct and indirect forms of taxation requires a vigorous government—something Hamilton knew all too well from his experience under the Confederacy. In turn, a vigorous government requires political leaders who are willing and able to enforce their policies by using the state's apparatus of coercion—that is, its armed forces. This Hamilton and his Federalist compatriots were quite willing to do.

The first serious test of the military capabilities of the new regime came in 1794 when farmers in North Carolina and western Pennsylvania rebelled against the collection of the excise tax on whiskey—the so-called Whiskey Rebellion.[91] Threatening to march on Pittsburgh, the

---

88. The so-called House Tax (officially known as "An Act to Provide for the Calculation of Lands and Dwelling Houses, and the Enumeration of Slaves within the United States") was enacted on July 9, 1798. It was the first direct tax enacted by Congress. While the states imposed direct taxes, the federal government had previously relied exclusively on indirect forms of taxation (i.e., tariffs and customs duties). Under the tax, dwellings were taxed at a rate of $0.10 per $100 of assessed value, with houses worth over $30,000 taxed at $1.00 per $100 of value and those worth less than $500 taxed at the rate of $.20 per $100 of value. Slaves were taxed at the rate of 50 cents each—regardless of age or sex, but exempting children, the aged, and the infirm. "Valuations of Land and Dwelling-houses and Enumeration of Slaves," Statutes at Large, ch. 70, July 9, 1798, 1:580–90. Debate over the tax is found in Annals of Congress of the United States, 5th Cong., 2nd sess., 8: 2049–55, 2058–61, 2172.

89. Legislation (the Direct Tax Act) providing additional bureaucracy to collect the House Tax was enacted on July 14, 1798. Assessors and their assistants were appointed by the treasury secretary as patronage positions.

90. Forsythe, *Taxation and Political Change*, 66. The efficiency of the customs service and the Treasury Department under Hamilton's reign is discussed in White, *The Federalists*, 507–16.

91. The standard history of the Whiskey Rebellion is Leland Baldwin, *Whiskey Rebels: The Story of a Frontier Uprising* (Pittsburgh: University of Pittsburgh Press, 1939). A more recent account is William Hogeland, *The Whiskey Rebellion: George Washington, Alexander Hamilton, and the Frontier Rebels Who Challenged America's Newfound Sovereignty* (New York: Scribner, 2006).

Pennsylvania farmers tarred and feathered local revenue collectors of the national government. Distillers refused to remit the tax. Hamilton favored a strong response from the outset.[92] After two years of patience in the face of rebellion, Washington finally responded in August 1794 by invoking martial law and calling up the militias of Pennsylvania and Virginia. There would be no replay of Shays' Rebellion under his watch. With Hamilton and General "Lighthorse Harry" Lee at his side, the president personally marched more than thirteen thousand militiamen and federal officers (an army larger than any he had commanded during the Revolutionary War) toward Pittsburgh in an overwhelming display of military force that smothered the rebellion in western Pennsylvania before it went any further. A state must be capable of enforcing its taxes and laws throughout its territory, and the Whiskey Rebellion gave Hamilton and his fellow Federalists the perfect opportunity to impress that essential message on the citizenry of the young republic.[93]

Notwithstanding the important Hamiltonian innovations in state structure and organization, the American state still possessed extraordinarily limited administrative capacity. Despite Federalist improvements to the military, the War Department consisted of just the secretary, six clerks, and various ordinance storehouses across the country.[94] In general, the central government exerted remarkably little control over the hinterlands.[95]

---

92. "My conviction is, that it is indispensable...to exert the full force of the law against the defenders, with every circumstance that can manifest the determination of government to enforce its execution....If this is not done, the spirit of disobedience will naturally extend, and the authority of the government will be prostrated." Alexander Hamilton quoted in Forsythe, *Taxation and Political Change,* 45.

93. Four years later, President Adams used the state militia and 500 men from the U.S. Army in eastern Pennsylvania against resistance to an internal tax on land and buildings. The so-called Fries's Rebellion (1799) was quickly suppressed and the leader, John Fries, sentenced to death for treason. He was later pardoned by Adams, which act of clemency deeply divided Federalists. The story of the rebellion is told in Paul Douglas Newman, *Fries's Rebellion: The Enduring Struggle for the American Revolution* (Philadelphia: University of Pennsylvania Press, 2004).

94. Kohn, *Eagle and Sword,* 290–91. The size of the bureaucracy of the War Department increased significantly between 1794 and 1789 under the Federalists; however, it was still tiny compared to those on the European Continent in the late eighteenth century.

95. The establishment of civil authority in the territories nominally under the jurisdiction of the new government commenced in 1787 when Congress enacted the Northwest Ordinance. A second territorial government was established south of the Ohio in 1790, and the Indiana Territory was created in 1800. The story of how the territorial government was implemented is told in White, *The Federalists,* 366–86.

Officials of the national government built a few roads, collected customs duties, maintained a basic military force, and delivered the mail with reasonable regularity, but did little else.[96] Like the states of medieval Europe, the eighteenth-century American state "lived lightly" off the land, extracting only minimal revenue from society to support itself. The revenue from the many taxes imposed by the national government in 1792 amounted to no more than 2 percent of GNP—"an extremely low tax burden for a central government in comparison with contemporary European standards."[97] The national government itself had a minor physical presence. In Philadelphia, the national government rented privately owned houses in which to conduct official business, while the president resided in the home of Robert Morris, which Washington complained was "inadequate to the commodious accommodation of my family."[98] In 1800, when the national government finally moved to its permanent capital, the physical plant of the American state remained negligible. The new City of Washington, erected along the banks of the Potomac River below Georgetown, was marked by empty boulevards, half-finished public buildings, few federal employees, and impassible streets.[99] Much of what had been built was destroyed by the British in 1812, and reconstruction was slow. What little existed hardly made for a capital worthy of the great nation that Hamilton

96. The Postal Service Act was signed by George Washington on February 20, 1792, establishing the Post Office Department. The statute provided the authority and means for a rapid expansion of the postal system from the Atlantic seaboard into the new western territories. This efficient national bureaucracy, which included a post office in nearly every local community, was completed by 1828. For a comprehensive study of the creation of the postal system and its impact on the development of the United States, see Richard R. John, *Spreading the News: The American Postal System from Franklin to Morse* (Cambridge: Harvard University Press 1995). The development of the "old postal regime" is the subject of Daniel P. Carpenter, *The Forging of Bureaucratic Autonomy: Reputations, Networks, and Policy Innovation in Executive Agencies, 1862–1928* (Princeton: Princeton University Press, 2001), 65–178.

97. Edwin J. Perkins, *American Public Finance and Financial Services, 1700–1815* (Columbus: Ohio State University Press, 1994), 232.

98. Quoted in White, *The Federalists,* 490. The Pennsylvania legislature approved funds for a residence for the executive, but it was not completed until Adams became president.

99. The haphazard planning and construction of the national's capital city in the early nineteenth century reflected the low esteem in which the government was held by the citizenry. See James Sterling Young, *The Washington Community, 1800–1828* (New York: Columbia University Press, 1966); see also Elkins and McKitrick, *The Age of Federalism,* 163–93. Young notes that the entire federal establishment (civilian and military) was comprised of only 9,237 persons in 1802, while the budget of the national government was only $7.8 million.

had envisioned, and the sorry physical condition of the city persisted for decades.[100] This was not a capital city befitting a great nation-state.

The politics of the period were similarly immature and undeveloped. The policies of Hamilton and the High Federalists quickly provoked the emergence of an opposition party. At the same time, the heated political battles over Hamilton's fiscal reforms (most particularly, protective tariffs) contributed to the fatal split within the Federalist ranks that led to the decisive defeat of Adams and the election of Jefferson in 1800, the collapse and virtual extinction of the Federalist Party by 1816, and the formation of a new national party system that would persist for decades. Overall, the American state that emerged during the ensuing decades of Republican hegemony more closely resembled Jefferson's vision of an agrarian republic than Hamilton's blueprint for a fiscal-military state modeled on Britain. Hamilton provided the design and inspiration to those who yearned for a powerful American state; notwithstanding his best efforts and important contributions, the forces of localism, states' rights, and limited government would prevail for another fifty years. The institutional legacy of decentralized federalism not only survived Hamilton's reign, it thrived in the era of Jeffersonian republicanism.

The Jeffersonian Republic

With Jefferson's election to the presidency in 1800 and the ascendance of the Republican Party, efforts by Federalists to establish a new political order came to an abrupt end. The new administration repealed the system of internal taxes erected by the Federalists, including the land tax and the despised excise tax on whiskey. The Jeffersonian republic was financed through a piecemeal system of customs duties, the sale of public lands, and

---

100. As late as 1842, an English visitor of renowned literary fame would eloquently describe the sorry state of the nation's capital: "It is sometimes called the City of Magnificent Distances, but it might with greater propriety be termed the City of Magnificent Intentions; for it is only on taking a bird's-eye view of it from the top of the Capitol, that one can at all comprehend the vast designs of its projector, an aspiring Frenchman. Spacious avenues, that begin in nothing, and lead nowhere; streets, mile-long, that only want houses, roads and inhabitants; public buildings that need but a public to be complete; and ornaments of great thoroughfares, which only lack great thoroughfares to ornament—are its leading features." Charles Dickens, *American Notes for General Circulation* (New York: J. Winchester, 1842), 21.

the tariff. As an impost on imported goods, the tariff was relatively easy to administer, requiring only control over the main points of entry into the country. That was important to Jefferson and the Republicans, who generally disliked a strong central government and the powers associated with it. The administrative capacity of a strong state is required to enforce internal taxes, especially an income tax, and because of this, such taxes were inimical to the Jeffersonian Republicans. Ironically, the protective tariff that they adopted is commonly associated with Hamilton's nationalist vision of manufacture, supposedly anathema to Jeffersonian republicanism.[101] But tariffs are enforceable through minimally intrusive means (i.e., a small number of customs agents in the major ports of entry), whereas the enforcement of internal taxes require a small army of assessors and tax collectors. During the 1790s, customs duties were imposed on a wide range of imported items at relatively low rates. Revenue from the tariff constituted about 90 percent of total federal revenue during this period.[102] Indeed, the tariff would be central to public finance throughout the nineteenth century. The Jeffersonian state relied on a minor tariff for its revenue. That revenue fluctuated in response to the vagaries of the economy, resulting in surpluses one year and deficits the next.[103]

During the Jeffersonian era, the states as well as the national government struggled to meet their financial commitments and obligations. The systems of taxation employed by the states, carryovers from the colonial period, were incapable of generating enough revenue to satisfy both current operations and fund the substantial debts they carried.[104] We know a good deal about the tax systems of the thirteen states from a report prepared

---

101. Hamilton's national economic plan is often erroneously associated with protectionism. His objective was to use economic incentives (e.g., subsidies) to stimulate key sectors of the economy rather than the protective tariffs that were common in the nineteenth century.

102. U.S. Bureau of the Census, *Historical Statistics of the United States: Colonial Times to 1970* (Washington, DC: U.S. Department of Commerce, 1975), series Y 352–257 ("Federal Government Receipts—Administrative Budget: 1789–1939"), part 2, 1106.

103. For a discussion of the failings of the tariff as a source of public revenue, see Roy G. Blakely and Gladys C. Blakely, *The Federal Income Tax* (New York: Longmans, Green, 1940), 2.

104. Even after assumption of their war debts, the states were burdened by debt. In 1787, Pennsylvania owed more than $1,845,000, while Virginia owed $2,766,000 in 1792. Figures from Ferguson, *Power of the Purse,* 180–81.

by the new treasury secretary, Oliver Wolcott, Jr.[105] In December 1796, in anticipation of establishing the national system of property taxation favored by the Federalists, Wolcott was directed by Congress to survey the various systems of taxation employed by the states. Congress's charge to Wolcott was to "report a plan for laying and collecting direct taxes by apportionment among the several states, agreeably to the rule prescribed by the constitution; adapting the same, as nearly as may be, to such objects of direct taxation, and such modes of collection, as may appear, by the laws and practices of the states, respectively, to be most eligible in each."[106] In the report Wolcott subsequently submitted to Congress, he provided a meticulous account of the laws and practices prevailing in the individual states and advised on the feasibility of retaining those state tax systems as the basis for an apportioned direct national tax on property. Ultimately, he weighed in against that option after concluding that the state tax systems were "utterly discordant and irreconcilable, in their original principles." Wolcott argued that to use the state tax systems as the basis for a federal tax would result in different taxation of the same things (persons and property) in different states. Even worse, it would again leave the national government dependent on the states to collect its taxes. As a good Federalist, Wolcott viewed such a system as little better than the system of requisitions that had "utterly failed under the late confederation."[107] This was precisely the system of taxation that the drafters of the Constitution of 1787 wished to repeal.

Were it not for the crushing burden of repaying the war debt, the traditional revenue sources of the national government would have been adequate to support its limited activities. Jefferson's secretary of treasury, Albert Gallatin, made great progress in reducing the national debt and increasing national reserves, even with the repeal of the internal taxes previously

---

105. Wolcott, a Connecticut Federalist, was appointed treasury secretary by Washington in February 1795 following Hamilton's sudden resignation. He was retained in office by Adams, but subsequently resigned in the wake of the Jefferson's landslide in the election of 1800.

106. Oliver Wolcott Jr., "Direct Taxes" (December 14, 1796), in Walter Lowrie and Matthew St. Clair Clark, comps., *American State Papers: Documents, Legislative, and Executive of the United States* (Washington, DC: Gales and Seaton, 1832–61), 3rd ser., Finance 1:414.

107. Wolcott, "Direct Taxes," 436–37. As previously noted, the Federalists enacted the national system of property taxation in July 1798. Wolcott's plan favored the taxation of land, while the 1798 tax was weighted toward the taxation of dwellings.

enacted by the Federalists.[108] By 1809, Gallatin managed to reduce the public debt to $57 million from the $83 million debt the Jeffersonians inherited when they took over the reins of government from the Federalists in 1801.[109] But the fiscal position of the national government took a sudden turn for the worse with the outbreak of the war with Britain in 1812.[110] The war strained the financial resources of the republic to the breaking point.

The military was not well prepared for the War of 1812. Under the Act of April 12, 1808, the authorized strength of the regular army (which stood at about 3,000 men during the Adams administration and Jefferson's first administration) had been increased to 9,921 men, but as of January 1812, only 5,260 men were on active duty.[111] The military lacked not only troops but supplies, officers, and professional staff. The entire administration of the U.S. Army was handled personally by the secretary of war, William Eustis, and the eight civilian clerks hired to assist him.[112] Once war was formally declared against Britain in June 1812, Congress enacted legislation authorizing an expansion of the army to 62,000 troops; however, the federal command was never able to muster anywhere near that number.[113] The maximum size of the U.S. Army during the war with Britain was reached in 1814 when 46,858 troops served on active duty under the command of 2,271 federal officers.[114] The vast majority of these were

108. For an account of Gallatin's fiscal policies, see Alexander Balinky, *Albert Gallatin: Fiscal Theories and Policies* (New Brunswick, NJ: Rutgers University Press, 1958).

109. U.S. Bureau of the Census, *Historical Statistics of the United States: Colonial Times to 1970,* series Y 335–338 ("Summary of Federal Government Finances—Administrative Budget: 1789–1939"), part 2, 1104.

110. The political wrangling prior to the War of 1812 and the crisis triggered by the conflict with Britain are described in Roger H. Brown, *The Republic in Peril: 1812* (New York: Columbia University Press, 1964); Richard Buel Jr., *Securing the Revolution: Ideology in American Politics, 1789–1815* (Ithaca: Cornell University Press, 1972).

111. Robert S. Quimby, *The U.S. Army in the War of 1812: An Operational and Command Study* (East Lansing: Michigan State University Press, 1997), 4. In 1794, the regular army had reached 5,800 men, but was reduced to 3,100 by 1796.

112. By the end of the War of 1812, the total number of civilian employees in the entire defense establishment was still only 190, including mechanics and other workmen in the army arsenals and navy yards. U.S. Bureau of the Census, *Historical Statistics of the United States: Colonial Times to 1970,* series Y 308–317 ("Paid Civilian Employment of the Federal Government, 1816 to 1970"), part 2, 1103.

113. Harry L. Coles, *The War of 1812* (Chicago: University of Chicago Press, 1965), 241.

114. Carter et al, eds., *Historical Statistics of the United States: Earliest Times to the Present* (New York: Cambridge University Press, 2006), table Ed26–47 ("Military Personnel on Active Duty, by Branch of Service and Sex: 1789–1995"), 5:5–354. The peak enrollment was in 1814. With

poorly trained volunteers contributed by the state militias, while the rest were "regulars" in the army. To supply and equip the troops, Congress enacted legislation authorizing $1 million for the regular army and another $1 million for the militiamen. Such emergency wartime expenses were initially financed through $5 million of public borrowing.

From the first, Gallatin realized that the revenue derived from the tariff and public borrowing would not be sufficient to finance a prolonged military conflict. Even prior to the outbreak of hostilities, Gallatin urged Congress to enact internal taxes (including excise taxes, a land tax, and even a stamp tax) and increase the tariff on imported goods in anticipation of the coming fiscal crisis, but his sound financial advice was rejected by his political opponents. With the formal declaration of war, it became clear even to the Jeffersonians in Congress that more money was needed than could be raised from borrowing or the tariff. During the first months of the war, the expenditures of the national government soared, while receipts declined. It is easy to see why expenditures soared as the military buildup commenced, but why did receipts decline? As a tax on imports, the tariff (the primary source of revenue for the national government) was particularly sensitive to levels of international trade, and the war itself caused a significant decline in receipts as foreign commerce declined. The effect was magnified because some 90 percent of foreign imports came from Britain, and that trade was cut off with the onset of the military conflict. The British naval blockade of the American coast caused receipts from the tariff to fall from $13 million in 1813 to $6 million in 1814.[115] In 1813, the national government had total revenue of $15 million, while expenditures exceeded $39 million. As a consequence, the national government ran large deficits during each year of the war, while the national debt soared from $45 million in 1811 to $127 million by 1815.[116]

---

most serving enlistments of less than six months, a large number of men passed through the service during the war with Britain. Mahon estimates that from 1812 to 1815, a total of 460,000 men served in the U.S. Army. John K. Mahon, *The War of 1812* (Gainesville: University of Florida Press, 1972), 384.

115. Jefferson imposed an embargo on foreign trade in 1808, and imports declined to one-fifth of what they had been in 1807. By 1814, imports and customs duties declined to one-tenth of the 1807 peak. Myers, *A Financial History of the United States*, 75–77.

116. U.S. Bureau of the Census, *Historical Statistics of the United States: Colonial Times to 1970*, series Y 335–338 ("Summary of Federal Government Finances—Administrative Budget: 1789–1939"), part 2, 1104.

The Jeffersonians generally wanted to fund the war deficit through borrowing, but new bank loans could not be obtained. Likewise, the Treasury Department was unable to raise any substantial revenue through the sale of long-term bonds. In response, Congress authorized the sale of $5 million of short-term Treasury notes. These notes were declared legal tender, and most were retired when used by note-holders for the payment of federal taxes. To finance the war effort, Gallatin again asked Congress to enact new internal taxes similar to those internal taxes of the Federalists that he had previously denounced in 1798. Initially Congress refused, forcing the national government to print paper money to keep the government operating. During the summer of 1813, Congress relented and enacted most of what Gallatin had requested the year before—taxes on land, dwellings, and slaves, as well as excise taxes on carriages, refined sugar, alcohol, and numerous other commodities (including a duty on imported salt).

Even with the revenue from these new taxes, the cost of the war continued to drain the government's reserves and undermine its financial position. As a last resort, Alexander J. Dallas, who replaced his friend Albert Gallatin as secretary of the treasury in 1813, recommended that Congress emulate the recent success of William Pitt the Younger, who as prime minister had implemented Britain's first income tax to finance its ongoing wars with France.[117] In January 1815, Dallas proposed what would have been the first national income tax in the United States to raise an additional $3 million for the war effort.[118] Later, he recommended a national inheritance tax. Had these two taxes been enacted, the fiscal foundation of the young republic might have been permanently fortified and the American state might have developed down a different path. As it was, the war with Britain ended in December 1815 before either proposal was taken up for consideration by Congress, and the national government returned to its

---

117. The income tax was enacted in 1799 and repealed in 1816 after the defeat of Napoleon's armies at Waterloo. For a summary of how Pitt introduced the income tax to Britain, see Margaret Levi, *Of Rule and Revenue* (Berkeley: University of California Press, 1988), 122–44; Edwin R. A. Seligman, *The Income Tax: A Study of the History, Theory, and Practice of Income Taxation at Home and Abroad* (New York: Macmillan, 1911), 57–115.

118. Dallas's proposal for a federal income tax and national inheritance tax is found in "Special Report on the State of the Finance, January 17, 1815," reprinted in *American State Papers* (Washington, DC: Gales and Seaton, 1832), 6:885–87.

traditional nineteenth-century sources of revenue—the tariff, excise taxes, and revenue from the occasional sale of public land.

With the return of peace, Republicans in Congress secured repeal of the internal taxes enacted during the war.[119] These were replaced with a system of indirect taxation of imports. With President Madison's approval, Treasury Secretary Dallas offered a proposal for a protective tariff that was adopted under the Tariff Act of 1816.[120] The new tariff regime served the federal government well for the next forty-five years. During this period, the tariff was the *only* federal tax and hence, was the principal source of revenue for the national government. Receipts from the tariff typically exceeded federal expenditures. When annual revenues came up short, the national government simply borrowed to make up the difference and usually repaid the money within a matter of years. From 1817 to 1857, the Treasury Department issued notes or borrowed fourteen times, always repaying such debts out of subsequent budget surpluses. This fiscal policy was facilitated by the chartering of the Second Bank of the United States in 1816 with $35 million in capital. Revenue from the tariff was supplemented by receipts from the sale of public land. These sales were sporadic and obviously not a replenishable source of revenue—although with the acquisition of 530 million acres pursuant to the Louisiana Purchase in 1803, it probably seemed as if the land would last forever. Land sales produced significant cash for the national government—$1 million in 1811, $4.9 million in 1834, $14.8 million in 1835, and the historic nineteenth-century peak of $24.9 million in 1836.[121] Accordingly, even with the repeal of the excise and property taxes enacted to finance the War of 1812, the national government was financially secure. By the time Andrew Jackson left

---

119. Republicans enacted a wide range of new excise taxes in 1815. These included duties on manufactured goods as well as an "annual duty" on watches and household furniture. These taxes are described in Robin L. Einhorn, *American Taxation, American Slavery* (Chicago: University of Chicago Press, 2006), 195–97.

120. The Tariff of 1816 was moderately protectionist, with exemptions or reduced rates for articles that could not be produced in the United States. The politics behind this legislation, which is generally considered to mark the beginning of protective tariff policy in the United States, is discussed in Forsythe, *Taxation and Political Change*, 68–72.

121. U.S. Bureau of the Census, *Historical Statistics of the United States: Colonial Times to 1970*, series Y 352–257 ("Federal Government Receipts—Administrative Budget: 1789–1939"), part 2, 1106.

the White House, the national debt was fully retired from surplus revenue derived from the tariff and customs duties.[122]

Notwithstanding the enormous revenue raised by the tariff, political resistance against the impost mounted. Southerners strongly opposed the Tariff of 1820 while public opinion in the North (led by New England textile interests) favored protection. Later, the infamous "Tariff of Abominations" of 1828 (a duty of nearly 50 percent on imported manufactured goods) provoked South Carolina to claim the power of nullification and threaten succession. Opposition throughout the South was strong. To resolve the crisis, the most offensive defects of the tariff were deleted by Congress in 1832, and the Compromise Tariff of 1833 reduced rates from an average of 33 percent to a uniform 20 percent.[123] Nevertheless, conflict over the tariff persisted for decades. Strife over tariff policy as well as the increasingly acrimonious debate over slavery and the nature of the relationship between the states and the national government undermined the stability of the antebellum political order. Ultimately, the conflict between these competing political and economic orders (North versus South) would be settled on the bloody battlefields of the Civil War. During that awesome military struggle as well as others that followed in the twentieth century, the political institutions and fiscal policy of the early American state were changed dramatically and permanently under the pressures of total war.

---

122. The national debt peaked at $127.3 million in 1816 following the War of 1812 and stood at $58.4 when Jackson took office in March 1829. Under fiscal policies pursued by Jackson's Treasury Department, the debt was retired as of January 1, 1835.

123. The definitive account of tariff policy from 1820 to 1860 remains F. W. Taussig, *The Tariff History of the United States: A Series of Essays* (New York: G. P. Putnam's Sons, 1894).

7

War and the Development of the American State

War is the parent of armies; from these proceed debts and taxes; and armies, and debts, and taxes are the known instruments for bringing the many under the domination of the few.

—James Madison, "Political Observations" (April 20, 1795)

The American state emerged from the wreckage of the Civil War. The state that early American nationalists had previously attempted to establish at the Constitutional Convention in 1787 had become a shell by 1860.... This antebellum government was not so much overthrown by the Civil War as rendered anachronistic.

—Richard Bensel, *Yankee Leviathan* (1990)

In the decades following the War of 1812, the United States experienced significant political change, although the American state itself remained a relatively weak political organization. To be sure, the *character* of the regime changed dramatically during this period. In antebellum America, the nascent party system that had first emerged with Jefferson's challenge to the Federalists and atrophied during the long period of Jeffersonian hegemony was revitalized by the election of Andrew Jackson in 1828. The so-called Age of Jackson was notable for the democratization of national political institutions and the emergence of a system of "spoils" (or patronage) and a functioning party system that provided a linkage between state and society.[1] Throughout his long political career, Martin Van Buren, secretary of state and vice president to Jackson prior to his own election to the presidency, orchestrated fundamental changes to the party system while at the same time clarifying the ideological differences between the Whigs and Democrats.[2] The institutionalization of political parties and electoral competition along with the emergence of democratic norms radically transformed the extant political order as the "rules of the game" were altered in fundamental ways.

In the early nineteenth century, national political leaders abandoned the highly restrictive reading of the Constitution advocated by Jefferson, who had argued that the national government lacked the constitutional authority to perform such basic functions as building roads and canals or establishing a national bank.[3] Under the tutelage of Whigs such as Henry Clay of Kentucky, political leaders embraced a more expansive reading of the constitutional powers delegated to Congress. Reflecting the emerging sentiment for a more active role for the national government, Congress inaugurated a program to distribute surplus revenue generated by the tariff to the local state governments to fund a program of internal improvements of Hamiltonian dimensions. The direct linkage between tariff revenue and internal improvements was central to Clay's so-called American System.[4]

---

1. The classic study of the Jacksonian era remains Arthur M. Schlesinger, Jr., *The Age of Jackson* (Boston: Little, Brown and Company, 1945). A recent comprehensive history of the transformation of American society between the War of 1812 and the Mexican War is Daniel Walker Howe, *What Hath God Wrought: The Transformation of America, 1815–1848* (New York: Oxford University Press, 2007).

2. Van Buren was a major figure in American politics in the first half of the nineteenth century but today is generally unappreciated. Joel Sibley refers to the Sly Fox of Kinderhook as "a transforming political figure in American history, a persistent and innovative practitioner of a new style of American politics." Joel H. Sibley, *Martin Van Buren and the Emergence of American Popular Politics* (Lanham, Md.: Rowman and Littlefield, 2002), xii.

3. When convenient, Jefferson invoked a broad reading of the constitutional powers of the president—for instance, when he acquired the vast Louisiana territory in 1803. Oddly, the purchase was opposed by many Federalists. The basis for Federalist opposition is explained in Richard Buel Jr., *Securing the Revolution: Ideology in American Politics, 1789–1815* (Ithaca: Cornell University Press, 1972), 266; Roger H. Brown, *The Republic in Peril: 1812* (New York: Columbia University Press, 1964), 159–61. Likewise, Jefferson read his constitutional powers broadly when he signed legislation in March 1802 creating the national military academy at West Point. As secretary of state, he had previously argued that Washington lacked authority to create just such an institution in the absence of specific authorization in the Constitution.

4. The specifics of Clay's plan for internal improvements are recounted in Maurice G. Baxter, *Henry Clay and the American System* (Lexington: University Press of Kentucky, 1995).

In an address to Congress as speaker of the House, Clay (a former Jeffersonian Republican who became a strong proponent of the tariff and internal improvements) extolled the virtues of the arrangement: "Of all modes in which a government can employ its surplus revenue, none is more permanently beneficial than that of internal improvements."[5] As Clay envisioned it, the national government would use its coercive powers to extract revenue from society via the tariff, at once raising public funds for internal improvements and simultaneously providing protection from foreign competition for nascent American industries. In this system of internal improvements, institutional development would be linked to, and dependent on, the American state's capacity for revenue extraction through indirect taxation.

Jefferson's own secretary of the treasury, Albert Gallatin, proposed a series of public improvement projects to be implemented by the national government. Gallatin's *Report on the Subject of Public Roads and Canals* (1808) offered a detailed plan for the construction of a network of national roads to link the East Coast and inland cities such as Detroit and St. Louis as well as an extensive system of canals and improvements to rivers to create a navigable waterway running from Massachusetts to North Carolina.[6] These projects, along with a number of lesser internal improvements, were estimated by Gallatin to cost more than $20 million and would be funded entirely by surplus revenue from the tariff. But Gallatin's ambitious plan was never implemented, as the War of 1812 put a halt to such endeavors. After the war, the mood shifted again, with James Madison vetoing legislation providing federal funding for internal improvements (the so-called Bonus Bill) in the final days of his presidency in March 1817.[7] Andrew

---

5. Henry Clay's 1818 speech to Congress is reprinted in William Letwin, ed., *A Documentary History of American Economic Policy Since 1789* (New York: W. W. Norton, 1972), 64. James Savage argues that Whigs such as Clay and Daniel Webster were savvy enough to realize that their only chance to fund a program of internal improvements was out of surplus funds, rather than through deficit spending. James D. Savage, *Balanced Budgets and American Politics* (Ithaca: Cornell University Press, 1988), 112.

6. United States Department of the Treasury, *Report of the Secretary of the Treasury, on the Subject of Public Roads and Canals, Made in Pursuance of a Resolution of Senate, of March 2, 1808* (Washington, DC: R. C. Weightman, 1808). Gallatin's plan is outlined in John Lauritz Larson, *Internal Improvement: National Public Works and the Promise of Popular Government in the Early United States* (Chapel Hill: University of North Carolina Press, 2001), 59–63.

7. "Veto Message of James Madison" (March 3, 1817), in *Veto Messages of the Presidents of the United States with the Action of Congress Thereon* (Washington, DC: Government Printing Office,

Jackson followed suit in 1830 with his own notorious veto of federal funding for a proposed national road linking the Ohio River to Lexington, Kentucky (the so-called Maysville Road). In his veto message, Jackson refused funds for the project on the traditional Jeffersonian grounds that the road was "purely of local character" (as it was located entirely within one state) and because he wished to "keep the movements of the Federal Government within the sphere intended" and curtail the "abuses of the powers of the Federal Government in regard to internal improvements."[8] Jackson followed up with vetoes of several lesser projects. Nevertheless, the fact that Congress was willing and able to pay for these internal improvements reveals much about the improved financial condition of the American state in the early nineteenth century. That it was private for-profit companies chartered by the state legislatures that built most of the roads and canals in the 1830s and the railroads in subsequent decades reveals even more about the limitations imposed on national political leaders by the decentralized federal system inherited from the Constitutional Convention of 1787.[9] After all, the national government had no administrative agencies or civilian employees of its own to build roads, canals, or railroads, while the states had the infrastructure but lacked the capital and manpower to carry off such themselves.[10] The national government would function as a

---

1886), 16–18. Despite previously approving appropriations for a National Road linking Baltimore and St. Louis, Madison called for a constitutional amendment authorizing federal contributions for internal improvements. Like Jefferson, he opposed stretching the interstate commerce clause to sanction federal support for building local roads and canals. The politics behind Madison's unexpected veto of the Bonus Bill are discussed in Larson, *Internal Improvement*, 67–69; Howe, *What Hath God Wrought*, 86–88.

8. "Veto Message of President Andrew Jackson" (May 27, 1830), in *A Compilation of the Messages and Papers of the Presidents, 1789–1897* (Washington, DC: Government Printing Office, 1896), 487. Like Madison before him, Jackson argued in his veto message that a constitutional amendment was necessary to give the national government the authority to construct internal improvements: "If it be the wish of the people that the construction of roads and canals should be conducted by the Federal Government, it is not only highly expedient, but indispensably necessary, that a previous amendment of the Constitution, delegating the necessary power and defining and restricting its exercise with reference to the sovereignty of the States, should be made."

9. For an account of the political issues relating to internal improvements and the role of the national government in promoting these, see Carter Goodrich, *Government Promotion of American Canals and Railroads, 1800–1890* (New York: Columbia University Press, 1960).

10. From 1816 to 1841, the federal civilian work force remained small, with anywhere from 69 percent to 79 percent consisting of postal officers. Richard R. John, *Spreading the News: The American Postal System from Franklin to Morse* (Cambridge: Harvard University Press 1995), table 1.1 ("Postmasters in the federal civilian work force, 1816–1841"), 3.

promoter of internal improvements, facilitating investment while leaving the work to private companies.[11]

After the signing of the Treaty of Ghent, which officially ended the War of 1812, the United States enjoyed a period of sustained peace and prosperity for more than thirty years. During this period, a good deal of the national military was again demobilized. The size of the U.S. Army (regulars and volunteer state militiamen) fluctuated between 5,600 and 11,000 men throughout the 1820s and 1830s. This was a minimalist force, with only 0.05 percent of the population of 15 million serving in the army in 1835.[12] Still the primary function of the federal government remained national defense, which accounted for 72 to 90 percent of total outlays of the national government in all but one year from 1808 to 1848.[13] The army was used mostly to suppress the occasional slave rebellion and pacify hostile Indian populations in the western territories.

The situation changed dramatically in April 1846 when war broke out with Mexico. The army was quickly bolstered by volunteers and reserves, ultimately reaching more than 60,000 men in uniform at the height of the conflict in 1848.[14] The number of federal officers was increased from 637 men immediately prior to the outbreak of war to 1,016 by 1848.[15] As a result of the sudden expansion of the military during the Mexican War, spending by the national government soared. Expenditures increased from $23 million in 1845 (when the national government enjoyed a $7 million surplus) to more than $57 million in 1847 (when the government ran a deficit of

---

11. In his account of economic development in Pennsylvania, Louis Hartz referred to such quasi-public works projects as reflecting a theory of "mixed enterprise." Louis Hartz, *Economic Policy and Democratic Thought: Pennsylvania, 1776–1860* (Cambridge: Harvard University Press, 1948), 289–302; see also Richard R. John, "Governmental Institutions as Agents of Change: Rethinking Political Development in the Early American Republic, 1787–1835," *Studies in American Political Development* 11 (fall 1997): 347–80.

12. George Q. Flynn, *The Draft, 1940–1973* (Lawrence: University of Kansas Press, 1993), 5.

13. Figures from Ira Katznelson, "Flexible Capacity: The Military and Early American State-building," in *Shaped by War and Trade: International Influences on American Political Development,* ed. Ira Katznelson and Martin Shefter (Princeton: Princeton University Press, 2002), 91.

14. Jack Bauer, *The Mexican War* (New York: MacMillan, 1974), 397. Justin Smith estimates that nearly 90,000 soldiers served during the Mexican War from 1846 to 1848, the majority of them volunteers who served relatively short enrollments. Justin H. Smith, *The War with Mexico* (New York: MacMillan, 1919), 2:318–19.

15. Carter et al., eds., *Historical Statistics of the United States,* vol. 5, table Ed26–47 ("Military Personnel on Active Duty, by Branch of Service and Sex: 1789–1995"), 5–354.

$30.7 million). Public debt jumped from a modest $16 million in 1845 to more than $63 million by the end of the war.[16] Despite this, the traditional nineteenth-century revenue system of the national government (the tariff, excise taxes, and revenue from the sale of public lands) was adequate to fund spending attributable to the war effort. Notably, the expansion of the military during the Mexican War was financed by the Polk administration entirely out of surplus revenue generated by the tariff and limited public borrowing, without recourse to tariff increases or new internal taxes.[17] This was a "limited war" that did not necessitate a full mobilization of manpower or societal wealth and, accordingly, had only a minor impact on institutional development. Following the conflict, budget surpluses were realized for eight straight years as the size of the military and spending by the national government were reduced to prewar levels. From 1848 to the Civil War, approximately 50 percent of total federal expenditures was consistently dedicated to military purposes.

During the 1840s, the political institutions that had emerged during the Jacksonian era remained relatively stable, this despite the intensity of partisan politics; however, the antebellum political order was gradually destabilized by the escalating controversy over the role of the national government in restricting slavery in the western territories. External military threats to the United States subsided following the war with Mexico, permitting long-standing "internal tensions" pertaining to slavery and states' rights to reemerge as divisive issues in the domestic political arena, thereby undermining "internal cohesion."[18] With the election of Abraham Lincoln in 1860 and the ascendance of the Republican Party in the North, those internal tensions erupted into overt hostilities as the political order that had prevailed during the first half of the nineteenth century suddenly and

---

16. Figures from U.S. Bureau of the Census, *Historical Statistics of the United States: Colonial Times to 1970* (Washington, DC: U.S. Department of Commerce, 1975), series Y 335–338 ("Summary of Federal Government Finances—Administrative Budget: 1789–1939"), part 2, 1104.

17. W. Elliot. Brownlee, *Federal Taxation in America: A Short History* (New York: Cambridge University Press, 1996), 22.

18. The importance of external military threats in creating "internal cohesion" is discussed in Michael C. Desch, "War and Strong States, Peace and Weak States?" *International Organization* 50 (spring 1996): 248. Desch argues that as external threats subsided during the 1850s, internal cohesion diminished and "internal tensions" over such divisive issues as slavery and states' rights, suppressed during the 1840s, reemerged with devastating consequences.

dramatically collapsed. The survival of the Union itself was imperiled by the secessionist movement that burst into armed conflict in the spring of 1861.[19] The four years of "total war" that ensued produced the most profound changes to the political order and national political institutions experienced in the history of the republic.[20]

Out of the chaos and terrible destruction of the Civil War, a powerful nation-state arose in North America. As James McPherson so eloquently put it: "The United States went to war in 1861 to preserve the *Union;* it emerged from war in 1865 having created a *nation.*"[21] At the height of the conflict, the American state possessed the largest and best equipped standing army in the world. This military colossus was financed by a robust system of revenue extraction buttressed by a sophisticated system of public borrowing. This "Yankee Leviathan" (as Richard Bensel calls it) was the belated fulfillment of Alexander Hamilton's vision of an American fiscal-military state modeled on eighteenth-century England. While the strong state created by the Republican Party would not long outlast the triumph of the Union armies, it left behind an institutional legacy that permanently altered the political order and economic institutions of nineteenth-century America. Most important, we can discern a direct connection between war, revenue, and state development during the period of intense state building that lasted from 1861 to 1865.

---

19. The forces that led to the secessionist movement are traced in William W. Freehling's authoritative studies, *The Road to Disunion,* vol. 1, *Secessionists at Bay, 1776–1854* (Oxford University Press, 1990); *The Road to Disunion,* vol. 2, *Secessionists Triumphant, 1854–1861* (Oxford University Press, 2007).

20. Whether the American Civil War was a "total war" is a matter of contention. Historians commonly referred to it as such until the publication of Mark E. Neely Jr., "Was the Civil War a Total War?" *Civil War History* 37 (March 1991): 5–28; see also Neely, *The Civil War and the Limits of Destruction* (Cambridge: Harvard University Press, 2007). Neely argues that in a total war, no distinction is made between civilians and soldiers. Notwithstanding the atrocities committed by both sides, such a distinction was generally preserved during the course of the conflict. Accepting this argument, many historians now refer to the Civil War as a "hard war." Still, based on the death, destruction, size of the armies, and extent of the mobilization of social resources, this was a total war. For a discussion of the issue, see James M. McPherson, "Was It More Restrained Than You Think?" *The New York Review of Books* 55 (February 14, 2008): 42.

21. James M. McPherson, *Abraham Lincoln and the Second American Revolution* (New York: Oxford University Press, 1990), viii.

Building a Fiscal-Military State

With the outbreak of armed hostilities in South Carolina on April 12, 1861, the national government in Washington immediately set about raising a large standing army under the command of the new Republican president. The day after the surrender of the federal garrison at Fort Sumter, Lincoln requested 75,000 volunteer state militiamen to serve under the scant 800 officers who remained in the federal army after the insurrection began.[22] The ranks of the U.S. Army swelled from 16,000 men in uniform in January 1861 (immediately prior to the outbreak of armed hostilities) to more than 700,000 soldiers by the end of 1861.[23] That was just the beginning of a vast mobilization of manpower. An estimated 2.1 million men served in the Union armies during the Civil War, with just over 1 million on active duty at the peak of the conflict in 1865.[24] During the same period, an estimated 600,000 to 750,000 men served in the military forces of the Confederate States of America.[25] The great armies that fought on the battlefields of the Civil War dwarfed those under Washington's command during the Revolutionary War as well as those that fought in the War of 1812 and the Mexican War. Raising such a large professional military required a wartime mobilization of the civilian population comparable to that undertaken during the Revolutionary War.[26] Some 37 percent of males in the North between the ages of fifteen and forty-four served

---

22. In January 1861, there were 1,098 commissioned officers in the U.S. Army, but 296 resigned their commissions and joined the Confederate forces when war broke out in April. Of these, 187 were graduates of West Point—Robert E. Lee being the most famous. E. B. Long, *The Civil War Day by Day: An Almanac, 1861–1865* (Garden City, NY: Doubleday, 1971), 709; Mark Mayo Boatner III, *The Civil War Dictionary* (New York: McKay, 1988), 495, 858.

23. Fred Albert Shannon, *The Organization and Administration of the Union Army, 1861–1865* (Cleveland: Arthur H. Clark, 1928), 27.

24. At the peak of the conflict in 1865, there were more than 1.062 million men in the Union army. Carter et al., eds., *Historical Statistics of the United States*, vol. 5, table Ed26–47 ("Military Personnel on Active Duty, by Branch of Service and Sex: 1789–1995"), 5–354.

25. Long, *Civil War Day by Day*, 705.

26. An estimated 9.8 percent of the population participated in the Civil War versus 10.4 percent during the Revolutionary War. Hugh Rockoff, "Veterans," in *Historical Statistics of the United States*, ed. Carter et al., 5–342. From 1860 to 1865, the population jumped from 31.5 million to 35.7 million. U.S. Bureau of the Census, *Historical Statistics of the United States*, series A 6–8 ("Annual Population Estimates of the United States: 1790 to 1970"), part 1, 8.

in the Union army during the course of the war.[27] Not surprisingly, there was a comparable increase in the size of the civilian bureaucracy of the national government. In January 1861, there were 2,199 federal employees in the capital city of Washington (compared to 1,533 in 1851). During the course of the Civil War, that contingent would nearly triple in size, while the size of the entire civilian bureaucracy of the national government swelled to nearly 50,000 employees.[28]

This rapid expansion of the federal army and the civilian bureaucracy, along with the enormous expenses incurred in mobilizing, equipping, and supplying the troops, resulted in an unprecedented increase in government spending. Expenditures of the national government soared from less than 2 percent of gross national product in the years immediately prior to 1860 to an average of 15 percent from 1861 to 1865.[29] During this period, the Union government spent an estimated $1.8 billion (in 1860 dollars) on the war effort.[30] Total outlays of the national government rapidly increased from $66.5 million in 1861 to $475 million in 1862 to nearly $1.3 billion in 1865.[31] The extraordinary explosion in governmental spending severely strained the reserves of the U.S. Treasury, resulting in an accumulated national debt of $2.7 billion by 1866.[32]

---

27. Theda Skocpol, *Protecting Soldiers and Mothers: The Political Origins of Social Policy in the United States* (Cambridge, MA: Belknap Press of Harvard University Press, 1992), 586, n5.

28. U.S. Bureau of the Census, *Historical Statistics of the United States,* series Y 308–317 ("Paid Civilian Employment of the Federal Government, 1816 to 1970"), part 2, 1103. Of the almost 50,000 civilians employed by the national government by the end of the Civil War, nearly 60 percent worked for the Post Office.

29. Brownlee, *Federal Taxation in America,* 23. By way of comparison, federal spending as a percentage of gross domestic product (GDP) dipped below 20 percent in the late 1990s for only the first time since the early 1970s.

30. Estimates of the economic cost of the Civil War vary greatly. Goldin and Lewis start with the known direct expenditures of the Union government for the war effort. These were $1.8 billion, with the states spending another $486 million. Also included are the loss of human capital and costs attributable to the draft. They estimate that the total direct cost of the Civil War to the North was $3.37 billion (in 1860 dollars). Claudia D. Goldin and Frank D. Lewis, "The Economic Cost of the American Civil War: Estimates and Implications," *Journal of Economic History* 35 (1970): 299–326.

31. U.S. Bureau of the Census, *Historical Statistics of the United States,* series Y 457–465 ("Outlays of the Federal Government: 1789–1970"), part 2, 1114.

32. U.S. Bureau of the Census, *Historical Statistics of the United States,* series Y 493–504 ("Public Debt of the Federal Government: 1791–1970"), part 2, 1118. In his Annual Message to Congress in December 1864, Lincoln downplayed the national debt, which stood at $1.74 billion as of July 1, 1863, by suggesting that since the debt was widely held, it was really a debt that citizens "owe to

From 1814 to 1861, the tariff was the primary source of federal revenue, generating more than 90 percent of the receipts of the national government, with the balance derived from customs duties, an assortment of federal excise taxes, and revenue from the sale of public lands. During this period, the traditional system of revenue financed a government of limited powers and functions. But the shortcomings of the revenue system became evident during periods of war, when imports and trade with foreign markets declined, thereby reducing public revenue precisely when the state needs it most. This occurred during the war with Britain in 1812 (although not in 1846, given the limited scope of the war with Mexico) and then again in 1861 when the Civil War broke out. This compelled the Union government to adopt a new revenue strategy to raise additional funds for the military campaign. As such, the Civil War was a stimulus for institutional innovation as well as an unprecedented expansion of the American state—both its military apparatus and its capacity for revenue extraction. The period of total war that lasted from 1861 to 1865 was a "crisis situation" that triggered an unprecedented growth of the state apparatus, greater penetration of society and the economy, and the adoption of a more aggressive system of revenue extraction. The Civil War was a watershed event in the history of the development of the American state.

In his definitive interpretation of the expansion of the authority and apparatus of the American state during the Civil War, Richard Bensel explains how political leaders in the North mobilized resources and built a new state apparatus in response to the secessionist challenge.[33] To be sure, the political leaders of the Confederate States of America faced an even greater challenge in building a new central state virtually from scratch. Ironically, the Confederacy employed a more statist approach in mobilizing societal resources than the Union, this notwithstanding a strong aversion to centralized political authority rooted in the South's commitment to state's rights and opposition to the transfer of local powers to the national government. In contrast to the statist approach employed by the Confederacy, the North relied primarily on market mechanisms and contracting with

---

themselves." Abraham Lincoln, "Annual Message to Congress" (December 6, 1864), in *Speeches and Writings 1859–1865* (New York: Library of America, 1989), 651–52.

33. Richard F. Bensel, *Yankee Leviathan: The Origins of Central State Authority in America, 1859–1877* (New York: Cambridge University Press, 1990).

private parties to supply their troops. In prior military engagements in the nineteenth century, military procurement had been a joint function of the national government and the states, with the state governments taking the initiative in arming and provisioning their volunteers and then turning to the national government for financial reimbursement for their expenses. During the first weeks of the Civil War, a similar arrangement spontaneously emerged. This was codified on July 27, 1861, when Lincoln signed into law an "indemnification act" providing that the national government would reimburse the states for "expenses properly incurred" in supplying, arming, and paying their troops.[34] Throughout 1861, however, federal officers took control of the state procurement offices and gradually assumed their functions. By early 1862, the North's procurement system was fully centralized under the command of a powerful new federal bureaucracy, the Quartermaster's Department of the U.S. Army, which purchased military supplies by entering into contracts with private manufacturers and suppliers. In his study of the Union procurement system, Mark Wilson argues that the creation of this national "military economy" in the North (i.e., the purchasing system under the Quartermaster's Department) had a lasting impact on the development of the American state.[35] The Quartermaster's Department was a professionalized administrative agency that, unlike other national political institutions, functioned largely outside the pressures of partisan politics and the patronage system, and as such, served as a model for would-be reformers of the American state later in the century.

As with military procurement, the South employed a more statist approach to the mobilization of manpower for the war effort than the Union government. The first military draft in American history was enacted by the Southern Confederacy in April 1862, predating by more than a year the conscription act passed by the Union government in March 1863.[36] Arguably, the Confederacy turned to conscription first because it lacked the economic resources of the North, which were used in the early years of the war to pay high bounties and monthly compensation to induce volunteers to join

---

34. Indemnity Act, July 27, 1861, ch. 21, 12 Stat. 276.

35. Mark R. Wilson, *The Business of the Civil War: Military Mobilization and the State, 1861–1865* (Baltimore: The Johns Hopkins University Press, 2006).

36. No fewer than five states in the North already had their own conscription laws in place by the fall of 1862. For an account of the enactment of the Union draft, see James W. Geary, *We Need Men: The Union Draft in the Civil War* (DeKalb: Northern Illinois University Press, 1991).

the armed forces.[37] Not only did the Confederacy adopt a draft before the Union government, it was more ruthless and unforgiving in the enforcement of its conscription policies. Overall, the Confederate state was a stronger state at the height of the war than the Union government as measured by the traditional indices of stateness: penetration of society, centralization of authority, control over persons within the territory of the state, and the capacity to appropriate resources from society. A state as strong as the Confederacy would not be seen again in America for more than seventy years. The fatal weakness of the Confederacy was its system of revenue extraction. The Confederacy enacted a tariff in 1861, but that impost failed to raise significant revenue. A direct tax of 0.5 percent on real and personal property was tried, but this too proved ineffective as the state governments, which were required to enforce the tax, were negligent in their collections. This forced the Davis administration to print more than $1.5 billion in Confederate notes to finance the war. The value of these notes declined significantly as inflation soared, forcing the Confederacy to appropriate private property for the war effort.

In the North, the strong state that emerged during the Civil War was a strikingly different political organization than the antebellum state from which it had evolved. The burst of state building and institutional innovation during the opening years of the conflict proved critical to the success of the Union in the military struggle against the Confederacy. With the victory of the Republican Party in the critical election of 1860 and the hasty departure of Southern Democrats from Congress the following spring, the Republican coalition that took control of the American state was free to restructure national political institutions without partisan opposition. To a greater extent than during any other period in American history (with the possible exception of the New Deal of the 1930s), state and party merged in the political institutions of the Union government. The culmination of Republican hegemony would be the campaign to remake society in the conquered South during the period of Reconstruction following the war, but before that, the "capture" of the national government by the Republican

---

37. Eugene C. Murdock, *One Million Men: The Civil War Draft in the North* (Madison: The State Historical Society of Wisconsin, 1971), 5, 24. Murdock calculates that the Union government in Washington paid out $300 million in bounties. This was in addition to an estimated $286 million in bounties paid by the northern states to meet their recruitment quotas.

Party produced a dramatic transformation of the political ideology, political order, and institutional apparatus of the national government in the North.

The Civil War brought a broad expansion of state authority as well as the triumph of the Republican Party's nationalist vision of political economy. Pursuant to the latter, the central state (firmly under the control of Republican nationalists) would, in Bensel's telling words, "sweep aside regional and local barriers to the development of a national capitalist market and directly assist in the construction of the physical and financial infrastructure necessary for that market."[38] The radical restructuring of the American economy during the Civil War was furthered by the Union government as it established a national currency, placed a large portion of the national debt with a new class of private finance capitalists, created a national banking system that superseded the state banks, taxed out of existence the notes of the local state-chartered banks that virtually functioned as currency, took the nation off the gold standard, and adopted paper money (the "Greenback") as legal tender.[39] In the face of relentless pressure to raise revenue for the war effort, political leaders turned to new forms of taxation that had been long resisted by powerful social and economic interests. By bolstering the state's capacity for revenue extraction and its capacity to borrow large amounts of money through the private capital markets, Republicans in the North permanently transformed the fiscal foundations of the American state. A comparable story of "revenue predation" (Margaret Levi's term) unfolded in the South, where the leaders of the Confederacy wielded all of the vast coercive powers of that political organization to marshal societal resources for the military campaign they waged.

A New Revenue Strategy for the Union Government

How did the leaders of the Union government secure new sources of revenue in response to the financial crisis resulting from the extraordinary

---

38. Bensel, *Yankee Leviathan,* 11.

39. The Greenback was authorized under the Legal Tender Act of 1862, portions of which were held unconstitutional by the Supreme Court in *Hepburn v. Griswold,* 75 U.S. 603 (1870). The court later reversed itself in a series of decisions known as the Legal Tender cases. The cases, the court's holding, and the coinage clause of the Constitution are discussed in Robert G. Natelson, "Paper Money and the Original Understanding of the Coinage Clause," *Harvard Journal of Law and Public Policy* 31 (summer 2008): 1017–82.

expansion of the state's administrative capacity and military apparatus during the Civil War? From the beginning, officials recognized that they faced an unprecedented demand for public revenue. The financial position of the national government was already in a weakened condition before the war broke out, having suffered two successive deficits following the Panic of 1857.[40] The government then ran a deficit of $50 million in 1860, further depleting the reserves of the Treasury. In the face of the impending military conflict, political leaders initially responded to the government's deteriorating financial position in the usual fashion—by bolstering the existing system of public revenue. This meant raising customs duties and tariff rates. In early 1861, Congress enacted the Morrill Tariff Act, which revised the Tariff of 1857 by broadly increasing rates on imported goods.[41] Named after its principal sponsor, Representative Justin Morrill of Vermont, an abolitionist who was one of the founders of the Republican Party in Vermont and an influential member of the Ways and Means Committee, the legislation was signed into law by the lame-duck Democratic president, James Buchanan, shortly before leaving office. This was the first of three increases to the tariff enacted during the Civil War. The Tariff Act of July 14, 1862, increased duties on certain manufactured goods. Subsequently, the Tariff Act of 1864 would impose duties that reached almost half of the total value of dutiable imports.[42] By 1865, the *average* rate of tax on dutiable imports soared to 48 percent.[43] The 1861 legislation marked the beginning of more than fifty years of continuous trade-protection policy implemented through the tariff. Even with steep increases in tariff rates, the Union government faced a $75 million deficit by the close of 1861, as receipts lagged behind the soaring military expenditures. Political leaders

---

40. The Panic of 1857 began in August with the failure of the Ohio Life Insurance and Trust Company, which led to the suspension of nearly all the major banks of New York. For a brief history of the financial crisis of 1857, see Margaret G. Myers, *A Financial History of the United States* (New York: Columbia University Press, 1970), 126–28, 138–40.

41. The Morrill Tariff Act passed the House during the 1859–60 session, but consideration by the Senate was postponed until the next session—after Lincoln's election. It then passed the Senate without material change. The most important changes implemented by the 1861 tariff were increased duties on iron and wool. For a description of the politics behind the Morrill Tariff Act, see F. W. Taussig, *The Tariff History of the United States: A Series of Essays* (New York: G. P. Putnam's Sons, 1894), 158–59.

42. Brownlee, *Federal Taxation in America*, 24.

43. Myers, *A Financial History of the United States*, 160.

quickly recognized that they needed to adopt an even more aggressive wartime revenue strategy or risk financial disaster.

Soon after Lincoln took office on March 4, 1861, he appointed Senator Salmon Chase of Ohio as his secretary of the treasury. Chase believed that the expansion of the Union army should be funded in the long-term through a combination of rate-increases for the tariff and excise taxes, expanded sales of public lands, and new public borrowing effected through the sale of long-term debt instruments by the Treasury. In the short-run, however, borrowing was the only way to rapidly raise funds for the war effort. In furtherance of that objective, Chase traveled to New York later that summer to meet with representatives of several large private banks. These banks would play a prominent role in selling Treasury debt instruments to private investors, beginning with an issue of $150 million of Treasury bonds that were placed with a syndicate of banks from New York, Boston, and Philadelphia. These sales of government debt instruments marked the emergence of a sophisticated new system of public borrowing arising out of a newly formed relationship between the state and private financial capitalists. The interests of creditor-financiers were now aligned with those of the American state based on their mutual interest in the survival of the national government to which they had loaned vast amounts of money during the war.[44]

With the outbreak of war, Lincoln, beleaguered Treasury officials, and the Republican leadership of Congress embarked on a campaign for a comprehensive restructuring of the fiscal powers of the American state. The lame-duck Thirty-sixth Congress had enacted an emergency measure authorizing a new issue of $25 million in twenty-year bonds. In April 1861, with the new Republican majority taking control of the national government, Secretary Chase proposed the sale of Treasury bonds and notes to raise another $15 million of revenue.[45] Despite this, Republicans recognized that borrowing alone would not be adequate to finance the war effort; new imposts would be required. When Congress reconvened on July 4, 1861, the Republican leadership took up the painful and difficult task of

---

44. As Bensel puts it, based on their loans to the Union government, the financiers were "brought into a clientele relationship with the state." Bensel, *Yankee Leviathan,* 163.

45. For a summary of Treasury borrowing during the first year of the Civil War, see Myers, *Financial History of the United States,* 149–53.

enacting new taxes—a task all the more difficult in a political system such as that of the United States, in which all the powerful economic interests of society are represented in the legislative branch of government. In such a political system of representative government, the business of enacting taxes becomes what Thomas S. Adams referred to as "a group contest in which powerful interests vigorously endeavor to rid themselves of present or proposed tax burdens."[46] The "contest" began in earnest when Chase proposed $20 million in new direct taxes, internal duties, and excise taxes. In response, Congress approved a direct tax of $20 million to be levied among the states in proportion to their populations—$15 million to the loyal states and $5 million to the states that had seceded. The latter allocation proved uncollectable as the southern states were already beyond the grasp of the Treasury Department.

Thaddeus Stevens of Pennsylvania, the powerful chairman of the House Ways and Means Committee, responded to the government's initiative with his own proposal for a direct national land tax to be allocated among the states based on population. This immediately provoked objections from representatives of western states, where agricultural interests were predominant and land abundant. In defense of his proposal, Stevens justified the "disagreeable" aspects of the proposed land tax by virtue of the need to "sustain the Government" against the attacks by the "rebels, who are now destroying or attempting to destroy this Government." He defended the revenue package as necessary in light of the Union's war effort, suggesting that "the annihilation of the Government is the alternative."[47] This was no exaggeration; the survival of the Union certainly was at stake,

---

46. In his 1927 presidential address to the Annual Meeting of the American Economic Association, Adams observed: "Modern taxation or tax making in its most characteristic aspect is a group contest in which powerful interests vigorously endeavor to rid themselves of present or proposed tax burdens." Thomas S. Adams, "Ideal and Idealism in Taxation," *American Economic Review* 18 (1928): 1. Adams was correct that powerful economic groups challenge tax policy in the political arena; however, he ignored the role of the state in defining the parameters of the "contest" and in negotiating an outcome acceptable to the groups. In the case of the Civil War income tax, the state's extraordinary demand for revenue was paramount in setting the agenda; interest groups were left to struggle among themselves in the legislative arena, each seeking to shift the burden of taxation elsewhere. Notably, those engaged in the contest were the wealthiest and most powerful in America. The Republican state was not targeting the poor, but the economically advantaged, most of whom were represented by the Republican Party itself.

47. Relevant portions of the debate are found in the Congressional Globe, 37th Cong., 1st sess. (July 24, 1861), 246–55.

and the revenue raised from these new taxes would be critical to the success of the armies of the North. Nevertheless, land taxation had been the traditional prerogative of the state governments, and such an intrusion into their domain by the national government was strongly resisted.

In the midst of the heated debate over the proposed land tax, Justin Morrill intervened by offering his own compromise proposal that included a new national income tax. By including an income tax (often referred to as an "income duty"), the burden of the proposed land tax could be greatly reduced. Still, this was a dubious strategy, as income taxation was itself a controversial issue that provoked deep political divisions exacerbated by regional conflicts. Opposition to income taxation was most intense in the Northeast (where most of the "moneyed men" lived), while support was strongest in the Midwest (where agriculture was predominant).[48] Throughout the nineteenth century, political conflict over the income tax would follow much these same geographical lines, reflecting the underlying economic division between agriculture and manufacturing interests. Nevertheless, in 1861 a substantial number of centrist Republicans viewed the income tax as a compromise that would avoid provoking the more intense regional conflict that was generated by the other options: a direct land tax, further tariff increases, or new federal excise taxes on such luxury "goods" as tobacco, whiskey, and slaves.

In the face of rising budget deficits, enough northern Republicans reluctantly acquiesced in Morrill's proposal for a national income tax to carry the House, which passed the bill on July 29 by a close vote of 77 to 60. The bill then went to the Senate, where Republican Senators faced the same unpleasant option of choosing between a tariff increase, the direct land tax, and the proposed income tax. In heated debate in the Senate, questions of equity were repeatedly raised by proponents of the income tax. James F. Simmons of Rhode Island, chairman of the Finance Committee, endorsed an income tax with a high personal exemption as more fair and equitable than a land tax: "Let us tax property in the last resort, when we have to

---

48. The opposition to the income tax was led in the House by Schuler Colfax of Indiana, a Republican who was elected Speaker of the House in 1863 and then served as vice president under Grant. The political maneuvering behind the enactment of the Civil War income tax is recounted in Edwin R. A. Seligman, *The Income Tax: A Study of the History, Theory, and Practice of Income Taxation at Home and Abroad* (New York: Macmillan, 1911), part 2, 430–80.

reach the poor as well as the rich, people of small means as well as those with large; but I do not believe this country has come to pass to be driven to a resource of such extreme measures." Senator William Pitt Fressenden, a Republican from Maine, agreed with that assessment, adding that the income tax would be "more equalized on all classes of the community, more especially on those who are able to bear them."[49] Be that as it may, the goal was to raise revenue by shifting the burden of taxation to the wealthiest citizens. This was a popular sentiment, and the bill quickly passed the Senate and was signed into law by President Lincoln on August 5, 1861.[50] With this, the United States had its first national income tax, imposed at a modest rate of 3 percent on annual income above a personal exemption of eight hundred dollars. The high personal exemption would shelter all but the wealthiest citizens from the grasp of the income tax. U.S. citizens residing abroad faced a higher tax rate of 5 percent, while interest paid on securities benefited from a preferential rate of 1.5 percent. The legislation included numerous excise taxes as well as an ad valorem tax on manufacturing and a gross receipts tax on railroads and steamship companies.

How do we explain the ready adoption of this national income tax by a government so thoroughly dominated by the Republican Party? Certainly, there was broad agreement in all quarters that the Union government was in dire financial straits and badly needed the revenue. The deteriorating financial situation, rather than the redistribution of wealth, was the immediate concern of those Republicans who voted for the income tax. Nevertheless, in selecting one tax over others, the Republican Congress in essence was deciding how to allocate the cost of the war among the major economic interests. That is because different taxes have different "distributions" (as economists would put it today). Debates such as this invariably are couched in the language of "fairness" and "equity," but in substance the politics of taxation in the national legislature is often little more than a mundane struggle to shift the economic burden of taxation to interests and groups located in someone else's state or district. This is the normal pattern of congressional tax policymaking that prevails during peacetime, when powerful interests struggle in the political arena to shift the burden of taxation to others, while the government advances tax policy through

49. Congressional Globe, 37th Cong., 1st sess. (July 24, 1861), 254, 255.
50. Act of August 5, 1861, chap. 45, sec. 49, 12 Stat. 309.

incremental adjustments to existing statutes.[51] Of course, the politics of taxation was anything but "normal" during the Civil War.[52] This was a period of total war and constitutional crisis. With the survival of the nation at stake, officials of the national government were forced to pursue a more aggressive revenue strategy that would secure new revenue sources. If this required increasing the burden of taxation on the wealthiest citizens, so be it.

In the midst of the military and constitutional crisis, national political leaders were able to impose new taxes on powerful economic interests that otherwise likely would have fended off such attacks on their property. To be sure, the Union government was never fully autonomous from society, and officials were never free to pursue a strategy of pure revenue predation. They still had to "negotiate" their wartime revenue strategy in the legislative arena with the representatives of powerful economic interests. This is an important consequence of the unique pattern of development experienced by the American state, one in which the democratization of American political institutions came prior to the development of the state's administrative capacities. Unlike the absolute monarchies of Europe, which achieved a significant degree of state autonomy prior to the democratization of the regime, the American state could not simply dictate its revenue policies to society by decree. Representatives of the various factions would have to negotiate compromises among themselves in the legislature. Nevertheless, Republican congressional leaders were ultimately successful in enacting an aggressive revenue strategy and restructuring the fiscal powers of the American state. The most powerful economic groups had little choice but to acquiesce in the Union government's demands for revenue in the midst of the crisis of total war. The military

---

51. This is the pattern of contemporary tax politics, which I have described in Sheldon D. Pollack, *The Failure of U.S. Tax Policy: Revenue and Politics* (University Park: Penn State Press, 1996), 243–65; see also Timothy J. Conlan, Margaret T. Wrightson, and David R. Beam, *Taxing Choices: The Politics of Tax Reform* (Washington, DC: Congressional Quarterly Press, 1990), 230–35; and "Solving the Riddle of Tax Reform: Party Competition and the Politics of Ideas," *Political Science Quarterly* 105 (1990): 193–217.

52. It has been said that "normal politics" is characterized by "muted conflict, by a limited number of established participants, by a well-defined institutional arena for decision-making, patterns of logrolling, negotiation, and compromise, and by implementation of decisions through routine administration." Dall W. Forsythe, *Taxation and Political Change in the Young Nation, 1781–1833* (New York: Columbia University Press, 1977), 119.

threat to the Union compelled powerful economic interests within the Republican coalition to accept, albeit grudgingly, a graduated income tax as well as a national inheritance tax, excise taxes on luxury goods, and higher tariff duties. This reflected the greater degree of autonomy of the state apparatus and the ability of political elites to pursue a more aggressive (almost predatory) revenue strategy during the period of total war from 1861 to 1865.

Public opinion was generally favorable to the national income tax, which was understood to be targeted at the wealthy, and not the average citizen. The editors of the *New York Times* praised this tax "levied upon a person's purse," as "probably one of the most equitable and bearable taxes that can be imposed." At the same time, they lamented the passing of the nineteenth-century Jeffersonian republic: "We must bid adieu to the golden era in our history in which we were scarcely conscious that we had a Government, so lightly did its burdens rest upon us, and enter upon that in which the almost sole problem of a statesman will be to make the credit balance the debt side of the national ledger."[53] This prophesy would prove highly accurate, as the financial burden of the national government never again would rest so lightly on the citizenry.

Notwithstanding enactment of the income tax in 1861, the impost never actually raised a single dollar. Secretary of Treasury Chase objected to the statute on the pragmatic grounds that the cost of implementation would be greater than the revenue derived from the tax. This was largely a result of the eight-hundred-dollar personal exemption, which was high enough to exempt most of the population from the tax.[54] In response to Chase's objections, the Ways and Means Committee in April 1862 reported a bill for a revised income tax, and the Senate took up the legislation in May. The Senate version included a slightly lower exemption and a progressive rate structure, which was ultimately adopted by the Conference Committee when it met to iron out the differences between the two bills. As enacted by Congress on July 1, 1862, the revised income tax was imposed at a rate of 3 percent on the "annual gains, profits or incomes" above six hundred dollars of all persons residing in the United States, "whether derived from any

---

53. *New York Times,* January 8, 1862, 4.

54. *Report of the Secretary of the Treasury for the Year 1861* (Washington, DC: Government Printing Office, 1861), 15.

kinds of property, rents, interest, dividends, salaries or from any profession, trade, employment or vocation carried on in the United States or elsewhere, or from any source whatever." The tax rose to 5 percent on income in excess of ten thousand dollars and on all income earned by U.S. citizens residing abroad. The income tax of 1862 was enacted as part of a comprehensive revenue package that included a tax on the income of certain kinds of corporations (i.e., the gross receipts of railroads, banks, trust companies, and insurance companies), established license fees for most professions, imposed excise taxes on such luxury goods as liquor, tobacco, yachts, jewelry, and carriages, and required stamp duties for most financial transactions.[55] The act expressly recognized a number of standard business deductions. In addition, the omnibus revenue package included a national gift tax and an inheritance tax on the receipt of property in the form of bequests and legacies.[56] Several other minor taxes were subsequently added to the Treasury's expanded arsenal. These included new excise taxes on iron, tobacco, whiskey, leather, and numerous luxury goods. In addition, ad valorem taxes were imposed at a rate of 3 percent on certain manufactured goods.[57] Collectively, these imposts created a robust revenue system, which along with the new system of public borrowing, financed the formidable armies assembled by the Union government. By July 1862, the Union government was emerging as a highly efficient fiscal-military state.

By the time the income tax of 1862 was implemented, the national debt had soared to $514 million.[58] With the public debt mounting year by year, a more comprehensive income tax statute was introduced in the spring of 1864 with the expectation of raising additional revenues. The Ways and Means Committee reported a bill that provided for a flat income tax rate of 5 percent. On the other hand, the first commissioner of Internal Revenue,

---

55. Act of July 1, 1862, ch. 119, 12 Stat. 432, 469–71.

56. Ibid., 12 Stat. 432, 483. The legislative history for the 1862 revenue act is found at Congressional Globe, 37th Cong., 2nd Sess. 1534 (1862). The nation's first experience with wealth transfer taxation was a federal inheritance tax in effect from 1797 to 1802.

57. These wartime excise taxes are discussed in Myers, *Financial History of the United States,* 157–58; Taussig, *Tariff History of the United States,* 163–64.

58. This trend would continue throughout the war, and as a consequence, the public debt of the Union government reached $2.76 billion by 1866. U.S. Bureau of the Census, *Historical Statistics of the United States,* series Y 335–338 ("Summary of Federal Government Finances—Administrative Budget: 1789–1939"), part 2, 1104. For an account of budget deficits and fiscal policy during the Civil War, see Savage, *Balanced Budgets and American Politics,* 123–31.

George S. Boutwell of Massachusetts, favored a progressive rate structure. In the pursuit of greater revenue, Boutwell recommended raising the tax rate to 5.5 percent on annual income in excess of twenty thousand dollars.[59] The House leadership accepted that controversial proposal, immediately triggering intense objections and a split within the Republican Party. On the floor of the House, Justin Morrill denounced the graduated income tax (as opposed to his flat tax of 3 percent) as reflecting the "spirit of agrarianism" and as contrary to the "very theory of our institutions," wherein "we make no distinction between the rich man and the poor man." He lamented that progressive tax rates "punish men because they are rich," and amount to nothing less than "seizing the property of men for the crime of having too much."[60] Representative Stevens raised similar objections, denouncing the progressive income tax as a "strange way to punish men because they are rich."[61] The point of enacting the income tax was not to "punish" the rich, but to raise revenue for the Union war effort. That said, it was obvious that the progressive rate structure was targeted at the wealthy, and not surprisingly, they and their representatives in Congress objected. Many moderate Republicans could live with an income tax, so long as it was not graduated.

Notwithstanding the challenges voiced in the Senate, the upper chamber followed the House in adopting a progressive rate structure with a maximum rate of 10 percent on income in excess of twenty-five thousand dollars (an enormous sum for an individual in 1864). To appease those Republicans from the Northeast who objected to the graduated rate structure, the Finance Committee agreed to lower the top rate to 7.5 percent on annual income in excess of ten thousand dollars. But a floor amendment pushed the maximum rate back up to 10 percent on income in excess of ten thousand dollars, and the Conference Committee adopted the House version. In the end, the income tax of 1864 was imposed at a rate of 5 percent on personal income above the exemption of six hundred dollars, with the rate rising to 7.5 percent on income above five thousand dollars and

---

59. *Report of the Commissioner of Internal Revenue for the Year ending June 30, 1863* (Washington, DC: Government Printing Office, 1864), 183–84.

60. Congressional Globe, 38th Cong., 1st sess. (1864), 1940.

61. Ibid., 1876.

reaching a maximum rate of 10 percent on income above ten thousand dollars.[62]

The income tax of 1864 was considerably more sophisticated than its predecessors. The number of preferences, deductions, exclusions, and exemptions in the statute increased. Most important, the base of the tax was greatly expanded. Reflecting this, more than 10 percent of households in the North would be subject to the income tax by the end of the war.[63] Receipts derived from the income tax rapidly increased from $2.74 million in 1863 to $20 million in 1864, $61 million in 1865, and $73 million in 1866. In total, the national income tax raised $220 million from fiscal year 1863 to 1867. While not an insignificant sum, this amounted to only 13 percent of federal receipts for the same period.[64] As such, the income tax was still a relatively minor source of federal revenue compared to the tariff, which remained the principal sources of revenue of the Union government. Even with the supplemental revenue from the income tax, annual expenditures greatly exceeded revenue, and the government was forced to borrow heavily to make up the difference. The Southern Confederacy faced the same problem, but borrowing was more problematic as the capital markets in the Northeast were closed to the South. Moreover, customs duties raised little revenue for the Confederacy on account of the Union naval blockade of southern ports. Accordingly, the Confederate government was forced to use more coercive and less efficient means of raising revenue, often seizing goods and supplies for the war effort. This had the negative effect of stifling trade and commerce in the South.[65]

Contrasting the two systems of revenue extraction in the North and the South is highly instructive. The reconstituted American state in the North resembled the English fiscal-military state of the eighteenth century in its organizational structure and methods of public finance, while

---

62. Act of June 30, 1864, ch. 173, sec. 116, 13 Stat. 223.

63. Brownlee, *Federal Taxation in America,* 27.

64. Figures from U.S. Bureau of the Census, *Historical Statistics of the United States,* table 3 ("Individual Income Tax Collections: 1863 to 1895"), part 2, 1091; ibid., series Y 352–357 ("Federal Government Receipts—Administrative Budget: 1789–1939"), part 2, 1106

65. "Major portions of the Confederate revenue system were not perceptibly different from partial confiscation, and they destroyed the forms of commerce from the flow of which, theoretically, they were intended to skim wealth." Bensel, *Yankee Leviathan,* 171.

the Confederacy functioned more as a desperate "stationary bandit" state that confiscated resources from its citizens through forced tribute, thereby stifling individual incentives for commerce and economic activity. Both states were powerful military organizations dedicated to territorial defense, and both wielded the coercive powers of the state to marshal societal resources to support their respective military forces. But the Union government employed a more efficient and sustainable system of revenue extraction. Moreover, it enjoyed superior resources (both economic and manpower) within its territory.[66] The greater population and economic resources of the North ultimately were critical to the success of the Union cause. With its burgeoning market economy and the administrative capacity to extract a share of the profits from private business enterprise via the income tax and customs duties, the Union government possessed all the essential features of a modern tax state. Officials of the Union government employed a variety of taxes to appropriate a share of the great wealth generated by the emergent industrial economy. By 1860, the United States ranked second only to England in industrial production, and most of that industrial capability was located in the Northern states.[67] With a strong industrial economy and a relatively significant number of wealthy individuals living within its territory, the Union government turned to the income tax to extract revenue. In turn, the industrial economy was stimulated by increased wartime spending by the Union and state governments. It was the perfect arrangement. Military spending fueled the economy, and the national government collected revenue for the war effort by taxing

---

66. Prior to the Civil War, the South enjoyed great prosperity. During the 1850s and 1860s, the South fell behind the North in population growth, urbanization, and manufacturing output. John D. Majewski, *A House Dividing: Economic Development in Pennsylvania and Virginia before the Civil War* (New York: Cambridge University Press, 2000), 2. A good deal of the North's manufacturing output was devoted to the new tools of warfare. Overall, the Civil War brought a "technological quantum leap" in weaponry that included the magazine-fed carbine rifle, mines, primitive submarines, and improved artillery, as well as the use of the railroads and telegraph for military purposes. A summary of the improvements in weaponry during the Civil War and the North's technological superiority over the South (based as it was on superior manufacturing and organizational capacity) is found in Eliot A. Cohen, *Supreme Command: Soldiers, Statesmen, and Leadership in Wartime* (New York: Free Press, 2002), 23–29.

67. Douglass C. North, *The Economic Growth of the United States, 1790–1860* (Englewood Cliffs, NJ: Prentice-Hall, 1961), v. North refers to the Civil War as a "costly and bitter interruption" to the steady economic growth that began decades before.

the profits of the owners of private capital. This was the fiscal engine that powered the Yankee Leviathan.

It is worth quoting at length from Bensel's assessment of the objectives and relative advantages of a state in adopting an efficient strategy for extracting revenue from a prosperous market economy during wartime:

> The search for new and more productive revenue sources during war encourages central states to reshape their taxation policies more closely to the form of societal production. While a state at peace may leave many sectors and activities untouched and concentrate levies on luxuries such as liquor and tobacco, a state at war is often compelled to extract revenue from almost all areas of societal production, thus molding the state apparatus in a way that compliments and exploits the strengths and organizing structures of economic activity.[68]

Herein lies the source of the immense power of the Union government that eventually overwhelmed the South. In the eighteenth century, England had first perfected the basic mechanisms by which the military apparatus of the state could be sustained by taxing a thriving commercial economy. This emerged as the basic organizing principle of the fiscal-military state in America created in the North. As we will see, similar mechanisms for extracting resources from the private wartime economy later would be employed by the American state during the fiscal crises occasioned by the two world wars of the twentieth century.

During the Civil War, Congress created an administrative apparatus to collect the new taxes adopted by the national government. This was the Bureau of Internal Revenue (precursor of the Internal Revenue Service), which was established by Congress pursuant to the Revenue Act of July 1, 1862.[69] With a network of 185 collection districts, the Bureau of Internal Revenue (a bureau within the Treasury Department) provided the American state with direct access to societal revenue sources unmediated by the state governments. As such, the revenue collection agency became a

---

68. Bensel, *Yankee Leviathan,* 96–97.

69. For an account of the creation of the Bureau of Internal Revenue (precursor agency of the Internal Revenue Service), see Joseph J. Thorndike, "An Army of Officials: The Civil War Bureau of Internal Revenue," *Tax Notes* 93 (December 24, 2001): 1739; see also John C. Chommie, *The Internal Revenue Service* (New York: Praeger, 1970), 10–12.

powerful tool of the national government. The Bureau of Internal Revenue began with three clerks working for the first commissioner of Internal Revenue, George S. Boutwell.[70] By January 1863, the bureau swelled to nearly four thousand employees. In 1861, the national government collected only $42 million in total receipts from all sources.[71] In 1866, the agency collected $310 million in taxes (excise, inheritance, and income) for the Union government—this compared to the paltry $41 million in taxes collected in 1863.[72]

Congress also created several other administrative agencies, which "facilitated societal penetration by the federal government" in support of the war effort.[73] These included the Department of Agriculture, the Bureau of Immigration, and the National Academy of Science. These agencies became part of the expanded administrative apparatus of the national government, which along with the sophisticated system of public borrowing, rudimentary system of central banking, and new national paper currency ("Greenbacks"), proved to be lasting institutional innovations. During the war, the Republican Congress enacted a homestead act, a system of land-grant colleges, and legislation providing for a transcontinental railroad. According to Bensel, the lasting legacy of the Civil War can be located in two specific areas: the furtherance of "economic development" (specifically, the hastened expansion of the industrial economy in the North) and the accelerated "modernization" (expansion, consolidation, and nationalization) of private economic organizations. Bensel further argues that the American Civil War had a negative impact, especially in the North, on "social democracy"—by which he means "the emergence of formal political organizations dedicated to a redistribution of wealth from upper to lower classes."[74] Other than pensions paid to Civil War veterans and their survivors (discussed further below), no significant social welfare benefits were

---

70. In 1902, Boutwell published his own account of events during his long tenure as commissioner of Internal Revenue. George S. Boutwell, *Reminiscences of Sixty Years in Public Affairs* (New York: Greenwood Press, 1968).

71. U.S. Bureau of the Census, *Historical Statistics of the United States,* series Y 352–357 ("Federal Government Receipts—Administrative Budget: 1789–1939"), part 2, 1106.

72. U.S. Bureau of the Census, *Historical Statistics of the United States,* series Y 358–373 ("Internal Revenue Collections: 1863–1970"), part 2, 1108.

73. Bruce D. Porter, *War and the Rise of the State: The Military Foundations of Modern Politics* (New York: Free Press, 1994), 261.

74. Bensel, *Yankee Leviathan,* 435–36.

provided to the citizenry by the national government prior to the New Deal of the 1930s. For his part, Mark Wilson suggests that the important legacy of the Civil War lies in its impact on the *organization* of business and government in the second half of the nineteenth century.[75] Wilson argues that the experience with the mobilization of manpower and resources during the Civil War established a successful "military model" for business organizations for the rest of the century and carried over as a model for would-be reformers of governmental institutions—for example, those seeking civil service reform pursuant to the campaign to end the "spoils" system.

The Fiscal Organization of the Postbellum American State

With the victory of the Union armies in the Civil War and the end of Reconstruction, the normal politics that had been suppressed during the national crisis reemerged and business interests within the Republican Party began to openly campaign for repeal of the wartime emergency taxes. In 1867, Congress enacted legislation that repealed a number of wartime internal excise taxes and recast the income tax as a flat 5-percent tax with a higher personal exemption of $1,000.[76] Thereafter, revenue from the income tax began to decline. The total amount collected under the income tax was $66 million in 1867; this declined to $41.5 million in 1868 and $34.8 million in 1869.[77] The impost was scheduled to expire altogether in 1870 under a sunset provision included in the original 1864 tax legislation. Surprisingly, a number of prominent Republicans advocated retention of the income tax. In his annual report delivered in December 1869, George Boutwell, who remained the commissioner of Internal Revenue, supported retaining the income tax, arguing that no substitute revenue source could be found that was as "just and equitable" and so little "burdensome" to taxpayers. Boutwell proclaimed the importance of income taxation for a modern activist government: "My opinion is that, so long as a large

75. Wilson, *The Business of the Civil War,* 208–25.

76. Act of March 2, 1867, 14 Stat. 478.

77. U.S. Bureau of the Census, *Historical Statistics of the United States,* table III ("Individual Income Tax Collections: 1863 to 1895"), part 2, 1091.

internal revenue is required by the official necessities of the government, a portion of that revenue should be collected from incomes. The reasons for this seem apparent and forcible. This tax reaches simply the profits of trade and business, and the increased wealth of the individuals from investment."[78] As Boutwell intimated, the most compelling justification for the income tax is that it provides the Treasury with a highly efficient tool to appropriate a share of the wealth and profits produced by the private economy.

In the Senate, John Sherman of Ohio, chairman of the Finance Committee, lobbied to retain the flat income tax as a permanent component of the system of public revenue of the national government. Sherman initially persuaded enough of his Republican colleagues to retain the income tax for another two years. Under the Act of July 14, 1870, the expiration date was pushed back to 1872, although the Civil War inheritance tax was repealed. Budget surpluses were realized by the national government from 1870 to 1872, lending further support to those who questioned the economic necessity of retaining the income tax. In the end, Congress allowed the impost to expire as scheduled in 1872. By that time, enthusiasm for the tax had waned even among its original supporters. The editors of the *New York Times* became disenchanted with the income tax and supported repeal, declaring that "the most judicious management cannot divest [the income tax] of an inquisitorial character, or obviate inequalities and injustice from its practical operation. It has been tolerated, just as various other obnoxious taxes were tolerated—because it was one of the inevitable burdens entailed upon us by a great war.... Let Congress redeem the session from utter barrenness by averting the vexation and unpopularity which will inevitably arise from the continued infliction of the impost."[79]

Just as the fiscal powers of the national government were reduced following the Civil War, so too was the military apparatus of the Yankee Leviathan retrenched. The great army of the North, with more than 1 million men in uniform in the spring of 1865, stood down after Lee's surrender at Appomattox. Fewer than 200,000 men were left carrying arms by the end of the year. Twelve months later, only 57,000 remained in the armed forces. Congress created a Joint Select Committee on Retrenchment

---

78. *Report of the Commissioner of Internal Revenue, for the Year ending June 30, 1869* (Washington, DC: Government Printing Office, 1869), XIV.

79. *New York Times,* January 19, 1871, 4.

to implement further tax cuts and reductions in the military budget at the request of President Andrew Johnson. During Johnson's turbulent tenure in office (1865–1869), the Union army stationed in the ten southern states to maintain order and supervise Reconstruction was restricted to 10,000 men. By the time of the Compromise of 1877, which effectively ended the military occupation of the South, the number of troops declined to fewer than 3,000.[80] By then, the entire U.S. Army was comprised of fewer than 24,000 men, and most of these were transferred to the western territories to maintain order and fight hostile Indian tribes. With the end of Reconstruction and the readmission of the southern states into the Union (along with their representatives in Congress), the period of Republican hegemony came to an abrupt conclusion. After 1877, Democrats reassumed control of virtually all political institutions in the southern states and emerged as viable competitors to the Republican Party at the national level. State and party were once again separate.

Notwithstanding the retrenchment of the military force and tax system, government expenditures remained at elevated levels after the Civil War. As previously discussed, a so-called displacement effect (or "ratchet effect") has been detected in the levels of government spending following many wars.[81] Such a ratchet effect can be discerned in the heightened spending by the national government after the Civil War. In the ten years prior to the Civil War, annual expenditures of the United States averaged less than $58 million. In 1865, expenditures by the Union government exceeded $1.3 billion. During the war years, the Union government spent more than $1.8 billion on the military campaign alone.[82] This extraordinary sum was more than the national government had previously spent in all of the prior seventy years of its existence. After the Civil War, annual spending by the national government never fell below $237 million and averaged $325 million during

---

80. Johnson's reconstruction policy is the described in Eric L. McKitrick, *Andrew Johnson and Reconstruction* (Chicago: University of Chicago Press, 1960); Eric Foner, *Reconstruction: America's Unfinished Revolution 1863–1877* (New York: Harper and Row, 1988); see also Niccole Mellow and Jeffrey K. Tullis, "Andrew Johnson and the Future of Politics," in *Formative Acts: American Politics in the Making,* ed. Stephen Skowronek and Matthew Glassman (Philadelphia: University of Pennsylvania Press, 2007), 153–70.

81. See notes 30 to 31 and accompanying text in chapter 3.

82. Goldin and Lewis, "The Economic Cost of the American Civil War," 304.

the period from 1865 to 1900.[83] As Bruce Porter observes: "The American state was simply larger and more activist after the Civil War than before. This new state activism was clearly a long-term effect of the war itself and not simply a secondary consequence of Reconstruction, for the shift in federal spending priorities continued after 1877."[84] This significant expansion in governmental spending and "activism" was another aspect of the institutional legacy of the Civil War.

How was the national government able to sustain these elevated levels of spending after the repeal of the income tax, inheritance tax, and the other emergency imposts enacted during the Civil War? With the end of the military conflict, officials of the American state returned to the traditional nineteenth-century sources of revenue: excise taxes, revenue from the sale of public land, customs duties, and the tariff. In particular, congressional Republicans retained the Civil War system of high protective tariffs. As Frank Taussig put it in his classic study of nineteenth-century tariff policy, the retention of the high wartime tariff rates "brought about gradually a feeling that such a system was a good thing in itself, and desirable as a permanent policy."[85] With increased international trade and commerce in the decades following the Civil War, the tariff again brought in significant revenue for the national government. Between the Civil War and the First World War, anywhere from 30 percent to 60 percent of federal receipts was derived from customs duties.[86] Revenue from the tariff alone exceeded annual federal expenditures, providing the national government for the first time in its history with the luxury of significant budget surpluses year after year. The massive public debt from the Civil War was cut in half in little more than twenty years and reduced to one third in less than thirty years.[87] The enormous revenues generated by the tariff led Henry George,

---

83. Figures from U.S. Bureau of the Census, *Historical Statistics of the United States,* series Y 335–338 ("Summary of Federal Government Finances—Administrative Budget: 1789–1939"), part 2, 1104.

84. Porter, *War and the Rise of the State,* 266. Porter argues that the increased spending was not a result of industrialization, but rather was based on experience from the Civil War.

85. Taussig, *Tariff History of the United States,* 194.

86. U.S. Bureau of the Census, *Historical Statistics of the United States,* series Y 352–357 ("Federal Government Receipts—Administrative Budget: 1789–1939"), part 2, 1106.

87. Figures from U.S. Bureau of the Census, *Historical Statistics of the United States,* series Y 335–338 ("Summary of Federal Government Finances—Administrative Budget: 1789–1939"), part 2, 1104.

the eclectic economist, to sardonically observe in 1883 that "the great question before Congress is what to do with the surplus."[88]

James Savage has suggested that in order to "reduce these enormous surpluses and legitimize the need for high tariffs, Republicans dramatically increased public expenditures in the late nineteenth century."[89] Republican politicians were wedded to a national policy of high protective tariffs and sought a politically advantageous mechanism for distributing the surplus revenue. What was that mechanism? A major portion of the surplus from the tariff was used to pay pensions to Civil War veterans and their survivors, the overwhelming majority of whom lived in the North and Midwest. Through the payment of pensions, public spending was targeted at segments of the population that were otherwise hostile to Republican tariff policy—for example, workers and consumers in the North as well as farmers in the West.[90] Robert Higgs argues that "in the absence of appreciable political leeway for tariff reduction the government's main response to the embarrassingly routine surpluses was to authorize greater and greater largess for the Civil War veterans and their (ever more distant) relatives."[91] Notwithstanding the distribution of what soon became very generous benefits, annual budget surpluses were still realized by the national government in every fiscal year from 1866 to 1893, as revenue from the tariff continued to pour into the U.S. Treasury.

The Civil War pension system was originally set up in 1862 when Congress authorized payments to disabled veterans as well as their widows and orphans. Under the original legislation, coverage extended to dependent mothers and sisters of the veterans, and later dependent fathers and brothers were added. While pensions had been provided to veterans of prior wars, starting with the Revolutionary War, benefits were much less generous and more limited in scope than those provided to Union veterans of the Civil War. In 1865, Congress expanded the pension system

---

88. Henry George, *The Complete Works of Henry George: Social Problems* (Garden City, NY: Doubleday, Page and Company, 1911), 168.

89. Savage, *Balanced Budgets and American Politics,* 122.

90. Richard F. Bensel, *Sectionalism and American Political Development, 1880–1980* (Madison: University of Wisconsin Press, 1984), 62–73.

91. Robert Higgs, *Crisis and Leviathan: Critical Episodes in the Growth of American Government* (New York: Oxford University Press, 1987), 97.

by establishing a "National Asylum" for disabled veterans.[92] By the 1870s, spending on Union veterans reached more than a third of a percent of the gross domestic product (GDP).[93] In 1878, Congress passed the Arrears of Pension Act, which authorized the Pension Bureau to reopen old cases and pay out benefits that were previously uncollected by an eligible veteran. This seemingly minor change resulted in a dramatic increase in spending on pension benefits.

As pension rules were increasingly liberalized and benefits expanded, the staff required to administer the pension system grew to more than fifteen hundred employees. In 1887, a magnificent brick building, designed by Montgomery C. Meigs, the army quartermaster general, opened in Washington to house the Pension Bureau. The grandeur of the building was symbolic of the importance of the pension program in American politics. Major changes to the pension system were again enacted under the Dependent Pension Act of 1890, pursuant to which Congress severed the link between war-related disability and pension benefits by providing benefits to anyone who served in the Union army for at least ninety days and later became disabled. In 1906, the statute was amended to expressly provide that old age was a disability that qualified for support; furthermore, pension benefits were raised.[94] During the period from 1880 to 1910, the national government devoted more than a quarter of its expenditures to pensions. At the peak of the program in 1893, there were 966,012 pensioners (most residing in the North), and the national government spent 41.5 percent of its total receipts on pension benefits. By 1910, some 28 percent of the male population over age sixty-five received pensions averaging $189 a year and more than 300,000 widows and orphans received benefits from the national government.[95]

In her seminal study of the Civil War pension program, Theda Skocpol refers to the postbellum national government as a "precocious spending state" that predated the social welfare programs of the New

---

92. The asylum was subsequently renamed the "National Home for Disabled Soldiers," more commonly known as the Old Soldiers Home.

93. Rockoff, "Veterans," in *Historical Statistics of the United States,* ed. Carter et al., 5–343.

94. U.S. Bureau of Pensions, *Laws of the United States Governing the Granting of Army and Navy Pensions* (Washington, DC: Government Printing Office, 1924), 43.

95. Theda Skocpol, "America's First Social Security System: The Expansion of Benefits for Civil War Veterans," *Political Science Quarterly* 108 (1993): 85, 114.

Deal by decades.[96] This was America's first system of income security for the disabled and elderly, albeit only those who had participated in the Union cause. Of course, this social welfare program was only temporary, as it inevitably phased out as more and more veterans died off after the turn of the twentieth century. That said, we must consider what forces were behind this important experiment in building a social welfare state in America. While accepting the claims of scholars (such as Savage and Higgs) who argue that the expansion of benefits was attributable to the need to distribute the tariff surpluses, as well as those who argue that the lobbying efforts by powerful interest groups such as the Grand Army of the Republic (GAR) were responsible for the expansion of pension benefits, Skocpol offers a broader explanation for pension policy. She attributes the impetus for Republican-sponsored efforts to expand pension benefits not to the budget surpluses per se, but rather to the "proclivity of the nineteenth-century U.S. political parties to enact distributive policies, which allowed the spread of sometimes carefully timed and targeted benefits to key supporters in their geographically widespread cross-class constituencies."[97] Given the relative parity between the two parties at the national level from 1877 until the realignment of the party system in 1896, Republicans used the surplus revenues distributed via pensions as a form of fiscal patronage to benefit their party.

The post–Civil War era was an exceptional period in the history of the finances of the United States, a rare time when perennial budget surpluses generated by the tariff drove domestic spending. The pension program was the product of those unique financial circumstances. With this program, the national government functioned as the precursor of the modern "transfer state." Officials used the coercive powers of the state to collect the tariff, customs duties, and other federal excise taxes, and then distributed a significant portion of that revenue to aged Union veterans and their survivors in the form of military pensions. Through this distributive policy, the Republican Party cultivated political support among those voters not directly benefiting from its national policy of protectionist tariffs. From a statist perspective, this was a highly ingenious arrangement that worked to enhance the legitimacy of the regime.

---

96. Skocpol, *Protecting Soldiers and Mothers,* 1.
97. Skocpol, "America's First Social Security System," 100–101.

Even though this postbellum revenue system generated perennial surpluses, it nonetheless had problems. Indeed, the tariff was a constant source of political controversy.[98] At its historic peak rate of 45 percent, the tariff was particularly beneficial to one section of the country (the Northeast) and one economic sector (manufacturing) at the expense of nearly everyone else. The high protective tariff imposed an economic burden on farmers in the South and Midwest as well as consumers and wage laborers in the Northeast by propping up prices for manufactured goods. This aggravated long-standing sectional cleavages that divided the country along geographical line.[99] Opposition to Republican tariff policy was strongest in the South and Midwest among the agrarian-based political parties, which gathered strength in the second half of the nineteenth century. These agrarian parties repeatedly made demands for reductions in the high tariff rates and a switch to a revenue system based on progressive income taxation.[100] Populists and egalitarians likewise embraced the graduated income tax and attacked protectionist tariff policy. Support for a progressive income tax was included in the platforms of the Greenback Party in 1877 and 1878, the National Greenback Party in 1880, the Greenback Labor and Antimonopoly parties in 1884, and the Union Labor Party in 1888. The Grangers, Knights of Labor, and the Farmers Alliance demanded restoration of an income tax, as did the Populist Party in each of its party platforms. From 1874 to 1894, no fewer than sixty-eight bills were introduced in Congress to enact a progressive income tax. In 1884, Democrats under Grover Cleveland capitalized on widespread opposition to the tariff and captured the White House.

Republican tariff policy also became an impediment to American industry seeking to penetrate international markets. High protective barriers to imports coming into the United States triggered comparable responses

---

98. For a discussion of the divisions over tariff policy as reflected in the platforms of the Democrats and third parties, see Richard F. Bensel, *The Political Economy of American Industrialization, 1877–1900* (New York: Cambridge University Press, 2000), 124–32.

99. The role of sectional conflict in influencing the development of American political institutions is the central theme of Bensel, *Sectionalism and American Political Development;* see also Bensel, *The Political Economy of American Industrialization,* 457–509.

100. For a discussion of the agrarian parties that supported the income tax and opposed the tariff, see Elizabeth Sanders, *Roots of Reform: Farmers, Workers, and the American State, 1877–1917* (Chicago: University of Chicago Press, 1999), 217–30. Sanders explores the impact of agrarian parties on the development of the American state.

abroad as foreign nations moved to close their markets to American manufacturers. In the long run, this hurt American industry. Consequently, political resistance to the tariff among business interests mounted during the latter half of the nineteenth century, even while generating a distinctive politics of interest group competition for preferences in tariff rate schedules. This is the familiar interest-group politics of logrolling and trade-offs that characterized congressional policymaking for the tariff in the early twentieth century.[101] Of course, income taxation produces political cleavages of its own. These are based not on sectional differences but rather disparities in income and wealth. The income tax pits the wealthy few against a majority of the population. A graduated rate structure, which increases the revenue derived from the income tax by shifting even more of the tax burden to the wealthy, only aggravates the division and political tension between the "haves" and "have-nots." This is a political cleavage easily exploited by Populist parties whose voting coalitions are mostly comprised of lower-income groups. Partly in response to widespread political pressure from Populists, who by then exerted considerable influence within the Democratic Party in the South and Midwest, key members of Congress moved in the early 1890s to resurrect the defunct Civil War income tax. At the same time, support for progressive income taxation came from a new generation of economists in the top American universities. Prominent among these was Edwin Seligman of Columbia University, who began his long and influential academic career writing about taxation in the early 1890s and promoting the resurrection of the graduated income tax.[102]

After heated debate, legislation for a new income tax was introduced in Congress as part of a reform bill that would reduce tariff rates previously

---

101. This politics of logrolling and vote trading over the tariff was observed by Elmer Schattschneider during the 1920s and 1930s. E. E. Schattschneider *Politics, Pressures, and the Tariff* (New York: Prentice-Hall, 1935).

102. See, e.g., Edwin R. A. Seligman, "The Theory of Progressive Taxation," *Political Science Quarterly* 8 (1893): 220. The role Seligman and other Progressives played in moving the United States from a system of public finance based on regressive consumption taxes to one based on a graduated income tax is the subject of Ajay K. Mehrotra, "Envisioning the Modern American Fiscal State: Progressive-Era Economists and the Intellectual Foundations of the U.S. Income Tax," *UCLA Law Review* 52 (August 2005): 1793; see also W. Elliot Brownlee, "The Transformation of the Tax System and the Experts," *National Tax Journal* 32 (1979): 47.

raised under the McKinley tariff bill of 1890.[103] The congressional coalition of Democrats in favor of the income tax was led by William Jennings Bryan of Nebraska and Benton McMillin of Tennessee, chairman of the House Ways and Means Subcommittee on Internal Revenue. William L. Wilson of West Virginia, Democratic chairman of the Ways and Means Committee, himself preferred tariff reduction to an income tax, but set in motion the legislative initiative.[104] The income tax was opposed by representatives of commercial and manufacturing interests in the Northeast. The six Republican members of the Ways and Means Committee (who did not participate in the markup) opposed the measure, and the vote followed strict partisan lines. Notwithstanding their objections, Congress enacted the Wilson Tariff Act of 1894 in August with strong turnout in both houses; voting followed party lines.[105] The income tax of 1894 imposed a flat tax of 2 percent on the gains, profits, and income of individuals above the four-thousand-dollar exemption. The legislation included a tax of 2 percent on the "net profits" or income of all corporations, companies, and associations doing business for profit in the United States.

The Populist victory was short-lived, however, as the Supreme Court held the income tax of 1894 an unconstitutional "direct" tax in the infamous case of *Pollock v. Farmer's Loan & Trust Co.* (1895).[106] The court reversed what was generally believed to be settled law as to the constitutionality of

---

103. For a discussion of the politics behind the McKinley tariff, see Joanne Reitano, *The Tariff Question in the Gilded Age: The Great Debate of 1888* (University Park: Pennsylvania State University Press, 1994), 127–37.

104. As chairman of Ways and Means, Wilson accepted a proposal from William Jennings Bryan to include an income tax in the tariff-reduction bill. Later he changed his mind and disassociated himself from Bryan. The strategy of linking an income tax to the tariff-reduction bill is recounted in Robert Stanley, *Dimensions of Law in the Service of Order: Origins of the Federal Income Tax, 1861–1913* (New York: Oxford University Press, 1993), 113–19.

105. Wilson Tariff Act of 1894, August 27, 1894, ch. 349, §73 et seq., 28 Stat. 570. A number of Republicans voted for the measure. The authoritative analysis of the partisan vote behind the bill is found in Stanley, *Dimensions of Law in the Service of Order,* 128–32. The legislation became law without the signature of President Cleveland, who favored tariff reduction but opposed the national income tax included in the legislation.

106. *Pollock v. Farmer's Loan and Trust Co.,* 157 U.S. 429c (1895); 158 U.S. 601 (1895) (rehearing). In an opinion written by Chief Justice Fuller, the Supreme Court held that the income tax was unconstitutional under Article 1, section 2 of the Constitution, which requires that "direct Taxes" must be apportioned among the states based on population.

income taxation.[107] In doing so, it thwarted a majority coalition intent on shifting the revenue strategy of the American state from excise taxes and a high protective tariff to progressive income taxation. For the time being, the court put a halt to this experiment in "socialism" targeted at the moneyed men. During the late nineteenth century, the Supreme Court also blocked numerous efforts by Progressives in the state legislatures to regulate the emerging national economy.[108] As Justice Holmes complained, the court was constitutionalizing its policy preferences by barring the states from legislating their own.[109] Whether in the pursuit of conservative or liberal economic theory, such efforts by the federal courts to regulate the modern industrial economy are doomed to failure because the judiciary lacks the administrative capacity, specialized expertise, and enforcement capabilities to enforce its rulings.

In response to this wave of judicial activism, Progressive reformers sought to remove economic regulation from the jurisdiction of the federal courts. This was the goal of legislation creating new national administrative agencies to regulate specific sectors of the economy or specific industries. Likewise, there were numerous attempts to restructure national institutions in response to changes in American society triggered by rapid urbanization and industrialization in the latter half of the nineteenth century. Reformers also attacked the patronage system by creating a professional nonpartisan bureaucracy pursuant to the Pendleton Civil Service Act of 1883. Similar efforts were undertaken to restructure the military and improve the organizational structure and level of professionalism of the army. Such attempts to reconstitute the American state have been aptly characterized as "patchwork" state building.[110] The limits of patchwork

---

107. When Congress considered enacting an income tax during the War of 1812, the consensus was that it was not a direct tax. The Supreme Court expressed this view in dictum in *Springer v. United States*, 102 U.S. 586 (1881). For a comprehensive review of this thorny issue, see Stanley, *Dimensions of Law in the Service of Order*, 136–75.

108. See, e.g., *Munn v. Illinois*, 94 U.S. 113 (1877); *Mugler v. Kansas*, 123 U.S. 623 (1887); *Allgeyer v. Louisiana*, 165 U.S. 578 (1897). Later, the court reversed the policy of the New York state legislature, which had enacted statutory restrictions on the hours and working conditions of bakery workers. *Lochner v. New York*, 198 U.S. 45 (1905).

109. In his famous dissent to *Lochner*, Holmes argued that "a constitution is not intended to embody a particular economic theory, whether of paternalism and the organic relation of the citizen to the State or of laissez faire."

110. The term patchwork state building is from Stephen Skowronek, *Building a New American State: The Expansion of National Administrative Capacities, 1877–1920* (New York: Cambridge University Press, 1982).

state building are all too obvious. While the outlines of a modern state began to emerge in America by the turn of the twentieth century, political power remained divided between the national government and the states. As Kimberley Johnson puts it, the "United States was precariously balanced between a continued dual federal system and a centralized modern state."[111] Notwithstanding the efforts of Progressive reformers, the American state remained a fragmented political organization dominated by patronage politics and political parties, lacking the "universal" professional bureaucracy, professional standing army, and revenue-extraction capacity possessed by the strong nation-states of nineteenth-century Europe.

The Birth of the Modern Income Tax

Following the Supreme Court's decision in *Pollock*, a campaign commenced in Congress to overturn the Court's ruling. Ironically, the initiative was set in motion by Nelson W. Aldrich, the conservative Republican chairman of the Senate Finance Committee, who in 1909 introduced a proposal for a constitutional amendment granting Congress the express authority to impose a direct income tax without regard to apportionment among the states based on population.[112] The proposal had the support of the Republican president, William Howard Taft.[113] With Progressive Republicans joining Democrats, the amendment was promptly approved by both houses of Congress.

---

111. Kimberley S. Johnson, *Governing the American State: Congress and the New Federalism, 1877–1929* (Princeton: Princeton University Press, 2007), 4.

112. The Democratic Party platform of July 7, 1908, called for a constitutional amendment specifically delegating to Congress the authority to levy a tax on the income of individuals and corporations: "We favor an income tax as part of our revenue system, and we urge the submission of a constitutional amendment specifically authorizing Congress to levy and collect a tax upon individual and corporate incomes, to the end that wealth may bear its proportionate share of the burdens of the Federal Government."

113. Taft and Aldrich apparently sought to deflate Populist enthusiasm for a highly graduated income tax by acquiescing in both a tax on corporate income and the future possibility of a moderate income tax enacted pursuant to the proposed constitutional amendment. For an account of the curious strategy pursued by Taft and Aldrich, see Jerold L. Waltman, *Political Origins of the U.S. Income Tax* (Jackson: University Press of Mississippi, 1985), 5–6.

The motivation and logic behind Republican support for retention of the Civil War income tax, enactment of the income tax of 1894, and the constitutional amendment to overturn *Pollock,* have long been a matter of speculation among scholars. After all, influential Republicans such as John Sherman, Thaddeus Stevens, and Justin Morrill supported the original Civil War income tax of 1862, which had a flat tax rate. Some moderate Republicans even endorsed the income tax of 1894. This contradicts the common perception that nineteenth-century tax policy was a Manichean struggle between, on the one hand, conservative Republicans opposed to all forms of income taxation, and on the other hand, Progressives and Populists who sought to use the income tax as a tool for achieving social justice. That certainly was the prevailing interpretation among a generation of Progressive historians of the income tax, who portrayed the enactment of the modern income tax as the culmination of a long political struggle for social justice against a reactionary movement they traced from the High Federalists to the modern-day Republican Party.[114] Even today, analysts tend to view nineteenth-century controversies over income taxation through the prism of contemporary politics, which supposedly pits liberal Democrats favoring tax hikes against conservative Republicans demanding tax-cuts for the rich. In fact, the partisan battle lines over federal tax policy were never so clearly drawn in the nineteenth century, nor are they today.

One convincing explanation for the seemingly contradictory behavior of those Republicans who gave qualified support for income taxation (as opposed to the Old Guard conservatives who consistently opposed all income taxes) is advanced by Robert Stanley, who argues that Republican "centrists" were willing to tolerate an income tax with low rates and even a mildly progressive rate structure as a strategy for deflecting the rising tide of populist agrarian agitation for more extreme measures to redistribute wealth. Such taxes never threatened the established economic order, nor could they ever have effected an appreciable redistribution of wealth. As Stanley puts it, "The early [income] tax was designed to preserve

---

114. Prominent examples include Edwin R. A. Seligman, *The Income Tax: A Study of the History, Theory, and Practice of Income Taxation at Home and Abroad* (New York: Macmillan, 1911); Sidney Ratner, *American Taxation: Its History as a Social Force in Democracy* (New York: W. W. Norton, 1942); Randolph E. Paul, *Taxation in the United States* (Boston: Little, Brown, 1954).

imbalances in the structure of wealth and opportunity, rather than to ame-
liorate or abolish them, by strengthening the status quo against the more
radical attacks on that structure by the political left and right."[115] This was
the scenario in 1913, when Republican centrists supported the proposed
constitutional amendment authorizing direct income taxation, thereby
hastening its passage through Congress.

The campaign for a constitutional amendment gathered momentum following the widespread electoral victories of the Democrats in 1912, which
gave the party control of the White House (for only the third time since the
Civil War) as well as both houses of Congress. Following the Democratic
landslide, the moderate Republicans who set in motion the amendment
process lost control of the outcome. With Democrats gaining majorities
in many state legislatures, ratification by the necessary thirty-six states became a foregone conclusion. On February 3, 1913, the Sixteenth Amendment became part of the U.S. Constitution. The amendment granted broad
powers to Congress with respect to taxation, thereby resolving once and
for all questions about the constitutionality of a direct (i.e., unapportioned)
income tax: "The Congress shall have power to lay and collect taxes on incomes, from whatever source derived, without apportionment among the
several States, and without regard to any census or enumeration."[116] With
this simple amendment, the national government finally gained the power
of direct taxation—a vital power that national political leaders had sought
since 1781 but were repeatedly denied by the state governments and the
Supreme Court.

Soon after he took office in the spring of 1913, the new Democratic president, Woodrow Wilson, pushed for tariff reduction and an income tax
statute under the authority of the new constitutional amendment. Later
that same year, legislation for an income tax was introduced pursuant to
tariff-reduction legislation.[117] The income tax proposal, drafted by Cordell
Hull (Democrat of Tennessee) who served on the House Subcommittee on
Internal Taxation, generated remarkably little debate in Congress. Much

---

115. Robert, *Dimensions of Law in the Service of Order,* viii.
116. U.S. Constitution, Sixteenth Amendment.
117. By this time, many insurgent Republicans (especially those from the Midwest) supported
tariff reform. The Republican platform of 1908 included a provision embracing "revision" of the
tariff, which was understood to mean tariff reduction.

of the discussion concerned the rate structure and the magnitude of the personal exemption. In the end, a mildly progressive rate structure was included along with a high personal exemption that would effectively exempt all but the wealthy from taxation. A number of Democrats in the Senate pressed for an even more progressive rate structure. Robert La Follette Sr., the maverick Republican from Wisconsin, proposed a maximum rate of 10 percent for the income tax and an inheritance tax with a maximum rate of 75 percent. But the Senate version was more moderate. The Conference Committee markup generally followed the Senate and was adopted on October 3 by both houses, with a handful of "insurgent" Republicans voting for the bill. The Underwood Tariff Act of 1913 was promptly signed by President Wilson.[118]

Few, if any, of those who voted for the income tax of 1913 believed at the time that it would be more than a supplemental source of revenue for the national government, which continued to rely for most of its revenue on the tariff, customs duties, and federal excise taxes. The new federal income tax included a generous personal exemption of $3,000 for single taxpayers and $4,000 for married couples. This exempted all but the wealthiest of citizens. The "normal" tax rate was only 1 percent on personal income between $3,000 and $20,000. On personal income above $20,000, a series of surtaxes took the maximum tax rate to 6 percent on income in excess of $500,000. While very few Americans earned $20,000 a year in 1913 (let alone $500,000), this made for a progressive tax, at least in theory. The Supreme Court would later hold that the progressive rate structure did not violate the "due process" clause of the Fifth Amendment to the U.S. Constitution.[119] For 1913, the first half-year under the new income tax, 0.8 percent of the population was subject to the tax and only 357,598 tax returns were filed.[120] This was attributable to the high personal exemptions.

---

118. Underwood Tariff Act of 1913, Oct. 3, 1913, ch. 16, 38 Stat. 114. When the income tax was enacted in 1913, the Bureau of Internal Revenue created a special "income tax unit" to collect revenue under the new impost. The creation of this unit and the revenue collected under the income tax in its first full year is noted in Treasury Department, *Annual Report of the Secretary of the Treasury on the State of the Finances for the Fiscal Year Ended June 30, 1914* (Washington, D.C.: Government Printing Office, 1915), 31–34, 149–51.

119. The constitutionality of the corporate business privilege tax was subsequently upheld by the Supreme Court in *Brushaber v. Union Pac. R.R. Co.*, 240 U.S. 1 (1916).

120. U.S. Bureau of the Census, *Historical Statistics of the United States*, series Y 402–411 ("Individual Income Tax Returns: 1913–1943"), part 2, 1110.

During the initial years of the income tax, only 2 percent of American households were required to pay tax.[121] Revenue amounted to a paltry $28 million in 1913.[122] The next year, revenue from the individual income tax increased slightly (constituting 7.4 percent of total federal revenue), but this was offset by a decline in revenue from the corporate income tax, which originally had been enacted in 1909 as a corporate business privilege tax.[123] The income tax was now a component of the revenue system of the American state; however, it was not yet a significant source of revenue. This would change dramatically with America's entry into the First World War, which brought major structural changes to the income tax and the entire fiscal system of the United States.

The Wartime Income Tax Regime

When war broke out in Europe in 1914, the United States enjoyed a balanced budget with only modest debt. National income and per capita income were by far the highest in the world.[124] With the onset of the war, however, trade and commerce with Europe declined dramatically. This had a substantial impact on receipts from the tariff and customs duties, which remained the primary source of revenue of the national government. Revenue from excise taxes on alcohol and tobacco also declined as many states adopted their own prohibition laws in advance of the national movement. As a result, monthly federal receipts declined precipitously from

---

121. Brownlee, *Federal Taxation in America,* 46.

122. The revenue collected in the first year of the income tax was reported in "Letter of the Secretary of the Treasury, William G. McAdoo," 63d Cong., 3d sess. (October 15, 1914), S. Doc. 623, 2.

123. Congress enacted a "business privilege tax" (in substance, a corporate income tax) of 1 percent on the net income of corporations earned "with respect to the carrying on or doing business." Act of August 5, 1909, 36 Stat. 112. The Supreme Court later held this to be an excise tax, rather than an unconstitutional "direct" income tax. *Flint v. Stone Tracy Co.,* 220 U.S. 107 (1911). The corporate excise tax raised $21 million in 1910 and $35 million in 1913 before it was replaced by the corporate income tax. Nearly 300,000 corporations filed returns for the corporate excise tax. U.S. Bureau of the Census, *Historical Statistics of the United States,* table 5 ("Collections Under the Corporate Excise Tax of 1909"), part 2, 1091; Ibid., series Y 381–392 ("Corporation Income Tax Returns: 1909 to 1970"), part 2, 1109.

124. Figures in Paul Kennedy, *The Rise and Fall of the Great Powers: Economic Change and Military Conflict from 1500 to 2000* (New York: Random House, 1987), 243.

$73.2 million in July 1914 to only $44.5 million in October.[125] The initial response by Congress was to raise federal excise taxes. Stop-gap legislation was passed to raise a projected $100 million in new revenue, but only half that much was realized. As the financial condition of the national government worsened, Treasury Secretary William G. McAdoo pressed Congress for structural changes to the income tax. As Wilson's chief financial advisor, McAdoo recommended using the income tax to ease the financial shortfall. This would be achieved by increasing tax rates and lowering personal exemptions to expand the tax base. In his State of the Union address to a joint session of Congress on December 7, 1915, Wilson outlined the new revenue strategy, which reflected McAdoo's recommendations: "By somewhat lowering the present limits of exemption and the figure at which the surtax shall begin to be imposed and by increasing, step by step throughout the graduation, the surtax itself, the income taxes as at present apportioned would yield sums sufficient to balance the books of the Treasury at the end of the fiscal year 1917 without making the burdens unreasonably or oppressively heavy." In addition, Wilson proposed increases in excise taxes on the production of gasoline, iron, and steel to ensure that "the industry of this generation should pay the bills of this generation."[126]

In January 1916, the House Ways and Means Committee took up a revenue proposal that included most of the modifications to the income tax requested by Wilson and McAdoo.[127] The chairman of the committee, Democrat Claude Kitchen of North Carolina, guided the bill through the House, which approved the legislation in July. The Senate gave its approval in August, and on September 7 the Congress adopted the mark of the conference committee, which included no Republican members. The next day, Wilson signed this major tax legislation. The Revenue Act of 1916 increased the "normal" income tax rate for individuals from 1 percent

---

125. Treasury Department, *Annual Report of the Secretary of the Treasury on the State of the Finances for the Fiscal Year Ended June 30, 1915* (Washington, DC: Government Printing Office, 1916), table G ("Statement Showing the Ordinary Receipts and Disbursements of the Government by Months, etc."), 228.

126. *Messages and Papers of the Presidents* (New York: Bureau of National Literature, n.d.), 8113.

127. For an account of the administration's revenue plan as well as the politics behind the 1916 legislation, see W. Elliot Brownlee, "Wilson and Financing the Modern State: The Revenue Act of 1916," *Proceedings of the American Philosophical Society* 129 (1985): 179–80.

to 2 percent, added a surtax of 1 percent on personal income in excess of twenty thousand dollars, and raised the maximum rate from 6 percent to 13 percent on income in excess of $2 million. The legislation included a progressive inheritance tax on estates greater than fifty thousand dollars.[128] Even before these tax hikes took effect, the Treasury Department requested additional revenues. These were authorized in legislation passed by Congress following Wilson's reelection. Rates for the federal estate tax were increased and a new "excess profits" tax of 8 percent was imposed on business corporations pursuant to the Revenue Act of March 3, 1917.[129]

With America's formal entry into the European war in April 1917, pressure mounted for even greater tax increases, with McAdoo requesting $3.5 billion from Congress as an initial one-year appropriation for the war. Both the treasury secretary and the president viewed the income tax as a tool for extracting a share of the profits realized by the domestic industrial economy, which had rebounded after 1915. Additional taxes were enacted by Congress that fall pursuant to the Revenue Act of October 3, 1917, which raised the normal income tax rate from 2 percent to 4 percent on taxable income in excess of three thousand dollars for single persons and four thousand dollars for married persons.[130] Personal exemptions were lowered to one thousand dollars for single taxpayers and two thousand dollars for married taxpayers. A surtax was enacted that reached 50 percent on income in excess of $1 million. Rates for the corporate income tax and the excess profits tax were also increased.

These tax increases were justified by the need to finance America's involvement in the global war. A draft was authorized in May 1917. With that, the size of the armed forces jumped from 179,376 men in 1916 to 643,833 in 1917. With America's formal entry into the war in 1918, nearly

---

128. Revenue Act of 1916, September 8, 1916, Pub. L. No. 64–271, ch. 463, 39 Stat. 756.

129. Revenue Act of 1917, March 3, 1917, Pub. L. No. 64–377, 39 Stat. 1000. Despite opposition from his supporters within the business community (e.g., Bernard Baruch, Jacob Schiff, and Clarence Dodge), Wilson favored using the excess profits tax to tax the profits generated by a heated wartime economy. W. Elliot Brownlee, "Tax Regimes, National Crisis, and State-Building in America," in *Funding the Modern American State, 1941–1995: The Rise and Fall of the Era of Easy Finance,* ed. W. Elliot Brownlee (New York: Cambridge University Press, 1996), 61–64.

130. Revenue Act of 1917, October 3, 1917, Pub. L. No. 65–50, ch. 63, 40 Stat. 300. For an account of the Revenue Act of 1917 and tax policy during the First World War, see Waltman, *Political Origins of the U.S. Income Tax,* 42–54; Steven A. Bank, Kirk J. Stark, and Joseph J. Thorndike, *War and Taxes* (Washington, DC: Urban Institute Press, 2008), 49–81.

2.9 million men served on active duty in the armed forces.[131] The overall size of the national government increased dramatically during the war, reaching 854,500 civilian employees in 1918—more than double the number from only four years earlier.[132] This expansion resulted in a significant increase in the expense of government. Indeed, the cost of the first full year of American participation in the war was greater than the total cost of operating the national government from 1791 through 1917. Charles Gilbert estimates that war expenditures from 1917 to 1920 totaled approximately $38 billion; total government expenditures increased from $742 million in 1916 to $18.952 billion in 1919—an astonishing increase of 2,454 percent in just three years.[133] During the course of the war, the national debt rose from $1.2 billion in 1914 to $25.5 billion in 1919.[134] This explosion in spending and debt by the national government demanded a new revenue strategy. As in the 1860s, the fiscal crisis triggered by the wartime mobilization of society led to fundamental changes to the revenue system of the American state.

During the First World War, congressional leaders learned that it was possible to significantly increase federal receipts through relatively minor adjustments to the federal tax code—specifically, by increasing income tax rates and lowering personal exemptions. Such techniques allow Congress to rapidly increase taxes during periods of war and immediately reduce them once the conflict ends. Proponents of the original 1913 statute seemed to grasp this, as the House Ways and Means Committee report noted that revenues from an income tax "readily respond to changes of rates," and

---

131. Carter et al., eds., *Historical Statistics of the United States,* vol. 5, table Ed26–47 ("Military Personnel on Active Duty, by Branch of Service and Sex: 1789–1995"), 5–355. During the First World War, the nation-states of Europe achieved historic levels for the wartime mobilizations of their populations. France and Germany mustered more than 13 percent of the population into the military, while Britain mobilized more than 9 percent. Niall Ferguson, *The Cash Nexus: Money and Power in the Modern World, 1700–2000* (New York: Basic Books, 2001), 29.

132. U.S. Bureau of the Census, *Historical Statistics of the United States,* series Y 308–317 ("Paid Civilian Employment of the Federal Government, 1816 to 1970"), part 2, 1102.

133. For a discussion of the impact of the First World War on expenditures and revenues, see Charles Gilbert, *American Financing of World War I* (Westport, CT: Greenwood, 1970), 65–74. In contrast, during the Civil War, expenditures reached a peak of $1.298 billion in 1865, up 1,847 percent from prewar levels.

134. U.S. Bureau of the Census, *Historical Statistics of the United States,* series Y 493–504 ("Public Debt of the Federal Government: 1791 to 1970"), part 2, 1117.

proclaimed this one of the most important features of the tax.[135] Senator John Sharp Williams pointed out that in light of the "elasticity" of the income tax, the government could easily "raise or lower revenue."[136] This was confirmed during the First World War as Congress dramatically raised rates for the individual income tax in pursuit of revenue for the war effort. Comparable adjustments to rates for the tariff would not have been nearly as effective, as international trade and commerce declined with the outbreak of war, reducing the revenue yield of the impost. In embracing the income tax, policymakers moved away from a revenue system that was, as Miguel Centeno puts it, "administratively simple" (i.e., indirect excise and customs duties) to a revenue system based on "more politically challenging, but potentially more lucrative, domestic sources of revenue" (i.e., direct income taxation).[137]

During the course of the war, the maximum rate for the individual income tax soared from 6 percent to 77 percent on income in excess of $1 million—an incredible expansion in such a short time. At the same time, the personal exemption was significantly reduced, thereby exposing a greater number of citizens to the tax. While less than 20 percent of the population was required to file tax returns during the war, this modest broadening of the tax base was sufficient to dramatically expand the revenue-raising capacity of the tax system. The individual income tax raised $178 million in 1916, $691 million in 1917, $1.1 billion in 1918, and nearly $1.3 billion in 1919.[138] The latter amounted to 31 percent of the total receipts of the national government.[139] Revenue from the corporate income tax increased nearly 300 percent during the same four-year period.[140] As such, the federal income tax played a major role in financing American military operations

135. House Committee on Ways and Means, 63d Cong., 1st sess. (April 21, 1913), H. Rept. 5, xxxvii.

136. Congressional Record, 63d Cong., 1st sess. (August 27, 1913), 50, pt. 4, 3806–3807.

137. Miguel Angel Centeno, *Blood and Debt: War and the Nation-State in Latin America* (University Park: Pennsylvania State University Press, 2002), 104.

138. U.S. Bureau of the Census, *Historical Statistics of the United States,* series Y 402–411 ("Individual Income Tax Returns: 1913 to 1943"), part 2, 1110.

139. Computations based on figures from U.S. Bureau of the Census, *Historical Statistics of the United States,* series Y 352–357 ("Federal Government Receipts—Administrative Budget: 1789 to 1939"), part 2, 1106.

140. U.S. Bureau of the Census, *Historical Statistics of the United States,* series Y 381–392 ("Corporate Income Tax Returns: 1909 to 1970"), part 2, 1109.

in Europe and the related expansion of the civilian bureaucracy.[141] But this was only the first stage in what would become a radical transformation of the revenue system of the American state in the twentieth century. Prior to the war, excise taxes and the tariff generated more than 90 percent of the revenue of the federal government. In 1914, the income tax provided only 9.7 percent of the receipts of the national government. This figure rose to 16 percent by 1916. During the height of the war in 1918, revenue from the wartime income tax (individual and corporate) and excess profits tax supplied fully 63.1 percent of federal receipts. In that year, revenue from the tariff and other excise taxes declined to just 28.7 percent of federal receipts.

Under the Wilsonian Democrats, the income tax emerged as the primary source of revenue for the national government, supplanting the tariff and excise taxes as the cornerstone of the federal revenue system. At the same time, Progressives sought to use the income tax to effect a mild redistribution of wealth. Their tax policy never posed a threat to the existing social order or the capitalist system. Instead, progressive income taxation served as a basic tool in what Elliot Brownlee refers to as Wilson's political strategy of "steering between socialism and unmediated capitalism."[142] The resulting "democratic-statist tax regime" was funded by revenue from the progressive income tax, the excess profits tax on corporations, and the federal estate tax, and thus was entirely dependent on the private capitalist economy. To administer these new taxes, expansion of the administrative apparatus was required. The staff of the Bureau of Internal Revenue (within the Treasury Department) increased from 4,000 to 15,800 between 1913 and 1920. At the same time, Treasury implemented a new strategy of massive borrowing from the public through the so-called Liberty Loan program.[143] The Federal Reserve Board (created in 1913) was used to control the money supply and national banking system, while the War Industries Board, the Food Administration (headed by Herbert Hoover), and

---

141. In 1913, the Bureau of Internal Revenue had only 4,000 employees collecting $344 million in revenue; by 1920, it had nearly 16,000 employees collecting $5.5 billion. Figures cited in Chommie, *The Internal Revenue Service,* 19.

142. Brownlee, *Federal Taxation in America,* 47–48.

143. Details of the Liberty Loan program are found in Myers, *A Financial History of the United States,* 281–83; Bank, Stark, and Thorndike, *War and Taxes,* 58–60.

the Petroleum Advisory Committee were used to manage the wartime economy.[144]

Significant changes to the national political institutions of the American state were implemented during the First World War, but institutional retrenchment followed in peacetime. The size of the military was dramatically reduced after 1919, and with that, the revenue needs of the American state declined. Despite this, government spending and taxes initially remained at elevated levels. This prompted the Republican candidate in the 1920 presidential election, Warren G. Harding, to campaign on the theme of a "return to normalcy," and after his election, tax reduction became the personal mission of his new treasury secretary, Andrew W. Mellon.[145] With a Republican back in the White House, pressure mounted on Congress to reduce income tax rates to prewar levels. Some conservatives lobbied for the outright repeal of the income tax, while others advocated that it be replaced with a national sales tax. Harding and Mellon resisted both extremes, advocating a moderate course of reducing income tax rates to prewar levels. In a speech before a joint session of Congress on April 12, 1921, Harding laid out the agenda for his new administration: "I know of no more pressing problem at home than to restrict our national expenditures within the limits of our national income, and at the same time measurably lift the burdens of war taxation from the shoulders of the American people."[146]

Implementing Harding's plan fell to Mellon, who would serve three successive probusiness Republican presidents at the helm of the Treasury Department. Throughout the 1920s, Mellon had a profound influence on the fiscal policies of the nation.[147] Early in his tenure at Treasury, he

---

144. The role of the War Industries Board, the Food Administration, and the Petroleum Advisory Committee in coordinating domestic production during the war is discussed in Robert H. Wiebe, *The Search for Order, 1877–1920* (New York: Hill and Wang, 1967), 298–301. In his "reinterpretation" of the period, historian Gabriel Kolko refers to such innovations as the Federal Reserve Board and the Federal Trade Commission as the "triumph of political capitalism." Gabriel Kolko, *The Triumph of Conservatism* (Chicago: Quadrangle Books, 1963).

145. Harding campaigned for a "return to normalcy" during the general election, leaving it to Mellon to implement tax policy during his brief tenure in office. Mellon presented his theories on taxation in his popular book, *Taxation: The People's Business* (New York: Macmillan, 1924).

146. Warren G. Harding, "Special Address to Congress," in *Messages and Papers of the Presidents* (New York: Bureau of National Literature, n.d.), 8937.

147. A recent biography of Mellon that provides a comprehensive account of his life and fiscal policies is David Cannadine, *Mellon: An American Life* (New York: Knopf, 2006).

supported efforts to rationalize the federal budget process implemented under the Budget and Accounting Act of 1921.[148] This legislation established executive control over the budget process by creating the Bureau of the Budget within the Treasury Department. It also created the General Accounting Office under the jurisdiction of the Comptroller General to provide for internal auditing of government accounts. Harding died in November 1923, but Mellon stayed the course for "tax normalcy" during the ensuing Coolidge administration. Remaining at the helm of Treasury, he proposed a 25-percent reduction in the tax on earned income, reducing the tax rate from 4 percent to 3 percent at the lower income brackets and from 8 percent to 6 percent at the upper income levels. Likewise, the special tax preference for capital gains was first unveiled during Mellon's long tenure as treasury secretary, as were numerous probusiness tax deductions such as the depletion allowance for oil and gas. The excess profits tax was repealed in 1921 and replaced with a moderate corporate income tax. Yet even as taxes were lowered, budget surpluses were realized and a significant portion of the war debt was retired. Simultaneously, the national government increased financial support for agriculture and federal highway construction during the 1920s. The trend toward lower taxes continued until the end of the decade, by which time rates were reduced to prewar levels. As John Makin and Norman Ornstein have observed, by the close of the 1920s "the federal government resembled what it had been in 1800 more than the institution that it would become by 1948."[149] That would soon change with the collapse of the domestic economy.

Tax Policy during the New Deal

Following the landslide electoral victory of Franklin D. Roosevelt and congressional Democrats in 1932, Republicans lost their already tenuous hold on Congress as well as the White House, and with that, control over the tax

---

148. Budget and Accounting Act of 1921, June 10, 1921, Pub. L. 67–13, ch. 18, 42 Stat. 20. Similar legislation was passed by Congress in 1920 but vetoed by Wilson based on concerns over the constitutionality of a provision granting the president removal power over the Comptroller General. The bill passed again in 1920 with minor changes.

149. John H. Makin and Norman J. Ornstein, *Debt and Taxes* (New York: Random House, 1994), 92.

policy agenda.[150] During the New Deal, the income tax became more than just an important source of public revenue; it emerged as a powerful tool and symbol of the highly partisan politics that dominated the era. Ironically, while the New Deal was a significant event in the history of the development of the American administrative state, it had a surprisingly minor long-term impact on federal tax policy, especially compared to the changes implemented in the 1940s during the Second World War. To be sure, tax policy was contentious and highly partisan during the 1930s, but the basic fiscal powers of the American state remained constant, notwithstanding the other historic political changes experienced during the decade.

On taking office, Roosevelt faced an extraordinary financial crisis resulting from the deepening economic depression that began with the crash of the stock market in October 1929. Federal receipts from the income tax (individual and corporate) had decreased sharply with the collapse of the national economy. Revenue from the income tax declined to 31 percent of total federal collections for 1934, down from 79 percent in 1930; furthermore, total federal collections declined from $3 billion to $1.6 billion from 1930 to 1932.[151] In 1931, the national government had suffered a budget deficit ($461 million) for the first time since 1919, and the national debt soared to $22 million as Roosevelt's first term began. The Hoover administration had advocated moderate income tax increases as well as a national sales tax to help balance the budget. The sales tax was rejected by congressional Democrats, but rate increases for the income tax were enacted by a bipartisan coalition under the Revenue Act of 1932.[152] When Roosevelt took office the next spring, he was more interested in balancing the federal budget by reducing governmental expenditures than increasing taxes on the wealthy. In fact, the administration initially relied on regressive excise taxes to raise badly needed revenue. The White House had no plans to wield the income tax as a tool to redistribute wealth or resolve the budgetary crisis.

---

150. Republicans retained control of the Senate and House following the 1930 mid-term elections, but special elections to fill vacancies gave Democrats a slim majority in the House. The 1932 elections finalized the shift in the balance of power for the 73rd Congress.

151. U.S. Bureau of the Census, *Historical Statistics of the United States,* series Y 358–373 ("Internal Revenue Collections: 1863 to 1970"), part 2, 1107.

152. Revenue Act of 1932, June 6, 1932, ch. 209, 47 Stat. 169. This legislation, which imposed the largest peacetime tax increase in the nation's history to date, also enacted several minor federal excise taxes. For a summary of Roosevelt's tax policy during the 1930s, see Brownlee, "Tax Regimes, National Crisis, and State-Building in America," 72–88.

Notwithstanding Roosevelt's initial reluctance to pursue rate increases for the income tax, the "soak-the-rich" rhetoric that emanated from radicals such as agrarian populist Huey Long in Louisiana and Father Charles Coughlin and his National Union for Social Justice, began to penetrate the New Deal philosophy.[153] Likewise, Roosevelt found himself increasingly under pressure from Progressives in the Senate led by Robert La Follette Jr. of Wisconsin. In response, Congress (with the support of the White House) raised rates for all individuals as well as the overall progressivity of the income tax under the Revenue Act of 1934.[154] This legislation also raised the federal estate tax to 60 percent on taxable estates greater than $10 million. In the Senate, both La Follette and Long pressed for even higher tax rates. They were initially opposed by Roosevelt, but his administration gradually adopted a more aggressive tax policy in response to the successes of Long and his agrarian populist movement, often referred to as the "Thunder on the Left."[155] In June 1935, the president unveiled to Congress his new tax policy agenda. First, he requested an inheritance tax that would apply to wealthy estates: "Inherited economic power is inconsistent with the ideals of this generation as inherited political power was inconsistent with the ideals of the generation which established our Government." Second, he asked for an increase in the surtax on personal income above $1 million: "Social unrest and a deepening sense of unfairness are dangers to our national life which we must minimize by rigorous methods.... Therefore, the duty rests upon the Government to restrict such incomes by very high taxes." Third, Roosevelt proposed a graduated rate structure for the corporate income tax to replace the flat 13.75 percent rate then in effect.[156] Roosevelt's initiative yielded results

---

153. For a history of these political movements, see Alan Brinkley, *Voices of Protest: Huey Long, Father Coughlin, and the Great Depression* (New York: Alfred A. Knopf, 1982). Roosevelt was pushed to support a national pension program by Dr. Francis Townsend, proponent of a widely popular old-age pension plan. See Edwin Amenta, *When Movements Matter: The Townsend Plan and the Rise of Social Security* (Princeton: Princeton University Press, 2006).

154. Revenue Act of 1934, May 10, 1934, ch. 277, 48 Stat. 680.

155. Long proposed a tax to cap personal wealth at $1.5 million. The revenue from this tax would provide a guaranteed income of $3,000 for every American family. Mark H. Leff, *The Limits of Symbolic Reform: The New Deal and Taxation, 1933–1939* (New York: Cambridge University Press, 1984), 123–24.

156. "A Message to the Congress on Tax Revisions," in *The Public Papers and Addresses of Franklin D. Roosevelt* (New York: Random House, 1938), 4:270.

in August 1935 as Congress enacted tax legislation that included most of what he had requested. The Revenue Act of 1935 increased the surtax on the wealthy, kicking in at 31 percent on income greater than $50,000 and rising to 75 percent on income greater than $5 million. The flat 13.75 percent rate for the corporate income tax was replaced with a graduated rate that rose from 12.5 percent on the first $2,000 of net income to 15 percent on income in excess of $40,000.[157]

In August, Congress enacted another major public policy in the Social Security Act of 1935.[158] This landmark legislation established a national income-maintenance program that pays benefits to current retirees out of payroll taxes collected from current workers as well as a national program of unemployment insurance.[159] The program was funded through a payroll tax of 2 percent on wages up to three thousand dollars (half of which was paid by the worker from wages and the other half by the employer). The tax was first collected in 1937. Benefits were initially paid out to a small number of qualifying retirees, as entire classes of workers were left uncovered by the legislation.[160] In the decades that followed, retirement benefits, the scope of coverage, and the payroll tax were gradually increased, thereby creating a comprehensive and extraordinarily expensive program—one that is part insurance and part social welfare.[161] In October 1935, Roosevelt took America down a path toward a system of retirement benefits that by the end of the twentieth century would consume nearly a quarter of the outlays of the national government.[162]

---

157. Revenue Act of 1935, August 30, 1935, ch. 829, 49 Stat. 1014.

158. Social Security Act of 1935, August 14, 1935, ch. 531, 49 Stat. 620.

159. By 1919, thirty-eight states had already adopted workers' compensation laws.

160. Death benefits were first paid out in 1937 to 53,236 beneficiaries, while the first monthly retirement benefits were paid in January 1940. Originally, only workers were covered, while nonworking surviving spouses, farm workers, the self-employed, and members of Congress were excluded. The Social Security Amendments of 1939 added survivors' benefits.

161. The classic account of the politics behind the enactment of the Social Security Act of 1935 is Martha Derthick, *Policymaking for Social Security* (Washington, DC: Brookings Institution, 1979). For an account of the expansion of the social welfare system, see Jacob S. Hacker, *The Divided Welfare State: The Battle over Public and Private Social Benefits in the United States* (New York: Cambridge University Press, 2002), 95–112, 142–45; Suzanne Mettler, *Dividing Citizens: Gender and Federalism in New Deal Public Policy* (Ithaca: Cornell University Press, 1998).

162. Office of Management and Budget, *Historical Tables, Budget of the United States Government, Fiscal Year 2009* (Washington, DC: Government Printing Office, 2008), table 4.2 ("Percentage Distribution of Outlays by Agency: 1962–2012"), 84.

Notwithstanding the fanfare, Roosevelt's programs failed to satisfy radicals on the Left, even while provoking an intense negative reaction from conservative Republicans. The opposition soon regrouped, and with the support of conservative Democrats, ushered through Congress legislation that reversed many of the tax policies enacted by Roosevelt's progressive coalition earlier in the decade. First, the Revenue Act of 1938 eased the tax burden on business corporations and lowered the tax on capital gains.[163] This was followed by the Revenue Act of 1939, which further reduced the tax burden on profitable businesses and wealthy individuals.[164] For all the sound and fury of the New Deal, Progressive Democrats were never able to use the income taxation to effect a significant redistribution of wealth. Despite the strong ideological overtones of the New Deal and its importance in the development of an administrative state, only relatively minor changes (e.g., higher tax rates) were made to the federal income tax during the 1930s. Mark Leff has aptly described tax policy during the New Deal as "symbolic reform"—that is, more political rhetoric than redistributive policy.[165] With the outbreak of the Second World War, however, the politics of the income tax shifted from a partisan "group contest" over who would bear the burden of taxation to a statist concern with raising the vast revenue needed for the global military campaign into which the United States was drawn.

The Emergence of a Modern Fiscal-Military State

On December 8, 1941, Congress approved a formal declaration of war on Japan in response to its attack on the U.S. naval base at Pearl Harbor in Hawaii.[166] Three days later, Germany and Italy declared war on the United

---

163. Revenue Act of 1938, May 28, 1938, ch. 289, 52 Stat. 447.

164. Revenue Act of 1939, June 29, 1939, ch. 247, 53 Stat. 862.

165. Leff, *The Limits of Symbolic Reform*. Leff provides a comprehensive account of tax policy during the New Deal. Ronald King agrees that New Deal tax policy did not threaten the economic regime: "Despite the redistributional imagery, helpful in regaining the political initiative and in stealing Huey Long's thunder, a careful consideration of the contents of the Roosevelt proposal [of June 1935] reveals no efforts either to undermine corporate capitalism or to share the wealth." Ronald F. King, *Money, Time, and Politics: Investment Tax Subsidiaries and American Democracy* (New Haven: Yale University Press, 1993), 113.

166. On December 8, the Senate unanimously approved the president's war resolution, while one lone dissenting vote was cast in the House by Jeannette Rankin of Montana.

States. Thus commenced America's entry into the global military conflict that already engulfed Europe and most of Asia. During the nearly four years of total war that followed, the United States emerged as a global superpower with the world's leading military and most advanced industrial economy. To finance the rapid buildup of the nation's military forces, national political leaders would create a powerful revenue system to tap the enormous wealth generated by the domestic economy. The American state was also forced to reorganize and redirect the industrial capacity of the nation to supply its military. This was necessary because "private industry had withdrawn almost entirely from the military sector" in the decades following the First World War.[167] With this great expansion of state capacity, the United States became the preeminent fiscal-military state in the world.

Even before America's official entry into the war, the Roosevelt administration took major steps to strengthen the nation's military capacity. In July 1940, in his acceptance speech before the Democratic Party convention in Chicago, Roosevelt raised the specter of a draft. At the time, the U.S. armed forces had only 458,365 personnel on active duty, with fewer than 269,000 men in the regular army, even as war had ravaged Europe for more than a year. In September, Congress enacted the Selective Training and Service Act of 1940, which required the registration of all men between the ages of twenty-one and thirty-five.[168] While the statute authorized a peacetime draft of 900,000 men, fewer than 630,000 men were drafted by the end of June 1941—this through a lottery system that imposed an obligation for twelve months of active service. In August, the term of service was extended to eighteen months. Then, with events in Europe and Asia spiraling out of control, a system of universal conscription was implemented to mobilize most of the civilian male population between the ages of eighteen and forty-five.

All the while, the military was expanded as war preparation commenced in earnest. In 1939, the armed forces of the United States consisted

---

167. Aristide R. Zolberg, "International Engagement and American Democracy: A Comparative Perspective," in *Shaped by War and Trade*, 43. Zolberg argues that to become a world power, the United States first "had to transform itself into a military-industrial state."

168. Selective Training and Service Act of 1940, September 16, 1940, ch. 720, 54 Stat. 885. The nation's first peacetime draft was approved in the Senate by 40 Democrats and 7 Republicans, and in the House, by 186 Democrats and 46 Republicans. "Final Roll-Calls on Draft Bill," *New York Times*, September 15, 1940, 31; Flynn, *The Draft, 1940–1973*, 15–18.

of 334,473 military personnel on active duty, with fewer than 190,000 men in the regular army. By the end of 1941, the number soared to 1.8 million and reached more than 12 million at the height of the war in 1945.[169] Over the course of the war, more than 15 million men and 350,000 women served in the armed forces of the United States.[170] This amounted to 5.5 percent of the population—slightly less than the percentages of the populations mobilized by Germany and England. On the home-front, much of the civilian population as well as the domestic economy was mobilized for the war effort.[171] Likewise, the civilian bureaucracy of the national government was greatly expanded. The number of civilian employees working in Washington nearly doubled from 1940 to 1945, while the total number of civilian employees rose from 1 million to 3.8 million.[172]

Reflecting this rapid expansion of the military and administrative apparatus of the American state occasioned by the nation's entry into the global war, governmental expenditures soared. Monthly payroll for federal civilian employees increased from $177 million for October 1940 to more than $642 million for October 1945. Total outlays of the federal government increased from $9.6 billion in 1940 to $14.0 billion in 1941; by 1945, the figure rose to $95 billion, of which $81.6 billion was devoted to national defense.[173] Expenditures of the federal government reached nearly 44 percent of annual GDP in 1943 and 1944.[174] Total war costs for the United States have been estimated at $664 billion, or 188 percent of the national

169. Carter et al., eds., *Historical Statistics of the United States,* vol. 5, table Ed26–47 ("Military Personnel on Active Duty, by Branch of Service and Sex: 1789–1995"), 5–355.

170. J. Garry Clifford and Samuel R. Spencer Jr., *The First Peacetime Draft* (Lawrence: University of Kansa Press, 1986), 3. An estimated 15 million persons served in the U.S. military forces during the Second World War out of a population of 138 million in 1945. U.S. Bureau of the Census, *Historical Statistics of the United States,* series A 6–8 ("Annual Population Estimates of the United States: 1790 to 1970"), part 1, chapter A ("Population"), 8.

171. For a comparison of the mobilization efforts of the Allies versus the Axis nations, see Mark Harrison, "The Economics of World War II: An Overview," in *The Economics of World War II: Six Great Powers in International Comparisons,* ed. Mark Harrison (Cambridge: Cambridge University Press, 1998), 1–42.

172. U.S. Bureau of the Census, *Historical Statistics of the United States,* series Y 308–317 ("Paid Civilian Employment of the Federal Government: 1816 to 1970"), part 2, 1102.

173. U.S. Bureau of the Census, *Historical Statistics of the United States,* series Y 472–487 ("Outlays of the Federal Government, by Major Function: 1940–1970"), part 2, 1116.

174. Office of Management and Budget, *Historical Tables, Budget of the United States Government, Fiscal Year 2009,* table 1.2 ("Summary of Receipts, Outlays, and Surpluses or Deficits as Percentages of GDP: 1930–2013"), 24.

economy.[175] The initial reaction to this extraordinary increase in government spending was similar to that for the Civil War and the First World
War—major tax increases were proposed. Even before war was declared,
President Roosevelt requested an additional $500 million in tax revenue
from Congress in anticipation of a projected deficit of $2.876 billion for
fiscal year 1941. This was provided under the Revenue Act of 1940 (enacted in June), which reduced personal exemptions for the income tax by
20 percent, imposed a relatively minor surtax on personal income over six
thousand dollars, increased corporate income tax rates from 19 percent to
22.1 percent, and increased federal excise taxes.[176] On July 1, 1940, Roosevelt
publicly requested a "steeply graduated excess profits tax, to be applied to
all individuals and all corporate organizations without discrimination."[177]
After debating throughout the summer, Congress enacted an excess profits
tax pursuant to the Second Revenue Act of 1940.[178] The excess profits tax
(with a maximum rate of 50 percent) was designed to tax business profits
attributable solely to increased defense spending, which had stimulated
the national economy.[179] The legislation increased the regular corporate
income tax from 22.1 percent to 24 percent.

Following his landslide victory in the 1940 presidential election, Roosevelt
pursued a wartime fiscal program based on increased public borrowing and
higher income taxation. He proposed that Congress further reduce personal exemptions, increase tax rates for the individual income tax, and expand the excess profits tax. Congress complied in the Revenue Act of 1941,
which implemented what was at the time the largest increase in federal
revenue in American history. This was achieved through lower exemptions
($750 for individuals and $1,500 for married couples) and higher tax rates
on middle-class taxpayers (reaching 77 percent on incomes over $5 mil-
lion). The federal estate and gift taxes were also increased. As government
spending for the war effort continued to rise, even greater tax increases

175. Carter et al., eds., *Historical Statistics of the United States,* vol. 5, table Ed168–179 ("Estimated Costs of U.S. Wars: 1775–1992"), 5–370.

176. Revenue Act of 1940, June 25, 1940, ch. 419, 54 Stat. 516.

177. *The Public Papers and Addresses of Franklin D. Roosevelt: 1940* (New York: Macmillan,
1941), 276.

178. Second Revenue Act of 1940, October 8, 1940, ch. 757, 54 Stat. 974.

179. For an account of the 1940 excess profits tax, see Carl Shoup, "Taxation of Excess Profits
III," *Political Science Quarterly* 56 (1941): 226; Bank, Stark, and Thorndike, *War and Taxes,* 87–90.

became necessary. The Revenue Act of 1942, enacted in November, raised normal income tax rates for individuals from 4 percent to 6 percent and added a progressive surtax that rose from 13 percent on net income in excess of $6,000 to 82 percent on net income in excess of $200,000. Personal exemptions were lowered to $500 for individuals and $1,200 for married couples, and a so-called Victory Tax of 5 percent was added.[180] This had the effect of expanding the reach of the income tax to include the vast majority of working Americans.

This expansion of the tax base was evidenced by the number of tax returns filed by individuals, which increased nearly eightfold from 1940 to 1945.[181] The total number of individuals subject to the income tax increased over the course of the Second World War, eventually reaching more than 74 percent of the population. No longer just a levy on the wealthy, the income tax was transformed from a "class tax" into a "mass tax."[182] Secretary of Treasury Henry Morgenthau Jr. glossed over the true nature of the new wartime revenue strategy when he boasted to Congress that "for the first time in our history, the income tax is becoming a people's tax."[183] This "people's tax" proved an extraordinarily effective tool that allowed the American state to extract enormous revenue from society for the war effort.

After 1942, tax rates continued to rise, eventually reaching 94 percent for individuals (on net income in excess of $2 million) and 40 percent for corporations. Consequently, revenue from the income tax continued to

---

180. Revenue Act of 1942, October 21, 1942, ch. 619, 56 Stat. 798. Brownlee argues that the Revenue Act of 1942 "represented agreement between Congress and Roosevelt on what became the core of a new tax regime—a personal income tax that was both broadly based and progressive." Brownlee, *Federal Taxation in America,* 93.

181. The number of tax returns filed by individuals rose from 3.9 million in 1939 to more than 40 million by 1943. U.S. Bureau of the Census, *Historical Statistics of the United States,* series Y 402–411 ("Individual Tax Returns: 1913–1943"), part 2, 1110.

182. The transformation of the income tax during the Second World War from an impost paid by only the wealthy few into a "mass tax" is described in John F. Witte, *The Politics and Development of the Federal Income Tax* (Madison: University of Wisconsin Press, 1985), 110–30. Efforts by the Treasury Department to publicize the obligations of middle-class taxpayers under the income tax during the war as well as to retain the impost after the war are discussed in Carolyn C. Jones, "Mass-Based Income Taxation: Creating a Taxpayer Culture, 1940–1952," in *Funding the Modern American State, 1941–1995,* ed. Brownlee, 107–47.

183. Senate Committee on Finance, Hearings on H.R. 7378, vol. 1, 77th Cong., 2d sess. (1942), 3.

swell. Federal receipts from the individual income tax rose from $892 million in 1940 to $18.4 billion in 1945, while receipts from the corporate income tax increased from $1.2 billion in 1940 to $16.0 billion in 1945.[184] During the same period, total receipts of the national government increased from $6.88 billion to $50.2 billion and receipts from federal excise taxes tripled.[185] Total receipts of the national government as a percentage of GDP increased from about 6 to 7 percent prior to the outbreak of war to 20.4 percent in 1945.[186] Yet even this enormous revenue was less than half the cost of the war effort. Consequently, the national government was forced to borrow ever greater amounts; public debt rose from $43.0 billion in 1940 to $259 billion in 1945.[187] The debt was placed through a sophisticated system in which the Treasury Department sold debt instruments to the American public as well as global capital markets.[188] The federal debt held by the public rose from less than $43 billion in 1940 to more than $235 billion in 1945.[189]

The administration of the federal revenue system was also radically transformed during the Second World War. The staff of the Bureau of Internal Revenue increased from twenty-two thousand to fifty thousand between 1940 and 1945, with the budget of the collection agency increasing from $60 million to $147 million.[190] Perhaps the most dramatic change

---

184. Office of Management and Budget, *Historical Tables, Budget of the United States Government, Fiscal Year 2009,* table 2.1 ("Receipts by Source, 1934–2013"), 30. The number of individual income tax returns filed from 1940 to 1945 increased from 14.6 million to nearly 50 million.

185. U.S. Bureau of the Census, *Historical Statistics of the United States,* series Y 343–351 ("Federal Government Receipts, by Source: 1940 to 1970"), part 2, 1105.

186. Office of Management and Budget, *Historical Tables, Budget of the United States Government, Fiscal Year 2009,* table 1.2 ("Summary of Receipts, Outlays, and Surpluses or Deficits as Percentages of GDP: 1930–2013"), 24.

187. U.S. Bureau of the Census, *Historical Statistics of the United States,* series Y 488–492 ("Public Debt of the Federal Government: 1791 to 1970"), part 2, 1117.

188. Federal wartime borrowing is described in Myers, *A Financial History of the United States,* 350–55. Between November 1942 and December 1945, the government sold $157 billion in bonds to individuals, corporations, and commercial banks. The expansion of the federal government's capacity to borrow during the war is recounted in detail in Bartholomew H. Sparrow, *From the Outside In: World War II and the American State* (Princeton: Princeton University Press, 1996), 109–25. More broadly, Sparrow argues that the Second World War had a "profound impact on the American state" as it transformed the bureaucracies of the federal government and "reconfigured the pattern of government-society relations." Ibid., 269.

189. Office of Management and Budget, *Historical Tables, Budget of the United States Government, Fiscal Year 2009,* table 7.1 ("Federal Debt at the End of the Year: 1940–2013"), 127.

190. Sparrow, *From the Outside In,* 132.

was the introduction of "withholding at the source," which required that employers withhold income tax from the paycheck of employees and remit the revenue to the federal government. Such a system had been first proposed by Cordell Hull of Tennessee, Democratic chairman of the House Ways and Means Committee, when the income tax was originally drafted in 1913. The model for withholding at the source was the British tax system, which required that tax be withheld at a flat rate from certain types of payments. In the face of strong opposition, withholding had been dropped from the 1913 tax legislation that established the modern income tax. The Roosevelt administration now pressed for withholding to speed up the collection of sorely needed revenue. The Social Security payroll tax was already collected from the wages of employees by their employers, and provided a model for extending the practice to the income tax. Congress approved this administrative innovation under the Current Tax Payment Act of 1943.[191] The legislation imposed an obligation on "payers" of wages, interest, and dividends, requiring them to withhold income tax at a statutory rate of 20 percent. Under the system, an individual's income taxes would be paid during the year thorough withholding (or quarterly estimated payments of tax), rather than with the filing of a tax return the following spring.[192]

This transformation of the income tax during the war gave the American state a powerful tool for revenue extraction that it has never relinquished. Whereas the partisan politics of the New Deal had failed to significantly alter the structure of the income tax regime, the crisis of total war brought about a radical restructuring of the entire fiscal system of the American state. While wage, price, and production controls were abandoned after the war, structural changes to the revenue system were not, as had been the case following the Civil War and the First World War. Despite modest rate reductions in 1946, the expanded rate structure and scope of the income tax were retained to finance high levels of military spending during the Cold War era. The expansionist trend for the income

---

191. Current Tax Payment Act of 1943, June 9, 1943, ch. 120, 57 Stat. 126.

192. With the introduction of withholding at the source in 1943, taxpayers were required to pay taxes for two years (1942 and 1943) in the same twelve-month period. The Roosevelt administration resisted proposals for relief from this "double payment," but in the end accepted a proposal from Beardsley Ruml, chairman of the New York Federal Reserve Bank, to forgive three-fourths of the 1942 income tax liability. Brownlee, *Federal Taxation in America,* 94–96.

tax experienced during the 1940s persisted in the postwar period, albeit at a slower pace. By 1950, fully 59 percent of the population was subject to the federal income tax; the figure increased to 81 percent by 1970. Revenue from the income tax amounted to 66 percent of total federal receipts in 1950.[193]

In the postwar era, the federal income tax would be used by politicians not just as the primary source of revenue for the American state, but also to implement social and economic policies that affect virtually all aspects of the lives of American citizens. It also raises the bulk of the revenue of the federal government. As we will see in the next chapter, the postwar American state is a fiscal-military colossus that consumes trillions of dollars a year. Raising that revenue is vital to the continued development of the American state.

---

193. Office of Management and Budget, *Historical Tables, Budget of the United States Government, Fiscal Year 2009,* table 2.1 ("Receipts by Source, 1934–2013"), 30.

FINANCING THE MODERN AMERICAN STATE

The Power of Nations is not now measur'd, as it has been, by Prowess, Gallantry, and Conduct. 'Tis the Wealth of Nations that makes them Great.

—DANIEL DEFOE, *Defoe's Review* (1705)

Taxes are the source of life for the bureaucracy, the army, the priests and the court, in short, for the whole apparatus of the executive power.

—KARL MARX, *The Eighteenth Brumaire of Louis Bonaparte* (1852)

The American state that emerged from the throes of the Second World War was a thoroughly transformed political organization. It bore little resemblance to the American state of the turn of the twentieth century, let alone its late-eighteenth-century predecessor. After nearly four years of total war during which the armed forces of Germany and Japan were vanquished by the Allies, the United States was suddenly the world's undisputed military superpower—rivaled only in Eastern Europe by a regional hegemon, the Soviet Union. With overseas "possessions" and military bases throughout the world, the United States was the only nation-state capable of projecting its military power globally. At the same time, with much of the industrial plant of Europe and Asia lying in ruins after the war, the United States possessed the foremost industrial economy in the world.[1]

---

1. In 1945, the industrial and agricultural production of Europe amounted less than half of what it had been in 1938. Rondo Cameron and Larry Neal, *A Concise Economic History of the World: From Paleolithic Times to the Present* (New York: Oxford University Press, 4th ed. 2003), 361.

America's wartime economy had grown an astonishing 142 percent from 1939 to 1945, as the gross domestic product (GDP) soared from $92.2 billion to $223 billion.[2] During the war, physical plant grew by nearly 50 percent and output of goods grew by more than 50 percent; by the end of the war, more than 50 percent of worldwide manufacturing took place within the United States.[3] Fueled by an efficient system of income taxation that allowed the national government to extract a substantial share of the wealth generated by the thriving domestic economy, the United States became the preeminent fiscal-military state in the world. If the sun was setting on the British Empire, the American Century had only just begun.

The Postwar American Military

Contrary to experience following prior wars, the United States retained a significant military force after the conclusion of the Second World War. While nearly two-thirds of the 12 million personnel on active duty in 1945 were discharged within one year of Japan's surrender on August 15, more than 1.6 million men and 18,000 women remained in uniform as late as 1949, with both Germany and Japan under continuing military occupation by the Allied forces.[4] Even with such an awesome military force, when war broke out in Korea in June 1950, it was necessary to call up reserve units to reinforce the regular army.[5] Authorization for the draft,

---

2. Figures from Bureau of Economic Analysis, United States Department of Commerce, *National Economic Accounts* ("Current-Dollar and 'Real' Gross Domestic Product," August 30, 2007).

3. William Ashworth, *A Short History of the International Economy since 1850* (London: Longman, 1975), 268.

4. The Allied occupation of western Germany did not officially end until 1955, although the military phase ended with the formation of the Federal Republic of Germany in May 1949. The occupation of Japan officially ended with the signing of the Treaty of San Francisco in September 1951. Bartholomew Sparrow argues that the rapid demobilization of so much of the army after the surrender of Japan "weakened the base from which [the United States] could negotiate with Joseph Stalin and the Soviet Union." Bartholomew H. Sparrow, "Limited Wars and the Attenuation of the State: Soldiers, Money, and Political Communication in World War II, Korea, and Vietnam," in *Shaped by War and Trade: International Influences on American Political Development,* ed. Ira Katznelson and Martin Shefter (Princeton: Princeton University Press, 2002), 270–71.

5. More than 240,000 personnel from the Organized Reserve Corps (renamed the Army Reserve in 1952) were called to active duty during the Korean War, although there is no record of how many of these actually served in the theater of war. Gordon L. Rottman, *Korean War Order of Battle: United States, United Nations, and Communist Ground, Naval, and Air Forces, 1950–1953*

which had temporarily expired in 1947, was reenacted by Congress under the Universal Military Training and Service Act of 1951. Thus universal conscription returned only six years after the end of the Second World War as American military forces were rapidly expanded. Some 1.79 million Americans ultimately served in the bloody Korean theater between June 1950 and July 1953, suffering more than 33,000 combat deaths.[6] As fighting dragged on during the two years of peace talks that culminated in the July 1953 cease-fire, the United States maintained more than 3.6 million servicemen on active duty worldwide. Other than during the peak years of the Second World War, this was the largest standing army ever assembled by the United States. If, as has been appropriately suggested, "military power is based largely on the size and strength of a state's army and its supporting air and naval forces,"[7] then the United States certainly was the most formidable military power in the world in the 1950s.

To cope with the increasing expenses that resulted from the expansion of military forces in Korea, federal taxes were raised by the Truman administration pursuant to the Revenue Act of 1950 and the Excess Profits Tax of 1950. Soon after, Congress enacted additional tax increases under the Revenue Act of 1951, which raised the maximum corporate rate to 52 percent and the maximum rate for individuals to 92 percent.[8] Caught up in a long Cold War and expensive arms race with the Soviet Union that would last for decades, the United States devoted more than 50 percent of its annual budget to national defense during the 1950s—considerably less than during the Second World War, when as much as 90 percent of the federal budget was allocated to national defense, but nearly five times the

---

(Westport, CT: Praeger, 2002), 4. For an account of events leading up to the Korean War as well as its broader meaning in international affairs, see William Stueck, *The Korean War: An International History* (Princeton: Princeton University Press, 1995).

6. Hannah Fischer, Congressional Research Service Report, *American War and Military Operations Casualties: Lists and Statistics* (Washington, DC: July 13, 2005), Table 1 ("Principal Wars in which the United States Participated: U.S. Military Personnel Serving and Casualties"), 2; U.S. Bureau of the Census, *Historical Statistics of the United States: Colonial Times to 1970* (Washington, DC: U.S. Department of Commerce, 1975), series A 856–903 ("Selected Characteristics of the Armed Forces, by War"), part 1, 1140.

7. John J. Mearsheimer, *The Tragedy of Great Power Politics* (New York: W. W. Norton, 2001), 56.

8. Revenue Act of 1951, Oct. 20, 1951, chap. 521, 65 Stat. 452. Tax legislation enacted during the Korean War is summarized in Steven A. Bank, Kirk J. Stark, and Joseph J. Thorndike, *War and Taxes* (Washington, DC: Urban Institute Press, 2008), 109–26.

percentage allocated to national security during the 1930s.[9] This commitment to military spending did not change much in the 1960s, when 43 to 50 percent of the annual budget remained devoted to national defense.[10] While that figure declined substantially during the 1970s and 1980s, the downward trend in military spending as a percentage of total spending was largely attributable to a sharp increase in discretionary spending on domestic programs during the same period. In absolute terms, military spending was rising, albeit at a slower pace.[11] Even still, with a booming domestic economy, military spending declined in relation to the economy during this period. As a percentage of gross domestic product (GDP), spending on national defense fluctuated in a range of 6 to 9 percent during the 1960s and 1970s (about what it was prior to the Second World War), and then dropped to 4 to 6 percent during the 1980s and 1990s, dipping to as low as 3 percent of GDP by 2000.

All the while, the size of the armed forces of the United States remained at elevated levels in the postwar era. Anywhere from between 2 to 3 million personnel were on active duty from 1951 until the collapse of the Soviet Union in 1991. Even following that historic event, the American military remained at near wartime levels. Notwithstanding initial optimistic predictions of future cost reductions, no substantial "peace dividend" was realized following the end of the Cold War, as 1.4 million men remained on active duty in the years following the demise of America's superpower rival.[12] Indeed, the new "uni-multipolar" world order proved less stable

---

9. Calculations based on figures from U.S. Bureau of the Census, *Historical Statistics of the United States,* series A 466–471 ("Budget Outlays of the Federal Government, by Major Function: 1900 to 1939"), part 1, 1115.

10. Figures from U.S. Department of Defense, *National Defense Budget Estimates for Fiscal Year 2007* (Washington, DC: March 2006), table 7–7 ("Defense Shares of Economic and Budgetary Aggregates"), 216.

11. During the Second World War, annual expenditures on national defense had reached a peak of $83 billion in 1945 (constituting 38 percent of GDP) as America was fully mobilized for war. By comparison, only $540 million was spent on national defense in 1934 and $1.6 billion (1.7 percent of GDP) in 1940 immediately prior to America's entry into the global conflict. After the war, spending on national defense temporarily declined, falling to $9.1 billion (3.6 percent of GDP) in 1949. The trend was reversed with the outbreak of war in Korea, with defense spending increasing each year in absolute terms. Spending for veterans benefits and services also increased after the Second World War, rising from $744 million in 1944 to $2.1 billion in 1945 to $6.6 billion in 1950. U.S. Bureau of the Census, *Historical Statistics of the United States,* series Y, 984–997 ("Expenditures for Veterans Benefits and Services: 1790 to 1970"), Part 1, 1147.

12. Conscription ended in the United States in 1973. Since then, the armed services have relied on volunteers to maintain the current level of 1.43 million on active duty.

than the bipolar system it replaced, as regional and ethnic conflicts broke out across the globe.[13] New enemies emerged in a world that remained, in the words of Daniel Patrick Moynihan, a very "dangerous place."[14] Largely in response to terrorist attacks on American soil in September 2001, the war in Iraq, and military operations in Afghanistan, defense spending surged 78 percent between 2000 and 2006, increasing from 3 percent of GDP to more than 4 percent. This translated into $553 billion spent on national defense in fiscal year 2007.[15] This vast sum represented nearly 20 percent of the total outlays of the national government and an astonishing 45 percent of worldwide military expenditures—more than the combined military spending of the next thirty-two nations.[16] Based on its budget and manpower, the military apparatus remains a major component of the postwar American state and is the principal source of its influence in international affairs.

The American Social Welfare State

While spending by the United States on national defense persisted at elevated levels in the postwar era, spending on domestic social programs increased even more—albeit less than in Western Europe. This amounted to a *double* ratchet-effect, as both postwar military expenditures and domestic spending significantly exceeded prewar levels—and the ratchet continues to turn. Since the 1960s, the national government has committed

---

13. The term *uni-multipolar* is from Samuel Huntington, who argued that while the United States was the world's only military superpower, there are other major powers (and numerous minor powers) in an international system in which no single nation dominates. Samuel P. Huntington, "The Lonely Superpower," *Foreign Affairs* 78 (March/April 1999): 35–49.

14. The reference is to a common theme in the speeches and writings of the late Senator Moynihan. See, e.g., Daniel Patrick Moynihan, *A Dangerous Place* (Boston: Little Brown, 1978).

15. Calculations based on figures from Office of Management and Budget, *Historical Tables, Budget of the United States Government, Fiscal Year 2009* (Washington, DC: Government Printing Office, 2008), table 3.1 ("Outlays by Superfunction and Function: 1940–2013), 54–55; table 6.1 ("Composition of Outlays: 1940–2013"), 125–25; Department of Defense, *National Defense Budget Estimates for Fiscal Year 2007* (Washington, DC: March 2006), table 7–7 ("Defense Shares of Economic and Budgetary Aggregates"), 216. For fiscal year 2009, the Bush administration proposed $585 billion for the Department of Defense—a 74-percent increase over 2001.

16. The United States accounts for 45 percent of military expenditures worldwide, with England, China, France, and Japan contributing between 4 to 5 percent each. Source: Stockholm International Peace Research Institute, *SIPRI Yearbook 2008: Armaments, Disarmaments and International Security* (New York: Oxford University Press, 2008), Appendix 5A ("Tables of Military Expenditures").

substantial revenues to domestic spending programs, including traditional "internal improvements" (e.g., federal highways, bridges, airports, dams) as well as a host of new domestic programs that did not even exist prior to the Second World War (e.g., federal aid to education, environmental protection, welfare and public housing for the poor, funding for scientific research, healthcare for the poor and elderly). Between 1970 and 1999, total expenditures of the national government in relation to GDP averaged 21 percent, with relatively little variation from year to year. This compares to an average of only 7.9 percent during the 1930s, a period during which government spending was actually expanding while the national economy contracted.[17] The recent expansion of government activities has been a nonpartisan phenomenon. Although conservative Republicans controlled the White House and both houses of Congress from 2000 to 2006, total expenditures of the national government in relation to GDP declined only slightly, averaging 19.5 percent during the period.[18] Like his predecessors in the White House (Republicans and Democrats alike), George W. Bush was unable to contain domestic spending, both discretionary and mandatory. Spending on the military soared even while taxes were cut.[19] Moreover, an expensive Medicare entitlement program for prescription drugs was enacted during Bush's second term at an estimated cost of more than $593 billion over ten years.[20] Overall spending on discretionary domestic programs increased 31 percent from 2001 to 2005 under the watch of the Republican Party. With the collapse of world financial markets and the domestic economy deep in recession, Congress authorized a $787 billion emergency fiscal package that would push the budget deficit for fiscal year

17. Based on figures from Bureau of Economic Analysis, United States Department of Commerce, *National Economic Accounts* ("Current-Dollar and 'Real' Gross Domestic Product," August 30, 2007); U.S. Bureau of the Census, *Historical Statistics of the United States,* series A 457–465 ("Budget Outlays of the Federal Government: 1789 to 1970"), part 1, 1114.

18. Office of Management and Budget, *Historical Tables, Budget of the United States Government, Fiscal Year 2009,* table 15.3 ("Total Government Expenditures as Percentages of GDP: 1948–2012"), 320–21.

19. The unprecedented wartime tax cuts enacted by the Bush administration and the Republican Congress are evaluated in Bank, Stark, and Thorndike, *War and Taxes,* 145–65.

20. The Congressional Budget Office estimated that the new drug prescription program, Title I of the Medicare Modernization Act of 2003 (Pub. L. 108–173), would cost the federal government $593 billion during the ten-year period from 2006 to 2015. Congressional Budget Office, "Updated Estimates of Spending for the Medicare Prescription Drug Program" (Washington, DC: March 4, 2005).

2009 over $1 trillion. Proclamations of the "end of the era of big government" proved eminently premature.[21]

What has been behind the long-term surge in federal spending in the postwar era? Elevated spending on defense certainly has contributed. The United States retains a large global military force, and its high-tech weaponry and equipment is extraordinarily expensive. The states of Western Europe, Canada, Australia, Japan, and Scandinavia have largely avoided this expense, as they maintain only minimal military forces. Italy devotes about 2 percent of total government expenditures to national defense, while Luxembourg dedicates only 1 percent. China, with the world's fourth largest military and an expanding economy, allocates just 2.1 percent of GDP to its military. But even more than the increased spending on the American military, the problem of budget shortfalls in the United States is largely attributable to soaring outlays for social welfare programs. And no social welfare program has expanded more in the postwar era than Social Security.

Due to improvements in diet and advances in medical care, Americans now live significantly longer than their parents and grandparents, with the average life expectancy of a sixty-five-year-old male now 16.3 more years compared to only 12.7 more years in 1940 (the first year monthly benefits were paid out under the Social Security program). The average life expectancy for an American born in the year 2000 is now nearly seventy-eight years—more than eight years longer than that of an American born fifty years earlier.[22] As a result of this extraordinary extension of life expectancy, the number of workers living to sixty-five years and beyond (long enough to collect Social Security benefits) has increased dramatically. In 1950, retirees collecting Social Security benefits comprised only 1.8 percent of the total population of the United States; by 2006, some 48.4 million persons (amounting to 16 percent of the population) were receiving monthly

---

21. Ironically, it was Bill Clinton, who in a radio address on January 27, 1996, proclaimed: "The era of big government is over." Less than six weeks later, the president announced his budget for fiscal year 1997, amounting to $1.6 trillion (22 percent of GDP). To be fair to Clinton, the size of the executive branch as measured by number of civilian employees (excluding post office workers) declined from 2.225 million when he took office in 1993 to 1.778 million when he left office in 2001. Office of Management and Budget, *Historical Tables, Budget of the United States Government, Fiscal Year 2009,* table 17.1 ("Total Executive Branch Civilian Employees: 1940–2007"), 329–30.

22. The average life expectancy at birth for Americans reached a record high of 77.6 years in 2003. U.S. Department of Health and Human Services, "Deaths: Preliminary Data for 2003," in *National Vital Statistics Reports* 53, no. 15 (February 28, 2005): 3.

benefits. With American workers living longer and retirees entitled to more generous benefits, the Social Security program faces long-term fiscal imbalance. Compounding the problem, the ratio of beneficiaries collecting benefits to workers contributing tax revenue to the Social Security Trust Fund (which is the immediate source of the revenue used to pay current beneficiaries) has steadily declined over the decades. The dramatic shift in demographics has had potentially disastrous consequences for the Social Security program. In 1945, five years after benefits were first paid, there were two beneficiaries for every hundred workers contributing payroll taxes; thirteen years later, there were sixteen beneficiaries for every hundred workers. By 1998, there were thirty beneficiaries for every hundred workers, and projections are that there will be fifty by the year 2031. This trend toward an untenable 2:1 ratio of workers to beneficiaries has undermined the financial solvency of the Social Security program.[23]

Even while the worker-to-beneficiary ration has declined, coverage under Social Security has progressively expanded. In 1965, the national government enacted new legislation providing healthcare benefits to the elderly (Medicare) and the poor (Medicaid). These programs (under the jurisdiction of the Social Security Administration) have added to the financial burden of the national government. Social welfare programs are structured differently and somewhat less generously in the United States than in Western Europe, but comparisons based on budget appropriations can be misleading. The national government in Washington indirectly absorbs a significant share of the cost of employer-provided pensions and healthcare insurance coverage for American workers through so-called tax expenditures.[24] Under the federal tax code, exclusions from income are provided to

---

23. Figures from Henry J. Aaron and Robert D. Reischauer, *Countdown to Reform: The Great Social Security Debate* (New York: Century Foundation Press, 1998), 56. A summary of the fiscal imbalance facing the Social Security program is found in C. Eugene Steuerle and Jon M. Bakija, *Retooling Social Security for the 21st Century: Right and Wrong Approaches to Reform* (Washington, DC: Urban Institute Press, 1994), 39–71. A comparable decline in the ratio of workers to retirees is taking place in Western Europe, with Switzerland and Germany facing the same untenable 2:1 ratio by the year 2040. See B. Guy Peters, *The Politics of Taxation: A Comparative Perspective* (Cambridge: Basil Blackwell, 1991), 83–85.

24. The concept of tax expenditures was first introduced to budget analysis by the Treasury Department in 1968. Subsequently recognized by statute, tax expenditures are defined as "those revenue losses attributable to provisions of the Federal tax laws which allow a special exclusion, exemption, or deduction from gross income or which provide a special credit, a preferential rate of tax, or a deferral of tax liability." Congressional Budget and Impoundment Act, Pub. L. No.

employees for the premiums for healthcare insurance and retirement fund contributions paid by employers on their behalf.[25] The tax expenditure for employer contributions for healthcare premiums and medical care (the largest single tax expenditure) is expected to cost the national government more than $168 billion in foregone tax revenue in fiscal year 2009, while the partial exclusion from income of Social Security retirement benefits will cost nearly $19 billion.[26] If slightly less generous in the overall benefits it pays to its citizens compared to the states of Western Europe, Australia, New Zealand, Canada, and Scandinavia, the United States nevertheless commits significant revenue and resources to social welfare programs through a combination of direct budget allocations and indirect tax expenditures. The result is a very expensive (albeit noncomprehensive) system of social welfare coverage. The modern American state is just as much a social welfare state as a military superpower.[27]

If America is a social welfare state, a good deal of its expenditures lies outside the oversight of the congressional budget process. Payment of most federal social welfare benefits is mandated by law to qualified persons, and

---

93–344, sec. 3(a)(3), 88 Stat. 298, 299 (1974). For a discussion of the politics behind tax expenditures, see Stanley S. Surrey, *Pathways to Tax Reform: The Concept of Tax Expenditures* (Cambridge: Harvard University Press, 1973); and Stanley S. Surrey and Paul McDaniel, *Tax Expenditures* (Cambridge: Harvard University Press, 1985).

25. Hacker stresses the importance of the "private" social benefits provided by employers in the United States, which benefits are subsidized by the national government through the income tax code. Jacob S. Hacker, *The Divided Welfare State: The Battle over Public and Private Social Benefits in the United States* (New York: Cambridge University Press, 2002). The use of tax expenditures to implement social policy is the subject of Christopher Howard, *The Hidden Welfare State: Tax Expenditures and Social Policy in the United States* (Princeton: Princeton University Press, 1997).

26. Office of Management and Budget, *Analytical Perspectives, Budget of the United States Government, Fiscal Year 2009*, table 19.3 ("Income Tax Expenditures Ranked by Total 2009–2013 Projected Revenue Effect"), 298.

27. Peter Gourevitch argues that after the Second World War, the United States became a "military state," a "welfare state," and a "regulatory state." Peter A. Gourevitch, "Reinventing the American State: Political Dynamics in the Post-Cold War Era," in *Shaped by War and Trade*, ed. Katznelson and Shefter, 307. Throughout this study, I have focused on the military and welfare functions of the American state, leaving to others to explain the rise of the regulatory state since the New Deal. Moreover, with respect to social welfare, I have focused on Social Security and Medicare, ignoring programs for the poor. As Theda Skocpol has observed, Americans typically draw a distinction between "Social Security" (retirement benefits, disability, medical coverage for the elderly) and "welfare" for the poor. Theda Skocpol, "The Limits of the New Deal System and the Roots of Contemporary Welfare Dilemmas," in *The Politics of Social Policy in the United States*, ed. Margaret Weir, Ann Shola Orloff, and Theda Skocpol (Princeton: Princeton University Press, 1988), 296.

appropriations for these programs are not included in the annual budget. At the same time, political constraints make it extremely difficult to cut back benefits.[28] Among the most expensive of the so-called entitlement programs are Social Security (i.e., Old Age, Survivors, and Disability Insurance) and Medicare. Since the 1960s, mandatory spending for these programs has expanded dramatically, threatening to overwhelm the rest of the federal budget. Total benefits paid out for Social Security and Medicare has increased from $1 million in 1937 to more than $952 billion in 2007 and exceeded $1 trillion in fiscal year 2008. Mandatory spending on Social Security as a percentage of total federal outlays increased significantly throughout the postwar era, rising from 14.4 percent in fiscal year 1965 to 19.1 percent by 1975. Annual spending on Social Security benefits alone now accounts for more than 20 percent of total federal outlays and is projected to reach 24.8 percent by 2013. This translates into 4.3 percent of GDP distributed to current retirees through the payment of Social Security (OASDI) benefits. Outlays for all mandatory programs now account for more than 53 percent of total federal spending (10.8 percent of GDP) and are projected to rise to an astonishing 60 percent by the year 2013.[29]

This surge in spending on entitlement programs has led economist Paul Krugman to quip that the federal government "has become a retirement program that does some military stuff and a bit of humanitarian stuff on the side."[30] A quick glance at the federal budget reveals that this is no joke. It is all the more remarkable given that little more than a 150 years ago the American state had only a minor military force and performed no social welfare functions at all. Today, Social Security and Medicare have transformed the American state into a massive "transfer state" that redistributes

---

28. In 1983, Congress approved amendments to the Social Security program that postponed the retirement age for recipients from 65 to 67 (with a gradual phase-in that began in 2000 and continues until 2022), Social Security Amendments of 1983, Pub. L. 98–21. This measure implemented an indirect reduction of benefits. For an account of the turbulent politics behind this legislation, see Aaron B. Wildavsky and Joseph White, *The Deficit and the Public Interest: The Search for Responsible Budgeting in the 1980s* (Berkeley: University of California Press, 1989), 310–30.

29. Office of Management and Budget, *Historical Tables, Budget of the United States Government, Fiscal Year 2009,* table 8.5 ("Outlays for Mandatory and Related Programs: 1962–2013"), 143; table 8.3 ("Percentage Distribution of Outlays by Budget Enforcement Act Category: 1962–2013"), 136; table 8.4 ("Outlays by Budget Enforcement Act Category as Percentages of GDP: 1962–2013"), 137.

30. Paul Krugman, *Fuzzy Math: The Essential Guide to the Bush Tax Plan* (New York: W. W. Norton, 2001), 49.

hundreds of billions of dollars annually across generations, collecting the money from young workers via the wage tax and distributing the proceeds to their parents and grandparents in the form of retirement and healthcare benefits.[31] But with fewer workers contributing taxes and more retirees collecting benefits, the system is financially unsustainable.

Financing the Postwar American State

One recurring theme of this study is that societal wealth does not translate directly into state capacity. To build a strong state, rulers must pursue a revenue strategy for extracting a share of societal wealth for the state. Greater societal wealth certainly makes revenue extraction easier and hence, is a precondition for building a powerful fiscal-military state.[32] Nevertheless, something more is required to convert societal wealth into state power. What is needed is efficient mechanisms of revenue extraction and skilled rulers who can implement their revenue strategies. Some rulers are more effective than others, and as we have seen, all rulers face constraints on their inclinations toward revenue predation.

The link between societal wealth and state power seems obvious, but actually it is difficult to specify. In his influential study on the dynamics of interstate relations, *The Tragedy of Great Power Politics* (2001), John Mearsheimer highlights the connection between military power and "wealth" (broadly conceived). Wealth is important because "a state cannot build a powerful military if it does not have the money and technology to equip, train, and continually modernize its fighting forces." Military power is based on the soldiers and equipment that comprise the state's armed forces, and acquiring and maintaining soldiers and equipment is incredibly expensive. Once the decision is made to acquire military power (e.g., a large and well-equipped army), enormous revenue is necessary to achieve that goal. But

---

31. The intergenerational impact of Social Security is a central theme of Laurence J. Kotlikoff, *Generational Accounting: Knowing Who Pays, and When, for What We Spend* (New York: Free Press, 1992); *Generational Policy* (Cambridge: MIT Press, 2003); and *The Coming Generational Storm* (Cambridge: MIT Press, 2004).

32. There is an extensive literature suggesting that military power is dependent on societal wealth. The relationship between societal wealth and military power is discussed in Robert Gilpin, *War and Change in World Politics* (New York: Cambridge University Press, 1981).

how does a state intent on acquiring a powerful military force go about converting societal wealth into military power? After all, societal wealth only constitutes the "latent power" of a state, not actual military power. As Mearsheimer properly notes, there is a strong correlation between latent power and actual power: "Wealth underpins military power and that wealth by itself is a good indicator of latent power."[33] As far as it goes, this is correct. But how do states convert latent power (based on societal wealth) into military power? As we have seen, the answer lies in the state's capacity to appropriate societal wealth through an effective revenue strategy and efficient mechanisms of revenue extraction. This is precisely what officials of the American state achieved during the Second World War, when they expanded the federal income tax and created a sophisticated system of public borrowing to convert "latent power" (i.e., the enormous wealth generated by the new industrial economy) into tangible military power—that is, airplanes, tanks, battleships, guns, and a well-equipped army of 12 million troops.[34]

Since the First World War, the income tax has been the principal source of revenue for the national government and hence, the fuel for its powerful military machine. During the Second World War, the American state became dependent on the revenue generated by this impost. That dependence persisted into the postwar era. At the same time, the United States used its considerable influence to press other nations to reduce tariffs and trade barriers in order to establish a new international order of nondiscriminatory world trade.[35] For better or worse, as protective tariffs were lowered, dependency on the income tax increased. In recent decades, a broad consensus has emerged among economists that some form of a consumption tax or value-added tax (VAT) would be more efficient than the present income tax (itself a hybrid form of a pure income tax). But with so much of the economy and government dependent on the current tax system, replacing the income tax with a national consumption tax or sales

---

33. Mearsheimer, *The Tragedy of Great Power Politics,* 67.

34. Airplanes, tanks, battleships, guns, and troops are the requisites for what Joseph Nye refers to as "hard power," which he contrasts with "soft power" (that is, the ability to exert influence in the international arena through diplomacy, persuasion, cultural contacts, and alliances). Joseph S. Nye, Jr., *Bound to Lead: The Changing Nature of American Power* (New York: Basic Books, 1990); and *Soft Power: The Means to Success in World Politics* (New York: Public Affairs, 2004).

35. Ashworth, *A Short History of the International Economy Since 1850,* 276–77.

tax is impossible.[36] It has been more than ninety years since America went down the path to a revenue system based on the income tax, and it would be very difficult and risky to make dramatic changes to the main source of revenue of the American state.

The importance of the federal income tax to the modern American state cannot be overstated.[37] The income tax is the cornerstone of the revenue system of the American state.[38] In fiscal year 2007, the income tax (individual and corporate combined) raised $1.5 trillion, amounting to nearly 60 percent of the total receipts of the national government, or 11.2 percent of the $14 trillion GDP of the United States, the world's largest economy. (This compares to the paltry 1.3 percent of GDP extracted by the federal government via the income tax in 1934.) At the same time, the Social Security wage tax contributed another $869 billion of revenue in fiscal year 2007, amounting to 33.9 percent of total receipts.[39] The latter tax is imposed

---

36. It should be noted that those European states that have a VAT use it to supplement the revenue from their national income taxes (personal and corporate). No advanced state in the world relies solely on a national sales tax or value-added tax for public revenue.

37. Like the national government, the states rely on income taxes for revenue. Local governments typically rely on real property taxes and sales taxes for most of their revenue. For a description of the tax bases of state and local governments in the United States, see Joseph A. Pechman, *Federal Tax Policy*, 5th ed. (Washington, DC: Brookings Institution, 1987), 256–98. State and local government expenditures amounted to 11.6 percent of GDP, while the federal government spent another 20 percent. Office of Management and Budget, *Historical Tables, Budget of the United States Government, Fiscal Year 2009*, table 2.3 ("Receipts by Source as Percentages of GDP: 1934–2013"), 35. A higher percentage of government expenditures are spent at the subnational level in the United States and other federal states, especially compared to the highly centralized unitary states such as France, Italy, and Spain. Peters, *Politics of Taxation*, 95.

38. The democracies of Western Europe rely less on income taxation than the United States. For example, France has traditionally relied on social security taxes and a value-added tax for most of its revenue. In 1985, the individual and corporate income taxes accounted for only 17.9 percent of total revenue. Source: Linda Stillabower, "Taxation in France," in *Comparative International Taxation*, ed. Kathleen E. Sinning (American Accounting Association, 1986). In 2005, the VAT raised 48 percent of total tax revenue, while the highly progressive personal income tax contributed 16 percent and corporate taxes another 12 percent. A controversial wealth tax (the *L'impôt de solidarité sur la fortune*) raises about 2 percent of total tax revenue. Source: Organization for Economic Cooperation and Development, *Revenue Statistics, 1965–2006* (Paris: OECD, 2007). For the European Community, total tax revenue as a percentage of GDP averages 40.8 percent. Among the nations of the EU, the figures range from 29 percent in Lithuania to 52 percent in Sweden, while France extracts 46 percent of GDP through taxes. Source: Eurostat, "Tax Revenue in the EU," in *Statistics in Focus, Economy and Finance, 31/2007* (Eurostat: March 20, 2007).

39. Office of Management and Budget, *Historical Tables, Budget of the United States Government, Fiscal Year 2009*, table 2.1 ("Receipts by Source: 1934–2013"), 31; table 2.2 ("Percentage

on wages and is withheld by the employer from the employee's paycheck and remitted to the federal government. Originally a flat impost of 2 percent on the first $3,000 of wages (half paid by the worker and half by the employer), the tax gradually expanded after its enactment in 1937. The combined wage tax increased to 3.0 percent in 1950 and then to 4 percent in 1954. It is currently imposed at the rate of 13.3 percent on the applicable annual "wage base" ($106,800 in 2009).

In fiscal year 2007, the combined revenue from the federal income tax and the Social Security wage tax amounted to more than $2.40 trillion, constituting 93.6 percent of total federal receipts and more than 17 percent of GDP. The balance of federal receipts (a mere $165 billion) was derived from an assortment of federal excise taxes ($65 billion), customs duties and fees ($26 billion), and the federal estate and gift tax ($26 billion).[40] These figures actually understate the American state's dependence on income taxation. Because the revenue from the wage tax is dedicated to paying current Social Security benefits, it falls to the income tax to raise virtually all the rest of the revenue that supports discretionary spending—everything that requires an annual appropriation in the budget, which includes all spending on the military, education, highway construction, agriculture, foreign aid, protecting the environment, enforcing the securities laws, consumer protection, and all sorts of regulation. The list goes on. All of these programs are dependent on the federal income tax. To date, the income tax has delivered.

Notwithstanding its many flaws and complexities, the tax system of the United States is the envy of rest of the world with respect to raising the enormous revenue required to operate a modern state. The vast array of tax laws enacted by Congress over the past nine decades has been codified into a single, unified edifice (the Internal Revenue Code). The tax code is administered by a powerful bureaucratic collection agency (the Internal Revenue Service) that has more than 100,000 permanent and 20,000 seasonal employees and an annual budget of $11.4 billion. The IRS collects

---

Composition of Receipts by Source: 1934–2013"), 33; table 2.3 ("Receipts by Source as Percentage of GDP: 1934–2013"), 35.

40. Office of Management and Budget, *Historical Tables, Budget of the United States Government, Fiscal Year 2009,* table 2.1 ("Receipts by Source: 1934–2013"), 31; table 2.5 ("Composition of 'Other Receipts': 1940–2013"), 46. The federal gift and estate tax raises about $26 billion a year—roughly 1 percent of the receipts of the federal government.

more than 96 percent of the receipts of the federal government and enforces the tax laws with an army of revenue agents backed by the Department of Justice, federal marshals, the federal judiciary, and ultimately the federal penal system. This system of revenue extraction, first devised in the nineteenth century and subsequently perfected in the twentieth century, is one of the most important manifestations of the power of the American state. At the same time, the revenue it generates is the main source of the power of the American state. This tax system is used by the American state to convert the "latent power" of societal wealth into state capacity. If, as Organski and Kugler argued, "taxes are exact indicators of governmental presence,"[41] then the modern American state has a significantly greater "presence" than its prewar incarnation.

The Modern Tax State

The revenue system of the American state, based on the federal income tax and Social Security wage tax, supports its expensive military and social welfare programs. This revenue system is perfectly suited for extracting vast amounts of revenue from a modern commercial economy. What is unique about this arrangement? Essentially, political leaders created the ideal type of what the Austrian economist Joseph Schumpeter referred to as the "tax state."[42] The fundamental principle of the tax state is simple: capital remains in private hands, while the state takes its own self-designated share of the profits of private business enterprises through various forms of taxation (e.g., income taxes, valued-added taxes, wealth transfer taxes). The state uses taxation to extract resources from society in a highly efficient and relatively unobtrusive manner, thereby providing a *stable* and *replenishable* source of public revenue. The tax state is, as Richard Bonney argues, a highly developed form of a fiscal state, one with an efficient system

---

41. A.F.K. Organski and Jacek Kugler, *The War Ledger* (Chicago: University of Chicago Press, 1980), 74.

42. Joseph A. Schumpeter, "The Crisis of the Tax State," (1918), reprinted in *International Economic Papers* 4 (1954): 5–38. As is evident from the title of his essay, Schumpeter questioned the ability of the tax state to raise sufficient revenue to satisfy the citizenry's expanding demand for public goods.

of taxation that enables it to repay its public borrowing, thereby assuring its long-term survival.[43]

In collecting tax revenues, the tax state "lives off" society—or, to be more precise, the wealth generated by the private economy. For this reason, Schumpeter viewed the tax state as an "economic parasite" of advanced capitalism. Notwithstanding, this is a highly efficient arrangement from the perspective of *both* state and society. The financial benefits are greatest where there is an advanced industrial economy as well as a bureaucracy capable of administering a comprehensive tax system. An efficient bureaucracy is needed to administer the kind of broad-based progressive income tax that alone can raise truly significant amounts of revenue. It is much more difficult to administer an income tax to millions of individuals and businesses than a system of indirect taxes, such as tariffs, customs duties, and excise taxes. Without adequate administrative capacity, there will be widespread noncompliance and "leakage" in an income tax system. At the same time, income taxation is itself conceivable only within the context of an advanced market economy (or Hamiltonian "commercial republic"), such as that which emerged in the United States by the middle of the nineteenth century. Preindustrial, agricultural societies (such as the nineteenth-century Jeffersonian "agrarian republic") simply will not generate enough revenue for the state coffers to make it worth enforcing an income tax on all but the wealthiest citizens.[44] At a minimum, there must be a significant number of workers who are wage earners and private businesses that are discrete legal entities. A national income tax would have been neither administrable nor particularly profitable in the United States in the late eighteenth and early nineteenth centuries, given its predominately agrarian economy. It was not very profitable during the Civil War even after industrialization had begun. Emerging nation-states generally lack the administrative capacity to enforce such a tax. This includes countries such as

43. "Richard Bonney, "Introduction," to Richard Bonney, ed., *The Rise of the Fiscal State in Europe, c. 1200–1815* (New York: Oxford University Press, 1999), 13. Bonney refers to four prevailing types of fiscal systems: the tribute state, the domain state, the tax state, and the fiscal state. The more common terminology, derived from Schumpeter, portrays an inexorable movement from the domain state to the tax state. The domain state of medieval Europe derived its revenue from the landed estates held by the crown. W. M. Ormond, "England in the Middles Ages," in *The Rise of the Fiscal State in Europe, c. 1200–1815,* ed. Bonney, 21.

44. See David Waldner, *State Building and Late Development* (Ithaca: Cornell University Press, 1999), 45.

China and Russia. Even developed nations such as France and Italy find it difficult to enforce a broad-based personal income tax in the face of widespread tax evasion and noncompliance.[45]

When the economy and the administrative apparatus of the state reach a sufficient degree of maturity, a "take-off" of sorts is reached.[46] This was first realized in the United States during the First World War—fifty years after the initial trial with a national income tax during the Civil War. Under the ideal arrangement, private business enterprises pay tribute (i.e., taxes) to the state, and in exchange the state provides the legal and structural framework for a stable market economy. This is the *quid pro quo* behind the revenue coalition that supports the modern tax state. Contrary to Schumpeter, the relationship between the tax state and the private economy is more aptly described as mutualism than parasitism. The income tax gives the state direct access to the profits generated by the private economy; the revenue generated by the tax is used to finance all the activities of a modern state (social welfare, as well as military), while the state itself avoids direct intervention in the private economy and free markets. The state pulls the levers of the tax system to manipulate and support the domestic economy, thereby steering clear of a host of economic and political problems that commonly arise where states nationalize all or specific sectors of their economies, or themselves engage in state entrepreneurship or central planning for the economy—specialized tasks for which states are poorly suited.[47] Private business enterprise flourishes within the context

---

45. Italy and France struggle to enforce their national income taxes in the face of widespread noncompliance. For this reason, they rely more than the United States on indirect taxes such as the VAT. The Italian tax system has recently been overhauled by the Italian Parliament (Law 80 of April 7, 2003). These reforms are not likely to alter the well-known reluctance of the Italian citizenry to comply with the national tax laws.

46. The notion of a "take-off" is borrowed from the theory of linear stages of economic development put forth in W. W. Rostow, *The Stages of Economic Growth: A Non-Communist Manifesto* (Cambridge: Cambridge University Press, 1960), chap. 2, "The Five Stages of Growth—A Summary," 4–16.

47. Schumpeter himself questioned the practicality of state entrepreneurial enterprises on the pragmatic grounds that the state cannot operate such ventures and produce a profit any greater than that of private owners, and probably will do worse: "Since the state must work with money capital just as any other entrepreneur, and since it can raise this money only through loans, it is unlikely that the remaining profit will be much larger than what could have been extracted from the same industry by direct and indirect taxes including taxes on the income of the industry." Schumpeter, "The Crisis of the Tax State," 24.

of a free-market economy established by the state through the use of its coercive powers to maintain such critical infrastructure as a legal system, an independent judiciary (vital for enforcing business contracts), a stable currency, and a national system of banking.[48] This reflects a fundamental tension inherent in the modern tax state. As Ronald King has pointedly observed, the modern tax state "is supposed to support and defend private property rights, yet it interferes with those rights in order to collect its own revenue. It is supposed to support a system of voluntary exchanges, yet it engages in mandatory expropriation."[49] The tax state is anything but a laissez-faire state.

Much of the tax revenue (i.e., "tribute") collected by the modern tax state is used to provide public goods (e.g., highways, national parks, the military, retirement benefits, etc.) to the citizens who pay those taxes. Citizens pay tribute that "buys" them the legal right to social welfare benefits. This creates a mutuality of interests between the state and the citizenry. The arrangement cultivates bonds of loyalty to the established political order, thereby enhancing the legitimacy of the regime. At the same time, the state itself, which depends on the continued success of the business community for its revenue, develops a strong interest in the vitality, prosperity, and expansion of the private economy.[50] The state becomes a caretaker or

---

48. The role of the modern state in fostering economic markets is the subject of Barry R. Weingast, "The Economic Role of Political Institutions: Market-Preserving Federalism and Economic Development," *Journal of Law, Economics, and Organization* 11 (1999): 1–31. Philip Bobbitt associates this new arrangement with what he refers to as the "market state." Philip Bobbitt, *Terror and Consent: The Wars for the Twenty-First Century* (New York: Knopf, 2008). Bobbitt contrasts the market state, which is an "emerging constitutional order" based on maximizing market relations and the increased privatization of state activities, with the established constitutional order of the traditional nation-states that derive their legitimacy from the "promise to improve the material welfare" of their citizens.

49. Ronald F. King, *Money, Time, and Politics: Investment Tax Subsidiaries and American Democracy* (New Haven: Yale University Press, 1993), 14. The central theme of King's important study is that after the Second World War, the policy of the national government has been to encourage economic expansion, using the income tax as "an instrument in support of capitalist accumulation" rather than the redistribution of wealth.

50. Charles Lindblom describes how the continued prosperity of the private economy and the success of the business community becomes almost a sacred cow within the political sphere. Charles E. Lindblom, *Politics and Markets: The World's Political Economic Systems* (New York: Basic Books, 1977), chap. 13 ("The Privileged Position of Business"), 170–88. Fred Block argues that "regardless of their own political ideology," state officials are dependent on the "maintenance of some reasonable level of economic activity." There are two reasons for this: "First, the capacity of the state to finance itself through taxation or borrowing depends on the state of the economy.

manager for the private economy, encouraging and cultivating industry and manufacturing out of a concern for its own economic well-being as well as that of its citizens.[51] The interests of the moneyed classes become aligned with those of the state, just as Hamilton sought two hundred years ago. The interests of private business, individual citizens, and the state all converge in the modern tax state.

In contrast to the American state, the former Soviet Union, with its inefficient state-owned and centrally managed economy (what may be referred to as economic Stalinism), offers a prime example of the failure of political elites to establish a stable and mutually beneficial relationship between state and society—or more properly in that case, party and society.[52] In the Soviet Union, the state overwhelmed and smothered society, much to the detriment of the nation as a whole. It is a highly unappealing model unlikely to be emulated by future generations of political elites, whether in economically developed or developing nations. The United States offers a far more attractive alternative, one which has been emulated (to varying degrees) by political elites in nations as diverse as South Korea, Singapore, Brazil, and postcommunist Eastern Europe. The only serious competitor is the corporatist model of the East Asian "capitalist developmental state," which relies on state-directed capital investment in key industrial sectors

---

If economic activity is in decline, the state will have difficulty maintaining its revenues at an adequate level. Second, public support for a regime will decline sharply if the regime presides over a serious drop in the level of economic activity, with a parallel rise in unemployment and shortages of key goods." Fred Block, "The Ruling Class Does Not Rule: Notes on The Marxist Theory of the State," in *Revising State Theory: Essays in Politics and Postindustrialism,* ed. Fred L. Block (Philadelphia: Temple University Press, 1987), 58.

51. Robert Gilpin perfectly describes the role of the modern state: "A fundamental and novel feature of the modern state is its role in the economy. Although there were important exceptions, the economic function of the pre-modern state was primarily to facilitate exploitation of the masses by the elite and to protect society from being exploited by foreign conquerors. In contrast, the primary function of the modern state has become the promotion of economic development through creation of internal technical infrastructure, removal of obstacles to the formation of a unified domestic market, and intervention in the economy in more direct ways. In effect, the state...liberated people to work and create wealth that could then be taxed for purposes of domestic welfare and national power." Robert Gilpin, *War and Change in World Politics* (New York: Cambridge University Press, 1981), 122–23.

52. Gerald Easter explains the sudden and unpredicted collapse of the Soviet Union, which he refers to as "the twentieth century's most feared state," in terms of the tenuous "personal networks" that linked that state to society. Gerald M. Easter, *Reconstructing the State: Personal Networks and Elite Identity in Soviet Russia* (New York: Cambridge University Press, 2000).

to stimulate national industrial development.[53] The critical difference between the two systems is the *degree* of government involvement in directing capital investment, with the East Asian states exercising considerably
greater and more direct control over the allocation of capital and investment during the formative stages of industrialization. Those nations with
strong liberal traditions favor the less intrusive market-mechanisms of the
tax state over East Asian corporatism or the Chinese version of authoritarian state capitalism.

In the United States, where building a strong central state came relatively late in the history of the nation (i.e., *after* industrialization and the
development of a mature capitalist economy), building a tax state was the
only politically expedient option for political leaders. Institutional obstacles and the prevailing political ideology prevented officials from penetrating society or controlling the economy through state-intervention or
outright ownership of the means of production, as the socialist parties of
Europe experimented with and the communist regimes in East Asia carried out with devastating effect. It was not long before political leaders in
America turned to the tax system not only to raise the revenue necessary
to finance state expansion, but also to manipulate the economy. From their
perspective, this was the optimal and rational course of action for several
reasons. For one thing, a deep-rooted antistate political ideology has permeated the regime from its inception, forestalling any possibility of *direct*
control or ownership of national industries by the American state. Even
the most basic regulation of the workplace by the national government was
thwarted by the U.S. Supreme Court as late as the 1930s.[54] In such a political climate, state entrepreneurial ventures, or even the nationalization

---

53. The success of Asian industrial policy (e.g., Japan) is described in Chalmers Johnson,
MITI and the Japanese Miracle: The Growth of Industrial Policy, 1925–1975 (Stanford: Stanford
University Press, 1982); and "Political Institutions and Economic Performance: A Comparative
Analysis of the Government-Business Relationship in Japan, South Korea, and Taiwan," in *The
Political Economy of the New Asian Industrialism,* ed. Frederic C. Deyo (Ithaca: Cornell University
Press, 1987). Johnson's model of the "developmental state" is sharply criticized in Robert Wade,
Governing the Market: Economic Theory and the Role of Government in East Asian Industrialization
(Princeton: Princeton University Press, 1990), 25–29.

54. Constitutional barriers to regulation of the workplace by state legislatures and the national government were enforced by the Supreme Court until the New Deal era. See, e.g., *Lochner
v. New York,* 198 U.S. 45 (1905); *Hammer v. Dagenhart,* 247 U.S. 251 (1918). *Hammer* was reversed
in *United States v. Darby,* 312 U.S. 100 (1941).

of limited sectors of the national economy, were never viable options for political elites, as they were in Europe, where strong labor parties and unions supported such initiatives. The constitution and legal framework of the American regime would not permit such penetrations of the "private" economy by the central state. Recall that the Supreme Court has held that even during periods of wartime national emergency, the U.S. Constitution prohibits the executive branch from nationalizing those sectors of the private economy most vital to national security, even on a temporary basis.[55] In this context, crafting a tax state was the best option available to national political elites seeking the additional revenue necessary to finance the building of a modern state.

The tax system of the American state has been commonly used by public officials in the postwar era not just as a source of revenue, but also as an instrument for implementing social policy and macroeconomic controls. In a political system that denies policymakers any means for *direct* means for centralized management of the national economy, the income tax provides officials with the means for *indirectly* influencing private economic activity. In the United States, the tax laws are used as a tool (albeit blunt and relatively inefficient) for manipulating private economic decision making and implementing national public policies.[56] This includes a wide range of public policies encouraged through tax preferences (employer-provided healthcare, life insurance, retirement benefits, home mortgage loans, wind-generated electricity, cars with hybrid engines—to name but a few) as well as a bipartisan commitment to stimulating capital formation via tax subsidies for business. That so many of the policies implemented through the tax code are also highly political and conflict with the policies pursued by technocrats (e.g., the Federal Reserve Board, experts in the Treasury Department, and advisors in the White House) is but one of the unfortunate consequences of our fractured and decentralized polity. Nevertheless, given the strong antistate ideology that dominates American political

---

55. In a controversial opinion, the Supreme Court ruled unconstitutional President Truman's executive order nationalizing segments of the steel industry during the Korean War. *Youngstown Sheet and Tube Co. et al. v. Sawyer,* 343 U.S. 579 (1952).

56. Elsewhere, I have argued that the excessive use of the tax code to implement public policy has undermined the coherence, stability, and integrity of the federal tax system. Sheldon D. Pollack, *The Failure of U.S. Tax Policy: Revenue and Politics* (University Park: Penn State Press, 1996), 11–29.

culture, it is rational for officials of the American state to implement public policy through tax expenditures inserted into the tax code, even as they themselves are dependent on the revenue the tax system generates.

The Fiscal Imbalance of the American State

The United States possesses a highly efficient system of revenue extraction that is used to support the state apparatus, which includes a powerful military force and a modern social welfare system. On account of the great expense of maintaining this global military colossus along with the rising costs associated with its social welfare programs (in particular, Social Security), the revenue-raising capacity of the federal tax system has been strained to the limit in recent decades. Arguably, the United States has already overextended its reach and devotes too much of its national resources to its military and retirement programs.[57] Federal spending now perennially outstrips the receipts of the national government—and the trend has only been exacerbated by the financial crisis that began in late 2008. In only six fiscal years between 1960 and 2007 has the national government *not* operated at a deficit. Consequently, the national debt has increased year by year, rising from $51 billion in 1940 to $260 billion in 1945 to $381 in 1970 to $1.1 trillion in 1982, ultimately surpassing $6.4 trillion in December 2008.[58] Because of this, questions arise as to whether the current system of public finance can continue to generate enough revenue to support the vast apparatus of the national government. Such a revenue failure would present a serious threat to the continued stability and development of the American state.

---

57. Paul Kennedy argues that when "Great Powers" such as the United States overextend their global reach and devote too much of their resources to military spending, they decline in relation to competitor states. Paul M. Kennedy, *The Rise and Fall of the Great Powers: Economic Change and Military Conflict from 1500 to 2000* (New York: Random House, 1987), 514–35.

58. Office of Management and Budget, *Historical Tables, Budget of the United States Government, Fiscal Year 2009,* table 7.1 ("Federal Debt at the End of the Year: 1940–2013"), 127–28. The total public debt held by the public as reported by the United States Department of the Treasury, Bureau of the Public Debt, stood at $6.85 trillion as of May 1, 2009. Total debt (including intragovernmental obligations held by various trust funds) stood at $11.15 trillion. In the postwar era, the European states also have regularly spent more than they raise in taxes. See Peters, *Politics of Taxation,* 79–81.

To a great extent, recent increases in discretionary spending have been a response to a series of unforeseeable tragic events: the terrorist attacks on September 11, the vast destruction left in the wake of hurricane Katrina, the prolonged war in Iraq, and the collapse of financial markets in 2008. But the problem goes deeper than the unavoidable spending on these national emergencies. For better or worse, American citizens (Republicans and Democrats alike) look to the federal government for protection not just from foreign invasion and terrorist attacks, but also from hurricanes, floods, earthquakes, pandemic viruses, global warming, starvation, beach erosion, and a host of other natural disasters. In the minds of many citizens, the proper role of the American state also includes protecting citizens from man-made inflictions—such as financial losses resulting from flawed investment strategies for retirement, the demise of private pension plans, the bankruptcy of private employers, the collapse of private investment banks, mortgage foreclosure, and numerous economic risks for which the American state is increasingly viewed as the insurer of last resort. Even many conservative Republicans accept as a legitimate state function the protection of citizens from alleged imperfections of markets—including seasonal fluctuations in the price of gasoline, the high cost of prescription drugs for the elderly, and risky mortgage lending practices. The role of the American state is now presumed to include bailing out the domestic automobile industry and commercial banking as well as bolstering the price of residential real estate. The American state no longer "lives off" the domestic economy; it now takes an active role in managing that economy through macroeconomic policies intended to maintain institutional stability and enhance economic prosperity for the benefit of both the private sector and the state itself.

For the national government to perform all of these sundry functions (military, social welfare, humanitarian relief, and insurer of economic risk), it must possess the capacity to raise trillions of dollars in revenue annually. To date, the American state has accomplished this Herculean task with the revenue from its robust system of public finance, based as it is on a broad-based progressive income tax, the Social Security wage tax, and massive public borrowing in global capital markets. How long this can continue is a matter of considerable doubt and uncertainty, as the national government now spends several hundred billion dollars more each year than it takes in, and arguably is already insolvent from a long-term actuarial perspective.

Addressing this fiscal imbalance is a matter of utmost importance for the continued vitality and long-term survival of the American state.

Does the American state face an inherent fiscal crisis, as some critics assert? More than thirty years ago, James O'Connor predicted a coming "fiscal crisis of the state" (by which he meant the "capitalist state") as the inevitable result of the "tendency for governmental expenditures to outrace revenues."[59] There is considerable truth in this observation. Elected officials in Washington have been unable to resist the urge to distribute all sorts of benefits to middle-class Americans to cultivate political support for their reelection campaigns. This imposes incredible pressure on domestic spending. The resulting fiscal imbalance may not be an irreversible "structural imbalance," but it certainly is difficult for the political process to change course once a particular path has been taken (e.g., the creation of the Social Security system or the adoption of an income tax versus a consumption tax). If the long-term fiscal crisis looming on the horizon strikes, one thing is certain: it cannot be blamed on the failings of the revenue system of the American state, which raises more than $2.5 trillion annually. Rather, the fiscal crisis can be traced to the enormous expansion of the American state during the twentieth century. With this expansion came an unquenchable demand for public revenue—more revenue than even this highly efficient tax system can generate within the constraints imposed by the democratic electoral system and the prevailing antitax public philosophy.[60]

While defense spending consumes a significant share of the federal budget, the great increase in spending on Social Security and Medicare is the most significant threat to the long-term fiscal position of the American state. While the revenue currently raised by the Social Security wage tax is enough to cover the cost of current benefits (and has generated annual surpluses ranging from $100 to $250 billion during the past ten years), receipts are projected to decline in relation to benefits paid out. The wage tax

---

59. James O'Connor, *The Fiscal Crisis of the State* (New York: St. Martin's Press, 1973), 2. For a discussion of the reasons put forth to explain why governments constantly run deficits, see Peters, *Politics of Taxation,* 119–24.

60. Arguably, the antitax public philosophy has restrained state building in the postwar era. See Julian E. Zelizer, "The Uneasy Relationship: Democracy, Taxation, and State Building Since the New Deal," in *The Democratic Experiment: New Directions in American Political Development,* ed. Meg Jacobs, William J. Novak, and Julian E. Zelizer (Princeton: Princeton University Press, 2003), 276–300.

is expected to bring in less than the expenditures paid out by 2018, thereby driving the Social Security Trust Fund "negative" until it is fully depleted by the year 2041.[61] With the baby-boomer generation approaching the age of retirement and an insufficient number of young persons contributing tax revenues to support their benefits, the program is in serious financial trouble. Social Security faces an estimated revenue shortfall of $3.8 trillion (present value) over the next seventy-five years.[62] At the same time, the Medicare system faces an equally dire future, as Medicare will experience a revenue shortfall of $6.2 trillion (present value) over the next seventy-five years.[63] The combined deficit for these two programs alone is estimated at more than 1.8 percent of GDP. Despite the best efforts of Congress in 1983 to restore financial solvency to Social Security, policymakers have yet to fully address the impending fiscal crisis attributable to this staggering unfunded liability of the American state. Increased deficit spending by the federal government in the wake of the failure of U.S. capital markets and the decline of the national economy that began in late 2008 are likely to seriously impair the financial position of the national government. Already the impact has been felt, as the U.S. government raised $44 billion less revenue in fiscal year 2008 than the prior year. Was this an aberration or the beginning of a dangerous trend?

Notwithstanding the uncertainty that lies ahead, past performance is unambiguous. The federal income tax provided the twentieth-century American state with the enormous revenue needed to wage two major global

---

61. The current surpluses generated by the excess of tax revenue over benefits paid (more than $185 billion in fiscal year 2006) have been "borrowed" by the U.S. Treasury and used to supplement general revenue. As Treasury debt obligations mature, the income tax must be increased for the government to meet its financial commitments. The Social Security Trust Fund presently has $1.9 trillion invested in "special issue" debt instruments of the U.S. Treasury.

62. United States General Accounting Office, "Social Security: Different Approaches for Addressing Program Solvency," (GAO/HEHS-98–33) (Washington, DC: U.S. General Accounting Office, July 1998). The Social Security and Medicare Trustees project that the combined shortfalls for Social Security and Medicare will amount to 0.7 percent of GDP over the next 75 years. That amounts to a projected deficit of $4.7 trillion over the 75-year period. *2007 Annual Report of the Board of Trustees of the Federal Old-Age and Survivors Insurance and Disability Insurance Trust Funds* (Washington, DC: Government Printing Office, 2007), 2–3. The Congressional Budget Office (CBO) projects a smaller budget shortfall for Social Security, amounting to 0.35 percent of GDP.

63. Annual costs for Medicare amounted to 3.1 percent of GDP in 2006 and are projected to surpass Social Security expenditures in 2028 and exceed 11 percent of GDP in 2081. *Summary of the 2007 Social Security and Medicare Trustees Reports* (Washington, DC: Government Printing Office, June 1, 2007).

wars as well as innumerable regional military actions, and in conjunction with the wage tax, financed the creation of a modern social welfare state. In times of war and peace, the American state has benefited from its extraordinarily robust system of public revenue. This system of revenue extraction, which supported the expansion of the American state during periods of both military conflict and reformist state building, was the main subject of this study. A crucial issue that must be addressed in future studies is whether the present arrangement is sustainable. Past experience does not guarantee continued success. The fiscal foundation of the American state has been weakened by the enormous unfunded liabilities of its social welfare programs and a military that has been maintained at wartime levels for most of the last sixty years. The extent of the damage remains to be seen.

Conclusion

The most perfect example of the modern State is North America.

—Karl Marx, "The German Ideology" (1845)

The primary function of the modern state has become the promotion of economic development through creation of internal technical infrastructure, removal of obstacles to the formation of a unified domestic market, and intervention in the economy in more direct ways.

—Robert Gilpin, *War and Change in World Politics* (1981)

The state is a political organization that claims a monopoly on violence within a given territory. To the extent that a particular state actually possesses such a monopoly (or something close to it), it is ideally situated to perform two vital functions: make war and collect tribute from those living under its jurisdiction. A good deal of the tribute collected is typically dedicated to the military apparatus of the state, which in turn, is used to forcibly extract revenue from society and sometimes, other nations. This is the basis of the powerful combination of fiscal and military powers behind the state. In essence, all states are fiscal-military organizations—some more efficient and successful than others.

In Europe, the driving force behind the development of the central state was the nearly constant warfare that plagued the continent for more than five centuries. The states of early modern Europe grew in size as their rulers built larger standing armies and an expanded administrative apparatus to deploy those forces. At the same time, the so-called military revolution in technology and weaponry that commenced in the middle of the sixteenth century rendered warfare an increasingly expensive enterprise. This trend favored certain types of states—specifically, those with the capacity to raise the enormous revenue needed to support large standing armies and acquire the expensive new instruments of warfare. The rising cost of warfare had a profound impact on state development in Europe as revenue extraction became increasingly critical to a state's survival in the new world order that emerged in the wake of the Peace of Westphalia of 1648.

The enormous cost of making war (as well as defending against it) forced the rulers of Europe to adopt more aggressive revenue strategies. Over time, the methods of revenue extraction became more regular, systematic, and efficient as rulers used their armed forces to provide protection to civilian populations in exchange for tribute. With the introduction of this system of "commercialized violence," regularized forms of taxation gradually replaced plunder and conquest as the primary source of public revenue. The modern nation-state—the product of this long process of institutional development—supplanted the feudal states and city-states of early modern Europe precisely because it was the most efficient form of political organization with respect to the exercise of the state's monopoly on violence (i.e., both internally and externally) and extraction of revenue from society. While modern states do more than just make war, the ability to perform *all* of the other governmental functions that modern states engage in (e.g., distributing social welfare benefits to citizens, delivering the mail, providing clean drinking water, paving road, etc.) ultimately depends on the capacity of the state to extract revenue from society.

In examining the long history of the development of the European state, we discerned strong evidence of a causal mechanism in which sustained war making led to state building and more aggressive revenue strategies. There may have been other causal mechanisms of state development that played out on other continents (such as the Asiatic model), but this is the process of state development that prevailed in Europe. Over time, it produced a highly effective and powerful political organization—the great nation-states that arose in Europe in the eighteenth century. Given this history, it was likely that state development would follow a similar path elsewhere. We turned to America to see if a similar causal mechanism of state development was present there. We found considerable evidence that it was. As in Europe, state building in America was stimulated during periods of sustained warfare, and both state building and war making required that political leaders adopt more aggressive revenue strategies to finance their expanded activities. The result was an enhanced state apparatus—that is, one better able to extract revenue and make war. A model based on the dynamic interaction between war, revenue, and state building is highly descriptive of the formation and development of the American state.

While there was no "military revolution" in America in the late eighteenth century comparable to that experienced in early modern Europe, the leaders of the former British colonies found themselves engaged in an all-out war with one of the dominant military powers in the world. This required a comprehensive mobilization of societal resources and the civilian population in the thirteen former English colonies. The threat of war was the main factor behind the initial decision to form a political union among the separate state governments. Thereafter, the minimal apparatus of the political union evolved into a rudimentary, albeit weak, state, during the course of the Revolutionary War. After independence from Britain was achieved, nationalists opened a new campaign—this time, for the creation of a stronger (but not necessarily strong) central state in a new federation of the thirteen separate states. What was their primary objective? Strengthening the military and revenue-extraction capacity of the national government of the American state. What was the basis for opposition by the Antifederalists? At the most fundamental level, they opposed efforts to build a European-style state in America.

If war played an important role in stimulating the initial formation of the American state, America was not Europe, and state building in America produced a different *kind* of state. The models and metaphors that are useful in describing the formation and development of the states of early modern Europe are strangely out of place in America. The Confederacy formed during the war with Britain was not foisted on the state governments by a warlord (or "stationary bandit") offering protection in exchange for tribute. Nor was the early American state imposed on the former colonies by a conquering foreign prince. Can the founding of the American state be characterized as a "protection racket" or was it a "social contract"? In essence, the founding was a social contract entered into for protection. This is quite distinct from a protection racket in which the would-be protector promises to cease inflicting violence on the population in exchange for tribute. The essence of a protection racket is extortion, not protection. The Confederacy was the product of a rational and voluntary decision made by autonomous "principalities" pursuant to which military protection from an external force would be provided as a collective good to the state governments by a new central state in exchange for limited access to their traditional sources of revenue. The national government was created primarily to provide military protection from the British, Indians, and other threatening foreign powers (e.g., Spain and France). From this perspective, the American state was less a protection racket than a protection league—one endowed with legitimacy and legality by the ratification process for the Constitution. Truth be told, very little revenue (or "tribute") was provided to the national government of the Confederacy by the state legislatures and only minimal protection was provided to the citizens by the national army. The early American state was a weak protection league. At the same time, local political leaders entered into a compact to create a national government that would protect their lives, liberty, and property—that is, to preserve the traditional rights of Englishmen. In this respect, the formation of the Confederacy expressed elements of a bona fide social contract.

Admittedly, the early American state bore only a slight resemblance to the Weberian ideal type of a state (i.e., a political organization claiming a monopoly on violence). During the Revolutionary War, the Congress struggled to exert a monopoly on violence within its territory—as vividly symbolized by the occupations of Philadelphia and New York by British troops. After the war, the Congress did not even *claim* a monopoly on violence within its own territory as the state governments retained their traditional militias and police powers. Indeed, most political and military power remained vested at the local level. The strategic bargain behind the formation of the first political union did not create a strong fiscal-military state in America. On the contrary, the Congress commanded only a small standing army and had little capacity to extract revenue from society on its own. The main function of the central state was military protection from the invading British troops. Only through a combination of skillful leadership and good fortune did America prevail in its war with England.

Without revenue, even skilled and dedicated rulers cannot build strong political organizations. Ideas and ideology may motivate leaders to rebel and found new states, but rulers need resources to build armies, navies, and bureaucracies. Without adequate revenue, the most enthusiastic efforts to build a strong state will inevitably fail. That is why the ability of rulers to devise and implement a successful revenue strategy is so critical to state development. In the case of the early American Republic, the national government lacked the capacity to extract revenue from society, and thus national political leaders had no viable revenue strategy. The local state governments retained their autonomy within the Confederacy, and local political leaders resisted efforts by the national government to encroach on their traditional sources of revenue. The national government of the Confederacy lacked both military powers and any viable means for extracting revenue from society. Under the Articles of Confederation, the Congress depended on the state governments for virtually all of its revenue. The resulting revenue shortages inhibited the development of the state apparatus. Notwithstanding efforts by political leaders such as Robert Morris and Alexander Hamilton to reconstitute the fiscal foundation of the Confederacy, the revenue-extraction powers of the national government were incapable of supporting further political development (i.e., creating a stronger state).

Attempts to fortify the revenue system of the national government of the Confederacy were repeatedly thwarted by the state governments, which jealously guarded their traditional sources of revenue. Provoked by the deteriorating fiscal and military position of the Confederacy, a group of nationalists met in the spring of 1787 to reconstitute the political order by building an American state with greater fiscal and military powers. As they convened in Philadelphia, nationalist leaders such as Hamilton, Madison, Adams, and Washington were mostly concerned with threats to public order (e.g., British troops in Canada, hostile Indians, and internal insurrections such as Shays' Rebellion) and the fiscal deficiencies of the regime. At the same time, they were motivated by a vision of politics that transcended the immediate situation. Ideas and skillful leadership mattered at the Constitutional Convention in 1787 as well as during the subsequent campaign for ratification of the new Constitution in the state legislatures, and the success of the nationalist vision resulted in the adoption of the constitutional blueprint for a stronger American state. The reconstituted national government was empowered to build its own standing army. Moreover, an independent power of taxation was conceded by the states to the new national government under the Constitution of 1787.

Even still, the American state remained extraordinarily weak compared to the states of late-eighteenth-century Europe. That is because the overwhelming majority of the founders did not want to build a European-type state in America (i.e., a centralized state with power consolidated under an executive). Rather, they sought to build a different kind of state in America—one that would avoid the "corruption" of Europe (i.e., large standing armies and national taxes). In the short-term, they succeeded.

Notwithstanding the success of the nationalists behind the movement for the Constitution of 1787 as well as Hamilton's subsequent fiscal innovations for the early American state, the national government remained relatively weak during the first decades of the Republic. Hamilton and his fellow Federalists made progress in bolstering the apparatus of the reconstituted American state, but much of what they accomplished was reversed by the Jeffersonian Revolution. The American state at the center of the political order established by the Democratic Republicans in the early nineteenth century remained one of limited powers and marginal administrative capacity. The main activities of the national government consisted in the administration of foreign affairs for the federation and the management of the vast western territories that came under the control and dominion of the national government in 1803. The small army of the national government was used mainly to pacify hostile Indian populations in the western territories.

Soon enough, a dynamic process of state building was set in motion in North America. Throughout the nineteenth century, warfare hardened the institutions of the American state. The process of state development was not a linear path toward a strong state but rather one of "punctuated equilibria"—periods of "long-term inertia" interrupted by "concentrated bursts of change" (i.e., state building during wartime). Following each episode of wartime state building, the national government was a bit more active and powerful—notwithstanding recurring periods of postwar retrenchment. This "ratchet effect" left the American state a stronger political organization with greater revenue-extraction capacity and military powers following each of its wars. The history of the development of the American state is closely (although not exclusively) connected to the expansion of the military and fiscal powers of the national government during sustained periods of warfare and systemic crisis. This has been the primary causal mechanism behind political development in the United States. But it was a cyclical process. For more than a century, geography provided isolation and protection from the powerful nation-states of Europe. This allowed institutional retrenchment following periods of wartime state building. For instance, during the War of 1812, the American state faced financial and military crisis. In response, political leaders adopted a more aggressive revenue strategy to support an expansion of the armed forces and the administrative apparatus of the central state. Yet, following the war, that revenue strategy was abandoned and the military was reduced to prewar levels. The national government returned to a system of indirect taxation (customs duties, excise taxes, and the tariff) and a minimalist national army, this notwithstanding the substantial increase in the size of the territory under its control.

This all changed dramatically with the outbreak of the Civil War. In the midst of total war and systemic crisis, the leaders of the Republican Party built a fiscal-military state with revenue-extraction capacity and standing armies previously unknown in North America. Societal resources and manpower were mobilized by the Union government (as well as the Southern Confederacy) for the war effort. While the Southern Confederacy was defeated and the Yankee Leviathan in the North was dismantled soon after the Union victory, the American state exercised considerably greater military and fiscal powers in the postbellum era.

The late-nineteenth-century system of public revenue (the tariff, customs duties, and excise taxes) brought in more than enough revenue to the national government, which enjoyed the luxury of perennial budget surpluses. During the same period, Progressive reformers sought to further enhance the administrative and regulatory powers of the national government in response to new environmental conditions (e.g., industrialization and urbanization) through a series of discrete institutional innovations (what Skowronek referred to as "patchwork reform"). Notwithstanding some successes in rectifying the deficiencies of the regulatory and administrative apparatus of the post–Civil War national government, it was not until the First World War that America again possessed a strong state with a large standing army and the capacity to extract revenue directly from society.

While yet another period of retrenchment followed the signing of the armistice with Germany in 1918, a strong fiscal-military state was constructed again during the Second World War. Significantly, the large standing army and robust system of revenue-extraction created during the war became permanent features of the American state after 1945. Likewise, the embryonic social welfare system created during the 1930s became a permanent component of the postwar American state. The social welfare system was greatly expanded in a second burst of reformist enthusiasm in the 1960s. Today, more than 20 percent of the outlays of the national government are dedicated to paying Social Security benefits alone. If the American state spends less on its social welfare programs than the states of Western Europe, it is still a modern social welfare state.

The American state devotes another 20 percent of its revenue (more than $500 billion) to national defense, something that distinguishes it from the modern democratic states of Western Europe, which abandoned their colonial empires and territorial ambitions after the Second World War. The United States, on the other hand, maintains the world's most powerful military force and a global military presence. How does the American state finance both its expensive social welfare programs and its powerful military, while most other nation-states can barely afford one or the other? The answer lies in the system of progressive income taxation resurrected by political leaders in the early twentieth century and perfected during the Second World War. The income tax is the centerpiece of a robust system of revenue extraction that provides the national government with an efficient means of penetrating society and appropriating wealth from the domestic economy—the prosperous "commercial republic" envisioned by Hamilton. By taxing private economic activity, the income tax raises nearly $1.5 trillion a year for the national government, which also relies on the Social Security wage tax and a sophisticated system of public finance through which it borrows hundreds of billions of dollars in international capital markets. (Ultimately, the capacity of the American state to borrow such vast sums from foreign governments and private investors is made possible by its capacity to impose and collect the taxes necessary to repay those loans.) Fueled by this enormous revenue, the American state became a fiscal-military colossus.

In little more than one hundred fifty years, the weak and fragile Confederacy of the United States of America developed into a global superpower—an institutional transformation comparable to anything witnessed on the European continent. To be sure, the modern American state, with its powerful army and enormous bureaucracy, is not the state imagined by the founders of the young Republic—with the possible exception of Alexander Hamilton, who from the beginning had visions of a strong American fiscal-military state modeled on that of eighteenth-century Britain. But the other founders rejected Hamilton's vision, creating instead a decentralized state of limited powers and authority.

The great irony is, notwithstanding the intentions of the founders, the same basic causal mechanism of state development that played out in early modern Europe gradually transformed American political institutions. Successive wars and military campaigns produced a strong and effective state in America, despite its highly decentralized federal structure. While the adoption of a federal constitutional system had a lasting impact on the development of the American state and produced a very different kind of state than in Europe, the end result was the same in many vital respects. In fact, the American state became the most efficient state in extracting revenue from society and maintaining a global military force, surpassing the states of Europe. While a good deal of stateness in America is still located at the local level (e.g., state militias, bureaucracies, and tax systems), early-nineteenth-century European notions of America as a "nonstate" state make little sense today. Indeed, they were rendered obsolete by the time of the Civil War. Today, America has an incredibly strong (albeit decentralized) state. It has a larger standing army than all the states of Western Europe combined and social welfare programs comparable to all but the most generous. It raises (and spends) more than three trillion dollars annually through a combination of taxation and public borrowing. An efficient system of revenue extraction supports a strong state apparatus. This reconstituted American state, Hamiltonian in its spirit and essential attributes, was not the state the founders intended for America; nevertheless, it is the state that developed in North America through the powerful causal mechanism of war, revenue, and state building.

BIBLIOGRAPHY

Ackerman, Bruce. "Taxation and the Constitution." *Columbia Law Review* 99 (January 1999): 1–58.

Alford, Robert R., and Roger Friedland. *Powers of Theory: Capitalism, the State, and Democracy.* New York: Cambridge University Press, 1985.

Almond, Gabriel A. "The Return to the State." *American Political Science Review* 82 (1988): 853–74.

Amenta, Edwin, and Theda Skocpol. "Redefining the New Deal: World War II and the Development of Social Provision in the United States." In *The Politics of Social Policy in the United States,* edited by Margaret Weir, Ann Shola Orloff, and Theda Skocpol, 81–122. Princeton: Princeton University Press, 1988.

Anderson, Fred, and Andrew Clayton. *The Dominion of War: Empire and Liberty in North America, 1500–2000.* New York: Viking, 2005.

Anderson, Perry. *Lineages of the Absolutist State.* London: Verso, 1974.

Ardant, Gabriel. "Financial Policy and Economics Infrastructure of Modern Nations and States." In *The Formation of National States in Western Europe,* edited by Charles Tilly, 164–242. Princeton: Princeton University Press, 1975.

Ashworth, William. *A Short History of the International Economy since 1850.* London: Longman, 1975.

Avineri, Shlomo. *Hegel's Theory of the Modern State*. Cambridge: Cambridge University Press, 1972.

Bailyn, Bernard. *The Ideological Origins of the American Revolution*. Cambridge, MA: Harvard University Press, 1967.

Bank, Steven A., Kirk J. Stark, and Joseph J. Thorndike. *War and Taxes*. Washington, DC: Urban Institute Press, 2008.

Barnett, Michael N. *Confronting the Costs of War: Military Power, State, and Society in Egypt and Israel*. Princeton: Princeton University Press, 1992.

Bates, Robert H. *Markets and States in Tropical Africa: The Political Basis of Agricultural Policies*. Berkeley: University of California Press, 1981.

———. *Prosperity and Violence: The Political Economy of Development*. New York: W. W. Norton, 2001.

Bean, Richard. "War and the Birth of the Nation State." *Journal of Economic History* 33 (March 1973): 203–21.

Becker, Robert A. *Revolution, Reform, and the Politics of American Taxation, 1763–1783*. Baton Rouge: Louisiana State University Press, 1980.

Bell, David A. *The Cult of the Nation in France: Inventing Nationalism, 1680–1800*. Cambridge, MA: Harvard University Press, 2001.

———. *The First Total War: Napoleon's Europe and the Birth of Warfare as We Know It*. Boston: Houghton Mifflin, 2007.

Bendix, Reinhard. *Nation-Building and Citizenship: Studies of Our Changing Social Order*. New York: Wiley, 1964.

Bensel, Richard F. *Sectionalism and American Political Development, 1880–1980*. Madison: University of Wisconsin Press, 1984.

———. *Yankee Leviathan: The Origins of Central State Authority in America, 1859–1877*. New York: Cambridge University Press, 1990.

———. *The Political Economy of American Industrialization, 1877–1900*. New York: Cambridge University Press, 2000.

Blakely, Roy G., and Gladys C. Blakely. *The Federal Income Tax*. New York: Longmans, Green, 1940.

Boatner, Mark Mayo, III. *Encyclopedia of the American Revolution*. New York: McKay, 1966.

———. *The Civil War Dictionary*. New York: McKay, 1988.

Bobbitt, Philip. *The Shield of Achilles: War, Peace, and the Course of History*. New York: Knopf, 2002.

———. *Terror and Consent: The Wars for the Twenty-First Century*. New York: Knopf, 2008.

Bolles, Albert S. *The Financial History of the United States, from 1774 to 1789*. New York: D. Appleton, 1879.

———. *The Financial History of the United States, from 1789 to 1860*. New York: D. Appleton, 1885.

Bonney, Richard, ed. *Economic Systems and State Finance*. New York: Oxford University Press, 1995.

———. ed. *The Rise of the Fiscal State in Europe, c. 1200–1815*. New York: Oxford University Press, 1999.

Boone, Catherine. *Merchant Capital and the Roots of State Power in Senegal, 1930–1985.* New York: Cambridge University Press, 1992.

Bowling, Kenneth R., and Donald R. Kenyon, eds. *Inventing America: Origins and Establishment of the First Federal Congress.* Athens: Ohio State University Press, 1999.

Braun, Rudolf. "Taxation, Sociopolitical Structure, and State-Building: Great Britain and Brandenburg-Prussia." In *The Formation of National States in Western Europe,* edited by Charles Tilly, 243–327. Princeton: Princeton University Press, 1975.

Brewer, John. *The Sinews of Power: War, Money, and the English State, 1688–1783.* London: Unwin Hyman, 1989.

Brown, Roger H. *The Republic in Peril: 1812.* New York: Columbia University Press, 1964.

———. *Redeeming the Republic: Federalists, Taxation, and the Origins of the Constitution.* Baltimore: Johns Hopkins University Press, 1993.

Brownlee, W. Elliot. "The Transformation of the Tax System and the Experts." *National Tax Journal* 32 (1979): 47–54.

———. "Wilson and Financing the Modern State: The Revenue Act of 1916." *Proceedings of the American Philosophical Society* 129 (1985): 173–210.

———. *Federal Taxation in America: A Short History.* New York: Cambridge University Press, 1996.

———, ed. *Funding the Modern American State, 1941–1995: The Rise and Fall of the Era of Easy Finance.* New York: Cambridge University Press, 1996.

Buel, Richard, Jr. *Securing the Revolution: Ideology in American Politics, 1789–1815.* Ithaca: Cornell University Press, 1972.

Burnham, Walter Dean. *The American Party Systems: Stages of Political Development.* New York: Oxford University Press, 1967.

Butterfield, L. H., Marc Friedlaender, and Mary-Jo Kline, eds. *The Book of Abigail and John Adams: Selected Letters of the Adams Family.* Cambridge, MA: Harvard University Press, 1975.

Cameron, David R. "The Expansion of the Public Economy: A Comparative Analysis." *American Political Science Review* 72 (1978): 1243–61.

Cameron, Rondo, and Larry Neal. *A Concise Economic History of the World: From Paleolithic Times to the Present.* 4th ed. New York: Oxford University Press, 2003.

Carnoy, Martin. *The State and Political Theory.* Princeton: Princeton University Press, 1984.

Carpenter, Daniel P. *The Forging of Bureaucratic Autonomy: Reputations, Networks, and Policy Innovation in Executive Agencies, 1862–1928.* Princeton: Princeton University Press, 2001.

———. "The Political Foundations of Bureaucratic Autonomy." *Studies in American Political Development* 15 (spring 2001): 113–22.

Centeno, Miguel Angel. *Blood and Debt: War and the Nation-State in Latin America.* University Park: Pennsylvania State University Press, 2002.

Chan, Michael D., *Aristotle and Hamilton on Commerce and Statesmanship.* Columbia: University of Missouri Press, 2006.

Chernow, Ron. *Alexander Hamilton.* New York: Penguin Books, 2004.

Clifford, J. Garry, and Samuel R. Spencer Jr. *The First Peacetime Draft.* Lawrence: University of Kansas Press, 1986.

Chommie, John C. *The Internal Revenue Service.* New York: Praeger Publishers, 1970.

Cohen, Youssef. *The Manipulation of Consent: The State and Working-Class Consciousness in Brazil.* Pittsburgh: University of Pittsburgh Press, 1989.

————. *Radicals, Reformers, and Reactionaries: The Prisoner's Dilemma and the Collapse of Democracy in Latin America.* Chicago: University of Chicago Press, 1994.

Cohen, Youssef, Brian R. Brown, and A.F.K. Organski. "The Paradoxical Nature of State Making: The Violent Creation of Order." *American Political Science Review* 75 (1981): 901–10.

Crankshaw, Edward. *Bismarck.* London: Macmillan, 1981.

Croly, Herbert. *The Promise of American Life.* New York: Macmillan, 1909.

Dauvergne, Peter, ed. *Weak and Strong States in Asia-Pacific Societies.* Canberra, Australia: Allen and Unwin, 1998.

Desch, Michael C. "War and Strong States, Peace and Weak States?" *International Organization* 50 (spring 1996): 237–68.

Dickson, P.G.M. *The Financial Revolution in England: A Study in the Development of Public Credit, 1688–1756.* New York: St. Martin's Press, 1967.

Dougherty, Keith L., *Collective Action under the Articles of Confederation.* New York: Cambridge University Press, 2001.

Downing, Brian M. *The Military Revolution and Political Change: Origins of Democracy and Autocracy in Early Modern Europe.* Princeton: Princeton University Press, 1991.

Edling, Max M. *A Revolution in Favor of Government: Origins of the U.S. Constitution and the Making of the American State.* New York: Oxford University Press, 2003.

Edling, Max M., and Mark D. Kaplanoff. "Alexander Hamilton's Fiscal Reform: Transforming the Structure of Taxation in the Early Republic." *William and Mary Quarterly* 61 (October 2004): 713–44.

Einhorn, Robin L. *American Taxation, American Slavery.* Chicago: University of Chicago Press, 2006.

Eisner, Marc Allen. *From Warfare State to Welfare State: World War I, Compensatory State Building, and the Limits of the Modern Order.* University Park: Pennsylvania State University Press, 2000.

Elkins, Stanley, and Eric McKitrick, *The Age of Federalism: The Early American Republic, 1788–1800.* New York: Oxford University Press, 1993.

Eloranta, Jari. "National Defense." In *The Oxford Encyclopedia of Economic History,* edited by Joel Mokyr. New York: Oxford University Press, 2003.

Elster, Jon. *Political Psychology.* New York: Cambridge University Press, 1993.

————. "A Plea for Mechanisms." In *Social Mechanisms: An Analytical Approach to Social Theory,* edited by Peter Hedström and Richard Swedberg, 45–73. Cambridge: Cambridge University Press, 1998.

Elton, G. R. *The Tudor Revolution in Government: Administrative Changes in the Reign of Henry VIII.* Cambridge: Cambridge University Press, 1953.

Ertman, Thomas. *Birth of the Leviathan: Building States and Regimes in Medieval and Early Modern Europe.* New York: Cambridge University Press, 1997.

Esping-Andersen, Gøsta. *The Three Worlds of Welfare.* Princeton: Princeton University Press, 1990.

Evans, Peter B., Dietrich Rueschemeyer, and Theda Skocpol, eds. *Bringing the State Back In.* New York: Cambridge University Press, 1985.

Farrand, Max, ed. *The Records of the Federal Convention of 1787.* Vols. 1–4. New Haven: Yale University Press, 1966.

Faust, Drew Gilpin. *The Creation of Confederate Nationalism: Ideology and Identity in the Civil War South.* Baton Rouge: Louisiana State University Press, 1988.

Ferguson, E. James. *The Power of the Purse: A History of American Public Finance, 1776–1790.* Chapel Hill: University of North Carolina Press, 1961.

Ferguson, Niall. *The Cash Nexus: Money and Power in the Modern World, 1700–2000.* Basic Books, 2001.

Finer, Samuel E. *The Man on Horseback: The Role of the Military in Politics.* New York: Praeger, 1962.

———. "State- and Nation-Building in Europe: The Role of the Military." In *The Formation of National States in Western Europe,* edited by Charles Tilly, 84–163. Princeton: Princeton University Press, 1975.

Fiske, John. *The Critical Period of American History, 1783–1789.* Boston: Houghton, Mifflin, 1888.

Flora, Peter, and Arnold J. Heidenheiner, eds. *The Development of Welfare States in Europe and America.* New Brunswick, NJ: Transaction Books, 1981.

Flynn, George Q. *The Draft, 1940–1973.* Lawrence: University of Kansas Press, 1993.

Fogelman, Robert W., and Stanley L. Engerman. *Time on the Cross: The Economics of American Negro Slavery.* Boston: Little Brown, 1974.

Ford, Worthington C., et al., eds., *Journals of the Continental Congress, 1774–1789.* Washington, DC: Government Printing Office: 1904–37.

Forsythe, Dall W. *Taxation and Political Change in the Young Nation, 1781–1833.* New York: Columbia University Press, 1977.

Foucault, Michel. *Discipline and Punish: The Birth of the Prison.* New York: Pantheon Books, 1977.

Fowler, William M., Jr. *Empires at War: The French and Indian War and the Struggle for North America, 1754–1763.* New York: Walker, 2005.

Freehling, William W. *The Road to Disunion.* Vol. 1. *Secessionists at Bay, 1776–1854.* New York: Oxford University Press, 1990.

———. *The Road to Disunion.* Vol. 2. *Secessionists Triumphant, 1854–1861.* New York: Oxford University Press, 2007.

Friedman, Lawrence M. *A History of American Law.* New York: Simon and Schuster, 1973.

———. *Crime and Punishment in American History.* New York: Basic Books, 1993.

Geddes, Barbara. *Politician's Dilemma: Building State Capacity in Latin America.* Berkeley: University of California Press, 1994.

Giddens, Anthony. *The Nation-State and Violence.* Berkeley: University of California Press, 1987.

Gilpin, Robert. *War and Change in World Politics.* New York: Cambridge University Press, 1981.

Glete, Jan. *War and the State in Early Modern Europe: Spain, the Dutch Republic, and Sweden as Fiscal-Military States, 1500–1660.* New York: Routledge, 2004.

Goldin, Claudia D., and Frank D. Lewis. "The Economic Cost of the American Civil War: Estimates and Implications." *Journal of Economic History* 35 (1970): 299–326.

Goldscheid, Rudolf. "A Sociological Approach to Problems in Public Finance." In *Classics in the Theory of Public Finance,* edited by Richard A. Musgrave and Alan T. Peacock, 203–13. New York: Macmillan, 1958.

Goldstone, Jack A. *Revolution and Rebellion in the Early Modern World.* Berkeley: University of California Press, 1991.

Goodrich, Carter. *Government Promotion of American Canals and Railroads, 1800–1890.* New York: Columbia University Press, 1960.

Gordon, Margaret S. *Social Security Policies in Industrial Countries: A Comparative Analysis.* New York: Cambridge University Press, 1988.

Gorski, Philip S. "Beyond Marx and Hintze? Third Wave Theories of Early Modern State Formation." *Contemporary Studies in Society and History* 43 (December 2001): 851–61.

———. *The Disciplinary Revolution: Calvinism and the Rise of the State in Early Europe.* Chicago: University of Chicago Press, 2003.

Grubb, Farley. "The U.S. Constitution and Monetary Powers: An Analysis of the 1787 Constitutional Convention and the Constitutional Transformation of the U.S. Monetary System." *Financial History Review* 13 (April 2006): 43–71.

———. "The Continental Dollar: What Happened to It after 1779?" NBER Working Paper No. 13770. Cambridge, MA: National Bureau of Economic Research, February 2008.

Guéhenno, Jean-Marie. *The End of the Nation-State.* Minneapolis: University of Minnesota Press, 1995.

Gumplowicz, Ludwig. *The Outline of Sociology.* Philadelphia: American Academy of Political and Social Science, 1899.

Hacker, Jacob S. *The Divided Welfare State: The Battle over Public and Private Social Benefits in the United States.* New York: Cambridge University Press, 2002.

Hamilton, Alexander. "Report Relative to a Provision for the Support of Public Credit" (1790), "Second Report on the Further Provision Necessary for Establishing Public Credit" (1790), and "Report on Manufacturers" (1791). *Reports of Alexander Hamilton.* New York: Harper and Row, 1964.

Harding, Neil, ed. *The State in Socialist Society.* Albany: SUNY Press, 1984.

Harrison, Mark. "The Economics of World War II: An Overview." In *The Economics of World War II: Six Great Powers in International Comparisons,* edited by Mark Harrison, 1–42. Cambridge: Cambridge University Press, 1998.

Hartz, Louis. *The Liberal Tradition in America: An Interpretation of American Political Thought since the Revolution.* New York: Harcourt, Brace, 1955.

Heclo, Hugh. *Modern Social Politics in Britain and Sweden: From Relief to Income Maintenance.* New Haven: Yale University Press, 1974.

Held, David. *Political Theory and the Modern State.* Stanford: Stanford University Press, 1989.

Henderson, Dwight F. *Congress, Courts, and Criminals: The Development of Federal Criminal Law, 1801–1829.* Westport, CT: Greenwood Press, 1985.

Hennock, E. P. *The Origin of the Welfare State in England and Germany, 1850–1914: Social Policies Compared.* New York: Cambridge University Press, 2007.

Hicks, Alexander. *Social Democracy and Welfare Capitalism: A Century of Income Security Politics.* Ithaca: Cornell University Press, 1999.

Higgs, Robert. *Crisis and Leviathan: Critical Episodes in the Growth of American Government.* New York: Oxford University Press, 1987.

Hintze, Otto. "Military Organization and the Organization of the State." In *The Historical Essays of Otto Hintze,* edited by Felix Gilbert, 178–215. New York: Oxford University Press, 1975.

Hooks, Gregory, and Gregory McLauchlan. "The Institutional Foundation of Warmaking: Three Eras of U.S. Warmaking, 1939–1989." *Theory and Society* 21 (1992): 757–88.

Howard, Christopher. *The Hidden Welfare State: Tax Expenditures and Social Policy in the United States.* Princeton: Princeton University Press, 1997.

———. *The Welfare States Nobody Knows: Debunking Myths About U.S. Social Policy.* Princeton: Princeton University Press, 2007.

Howard, Michael E. "War and the Nation-State." *Daedalus* 108 (1979): 101–10.

———. *The Causes of Wars and Other Essays.* Cambridge, MA: Harvard University Press, 1983.

Howe, Daniel Walker. *What Hath God Wrought: The Transformation of America, 1815–1848.* New York: Oxford University Press, 2007.

Hui, Victoria Tin-bor. *War and State Formation in Ancient China and Early Modern Europe.* New York: Cambridge University Press, 2005.

Huntington, Samuel P. "Political Development and Political Decay." *World Politics* 17 (1965): 386–430.

———. *Political Order in Changing Societies.* New Haven: Yale University Press, 1968.

———. *American Politics: The Promise of Disharmony.* Cambridge, MA: Belknap Press, 1981.

Jacobs, Meg, William J. Novak, and Julian E. Zelizer, eds. *The Democratic Experiment: New Directions in American Political Development.* Princeton: Princeton University Press, 2003.

Jensen, Merrill. *The Articles of Confederation: An Interpretation of the Social-Constitutional History of the American Revolution, 1774–1781.* Madison: University of Wisconsin Press, 1940.

———. *The New Nation: A History of the United States during the Confederation, 1781–1789.* Boston: Northeastern University Press, 1950.

———. *The Founding of a Nation: A History of the American Revolution, 1763–1776.* New York: Oxford University Press, 1968.

Jillson, Calvin C., and Rick K. Wilson. *Congressional Dynamics: Structure, Coordination, and Choice in the First American Congress, 1774–1789.* Stanford, CA: Stanford University Press, 1994.

John, Richard R. *Spreading the News: The American Postal System from Franklin to Morse.* Cambridge, MA: Harvard University Press 1995.

———. "Governmental Institutions as Agents of Change: Rethinking Political Development in the Early American Republic, 1787–1835." *Studies in American Political Development* 11 (fall 1997): 347–80.

Johnson, Chalmers A. *Revolutionary Change.* Boston: Little, Brown, 1966.

Johnson, Kimberley S. *Governing the American State: Congress and the New Federalism, 1877–1929.* Princeton: Princeton University Press, 2007.

Karl, Terry Lynn. *The Paradox of Plenty: Oil Booms and Petro-States.* Berkeley: University of California Press, 1997.

Katsaro, Thomas. *The Development of the Welfare State in the Western World.* New York: University Press of America, 1995.

Katzenstein, Peter J., ed. *Between Power and Plenty: Foreign Economic Policies of Advanced Industrial States.* Madison: University of Wisconsin Press, 1978.

Katznelson, Ira, and Martin Shefter, eds. *Shaped by War and Trade: International Influences on American Political Development.* Princeton: Princeton University Press, 2002.

Katznelson, Ira, and Aristide R. Zolberg, eds. *Working-Class Formation: Nineteenth-Century Patterns in Western Europe and the United States.* Princeton: Princeton University Press, 1986.

Keegan, John. *The Face of Battle: A Study of Agincourt, Waterloo, and the Somme.* New York: Penguin, 1978.

———. *A History of Warfare.* New York: Alfred A. Knopf, 1994.

Kennedy, Paul. *The Rise and Fall of the Great Powers: Economic Change and Military Conflict from 1500 to 2000.* New York: Random House, 1987.

Kestnbaum, Meyer, and Theda Skocpol. "War and the Development of Modern National States." *Sociological Forum* 8 (1993): 661–74.

Kimmel, Michael S. *Absolutism and Its Discontents: State and Society in Seventeenth-Century France and England.* New Brunswick, NJ: Transaction, 1987.

King, Ronald F. *Money, Time, and Politics: Investment Tax Subsidiaries and American Democracy.* New Haven: Yale University Press, 1993.

Kohn, Richard H. *Eagle and Sword: The Federalists and the Creation of the Military Establishment in America, 1783–1802.* New York: Free Press, 1975.

———. *The United States Military under the Constitution of the United States, 1789–1989.* New York: New York University Press, 1991.

Krasner, Stephen D. *Defending the National Interest.* Princeton: Princeton University Press, 1978.

———. "Approaches to the State: Alternative Conceptions and Historical Dynamics." *Comparative Politics* 16 (1984): 223–46.

———. *Sovereignty: Organized Hypocrisy.* Princeton: Princeton University Press, 1999.

Kromkowski, Charles A. *Recreating the American Republic: Rules of Apportionment, Constitutional Change, and American Political Development, 1700–1870.* New York: Cambridge University Press, 2002.

Kruman, Marc W. *Between Authority and Liberty: State Constitution Making in Revolutionary America.* Chapel Hill: University of North Carolina Press, 1997.

Labunski, Richard. *James Madison and the Struggle for the Bill of Rights.* New York: Oxford University Press, 2007.

Lane, Frederic C. *Profits from Power: Readings in Protection Rent and Violence-Controlling Enterprises.* Albany: State University of New York Press, 1979.

Larson, John Lauritz. *Internal Improvement: National Public Works and the Promise of Popular Government in the Early United States.* Chapel Hill: University of North Carolina Press, 2001.

Levi, Margaret. "A Theory of Predatory Rule." *Politics and Society* 10 (1981): 431–65.

——. *Of Rule and Revenue.* Berkeley: University of California Press, 1988.

——. "Why We Need a New Theory of Government." *Perspective on Politics* 4 (2006): 5 19.

Levinson, Sanford. *Our Undemocratic Constitution: Where the Constitution Goes Wrong (And How We the People Can Correct It).* New York: Oxford University Press, 2006.

Lieberman, Robert C. "Ideas, Institutions, and Political Order: Explaining Political Change." *American Political Science Review* 96 (December 2002): 697–712.

Madison, James. *Notes of Debates in the Federal Convention of 1787 Reported by James Madison.* New York: W. W. Norton, 1966.

Maier, Pauline. *American Scripture: Making the Declaration of Independence.* New York: Knopf, 1997.

Majewski, John D. *A House Dividing: Economic Development in Pennsylvania and Virginia before the Civil War.* New York: Cambridge University Press, 2000.

Makin, John H., and Norman J. Ornstein. *Debt and Taxes.* New York: Random House, 1994.

Maman, Daniel, Eyal Ben-Ari, and Zeev Rosenhek, eds. *Military, State, and Society in Israel.* New Brunswick, NJ: Transaction, 2001.

Mann, Michael. *The Sources of Social Power.* Vol. 1. *A History of Power from the Beginning to A.D. 1760.* New York: Cambridge University Press, 1986.

——. *States, War, and Capitalism: Studies in Political Sociology.* Oxford: Basil Blackwell, 1988.

——. *The Sources of Social Power.* Vol. 2. *The Rise of Classes and Nation States, 1760–1914.* New York: Cambridge University Press, 1993.

Mansfield, Harvey C., Jr. *America's Constitutional Soul.* Baltimore: Johns Hopkins University Press, 1991.

Marston, Jerrilyn Greene. *King and Congress: The Transfer of Political Legitimacy, 1774–1776.* Princeton: Princeton University Press, 1987.

Mayhew, David R. "Wars and American Politics." *Perspectives on Politics* 3 (September 2005): 473–93.

McAdam, Doug, Sidney Tarrow, and Charles Tilly. *Dynamics of Contention.* New York: Cambridge University Press, 2001.

McCoy, Drew R. *The Elusive Republic: Political Economy in Jeffersonian America.* Chapel Hill: University of North Carolina Press, 1980.

McCusker, John J., and Russell R. Menard. *The Economy of British America.* Chapel Hill: University of North Carolina Press, 1985.

McDonald, Forrest. *We the People: The Economic Origins of the Constitution.* Chicago: University of Chicago Press, 1958.

——. *E Pluribus Unum: The Formation of the American Republic, 1776–1790.* Boston: Houghton Mifflin, 1965.

——. *Novus Ordo Seclorum: The Intellectual Origins of the Constitution.* Lawrence: University Press of Kansas, 1985.

McKitrick, Eric L. *Andrew Johnson and Reconstruction.* Chicago: University of Chicago Press, 1960.

McNeill, William H. *The Pursuit of Power: Technology, Armed Force, and Society since A.D. 1000.* Chicago: University of Chicago Press, 1982.

McPherson, James M. *Abraham Lincoln and the Second American Revolution*. New York: Oxford University Press, 1990.

Mearsheimer, John J. *The Tragedy of Great Power Politics*. New York: W. W. Norton, 2001.

Mehrotra, Ajay K. "Envisioning the Modern American Fiscal State: Progressive-Era Economists and the Intellectual Foundations of the U.S. Income Tax." *UCLA Law Review* 52 (August 2005): 1793–1866.

Mettler, Suzanne. *Dividing Citizens: Gender and Federalism in New Deal Public Policy*. Ithaca: Cornell University Press, 1998.

Migdal, Joel S. *Strong Societies and Weak States: State-Society Relations and State Capabilities in the Third World*. Princeton: Princeton University Press, 1988.

——. *State in Society: Studying How States and Societies Transform and Constitute One Another*. New York: Cambridge University Press, 2001.

Miliband, Ralph. *The State in Capitalist Society*. New York: Basic Books, 1969.

——. *Class Power and State Power*. London: Verso, 1983.

Milkis, Sidney M. *The President and the Parties: The Transformation of the American Party System since the New Deal*. New York: Oxford University Press, 1993.

——. *Political Parties and Constitutional Government: Remaking American Democracy*. Baltimore: Johns Hopkins University Press, 1999.

Mink, Gwendolyn. *Old Labor and New Immigrants in American Political Development: Union, Party, and State, 1875–1920*. Ithaca: Cornell University Press, 1986.

Moe, Terry. "Power and Political Institutions." *Perspective on Politics* 3 (2005): 215–33.

Moore, Barrington, Jr. *Social Origins of Dictatorship and Democracy: Lord and Peasant in the Making of the Modern World*. Boston: Beacon Press, 1966.

Morison, Samuel Eliot, Henry Steele Commager, and William E. Leuchtenburg. *The Growth of the American Republic*. 7th ed. New York: Oxford University Press, 1980.

Morris, Richard B. *The Forging of the Union, 1780–1789*. New York: Harper and Row, 1987.

Musgrave, Richard A., and Alan T. Peacock, eds. *Classics in the Theory of Public Finance*. New York: Macmillan, 1958.

Myers, Margaret G. *A Financial History of the United States*. New York: Columbia University Press, 1970.

Natelson, Robert G. "Paper Money and the Original Understanding of the Coinage Clause." *Harvard Journal of Law and Public Policy* 31 (summer 2008): 1017–82.

Neely, Mark N., Jr. "Was the Civil War a Total War?" *Civil War History* 37 (March 1991): 5–28.

——. *The Civil War and the Limits of Destruction*. Cambridge, MA: Harvard University Press, 2007.

Nettl, J. P. "The State as a Conceptual Variable." *World Politics* 20 (1968): 559–92.

Nettles, Curtis P. *The Emergence of a National Economy, 1775–1815*. New York: Holt, Reinhart, and Winston, 1962.

Neuberger, Benyamin. "The Western Nation-State in African Perceptions of Nation-Building." *Asian and African Studies* 11 (1976): 241–61.

Newman, Paul Douglas. *Fries's Rebellion: The Enduring Struggle for the American Revolution*. Philadelphia: University of Pennsylvania Press, 2004.

Nisbet, Robert A. *Twilight of Authority*. New York: Oxford University Press, 1975.

Nordlinger, Eric A. *On the Autonomy of the Democratic State.* Cambridge, MA: Harvard University Press, 1981.

North, Douglass C. *The Economic Growth of the United States, 1790–1860.* Englewood Cliffs, NJ: Prentice-Hall, 1961.

——. *Structure and Change in Economic History.* New York: W. W. Norton, 1981.

——. *Institutions, Institutional Change, and Economic Performance.* New York: Cambridge University Press, 1990.

North, Douglass C., and Robert P. Thomas. *The Rise of the Western World: A New Economic History.* Cambridge: Cambridge University Press, 1973.

North, Douglass C., and Barry R. Weingast, "Constitutions and Commitments: The Evolution of Institutions Governing Public Choice in Seventeenth-Century England." *Journal of Economic History* 49 (December 1989): 803–32.

Novak, William J. "The Myth of the 'Weak' American State." *American Historical Review* 113 (June 2008): 752–72.

O'Brien, Patrick K., and Philip A. Hunt. "The Rise of the Fiscal-Military State in England, 1485–1815." *Historical Research* 66 (1993): 129–76.

Olson, Mancur. *Power and Prosperity: Outgrowing Communist and Capitalist Dictatorships.* New York: Basic Books, 2000.

——. *The Rise and Decline of Nations.* New Haven: Yale University Press, 1981.

Organski, A.F.K. *The Stages of Political Development.* New York: Knopf, 1965.

Organski, A.F.K., and Jacek Kugler. *The War Ledger.* Chicago: University of Chicago Press, 1980.

Orren, Karen. *Belated Feudalism: Labor, the Law, and Liberal Development in the United States.* Cambridge: Cambridge University Press, 1991.

Parker, Geoffrey. "The 'Military Revolution,' 1560–1660—a Myth?" *Journal of Modern History* 48 (1976): 195–214.

——. *The Military Revolution: Military Innovation and the Rise of the West, 1500–1800.* Cambridge: Cambridge University Press, 1988.

Paul, Randolph E. *Taxation in the United States.* Boston: Little, Brown, 1954.

Peacock, Alan T., and Jack Wiseman. *The Growth of Public Expenditure in the United Kingdom.* Princeton: Princeton University Press, 1961.

——. "Approaches to the Analysis of Government Expenditure Growth," *Public Finance Quarterly* 7 (1979): 3–23.

Perkins, Edwin J. *American Public Finance and Financial Services, 1700–1815.* Columbus: Ohio State University Press, 1994.

Peters, B. Guy. *The Politics of Taxation: A Comparative Perspective.* Cambridge: Basil Blackwell, 1991.

Pierson, Paul. "When Effect Becomes Cause: Policy Feedback and Political Change." *World Politics* 45 (July 1993): 595–628.

——. "Increasing Returns, Path Dependence, and the Study of Politics." *American Political Science Review* 94 (June 2000): 251–67.

——. *Politics in Time: History, Institutions, and Social Analysis.* Princeton: Princeton University Press, 2004.

Pocock, J.G.A. *The Machiavellian Moment: Florentine Political Thought and the Atlantic Republican Tradition.* Princeton: Princeton University Press, 1975.

Poggi, Gianfranco. *The Development of the Modern State: A Sociological Introduction.* Stanford: Stanford University Press, 1978.

——. *The State: Its Nature, Development, and Prospects.* Cambridge, UK: Polity Press, 1990.

Polanyi, Karl. *The Great Transformation: The Political and Economic Origins of Our Time.* New York: Rinehart, 1944.

Pollack, Sheldon D. *The Failure of U.S. Tax Policy: Revenue and Politics.* University Park: Penn State Press, 1996.

——. *Refinancing America: The Republican Antitax Agenda.* Albany: State University of New York Press, 2003.

Polsby, Nelson W. "The Institutionalization of the U.S. House of Representatives." *American Political Science Review* 62 (1968): 144–68.

Porter, Bruce D. *War and the Rise of the State: The Military Foundations of Modern Politics.* New York: Free Press, 1994.

Pye, Lucian W. "The Concept of Political Development." *Annuals of the American Academy of Political and Social Science* 358 (1965): 1–13.

Rabushka, Alvin. *Taxation in Colonial America.* Princeton: Princeton University Press, 2008.

Rakove, Jack N. *The Beginnings of National Politics: An Interpretive History of the Continental Congress.* New York: Knopf, 1979.

Rasler, Karen A., and William R. Thompson. "War Making and State Making: Governmental Expenditures, Tax Revenues, and Global Wars." *American Political Science Review* 79 (1985): 491–507.

——. *War and State Making: The Shaping of Global Powers.* Boston: Unwin Hyman, 1989.

Ratner, Sidney. *American Taxation: Its History as a Social Force in Democracy.* New York: W. W. Norton, 1942.

Reitano, Joanne. *The Tariff Question in the Gilded Age: The Great Debate of 1888.* University Park: Pennsylvania State University Press, 1994.

Riker, William H. "The Senate and American Federalism." *American Political Science Review* 49 (June 1955): 452–69.

——. *Soldiers of the States: The Role of the National Guard in American Democracy.* Washington, DC: Public Affairs Press, 1957.

——. *The Theory of Political Coalitions.* New Haven: Yale University Press, 1962.

——. *Federalism: Origin, Operation, Significance.* Boston: Little, Brown, 1964.

——. "Federalism." *The Handbook of Political Science.* Vol. 5. *Government Institutions and Processes,* edited by Fred I. Greenstein and Nelson Polsby. Reading, MA: Addison Wesley, 1975.

——. "Comments on Vincent Ostrom's Paper." *Public Choice* 27 (1976): 13–15.

——. *The Development of American Federalism.* Boston: Kluwer, 1987.

Rimlinger, Gaston V. *Welfare Policy and Industrialization in Europe, America, and Russia.* New York: Wiley, 1971.

Roberts, Michael. "The Military Revolution, 1560–1660." In *Essays in Swedish History,* edited by Michael Roberts, 195–225. Minneapolis: University of Minnesota Press, 1967.

Robertson, David Brian. "Madison's Opponents and Constitutional Design." *American Political Science Review* 99 (2005): 225–43.

———. *The Constitution and America's Destiny.* New York: Cambridge University Press, 2005.

Ross, Dorothy. *The Origins of American Social Science.* New York: Cambridge University Press, 1991.

Rutland, Robert A., ed. *The Papers of James Madison.* Chicago: University of Chicago Press, 1975.

Sanders, Elizabeth. *Roots of Reform: Farmers, Workers, and the American State, 1877–1917.* Chicago: University of Chicago Press, 1999.

Savage, James D. *Balanced Budgets and American Politics.* Ithaca: Cornell University Press, 1988.

Schofield, Roger. *Taxation under the Early Tudors, 1485–1547.* Oxford: Blackwell Publishing, 2004.

Schumpeter, Joseph A. "The Crisis of the Tax State." 1918; reprinted in *International Economic Papers* 4 (1954): 5–38.

Seligman, Edwin R. A. "The Theory of Progressive Taxation." *Political Science Quarterly* 8 (1893): 220–51.

———. *The Income Tax: A Study of the History, Theory, and Practice of Income Taxation at Home and Abroad.* New York: Macmillan, 1911.

Shafer, D. Michael. *Winners and Losers: How Sectors Shape the Development Prospects of States.* Ithaca: Cornell University Press, 1994.

Shapiro, Ian, Stephen Skowronek, and Daniel Galvin, eds. *Rethinking Political Institutions: The Art of the State.* New York: New York University Press, 2006.

Sharp, James Roger. *American Politics in the Early Republic: The New Nation in Crisis.* New Haven: Yale University Press, 1993.

Shefter, Martin. *Political Parties and the State: The American Historical Experience.* Princeton: Princeton University Press, 1994.

Sibley, Joel H. *Martin Van Buren and the Emergence of American Popular Politics.* Lanham, Md: Rowman and Littlefield, 2002.

Skocpol, Theda. "Wallerstein's World Capitalist System: A Theoretical and Historical Critique." *American Journal of Sociology* 82 (1977): 1075–90.

———. *States and Social Revolutions: A Comparative Analysis of France, Russia, and China.* New York: Cambridge University Press, 1979.

———. *Protecting Soldiers and Mothers: The Political Origins of Social Policy in the United States.* Cambridge, MA: Belknap Press, 1992.

———. "America's First Social Security System: The Expansion of Benefits for Civil War Veterans." *Political Science Quarterly* 108 (1993): 85–116.

———. *Social Policy in the United States: Future Possibilities in Historical Perspective.* Princeton: Princeton University Press, 1995.

Skowronek, Stephen. *Building a New American State: The Expansion of National Administrative Capacities, 1877–1920.* New York: Cambridge University Press, 1982.

———. *The Politics Presidents Make: Leadership from John Adams to George Bush.* Cambridge, MA: Harvard University Press, 1993.

———. "Order and Change." *Polity* 28 (fall 1995): 91–96.

Skowronek, Stephen, and Matthew Glassman, eds. *Formative Acts: American Politics in the Making.* Philadelphia: University of Pennsylvania Press, 2007.

Skowronek, Stephen, and Karen Orren. *The Search for American Political Development.* New York: Cambridge University Press, 2004.

Smith, Rogers M. "Beyond Tocqueville, Myrdal, and Hartz: The Multiple Traditions in America." *American Political Science Review* 87 (1993): 549–56.

———. *Civic Ideals: Conflicting Visions of Citizenship in U.S. History.* New Haven: Yale University Press, 1997.

Sparrow, Bartholomew H. *From the Outside In: World War II and the American State.* Princeton: Princeton University Press, 1996.

Steinberger, Peter J. *The Idea of the State.* New York: Cambridge University Press, 2004.

Steinmo, Sven. *Taxation and Democracy: Swedish, British, and American Approaches to Financing the Modern State.* New Haven: Yale University Press, 1993.

Stepan, Alfred. *The State and Society: Peru in Comparative Perspective.* Princeton: Princeton University Press, 1978.

———. *Rethinking Military Politics.* Princeton: Princeton University Press, 1988.

Steuerle C. Eugene, and Jon M. Bakija. Retooling Social Security for the Twenty-First Century: Right and Wrong Approaches to Reform. Washington, DC: Urban Institute Press, 1994.

Stinchcombe, Arthur L. "The Conditions of Fruitfulness of Theorizing about Mechanisms in Social Science." *Philosophy of Social Science* 21 (1991): 367–88.

Strayer, Joseph R. *On the Medieval Origins of the Modern State.* Princeton: Princeton University Press, 1970.

Swenson, Peter A. *Capitalists against Markets: The Making of Labor Markets and Welfare States in the United States and Sweden.* New York: Oxford University Press, 2002.

Taussig, F. W. *The Tariff History of the United States: A Series of Essays.* New York: G. P. Putnam's Sons, 1894.

Taylor, Michael. "Rationality and Revolutionary Collective Action." In *Rationality and Revolution,* edited by Michael Taylor, 63–97. Cambridge: Cambridge University Press, 1988.

Thies, Cameron G. "War, Rivalry, and State Building in Latin America." *American Journal of Political Science* 49 (July 2005): 451–65.

Thorndike, Joseph J. "An Army of Officials: The Civil War Bureau of Internal Revenue." *Tax Notes* 93 (December 24, 2001): 1739–61.

Tilly, Charles. "Reflections on the History of European State-Making." In *The Formation of National States in Western Europe,* edited by Charles Tilly, 3–83. Princeton: Princeton University Press, 1975.

———. "War Making and State Making as Organized Crime." In *Bringing the State Back In,* edited by Peter B. Evans, Dietrich Rueschemeyer, Theda Skocpol, 169–91. New York: Cambridge University Press, 1985.

———. *Coercion, Capital, and European States: AD 990–1990.* Cambridge, UK: B. Blackwell, 1990.

———. "Mechanisms in Political Processes." *Annual Review of Political Science* 4 (June 2001): 21–41.

Tocqueville, Alexis de. *The Old Regime and the Revolution.* New York: Harper and Brothers, 1856.

Turkel, Gerald. "Michel Foucault: Law, Power, and Knowledge." *Journal of Law and Society* 17 (summer 1990): 170–93.

——. *Dividing Public and Private: Law, Politics, and Social Theory.* Westport, CT: Praeger, 1992.

Van Creveld, Martin. *The Rise and Decline of the State.* Cambridge: Cambridge University Press, 1999.

Ver Steeg, Clarence L. *Robert Morris: Revolutionary Financier.* Philadelphia: University of Pennsylvania, 1954.

Wade, Robert. *Governing the Market: Economic Theory and the Role of Government in East Asian Industrialization.* Princeton: Princeton University Press, 1990.

Waldner, David. *State Building and Late Development.* Ithaca: Cornell University Press, 1999.

Wallerstein, Immanuel. *The Modern World System.* New York: Academic Press, 1974.

——. *The Capitalist World Economy.* Cambridge: Cambridge University Press, 1979.

Weingast, Barry R. "The Economic Role of Political Institutions: Market-Preserving Federalism and Economic Development." *Journal of Law, Economics, and Organization* 11 (1999): 1–31.

Weinstein, James. *The Corporate Ideal in the Liberal State, 1900–1918.* Boston: Beacon Press, 1968.

Weir, Margaret, Ann Shola Orloff, and Theda Skocpol, eds. *The Politics of Social Policy in the United States.* Princeton: Princeton University Press, 1988.

White, Leonard D. *The Federalists: A Study in Administrative History.* New York: Macmillan, 1948.

——. *The Jeffersonians: A Study in Administrative History, 1801–1829.* New York: Macmillan, 1951.

——. *The Jacksonians: A Study in Administrative History, 1829–1861.* New York: Macmillan, 1954.

——. *The Republican Era, 1869–1901: A Study in Administrative History.* New York: Macmillan, 1958.

Wiebe, Robert H. *The Search for Order, 1877–1920.* New York: Hill and Wang, 1967.

Wildavsky, Aaron B., and Carolyn Webber. *A History of Taxation and Expenditure in the Western World.* New York: Simon and Schuster, 1986.

Wilentz, Sean. *The Rise of American Democracy: Jefferson to Lincoln.* New York: W. W. Norton, 2005.

Wills, Garry. *Inventing America: Jefferson's Declaration of Independence.* New York: Vintage Books, 1978.

——. *Explaining America: The Federalist.* Garden City, NY: Doubleday, 1981.

Wilson, Mark R. *The Business of the Civil War: Military Mobilization and the State, 1861–1865.* Baltimore: Johns Hopkins University Press, 2006.

Witte, John F. *The Politics and Development of the Federal Income Tax.* Madison: University of Wisconsin Press, 1985.

Wong, R. Bin. *China Transformed: Historical Change and the Limits of European Experience.* Ithaca: Cornell University Press, 1997.

Wood, Gordon S. *The Creation of the American Republic, 1776–1787.* New York: W. W. Norton, 1972.

———. *The Radicalism of the American Revolution*. New York: Knopf, 1992.

———. *Revolutionary Characters: What Made the Founders Different*. New York: Penguin Press, 2006.

Young, James Sterling. *The Washington Community, 1800–1828*. New York: Columbia University Press, 1966.

Zolberg, Aristide R. "Origins of the Modern World System: A Missing Link." *World Politics* 33 (1981): 253–81.

INDEX

by managerial change, which boiled down to new groups taking control of the factory. These new groups rejected the Tsitsihar model and tried to install new committees of cadres, technicians, and workers to run the factories. In late 1966, through 1967, and into 1968 this seizure of factories continued.[29] The new committees tackled not only routine production in the shop but also family child-care, the role of women, and worker education—issues far removed from everyday factory operations.[30] The new committees also encouraged worker involvement in planning factory-output quotas for the annual plan. They frequently held study sessions to discuss Maoist-Marxist texts. Whether all modern enterprises became managed by these new committees is not clear. Struggle continued, however, and in 1977 violent outbreaks in Hankow, Foochow, and Shihchiachuang erupted and even forced many factories to close down for long periods. Industrial production in that year came to a standstill in many areas.

In late 1977 and early 1978 the situation rapidly reversed. The new party leadership of Hua Kuo-feng and Teng Hsiao-p'ing quietly restored managerial control to cadres and managers. Worker participation in management receded. The party ordered that revolutionary committees be disbanded and wages increased. Bonuses and material incentives again surfaced. In spring of 1978 several science and technology conferences convened to take stock of how to speed up the education and training of scientists and technical manpower and how to promote pure research in industry and agriculture. Yet the "learn from Ta-ch'ing" model continued to be soft-pedaled. Publications appeared extolling the virtues of the Ta-ch'ing organizational spirit and its adoption by industry throughout the economy.

In 1978 the party announced a new Ten-Year Economic Plan and set ambitious goals to make China a modern economic power by the turn of the century. By 1985 agriculture would be more than 85 percent mechanized for major phases of farming; grain output would reach 400 million tons or a 4 percent annual growth rate; industrial output would grow at 10 percent per annum; metallurgy, petrochemicals, and transport would be further modernized. For these targets to be achieved, the economy would continue to generate high saving and capital accumulation rates. China will continue to acquire new capital equipment and machinery from abroad and steadily add this new vintage to its current stock. The party gambled that this method of capital accumulation would guarantee a high productivity for capital.

SUMMARY: SOCIALISM CHINESE-STYLE

Paradox and contradiction have persistently characterized Chinese economic planning and organization. Party cadres contended land reform would liberate the productive forces of agriculture. But within five years farm production was slowing down and some households were amassing land once again; these two developments prompted the party to scuttle family farming and establish team farming in its place. Under the three-tier-managerial commune system, communes were expected to meet or surpass certain targets, yet they had great latitude of choice to set their accumulation fund target and how much to distribute for consumption from current production. The state appears eager to promote agricultural science and technological research, but the party actively encourages every county to establish Ta-chai brigades within every commune and acquire the spirit of "bitter struggle" and sacrifice.

The party has often demanded that the people demonstrate greater self-reliance in production. Yet the state shops in foreign markets to buy the most modern equipment and machinery to build entire factories in far-flung parts of the country. In industry the party first experimented with Soviet enterprise management, then rejected it to opt for committee-type factory supervision in the late 1960s, and recently has ordered that single-management responsibility be restored. The state now presses for the revival of modern education and scientific research in institutes and universities to develop industrial technology. Yet the party continues to insist that industry adopt the "learn from Ta-ch'ing" organizational experience. In price controls the state gradually raised the prices of farm products and reduced those of industrial products so that commune purchasing power gradually increased. Yet party cadres urge workers to accept high accumulation fund targets and save a high proportion of their personal income in branches of the People's Bank. This flexibility and experimentation in organizational management has prevented resource and commodity scarcities from becoming too serious. At the same time the economy continues to plough back a very high proportion of its current output for capital goods production.

QUESTIONS FOR DISCUSSION

1. How did the Communist party establish economic controls so quickly over the private sector in order to introduce economic planning in 1953?
2. What kinds of economic problems are likely to arise under a planned economy that attempts to achieve a high rate of saving and capital formation?
3. Compare and contrast the state's policies to develop agriculture during the 1950s and after 1962?
4. What kind of financial policies did the Communist party introduce to channel more resources to capital investment? Compare monetary and fiscal policies, and discuss how one complements the other.

5. How has the state been able to achieve such a high rate of capital formation over the past quarter century? Is this likely to continue, and if not, why?
6. What is the relationship between capital accumulation and rapid industrial development? Is capital formation and the expansion of "producer goods" industries the same phenomenon?
7. What were the "learn from Ta-chai" and "learn from Ta-ch'ing" campaigns? What were these campaigns supposed to achieve? Have they had any influence on agricultural and industrial development?

NOTES

1. Mao Tse-tung, "K'ang-jih-ch'i ching-chi wen-t'i ho ts'ai-cheng wen-t'i" [Economic and Financial Administrative Problems during the Anti-Japanese Period], in *Mao Tse-tung hsüan-chi* [The Collected Works of Mao Tse-tung] , 5 vols. (Peking: Jen-min ch'u-pan-she, 1955), vol. III, pp. 913–18.
2. The Communist party held a conference on the land issue on 13 September 1947 and drew up a document referred to as "The Outline Land Law of China," which was comprised of sixteen articles and was published on 10 October 1947. This document served as the basic guideline for carrying out the first stage of land reform.
3. The best account of village land reform in north China is William Hinton, *Fanshen: A Documentary of Revolution in a Chinese Village* (New York: Random House, 1968), pp. 103–232, from which the remarks in this section are taken.
4. Norinshō Nochibu, *Chūgoku kaihō chiku tochi kaikaku kankei shiryoshi* [A Collection of Materials Related to Land Reform in the Liberated Base Areas of China] (Tokyo: Gaimushō, 1949), p. 95.
5. A good illustration of a village undergoing land reform in southeast China can be found in C. K. Yang, *A Chinese Village in Early Communist Transition* (Cambridge, Mass.: M.I.T. Press, 1959), chapter 9.
6. William Brugger, *Democracy and Organization in the Chinese Industrial Enterprise 1948–1953* (Cambridge: Cambridge University Press, 1976), pp. 112–20.
7. Richard L. Walker, *China under Communism: The First Five Years* (New Haven: Yale University Press, 1955), p. 80.
8. This assertion is based upon the unpublished findings contained in Charles R. Roll, Jr., "The Distribution of Rural Incomes in China: A Comparison of the 1930s and the 1950s," thesis in partial fulfillment of the requirements for the degree of Doctor of Philosophy, presented to the Department of Economics, Harvard University, Cambridge, Mass., 1974, p. 46.
9. Ibid., p. 139. Roll has measured the Gini coefficient of rural-household-income inequality for the 1930s and for 1952 and has found that the coefficient declined roughly 30 percent.

10. Shao-er Ong, "A Study of Agricultural Taxation in Communist China," Department of Asiatic Studies, University of Southern California, Los Angeles, 1952 (mimeographed), p. 100 and chapter 3.

11. Dwight H. Perkins, *Market Control and Planning in Communist China* (Cambridge, Mass.: Harvard University Press, 1966), p. 41. The discussion that follows is based upon this excellent study of agricultural financing of industrial development.

12. Jung-Chao Liu, "Wages and Profits of Selected Industries in China," *Economic Development and Cultural Change* 26, no. 4 (July 1978): 747–61.

13. See John G. Gurley, *China's Economy and the Maoist Strategy*–(New York and London: Monthly Review Press, 1976), p. 163. The discussion in this paragraph comes from Gurley's lucid review of various economic studies written about China.

14. Bryant G. Garth and editors of the *Stanford Journal of International Studies,* eds., *China's Changing Role in the World Economy* (New York: Praeger, 1975), p. 29.

15. Thomas G. Rawski, "The Growth of Producer Industries, 1900–1971," in Dwight H. Perkins, ed., *China's Modern Economy in Historical Perspective* (Stanford, Calif.: Stanford University Press, 1975), pp. 221–32.

16. Solomon Adler, *The Chinese Economy* (New York: Monthly Review Press, 1957), chapter 8.

17. The discussion in this paragraph is based upon Vaclav Smil, " 'Energy in China' Achievements and Prospects," *China Quarterly* 65 (March 1976): 54–81.

18. The information in these next paragraphs is based in part on Ramon H. Myers, "Wheat in China—Past, Present and Future," *China Quarterly* 75 (June–July 1978): 297–333.

19. Examples of such waste and inefficiency are described by the U.S. team that visited China to observe rural small-scale industry in 1975. See the American Rural Small-Scale Industry Delegation, *Rural Small-Scale Industry in the People's Republic of China* (Berkeley: University of California Press, 1977), especially chapter 4.

20. The discussion in this paragraph relies heavily upon Alexander Eckstein, *China's Economic Revolution* (Cambridge: Cambridge University Press, 1977), pp. 146–47.

21. These observations on the Chinese banking system are based upon John G. Gurley, *China's Economy,* chapter 6.

22. Information in this paragraph is drawn from Choh-ming Li, *Economic Development of Communist China* (Berkeley: University of California Press, 1959), chapter 6.

23. Franz Schurmann, *Ideology and Organization in Communist China* (Berkeley: University of California, 1966), p. 324.

24. These two developments are the major factors prompting the sudden shift toward collectivizing farming. They are described by Su Hsing, "T'u-ti kai-ke i-hou wo-kuo nung-ts'un she-hui chu-i ho tzu-pen chu-i liang-t'iao tao-lu ti tou-cheng" [The Struggle between the Two Roads of Socialism

and Capitalism in Chinese Rural Society after Land Reform], *Ching-chi yen-chiu*, [Economic Research] 7 (1965): 12–26 and 8 (1965): 1–13.

25. *Yung Ta-chai ching-shen wei ts'ai-cheng chin-jung* [Rely upon the Ta-chai Spirit for Making Financial Policy] (Peking: Chung-kuo ts'ai-cheng ching-chi ch'u-pan-she, 1977), p. 5.

26. Ibid., 83.

27. This section is based upon information in Stephen Andors, *China's Industrial Revolution* (New York: Pantheon Books, 1977), chapter 6.

28. *Yung Ta-ch'ing ching-shen wei shih-yeh ts'ai-wu* [Rely upon the Ta-ch'ing Spirit to Carry Out Enterprise Financing] (Peking: Chung-kuo ts'ai-cheng ching-chi ch'u-pan-she, 1977), p. 16. The industrial enterprises at Ta-ch'ing between 1965 and 1976 were supposed to have reduced their average costs by 50 percent, and the value of production was supposed to have increased 4.4 times or roughly 16.5 percent per annum, which was much faster than the average industrial growth rate for the country. Chinese organizers boasted that "in 17 years [since 1960] we have developed a great oil field, constructed a modern network of enterprises, and set forth upon a new road to enable our country to develop more and more of its natural wealth." See p. 16.

29. Stephen Andors, *China's Industrial Revolution*, pp. 168–85.

30. Charles Hoffmann, "Worker Participation in Chinese Factories," *Modern China*, 3, no. 3 (July 1977): 308–09.

SELECTED READINGS

1. Alexander Eckstein. *China's Economic Revolution.* Cambridge: Cambridge Univeristy Press, 1977.

2. Stephen Andors. *China's Industrial Revolution.* New York: Pantheon Books, 1977.

3. John G. Gurley. *China's Economy and the Maoist Strategy.* New York: Monthly Review Press, 1976.

4. Dwight H. Perkins. *Market Control and Planning in Communist China.* Cambridge, Mass.: Harvard University Press, 1966.

5. William Brugger. *Democracy and Organization in the Chinese Industrial Enterprise 1948–1953.* Cambridge: Cambridge University Press, 1976.

6. Alexander Eckstein. *China's Economic Development: The Interplay of Scarcity and Ideology.* An Arbor: University of Michigan Press, 1976.

7. Ramon H. Myers. "Scarcity and Ideology in Chinese Economic Development." *Problems of Communism* 27 (March–April 1978): 86–96.

8. ———. "Wheat in China—Past, Present and Future." *China Quarterly* 75 (June–July 1978): 297–333.

9. Choh-Ming Li. *Economic Development of Communist China.* Berkeley: University of California Press, 1959.

10. Bryant G. Garth and editors of *Stanford Journal of International Studies*, eds. *China's Changing Role in the World Economy*. New York: Praeger, 1975.

11. "Studies in Chinese Economic Planning (I)." *Chinese Economic Studies* 10, no. 3 (Spring 1977) : 1–103.

12. "Studies in Chinese Economic Planning (II)." *Chinese Economic Studies* 11, no. 2–3 (Winter–Spring 1977–78): 1–167.

Performance and Prospects

8

Within a decade of unifying China, the Communist party had eliminated private property, redistributed both tangible property and its income among the poor, and created new organizations of production and exchange. At first the economy achieved extremely high growth rates for various economic sectors, but these owed as much to rapid economic recovery after more than a decade of war and decline as to the great public campaigns to mobilize the nation's resources to meet the new challenges set by the party. Like the managers of the elite households of the past who had accumulated enormous wealth and managed it prudently and skillfully, state officials also established very high rates of saving and capital investment for this poor economy. Every organization and enterprise balanced its budget and maintained a high capital-accumulation-to-income ratio. Through high investment each year the state greatly expanded its producer industries in cities and built small-scale industries in the countryside. The latter, really a form of modernizing traditional rural handicraft, exemplifies the pattern of the past. China also directly purchased new capital from abroad to build her machine-tool, metallurgical, chemical fertilizer, and petrochemical industries. The state will undoubtedly continue these strategies of accumulating capital, borrowing advanced technology from abroad, and pursuing a balanced type of economic growth that so far have won for China acclaim throughout much of the world.

In many respects, then, China's modern economic growth experience stands as unique among developing countries. Great proverty and backwardness characterized this huge, populated country in 1949. Yet by the late 1970s China adequately fed, housed, and clothed its people, provided them with sufficient preventative medical care to bring serious epidemics under control, and put everyone to work. Chinese society appears orderly, calm, yet exuding great energy to improve itself. However, these past three decades have not been without severe human costs. Land reform and the cooperativization of agriculture claimed hundreds of thousands of lives—perhaps millions. Ruthless political campaigns have crushed any form of dissent or independent expression and invariably led to a spillover of human traffic into labor camps. The labor camps with their untold millions do exist. A pervasive totalitarian control over thought and action dominates every nook and cranny of society and economy alike. Yet China's economic achievements must be viewed as remarkable within this context of high human cost. They are not likely to be duplicated or surpassed by many other countries also striving to modernize quickly.

Has economic growth exhibited distinctive trends of acceleration or retardation? Has this economic transformation been smooth or stormy in terms of setbacks in production or cyclical downswings of extreme severity? Have resources been squandered or used efficiently? Have consumers been able to share some of the gains from rapid economic growth? If so, have these gains taken the form of longer life span, employment security, health improvement, greater consumption of consumer goods, or elevation of status and material living standard of traditionally deprived groups such as women? Finally, what are the economic development prospects for China during the final decades of this century as its population crosses the one billion mark?

TABLE 8–1. *Average Annual Rates of Economic Growth 1949–1977*

Indicator of Economic Performance	1949–1952	1952–1957	1957–1965	1965–1970	1970–1975	1975–1977
Gross National Product	19%	7%	4%	7%	7%	4%
Agricultural Production	16	4	–	5	3	-1
Industrial Production	34	16	9	10	10	7
Construction Activity	28	21	8	8	9	7
Modern Transport	35	21	7	8	9	7
Foreign Trade (Exports)	0	3	3	1	28	5
Foreign Trade (Imports)	36	7	3	4	27	-2

Source: National Foreign Assessment Center, *China: Economic Indicators* (Washington, D.C.: Central Intelligence Agency, 1978), pp. 3 and 5.

ECONOMIC TRENDS AND CYCLES

Although the average, long-term growth of the economy has been very rapid—as has that of its subsectors of agriculture and industry—the definite periods of rapid growth and slowdown deserve mention. In table 8–1 we observe that between 1949 and 1952 economic growth was most rapid. In 1949 the economy had run down; unemployment was in the tens of millions; and production at a near standstill. Any reckoning from a benchmark of near-zero annual growth over a period of rapid, intense economic recovery with resources returning to work will produce very high growth rates. From 1952 until 1957 the state launched its industrial drive and reorganized agriculture. Trade remained brisk with the Soviet Union; industrial production surged forward; and even agriculture obtained a most respectable 4 percent annual growth rate considering the enormity of the organizational change taking place in the countryside.

The Rocky Road of Economic Transformation

The economy began faltering after 1958 when massive campaigns to mobilize the population to surpass the "advanced" countries in coal and steel production seriously disrupted planting of crops. Several years of bad harvests followed. Agricultural production declined, and the country stood on the brink of famine. Raw material shortages and the misallocation of factory workers to "backyard" steel production also slowed up industrial production. China's rupture with the Soviet Union did not help matters, and trade fell off as well.

The party relaxed its controls over the communes in the early 1960s and even permitted the revival of free markets; the state allocated more funds to agriculture and even lowered prices of industrial commodities that trading companies sold to communes. By 1965 farm production reached the previous 1957 high, and for the next five years good weather, the spread of new seeds, and a burst of irrigation development raised the farm production growth rate to a high 4 percent per annum. Although violence erupted in many factories when new groups seized managerial control, the high investment rate underway kept industry's growth rate at a high level. Meanwhile, the leadership's stress on China's becoming more self-reliant did not encourage foreign trade expansion. From 1970 to 1975 the state shifted its stance and purchased heavily from abroad and also pushed its exports to pay for these imports. The overall pace of economic development resembled that of the mid-1950s, and it seemed that the country was resuming on its road of modernizing the economy. But the years 1975 and 1976 witnessed sharp infighting within the party leadership between "radical" and "moderate" factions, a great earthquake in the north, and widespread disorders in cities, which paralyzed many factories. Industrial production came to a standstill; trade fell off; and poor weather prevented output on the communes from expanding.

Between 1957–1965 and 1975–76, in particular, resource scarcities were aggravated by political policies that were often the product of factional strife with the Communist party. In 1958 Mao Tse-tung envisioned massive campaigns to mobilize the people and reeducate them in a new work ethic and life-style. The masses were to work harder and longer, limit their consumption, and participate in endless meetings in order to better absorb the party's ideology. The mass mobilization campaigns that materialized only strained the economy's capacity to produce enough of the goods demanded by the state—particularly farm products in the years 1958 through 1960 and industrial products in 1975–76. Various party factions naturally interpreted differently the extent and causes of these economic difficulties and proposed their respective solutions. Factional conflicts and personal rivalries even led occasionally to conspiratorial attempts to seize power within the party as seen by the activities of Madame Chiang Ch'ing and her followers after the death of Mao.

Political debate and power struggle have produced several downturns in economic activity and retarded development. Nevertheless, the long-terms trends for high agricultural and industrial growth have not showed any signs of slowing down since 1960. These growth rates have not been as high as those of the first decade of modern economic growth when idle resources returned to work and the economy was still "catching up," so to speak, after nearly two decades of economic stagnation and decline.

PRODUCTION AND EFFICIENCY

The advent of modern economic growth means the application of science and technology to production and distribution. Their contribution increases output by enabling more output to be produced from current resources than would normally have been the case in the recent past. In other words technological improvement allows a fixed combination of labor, capital, and materials to produce a larger amount of output than before. The rising productivity of a single resource—like labor or land—has always been a key quantitative indicator showing the productivity of an industry or economic sector. In recent years economists have tried to measure the contribution of all factors of production that supply goods and services and thus measure the productivity of all resources used in production or what we will refer to here as *total factor productivity*. If the value of land, labor, and capital used in production can be accurately measured in terms of how much of all three were required to produce a certain output, then by dividing the value of that output by the total value of land, labor, and capital used in its production, we obtain a measure of the productivity of all productive factors or total factor productivity.

Total Factor Productivity

Recent studies have concluded that when countries initiate their modern economic growth, total factor productivity begins to rise significantly for both agriculture and industry.[1] This merely means that an economy successfully has applied modern technology to the organizations of production and distribution and that a major break with tradition has occurred. Let us assume however, that total factor productivity declined precisely when rapid growth rates were being achieved. How do we interpret these results? One interpretation is that too many resources were being utilized in the sector where total factor productivity declined, and more resources could be reallocated elsewhere with the prospect that these would increase production more rapidly. If that plan proved impossible, labor might be allowed more leisure, or other resources could be reduced so as to cut waste. If total-factor-productivity decline still persisted, then the economy was misallocating scarce resources and using them inefficiently. Another interpretation says that resources are being used inefficiently and improved organizational efficiency of these resources would greatly increase output beyond existing levels. What have been the trends for total factor productivity in Chinese industry and agriculture since the early 1950s?

We possess some crude estimates for total factor productivity that must be seriously interpreted until further study revises them or refutes them altogether. Thomas Rawski's recent study of the producer industries gives such a measure for the 1950s until 1965.[2] These industries covered mining, metallurgy, fuels and power, metal processing, basic chemicals and building materials. Between 1953 and 1957 the input growth measure covered estimates for employment, the wage bill, and fixed and working capital. Different weights were applied to combine these inputs into an aggregate input index that when divided into the index for gross production value gave several measures for total-factor-productivity indexes. These indexes rose— the lowest by 18 percent and the highest by 63 percent over this period. Therefore, total factor productivity in producer industries rose rapidly in the 1950s so that the rising productivity of all inputs contributed considerably to the expansion of output itself.

After the economic setbacks of late 1958 through 1961, demand for industrial producer goods weakened, and excess capacity emerged. To balance demand and supply in the producer goods' sector, assembly lines were altered; skilled workers were deployed to other industries; and new product lines were developed. These changes required severe adjustments, which greatly slowed up productivity. One foreign observer in 1966 reported that many industrial plants were poorly organized.[3] Whether or not total factor productivity in producer goods' industries resumed an upward course in the late 1960s and early 1970s is problematic. As far-reaching managerial changes took place after 1966, an upward trend for total factor productivity as rapid as that of the 1950s is unlikely; in fact, a steady decline in total factor productivity probably took place.

Agricultural Productivity   Four independent studies covering different time periods since 1952 have concluded that total factor productivity in agriculture steadily declined.[4] These studies have used roughly
the same output growth measures, and while the overall procedure to
compute an aggregate input index was similar in each study, different
input estimates were reached. The surprising conclusion is that these
different estimates still did not show any trend for total factor productivity in agriculture to rise—either during the growth spurt of the
1950s or later in the 1960s. These estimates show that mobilization of
labor during the 1950s and rapid introduction of new capital in the
1960s made for an aggregate input index that rose much more rapidly
than the output index for food grains. Possibly, an output index including fibers and livestock might conceivably show a growth rate approximate to that of the input index, which would yield either little or
no rise in total factor productivity. Until new studies are completed,
these findings can only be interpreted as follows.

Use of Resources   The state successfully mobilized resources in agriculture to accelerate the growth rate of production far in excess of
the long-term traditional growth rate. Both women and men worked
on production teams, and their year-long employment exceeded that of
the labor by family farms in the presocialist era. Of course, men and
women worked longer hours because land was farmed virtually all
year round by the late 1960s, and an enormous quantity of work-days
were required to fertilize and irrigate fields. Leisure seems to have
been curtailed in order to employ more labor to increase the growth
rate of production. Labor productivity has not been increased, and the
trend since 1952 is similar to the long-term labor productivity trend
during the Ch'ing period: constant. The supply of farm capital greatly
increased, but its efficient use has been questionable. For example,
the two-wheeled share ploughs that were manufactured in 1958
proved to be unusable in villages because of faulty design.[5] In 1959
many poorly conceived irrigation projects merely contributed to flooding and waterlogging of land in subsequent years.[6] Waste of capital
and substitution of labor for leisure appear to be the two main ways
that farm inputs have been utilized in agriculture to prevent total factor productivity from rising. In other words, the same output could
possibly be produced in agriculture by a more efficient use of labor and
capital, and rural welfare would be increased through greater leisure
time.

    The discerning reader will point out that historically, total factor
productivity in agriculture never rose anyway, so that the same trend
is likely to persist during the transition to modern economic growth—
particularly when this huge rural population remains rooted to the

land. After the passage of more time, the steady application of modern technology to agriculture is bound to pay off, so that total factor productivity will eventually rise. This observation might be true, but it should be pointed out that two Chinese territories prior to 1949 experienced rising total factor productivity in agriculture: Taiwan and the Liaotung peninsula. Both of these regions were controlled by Japan, and because these two colonies enjoyed peace and efficient administration, family farming prospered. The Japanese merely protected traditional property rights, simplified the collection of the land tax, improved transportation and marketing, expanded irrigation, promoted primary education, and made available to farmers modern farm technologies such as high-yield seeds and new fertilizers. This rural strategy apparently had a high payoff because not only did farm production increase at growth rates exceeding 3 percent per year but total factor productivity played an important contributing role in this achievement.[7] In other words alternative strategies have been used in Chinese agriculture. The introduction of new capital and technology for seed, fertilizer, and irrigation improvements rapidly increased farm production; total factor productivity rose; and real income for farmers also rose fairly rapidly. The strategy of reorganizing family farming into team farming led to massive mobilization of labor and other resources. The result was also a rapid growth in farm production but no visible rise of total factor productivity.

WELFARE AND EMPLOYMENT

For a backward, densely populated economy trying to increase production, raise employment, and improve welfare, the achieving of efficient resource use and allocation is only one of several measures of performance. The Chinese economy from time to time certainly has been extraordinarily wasteful of scarce capital and lavish in its use of abundant labor. On other accounts the state has achieved certain goals—that is, equalizing income distribution, raising the living standards of the masses, and reducing unemployment—that underdeveloped countries would very much like to duplicate. These achievements have not been without their costs. Every organization exerts firm control over its members. The uniformity of consumer habits such as everyone—irrespective of sex or age—wearing the same kind of clothes, the conformity to prescribed work habits and routine, and the adherence to a single ideology are the well-known features of this totalitarian system in which the party attempts to regulate everything an individual does or thinks.

Urban and Rural Salaries

By 1957 the unequal distribution of wealth and income of the past had been greatly reduced. For example, what little evidence is available for household income distribution of rural communities in the early 1950s shows a Gini coefficient measure for inequality of only .17 to .25—compared to the very high prewar measures of around .7 or .8.[8] Although some redistribution of property rights did occur in cities whereby very wealthy families were dispossessed, nothing approaching the income redistribution of villages occurred in the wards within cities. Income variation in the cities, of course, was bound to be higher than in the villages because of the wider range of existing skilled and unskilled jobs and their associated wages. Visitors to China in recent years have reported monthly wages from as low as 42 yuan per month to as high as 124 yuan per month in Shanghai machine-tool plants. The average urban industrial worker perhaps earned around 50 yuan per month in the early 1970s. How do these urban salaries compare to those in communes?

Workers on the most advanced communes earned monthly wages of around 42 yuan. At first sight the rural-urban income difference appears very small. But these advanced communes made up perhaps less than 5 percent of the countryside's communes.[9] The monthly worker's wage for very poor communes during the mid-1970s was about 12 yuan per month. It is likely that for much of the countryside the average monthly wage at best was only one-third of the urban worker's monthly income. The income gap was much higher in the pre-1949 period, so that considerable income difference between countryside and city had been eliminated. Income differences within communities certainly will not be entirely eliminated. Like families in traditional times, today's rural family pools its income, redistributes it to members, and saves the remainder for major outlays to purchase a bride, pay for a funeral, or buy a house. Families fortunate enough to have sons and daughters working naturally earn more income than those of widows or those with members in the armed forces. Every organization uses a portion of its welfare fund to supply grain and some cash to those families with very low earning power. Such decisions to redistribute are made within the economic organization to which the household belongs—not by the central government.

Material Standard of Living

Per capita real income as expressed in 1977 U.S. dollars is supposed to have risen from 162 U.S. dollars in 1952 to 288 U.S. dollars in

1970, and to 377 U.S. dollars in 1977 or a 3.2 percent rate of growth for the twenty-five year period.[10] If correct, these figures represent a rapid, sustained improvement in material living conditions, but we should recall that extreme poverty and commodity scarcity prevailed in the early 1950s. If the growth rate reflected in these figures continues until the year 2000, per capita real income would roughly double to nearly 800 U.S. dollars (in U.S. dollars for 1977), which by contemporary income standards for many countries is still extremely poor. What does the present near-400 U.S. dollar income level really mean in living standard terms for the rural and urban workers of this society?

The very high rate of capital accumulation set by the party naturally permitted only a very slow expansion of consumer goods and services. The expansion of food, fibers, and raw materials from agriculture has matched that of population growth, but the private sector must compete with the state for how these goods will be distributed for food, clothing, and shelter. A portion of farm output is traded abroad to purchase capital goods; another portion is used as intermediate products for production. The remainder must then be rationed among the population each year. The industrial sector produces a small supply of consumer goods, of which bicycles, radios, watches cameras, and fabrics are much in demand. Their supply is insufficient to go around, except to those few families who have pooled household savings over several years, accumulated sufficient ration coupons, and perhaps even obtained the required letter of official authorization from the household's organization unit to buy the item in question.

Let us consider the example of bicycles. China now produces nearly 6 million bicycles each year, perhaps 8 million watches, and over 15 million radio sets. Although the rate of growth of consumer goods' production exceeds that of population growth, the country's existing huge population simply means that many decades must pass before every household can be guaranteed even these ordinary consumer goods. Between 1960 and 1975 perhaps between 35 to 40 million bicycles were added to the Chinese economy, if we assume a bicycle has fifteen years of use before replacement.[11] Unless the capacity for consumer goods' production is greatly increased, the net addition of consumer goods each year will still not be enough to reach every household until well into the next century.

A Complex Rationing System More serious is the long-standing, severe rationing for ordinary but essential articles like grain, cotton, sugar, cooking oil, and soap. The state has been forced to ration these among a population growing at around the annual rate of growth of 2 percent. In 1975 the population under fifteen years of age was perhaps as high as 358 million people or 38 percent of the total population. As these young people became adults, the demand for essential goods will become even more intense. These and other consumer goods are rationed by a complex system, which outsiders still do not properly understand. The following is a description of this system based upon reports of recent visitors to China.[12]

Upon receiving wages, each working person also obtains monthly ration coupons for specific commodities from his or her economic organization. These coupons can be exchanged between individuals by their own individual preference. When an individual has collected a sufficient number of these coupons and also has the required cash sum in hand, he or she can buy the item in question. Households might pool their ration coupons and cash to purchase a bicycle or camera.

For ordinary food, fibers, and cooking oil each employed household receives ration coupons sufficient to maintain necessary nutritional standards. Only between 1959 and 1962 did serious nutritional difficulties develop. At that time rationing of essentials became even more rigid and goods extremely scarce. In that same period many more diseases became prevalent, and the death rate rose slightly. But that has been the only period of extreme shortage of any serious kind. Since then, the extent of individual commodity rationing is not clear. In the south, working teenagers and adults in cities receive a monthly rice ration, which, depending upon the work they perform, ranges from 28 to 66 pounds of dry and uncooked rice. Individuals receive ration coupons for as much as 6 yards of basic, average-quality cotton each year. This varies from region to region. Fresh meat is available only in limited quantities, except at holidays. In Peking the ration for cooking oil is half a kilogram a month; in many other cities the ration is only half that. The soap ration is apparently two bars per person each year. Laundry powder is nearly unobtainable. Toothpaste is a luxury item, and those who can afford it must submit a used tube upon purchase.

These fragmentary reports on household income and food availability suggest spartan living conditions for a society long-accustomed to scarcity and poor-quality goods and services. In fact, overall living standards—compared with those of the past during a stable, average period—do not seem to show very much improvement. For example, in 1975 a comparison of household income, food prices, and the estimated food consumption on a per capita basis for various cities showed that a family of five could still expect to spend around 60 percent of its household wage income for food alone.[13] If such a household expenditure pattern was typical throughout the country, it is roughly equivalent to the average household food expenditure pattern for urban workers and villagers during the 1920s and 1930s.

But other welfare considerations that were absent in the past must be taken into account. In 1975 Chinese workers could depend upon permanent employment. Each household affiliated with an economic organization—that is, a commune or factory—was guaranteed a stable supply and distribution of food. And finally, the commune or factory worker received a steady income, which gradually purchased more each year as prices for certain goods were reduced. These are important, new gains that this socialist regime has made available for all households. Natural catastrophes that beset the economy in former times do not carry the same high, human costs of displaced workers who are homeless and without food. State organizations now respond to bad weather or crises by contributing resources to the stricken area. People without work are quickly allocated to new jobs and new organizations. In the past the north was frequently hard hit by poor weather and flooding so that hundreds of thousands lost their homes and were unemployed. By the early 1970s the regime had succeeded in making the provinces of Hopei, Shantung, and Honan self-sufficient in food grain production.[14] To be sure, since 1960 the country has imported large quantities of wheat each year to the cities of Shanghai and Tientsin—the latter to supply Peking. This anomaly arose because of the inability of the transportation and storage system to make sufficient grain available to the urban inhabitants of these three huge metropolitan areas, which perhaps embrace nearly 18 million persons. Rather than invest in more transport and storage facilities to eliminate food grain imports, the regime apparently finds it rational and economical to still import wheat.

Urban and Rural Work Force Prewar unemployment had been extremely high and even worsened during the war years. After 1950 seasonal unemployment in the countryside continued, and urban unemployment remained severe until the early 1960s because of the spillover of unemployed and those fleeing collectivization in the villages. Yet labor participation in the rural work force had increased as team farming mobilized idle hands for winter projects of water control, building construction, and fertilizer production. The urban industrial work force, meanwhile, had expanded in proportion to the new projects and factories initiated through economic planning. But not until the early 1960s had any semblance of near-full employment been achieved in the cities. The main reason for this was that the party had ordered many recent arrivals from villages to return to their homes, and communes prevented workers from freely setting off to the cities.

Between 1957 and 1975 the total labor force, which perhaps comprised only around 45 percent of the population, expanded from around 280 million to nearly 420 million people.[15] Nonagricultural employment more than doubled and seemed to keep even with the population growth rate of around 2 percent per year. If these figures are accurate, they imply that nonagricultural employment as a share of the work force rose from 15 to 26 percent over this period. This seems plausible even though the urban population between 1957 to 1975 probably grew only from 92 to 150 million people. The reason for this more rapid growth of the nonagricultural work force, while urban population expanded at only around 2.8 percent per annum, was the increased entry and greater participation of younger people in the nonagricultural labor force.

Some unemployment currently exists alongside these high employment conditions. The first example occurs in the form of youths originally sent to work and live in the countryside in the late 1960s and early 1970s. However, they fled their rural economic units and returned to the towns and cities to find work but are compelled by circumstances to live a sort of semilegal life. Secondly, voluntary underemployment also exists in rural households in which members refuse to participate in team labor because what they earn does not buy consumer goods of any value. Many households can afford to get by if the "wife stays home and minds the pigs and the cabbages and the husband stays home one day out of three" from participating with his production team.[16] Yet these are voluntary forms of unemployment.

Certainly by 1962 involuntary unemployment probably had almost disappeared in China—a remarkable feat not achieved anywhere in the world by developing countries of the same low per capita income as China's. Economic organizations always find work for their members, even if it is temporary "make work"-type schemes. And periodic campaigns to mobilize mass participation for large-scale projects such as road construction, tree planting, drainage works, irrigation, or flood control are perennially taking place. Another distinctive feature, which is currently taking place and is expected to continue into the future, accounts for much of the high labor-force participation in the countryside: This is the creation of small-scale industry in the communes.

Expansion of Nonagricultural Work Force Communes are currently expanding small-scale industrial production by establishing enterprises both at the county and township levels and at the brigade or old village level. Brigades are trying to expand the same service and administrative activities already developed at the commune seat—that is, schools, hospitals, cultural centers, distribution networks, and administration. Labor teams are also being formed to rebuild all households in every brigade. These developments require more nonagricultural employment. As a result more and more household members in communes work part-time on production teams in the fields and then shift to small-scale factories to learn new industrial skills. As the nonagricultural work force expands, agricultural work force participation will slow up and eventually cease when population growth becomes stabilized by the reduction of the birth rate to equal the death rate. This, of course, is not likely to be achieved until well after the turn of the century. So far China has avoided the transfer of millions of people from villages to medium- and large-size cities, and the amenities of urban culture are gradually being introduced to the countryside from the cities.

ECONOMIC DEVELOPMENT PROSPECTS

Accommodative Policies

For the past thirty years the leadership has relied principally upon transformative policies to attack the problem of resource and commodity scarcities.[17] These policies initiated sudden, radical organizational changes, involved mobilization tactics, and emphasized normative and coercive rather than remunerative sanctions. Such policies are animated by a voluntaristic faith that the status quo is malleable and can be vastly altered. The death of Mao was followed by an attempted coup d'etat and squashed by a new leadership that then formulated policies we can refer to as *accommodative*. In the case of accommodative policies, human conditions are perceived as more tractable. These policies meet the problem of scarcity more gradualistically; they stress remunerative sanctions such as material incentives.

The Maoist transformative policies produced new organizations, such as the commune system, and generated the new models of "learn from Ta-chai" and "learn from Ta-ch'ing" by which agriculture and industry were to be developed. China's rich organizational heritage also contributed to the flexible, decentralized manner in which these new organizations now operate. In 1977 and 1978 the new, post-Mao leadership expressed a commitment to acquire modern technology and graft this upon the organizations of production and distribution. The numerous policy changes that have recently materialized in factory management, higher education, and foreign trade strongly suggest that accommodation, rather than transformation, will shape the Chinese economy until the end of this century and probably well into the next.[18] Within this political-cultural context, then, what are the future prospects for developing the Chinese economy?

Future economic development first of all depends upon peace and order. Political instability or decay invariably leads to the disruption of production and exchange, to unemployment, and eventually to social violence, and last of all, to further economic decline. If the Chinese polity remains stable and the leadership pursues accommodative policies, what then?

Projected Annual Growth Rates

In early 1978 the leadership projected that for the next seven years industrial production must grow at 10 percent per year and agricultural production at 4 percent. In fact we have every reason to believe the regime would like to sustain these growth rates until the end of the century. These growth rates approximate those achieved between 1965 and 1975 (see table 8–1), and they are probably the maximum that can be expected. The very high growth rates of the early and mid-1950s cannot be repeated as they represented the mobilization of idle resource. Whether these high, projected growth rates can be achieved and sustained is another matter.

If these growth rates are achieved and the service sector expands as in the recent past, the economy's GNP can be expected to grow at around 6 percent per annum. Further, if we assume the population growth slows from a long-run average of 2 percent to around 1.5 percent, then real income per capita will grow at around 4.5 percent per year so that over a twenty-two-year period per capita income will rise about 160 percent over its 1978 level. This would be an impressive performance for this economy of huge population size whose government strives to maintain tight political, social, and ideological control.

But are the projected annual growth rates of 10 and 4 percent for industry and agriculture attainable? Much depends upon the performance of agriculture. Agriculture supplies roughly 75 percent of the raw materials for the industrial sector.[19] It and mining contribute more than two-thirds of the value of the country's exports. The continued growth of the 950 million population in 1976–77 at around 1.5 percent each year implies that an additional 15 million people each year must be fed, clothed, and housed. This burden will not grow lighter until well into the next century. Therefore, agriculture's actual growth will determine the pace of industrial development, export performance, and the health of the economy. Can agriculture grow at 3 or even 4 percent per annum? Some Western economists say no.[20] They contend rice yields are already as high as those in Japan and Taiwan, the world's highest. Irrigation in the south has already reached its maximum. Huge capital investments for water control and irrigation are yet required for the northern regions. These assertions seem valid, but other considerations temper these claims.

Increased Use of Modern Agricultural Methods   First, the scope to harness modern science to agriculture still remains enormous. For example, high-yielding, early-maturing, and disease-resisting seeds have yet to be developed for coarse grains. Progress along these lines for wheat, rice, and cotton far exceeds that for millet, corn, maize, and sorghum. The same holds true for soybeans. The fertilizer-seed response ratio for these coarse grains is high, and if proper plant care and irrigation can be maintained as chemical fertilizers are applied along with new seeds, yields can be increased prodigiously.[21] Another example is that of improving irrigation, planting, and fertilizing of the currently high-yield wheat, rice, and cotton crops. Yields in many areas can still be raised and thereby can be brought closer to the highest yields obtained in the most fertile areas.[22]

Additional Cropping and New Research Strategies   Second, while only 15 percent of the land area is farmed, even this land can be cropped more intensively than is presently the case. In the northeast, north, northwest, and southwest double-cropping can be greatly extended. In central and southeast China triple-cropping still can be greatly expanded. These developments depend upon the availability of water and fertilizer supply. The new chemical fertilizer plants constructed between 1973 and 1976 will soon be supplying the entire country. At present green-cover crops grow on roughly 20 percent of the land in many areas during a single-cropped season. These can be replaced with food grains or fibers as chemical fertilizer becomes available, and thus more land is freed for crops.

Finally, stricter attention to proper water application for different soils will improve yields. Communes still do not undertake soil studies to relate water and fertilizer application to the soil. These surveys and experiments can only be conducted on communes if the supply of scientists and technicians increases. In particular, new research strategies aimed at speedy, accurate assessment of seed-breeding results must be developed, but these practices have not been introduced yet.

To sum up, very considerable new technological change will be required to produce a 4 percent annual growth rate. In the light of current organizational inefficiencies and difficulties, China will be fortunate to maintain an annual growth rate between 2 and 3 percent.

Industrial Growth and Capital Replacement   To develop future prospects in industry, geological exploration for petroleum and nonferrous metals is gradually uncovering new, rich sources that eventually will make China as favorably resource-endowed as the United States and the Soviet Union. The capital investment to extract, transport, process, and distribute these materials will be enormous and demand up-to-date modern technology. China gradually can acquire this capital from abroad; the only limitation is her ability to pay. For the next decade or so, China will find it increasingly difficult to pay for such new imports and still maintain the recent high rates of saving and capital investment required to expand its industrial capacity and still develop new petroleum and nonferrous metal sources. If raw material shortages emerge and China must depend upon their import, industrial growth would be greatly affected and very likely reduced.

A critical problem will be that of capital replacement in the near future. When capital-replacement demand increases at the same time as new capital requirements bulk large, severe shortages and imbalances might materialize to affect industrial expansion. The capital stock installed in the machine-tool and metallurgical industries established in the 1950s might have to be replaced by the late 1980s and early 1990s. New capital investment demand at that time perhaps would take precedence, so that the productivity decline for older capital accelerates. This might reduce the rate of industrial growth to perhaps 6 percent—a rate more in line with that of mature industrialized societies.

SUMMARY: CHINA'S COMMITMENT TO MODERN ECONOMIC GROWTH

China's unique economic development performance of the past three decades owes much to its organizational heritage and the leadership's ability to innovate with new organizations and controls to mobilize the country's resource. Although China remains a command economy, its planners and organizers have demonstrated how price and wage adjustments can be introduced to encourage economic organization to maintain full employment, achieve a very high rate of saving, and yet modestly increase consumption. Lower-level economic organizations like those in the communes have considerable autonomy to make decisions affecting their constituents. China will continue to surprise the West. Meanwhile, this huge country of nearly a billion people remains committed to achieving modern economic growth and mastering all its complexities.

QUESTIONS FOR DISCUSSION

1. Is the economic behavior that influences investment and saving decisions in capitalist economic systems the same as in command economies such as the People's Republic of China? What factors account for the growth fluctuations in the Chinese economy since 1949?
2. What economic indicators can be compiled or computed to measure the performance of an economy that begins to experience modern economic

growth? If these components are applied to the Chinese economy for the period since 1949, what results emerge?

3. What kind of system for allocating consumer goods has developed in the Chinese economy? Has it worked efficiently?

4. What is likely to be the predominant constraint affecting long-term economic growth in China? How does this factor influence economic growth prospects?

NOTES

1. For Western countries and Japan, total factor productivity rose in the early period of modern economic growth. Such an increase was not the case in agriculture in the Soviet Union in the pre–World War II era, and only by the 1960s did total factor productivity begin to rise very slowly.

2. Thomas G. Rawski, "The Growth of Producer Industries, 1900–1971," in Dwight H. Perkins, ed., *China's Modern Economy in Historical Perspective* (Stanford, Calif.: Stanford University Press, 1975), p. 224.

3. Ibid., p. 231.

4. For the period 1953–1957 A. Tang's findings showed total factor productivity (TFP) fell by 6 percent; Kang Chao's study showed TFP declining 8 percent; N. R. Chen's study for Manchuria showed a decline of TFP at 9 percent. For the 1957–1965 period A. Tang's study showed TFP declining another 8 percent. For the 1965–1972 period the preliminary study by Bobby A. Williams showed TFP declining 19 percent. See A. Tang, "Input-Output Relations in the Agriculture of Communist China, 1952–1965," in W. A. Douglass Jackson, ed., *American Policies and Problems in Communist and Non-Communist Countries* (Seattle: University of Washington Press, 1971), p. 285. Kang Chao, *Agricultural Production in Communist China 1949–1965* (Madison: University of Wisconsin Press, 1970), pp. 227 and 238. Nai-Ruenn Chen, "Agricultural Productivity in a Newly Settled Region: The Case of Manchuria," *Economic Development and Cultural Change* 21, no. 1 (October 1972): 90, 94. Bobby A. Williams, "China: Grain Output Growth and Productivity, 1957–72," unpublished report prepared for Central Intelligence Agency, Washington, D.C., 1974, table 13.

5. Kang Chao, Agricultural Production, pp. 101 and 103.

6. Ibid., pp. 128–29.

7. For the Liaotung Peninsula, see Ramon H. Myers and Thomas R. Ulie, "Foreign Influence and Agricultural Development in Northeast China: A Case Study of the Liaotung Peninsula, 1907–45," *Journal of Asian Studies* 31, no. 2 (February 1972): 329–50. For Taiwan, see Samuel Pao-San Ho, "Agricultural Transformation under Colonialism: The Case of Taiwan," *Journal of Economic History* 28, no. 3 (September 1958): 315.

8. For measures of income distribution in rural communities during the 1950s, see Mark Blecher, "Income Distribution in Small Rural Chinese Communities," *China Quarterly* 68 (December 1976): 797–816.

9. Jan S. Prybyla, "A Note on Incomes and Prices in China," *Asian Survey* 15, no. 3 (March 1975): 266–78.

10. National Foreign Assessment Center, *China: Economic Indicators* (Washington, D.C., Central Intelligence Agency, 1978), p. 1.

11. The estimate of net bicycle production since 1960 is based upon information in *China: Economic Indicators,* 1977, p. 25. I assumed no replacement for those bicycles produced during the 1950s.

12. The account here is based entirely upon material gathered and presented by Ross H. Munro, "China's Rigid Rationing," *Washington Post,* 27 November 1977, p. C5.

13. W. Klatt, "Cost of Food Basket in Urban Areas of the People's Republic of China," *China Quarterly* 70 (June 1977): 407–08.

14. Kenneth R. Walker, "Grain Self-sufficiency in North China, 1953–75," *China Quarterly* 71 (September 1977): 555–90.

15. These estimates and the discussion that follows come entirely from Thomas G. Rawski, "Industrialization, Technology and Employment in the People's Republic of China," report prepared for World Bank, Washington, D.C., 1977 (mimeographed), p. 144.

16. Ross H. Munro, "Why China's Peasants Don't Want to Work," *San Francisco Chronicle*, 29 July 1977, p. 12.

17. These policies are discussed in Ramon H. Myers, "Scarcity and Ideology in Chinese Economic Development," *Problems of Communism 27* (March–April 1978): 94–96.

18. For example, committees to supervise factories have begun to be abolished; the selection of qualified students by examinations for normal university education has resumed; the Chinese have actively shopped in international markets for modern capital and weaponry.

19. Allen S. Whiting and Robert F. Dernberger, *China's Future: Foreign Policy and Economic Development in the Post-Mao Era* (New York: McGraw-Hill, 1977), p. 148.

20. Ibid., pp. 126–34.

21. The figure depicting "Food Grain Yield Reponse to Fertilizer in China, 1970s–1980s" shows the yield response to fertilizer input for the first

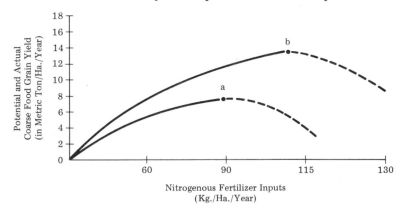

Potential and Actual Coarse Food Grain Yield (in Metric Ton/Ha./Year)

Nitrogenous Fertilizer Inputs (Kg./Ha./Year)

wave of seed varieties introduced during the 1970s as shown by the curve *oa*. As more fertilizer is applied, yield levels off. If other high-yield seeds with more response to chemical fertilizers are developed, further yield increase could take place along curve *ob*. Such a prospect might develop during the 1980s as the supply of scientists and technicians make more vigorous efforts to produce new seed varieties.

22. Ramon H. Myers, "Wheat in China—Past, Present, and Future," *China Quarterly* 75 (June–July 1978): 297–333.

SELECTED READINGS

1. Allen S. Whiting and Robert F. Dernberger. *China's Future: Foreign Policy and Economic Development in the Post-Mao Era.* New York: McGraw-Hill, 1977.

2. Victor D. Lippit. "Economic Development in Meiji Japan and Contemporary China: A Comparative Study." *Cambridge Journal of Economics* 2 (1978): 55–81.

3. U.S. Congress. Joint Economic Committee. *China: A Reassessment of the Economy.* Washington, D.C.: Government Printing Office, 1975.

4. National Foreign Assessment Center. *China: Economic Indicators.* Washington, D.C.: Central Intelligence Agency, 1977.

5. U.S. Department of Agriculture. *People's Republic of China: Agricultural Situation, Review of 1977 and Outlook for 1978.* Washington, D.C.: U.S. Department of Agriculture, 1978.

6. John S. Aird. "Recent Provincial Population Figures." *China Quarterly* 73 (March 1978): 1–44.

Epilogue

On 15 December 1978 President Carter announced that on 1 January 1979 the United States would recognize the People's Republic of China as the sole legal government of China and terminate diplomatic relations and the Mutual Defense Treaty between the United States and the Republic of China. A new era in Chinese-American relations had begun.

Future economic relations between the two countries must be appraised within the context of recent changes taking place in the PRC. These changes can be summed up in the conclusions emerging from the Third Plenary Session of the Chinese Communist party's Central Committee in December 1978. The state intended to give top priority to modernization and terminate "the large-scale nationwide mass movement to expose and criticize Lin Piao and the Gang of Four."[1]

Party leaders after the Third Plenary Session pointed out that to carry out the four modernization goals, the "productive forces" in the economy had to be developed. But how? The party proposed reforming management and establishing conditions of calm and stability so that economic organizations could become more productive. In other words the party was tacitly abandoning its time-honored strategies of the "campaign" and "class struggle" and concentrating on seeking the most talented persons to manage economic organizations. This meant encouraging scientific and technological research and upgrading education.

REASONS FOR CHANGES IN CCP POLICY

Why had China suddenly become so concerned about modernizing its defense, its economy, its polity, and its educational system? Perhaps the post-Mao leadership recognized that China was suffering from two very fundamental weaknesses. First, its defense capabilities were appallingly weak compared to those of other modern states—especially the Soviet Union, which in recent years loomed more threateningly to China. China's invasion of Vietnam in early 1979 further impressed upon that leadership certain, glaring deficiencies. In modern transport equipment, aircraft, and weaponry-military components, the Vietnamese often exhibited their superiority over the Chinese.

More important, however, was the problem of economic backwardness. The economy has long suffered a serious problem perhaps best described as having very little resource productivity to increase the production of more goods and services. That is to say, the creation of more modern machinery to produce capital goods and the expansion of capital formation in agriculture during these past decades has never achieved an increase of total factor productivity of land, labor, and capital. To the contrary, China has produced more output only by adding labor and capital to her economy. Unless this economy achieved higher productivity from its resources so that productivity, as well as the expansion of resources, produced greater output, China would merely continue to waste its scarce resources and produce far less than it actually could produce.

For these two reasons the party leadership in 1978 decided to take advantage of the new relations that China might establish with Japan, the United States and Western European countries. Therefore, various Chinese leaders traveled abroad; numerous foreign officials and business people visited China; and the government reached agreements with Japan to conclude a treaty terminating World War II and with the United States to normalize relations between the two countries. China's new foreign policy reflects its new domestic policies, and as long as the current leadership remains in power, modernization will undoubtedly remain the nation's primary goal.

CHINA'S NEW ECONOMIC GROWTH STRATEGY

In 1978 China's leaders initiated policies of accommodation rather than transformation. Instead of relying upon massive campaigns and appeals to popular volunteerism, the party has gradually taken steps to improve the management of economic organizations in order to make them more productive. Toward this end the leadership has sought to produce a large supply of scientists, technocrats, and managers and to acquire the most advanced technology from abroad for its economic organizations. Three strategies are self-evident.

First, the state has given priority to building "key research institutions" to serve as models to guide other institutions in planning and managing the economy and in developing science and technology. One such "key" institution is Hofei (in Anhwei province), the site of the University of Science and Technology, which already includes an institute of research in optical precision machinery, and a plasma physics research institute, and which will eventually include new institutes of solid state physics and of metal corrosion research, a scientific instruments plant, and a computer mathematics and technology research unit. Such a multipurpose site combines basic science research and its application to industry and agriculture.

Second, the state has reopened schools and universities closed since the cultural revolution. In July 1978 national college entrance examinations were held, and these are expected to be repeated every year. Steps are also under way to send researchers and advanced students on extended tours to Japan, North America, and Western Europe to receive additional training. By the mid-1980s China is expected to have as many as 10,000 of these students studying abroad.

Third, China has begun to purchase more plants and equipment from advanced countries for its metallurgical, petrochemical, and transportation industries. By obtaining the most advanced capital and its embodied technology, China's leaders hope to transfer the best technical practices of the West to revitalize China's economy.

FINANCING THE NEW GROWTH STRATEGY

The transfer of technology from the West will be expensive. How can a poor country like China afford it? Estimates vary greatly on the required funding to increase China's industrial capacity over the next decade from as high a figure as 600 billion U.S. dollars to as low as 250 billion U.S. dollars. Whichever the true amount, it is believed that China's domestic savings and expanded foreign trade earnings will still not be sufficient to pay for the capital it intends to buy. In fact, in early 1979 China began negotiating for credit from the United Kingdom, France, and Japan. Business leaders from the United States visited China and signed contracts that involve the building of hotels and a steel complex by advancing credit. While it is too soon to project the exact amount China intends to borrow, its capacity to repay such credits will depend upon what it can sell abroad and how rapidly these new industries can prosper and make a profit. What are China's trade prospects in general and with the United States in particular?

CHINESE TRADE PROSPECTS

From 1971 to 1975 the dollar value of Chinese trade tripled, and the non-Communist share of China's trade rose to nearly 85 percent—the largest share for any Communist country's trade. During the 1970s China's annual growth rate of exports to non-Communist countries in constant U.S. dollars has been around 30 percent per annum, and such a growth rate is not likely to be exceeded during the 1980s. In fact, if Western countries insist upon establishing fixed quotas for textiles and processed food from China, the nation will be fortunate to increase exports in constant-dollar terms at even this very rapid rate of growth.

It should be emphasized that such an export growth would still only pay for the usual items—chemical fertilizers, agricultural commodities, and such industrial supplies as steel, nonferrous metals, and petrochemicals—that China normally purchased during the 1970s. China, of course, can export only more petroleum, raw materials, textile products, and processed food—the same items sold during the 1970s. But these commodities, except for petroleum, are not likely to rise in value, nor are they highly income-inelastic demanded goods that will net China higher proceeds.

China's petroleum export capability depends upon how rapidly oil can be located and produced—compared to its overall domestic demand. If supply can rise faster than domestic demand, a rising surplus for export will net China more foreign exchange. Yet the most optimistic projections of future exports and earnings indicate that China will not be a major supplier of petroleum until the end of this century. By that time the supply and demand for world energy might significantly change so that petroleum will have become only one of several major energy sources.

CHINA AND U.S. TRADE PROSPECTS

In 1976 and 1977 the United States moved up from eighth to seventh among China's top 10 trading partners, but in 1977 it had only 5 percent of the top 10 trading partners' share of China's trade. The United States certainly can elevate its ranking and possibly even surpass West Germany, which ranked third among China's trading partners in 1977. Still, that move would mean the United States could claim only around 10 percent of the top 10 trading partners' share of China's trade. The United States is not likely to ever capture as high as 20 percent of total Chinese trade. If China's total trade with the non-Communist world expands faster than in the 1970s, the United States may be able to expand its share of China's trade without having to displace other competitors. But is this likely to be the case?

If China's total trade grows only at the same rate as during the 1970s, the prospects for Chinese and U.S. trade expansion are modest, not great. In 1977 the total trade of the United States with China was nearly 400 million U.S. dollars, and in 1978 it reached around 1 billion. Whereas the by-products of normalization—modest credit and more liberal terms for exports to the United States—will encourage tal trade to rise to 2 billion or more in 1979, it is unlikely that by the mid-1980s total trade will expand beyond 4 or 5 billion U.S. dollars— if that much. When we compare this prospect with the total trade of the United States and Republic of China in 1978, a total of 7 billion U.S. dollars, we see that future economic ties between the PRC and the United States will expand very slowly.

NOTES

1. See the communique of the Third Plenary Session of the Eleventh CCP Central Committee on 22 December 1978, which appeared in *Peking Review* 52 (29 December 1978):6–16.

Appendix

Dynastic Dates

Sung and Chin Dynasties	960–1179 A.D.
Yüan (Mongol) Dynasty	1280–1368
Ming Dynasty	1368–1644
Ching Dynasty	1644–1911
Republican Period	1911–1949
Communist Period	1949–

Weights and Measures

Weights

1 catty = 1.1 pound
2 catties = 1 kilogram
100 catties = 1 picul
20 piculs = 1 metric ton
2000 catties = 1 metric ton

Area

1 mow = 0.1647 acre
6 mow = 1 acre (approx.)
15 mow = 1 hectare

Capacity

1 shih = 100 litres
10 tou = 1 shih
10 sheng = 1 tou

Currencies

During the Ch'ing period, 1000 copper cash coins = 1 silver tael as set at the imperial mints.

The Haikwan tael was purely a money of account and not an existing currency. It was used in the Chinese customs for levying duty from the late nineteenth century to the early 1930s and was calculated to have 583.30 grams of silver 1,000 fins. The exchange rate for the Haikwan tael and U.S. dollar fluctuated annually. The Kuping tael was roughly the same value as the Haikwan and other tael units. During the 1930s, 1 tael = 1.5 yuan (approximately).

The Chinese dollar or Chinese standard dollar or *Fa-pi* was legal tender in China in the late 1930s until 19 August 1949. In the pre-1937 period, every Chinese dollar of $1.558 equaled one Haikwan tael. A yuan or one Chinese dollar in 1933 = $0.26 (1933 U.S. dollar).

After 19 August 1948, the Gold Yuan (G.Y.) replaced the *Fa-pi* but was abandoned July 1949.

After 1949 the People's Republic of China introduced the new currency, the *ten-min-pi,* whose unit the yuan in 1952 = $0.427 (1952 U.S. dollar).

Table of Major Economic Events in China

Date	Economic Event	Implications
Nov. 8, 1644	Additional tax levies of late Ming removed and land taxes collected according to tax registers of early Ming (ca. 1400).	Beginning of land tax reform to fix tax rates at very low level.
1699	Resumption of English tea trade at Canton.	Small silver import produced by trade.
1745	Last province (Shensi) to adopt tax reform for combining poll and land tax.	Conclusion of major land tax reform.
1816–1817	First recorded opium imports.	Stage set for imbalance of trade and silver outflow.
1825–1826	Large silver exports that sparked official concern of silver shortage.	Gradual beginning of monetary deflation.
1840	First Opium War between England and China.	China's international relations will begin to change.
Aug. 1842	Treaty of Nanking concluding Opium War.	Opening of five ports for foreign trade; payment to England of 12 million silver dollars war indemnity.

Date	Economic Event	Implications
1850	Taiping rebellion.	Fifteen years of internal rebellion.
1858	Treaty of Tientsin ending second Anglo-Chinese War in Canton.	Opening of eleven more ports to foreign trade.
1862	Military arsenals in Shanghai and Soochow established by Li Hung-chang.	Beginning of self-strengthening effort.
1864	Taiping leader Hung Hsiu-ch'uan defeated.	Resumption of peace and economic recovery efforts.
1865	Hong Kong–Shanghai Bank in Hong Kong established by the English.	Important institution financing English commerce.
1869	Establishment of Machine Works Factory at Foochow.	Further Ch'ing efforts at self-strengthening.
1872	Creation of *Chao-shang-chü* for management of Chinese Merchant Steamship Company.	Ch'ing state efforts at self-strengthening.
1876	Cheefoo Treaty.	Opening of four more ports.
1877	Opening of Kaiping Coal Mine.	Li Hung-chang's efforts to develop resources.
1878	Cotton-spinning mill established by Tso Tsung-tang in Lanchow of Kansu province.	
1879	First telecommunication line between Tientsin and T'ai-ku established.	
1881	Machine works established at Kirin province in Manchuria.	
1884	Sino-French War in Annam.	Loss of China's sphere of influence in Indo-China.
1888	Completion of the T'ang-shan–to–Tientsin railroad that was financed and constructed by the British.	Beginning of railroad development in north China.
1889	Establishment of cotton-weaving factory and ironworks in Kwangtung by Chang Chih-tung.	Further self-strengthening efforts by provincial officials.
1890	Government funds used by Chang Chih-tung to construct an iron and steel factory at Han-yang in Hupeh province, to merge with an iron mine in	

Date	Economic Event	Implications
	Ta-yeh (Hupeh) in 1894, and then to combine with the P'ing-hsiang coal mine in Kiangsi and become the Han-yeh-p'ing Corporation in 1908.	
1893	Opening of railway between Peking and Shan-hai-kuan in south Manchuria.	
1894	First Sino-Japanese War.	Setting of stage for foreign capital to enter China.
1895	Treaty of Shimenoseki concluding war.	Giving right to foreigners to build factories in China.
1898	Concessions in Kiachow Bay granted to Germany; acquisition of Liaotung peninsula by Russia; acquisition of Weihai-wei in Shantung by England.	Spreading of foreign imperialism.
1899	Boxer outbreak in north China.	Further weakening of Ch'ing empire.
1901	Throne memorialized by Chang Chih-tung and Liu K'un-i urging China to reform as Meiji Japan did after 1867.	Urging by officials of large-scale imperial reform.
1902	Creation of British-American Tobacco Company with capital of 25 million pounds sterling.	
1903	*Shang-pu* (Department of Commerce) set up by Ch'ing state to revise commercial laws and encourage Chinese business development.	First major Ch'ing economic reform effort.
1904	Tsingtao-Chinan railway completed; iron from Han-Yeh p'ing Iron and Coal Works bought by Japan.	Further foreign economic influence.
	Bank of China established.	Further Ch'ing government economic reforms.
1905	Sun Yat-sen's T'ung Meng Hui revolutionary group created.	Beginning of Sun's efforts to topple the Ch'ing.
1906	Rules promulgated for establishing a constitution.	Evidence of further Ch'ing political reforms.
	Japanese South Manchurian Railway created.	Setting up of powerful instrument of Japanese imperialism.

Date	Economic Event	Implications
1907	Bank of Communications established; number of new industrial corporations in east central China created by private capital.	
1908	Movement to purchase foreign railway rights launched by Ch'ing government.	Ch'ing state's attempt to restore national control over railroad systems.
1909	Convening of provincial assemblies.	First step toward constitutional democracy.
1910	State proclamation to convene a national assembly.	
1911	Outbreak of revolution and overthrow of Ch'ing government by Sun Yat-sen and supporters.	
1912	Attempts by Republic of China to consolidate its foreign loans and to finance by borrowing.	Efforts by new government to rationalize its finances.
1914	Promulgation of new mining law population; census undertaken and a rural population of 358,413,000 reported (90 percent of country's total population); Japanese rapidly increasing their investment.	
1915	Signing of 21 Demands Treaty giving Japan greater sphere of influence within China.	
1917	New Kwangtung government set up; political disintegration begun. Cultivated area of 91 million hectares reported in new crop survey by the Ministry of Agriculture and Commerce.	Continued efforts by Republican government to carry out economic surveys and collect relevant economic data.
1918	45.9 million rural households reported in survey of family farms by Ministry of Agriculture and Commerce; Bank of China reorganized; foreign customs and tariff rules revised; loan of 230 million yen granted by Japan.	

Date	Economic Event	Implications
1919	May Fourth Cultural Movement at National Peking University begun. Establishment of Kuomintang political party.	Budding nationalism.
1920	Outbreak of warlord violence in north China; 440 million people reported by postal service population census; new income tax system and rules established by Finance Ministry.	
1921	Sun Yat-sen elected president by Kwangtung government; famous *Industrial Plan* for developing resources published by Sun; first convention of Chinese Communist party held; labor movement becoming more active.	Formation of new nationalist forces in south.
1923	Soviet support for party sought by Sun; Peking-Hankow railway paralyzed by labor strike; new factory laws promulgated; various warlord armies' spheres of influence expanded; survey of rural work force wages published.	
1924	First convention of Kuomintang (KMT) held; attempt by KMT to co-opt peasant violence in various parts of the south; decline in family-owned farms shown by new government rural survey; increase shown in Japanese textile factories.	Decline of effective local government rule reflected in rural uprisings in the southeast.
1925	Great strike in Japanese textile factories in Shanghai, Tsingtao, and Tientsin; new Chinese National Bank established.	Year of great instability in city-port areas.
1926	Control in KMT gained by Chiang Kai-shek who launched military drive to the north to defeat the northern warlords; promulgation of antistrike bill; rent reduction law proposed by	

Date	Economic Event	Implications
	KMT; population of 485 million reported by postal service census.	
1927	Convention of KMT in Wuhan; Hankow foreign concession zone recovered; Wuhan and Nanking KMT forces joined; agricultural population of 335 million or 84 percent of national population reported in rural census by KMT Central Land Commission; 201 county agricultural associations, 1,102 district agricultural associations, and 4,011 village agricultural associations with a grand total of 9.1 million members reported in 17 provinces by Wuhan government's Peasant Bureau figures; between 1919 and 1927 a drop in cotton production from 9.0 to 6.7 million piculs (20 piculs = 1 metric ton) and a decline in cotton acreage from 33 to 27 million mou (6 mou = 1 acre) reported in the Cotton Manufacturers Association's published data; since 1904 more than 20,000 Chinese students schooled in Japan; in 1927, 8,000 students reported by the government as studying overseas.	KMT ascension to power in east central China.
1928	Entry of the Chinese Revolutionary Army of the KMT into Peking; the Sixth Plenum of the Chinese Communist party convened in Moscow; Chiang Kai-shek chosen chairman of the KMT; plan for national highways established by the KMT government's Communication Bureau; Shanghai Central Bank created; highest amount of national military expenditures reached by growth	Beginning of nation building under KMT.

Date	Economic Event	Implications

from 203 million yuan in 1918 to 800 million yuan in 1928 (annual prices); a total of 155,069 unemployed industrial workers, or 6.45 percent of the registered labor union rolls, announced by the Shanghai Municipal Statistical Bureau; Between 1927 and 1928, 9 million deaths from starvation in Shantung, Hopei, and Honan reported by famine relief associations; 120 modern, cotton textile factories in existence—the same number as in 1923—with 3.8 million spindles; coal production's highest amount of 25 million tons reached.

1929 — Law for standardizing weights and measures promulgated; customs duties regulations revised; Chiang Kai-shek opposed by various factions within KMT; cotton textile industry strike in Shanghai; 37 million people reported to be starving throughout north China. — Breakdown of unity in **KMT**.

1930 — Foreign investment in China estimated at 700 million pounds sterling.

1931 — New tariff structure introduced and tariff autonomy sought; second annihilation campaign against Communist Red Army launched; National Economics Commission created; Kwangtung national government set up by Hu Han-min and ties with Chiang broken; new factory laws promulgated; outbreak of Manchurian incident; agreement by Kwangtung and Nanking to set aside their differences; survey of Ting county in Hopei completed; cooperative

Date	Economic Event	Implications
	movement in countryside launched by KMT.	
1932	Fourth annihilation campaign against Communist Red Army; Manchukuo puppet state established by Japanese; decline in exports caused by world depression; Likin tax abolished.	Punishing effects on foreign trade and domestic commerce brought about by world depression.
1933	Commission for establishing a constitution formed; rural reconstruction commission created; fifth annihilation campaign against Communist Red Army; numerous economic construction projects launched in Kiangsu and Chekiang.	
1934	Land Commission created; breakout by Communists and the beginning of their long march; rural loans increased by Farmers' Bank; huge outflow of silver prompted by U.S. Treasury purchase of silver, setting off deflationary spiral.	
1936	National Economics Construction Commission created to revive agrarian economy and develop resources; signs of improvement beginning to show in economy.	
1937	Second Sino-Japanese War.	
1938	Massive KMT government reorganization and retreat to Chungking; Chin-Ch'a-Chi liberated base areas in Shansi, Hopei, and Honan established by Chinese Communist armies; rules for lowering land rent introduced by party; issuing of war bonds to finance war effort begun by KMT government.	Rise of Communist power in the north.
1939	KMT government's bond issuing given up and the printing of paper money in large quanti-	Setting of stage for severe inflation in KMT-ruled China.

Date	Economic Event	Implications
	ty begun; rent reduction program in T'ai-hang mountain liberated base area introduced by Communists.	
1940	Essay issued by Mao Tse-tung on *New Democracy*, outlining how Communist party will dominate in new society in coalition with other political parties.	Mao's strategy for united front under Communist party aegis.
1941	$500 million credit to Nationalist Chinese granted by United States; rules issued by Communists on land use in their north China, liberated base zones; exchange and trade controls introduced by KMT offset by the quick emergence of a flourishing black market.	Weakening of KMT's economic control and growth because of inflation.
1942	Continuation of Communist-issued rules for cadres to deal with tenant and farmer-owner lands in their liberated base areas; U.S. Treasury agreement to provide $20 million of gold to Nationalists for sale within China to check inflation.	
1943	Worsening of inflation in areas under KMT control; vigorous attempt by Communists to deal with inflation in their areas of control.	Manifestation of mounting corruption and ineptness within KMT.
1944	New laws issued by Communists pertaining to tenant land and land ownership in Shen-Kan-Ning, or northwest, liberated base areas.	
1945	Talks between Communists and KMT leaders in Chungking; war ended and coastal ports reoccupied by KMT troops; move by Communists into Manchuria.	
1946	Worsening of inflation in Nationalist China.	

Date	Economic Event	Implications
1947	Raging of civil war.	
	Decision by Communists to introduce land reform.	Beginning of land reform for the north.
1948	Land reform introduced throughout areas under Communist control; $570 million aid granted by United States.	
1949	More moderate land reform in central China introduced by Communist party; KMT defeated and task of reunifying China under Communist party control begun; conference to restore national railroad system convened; Science Academy created; conference for educational work convened.	Beginning of new socialist era.
1950	Signing of thirty-year friendship treaty with Soviet Union; various laws promulgated on land, labor, and private business; movement opposing American involvement in Korea begun.	Increased cooperation between China and Soviet Union.
1951	National Planning Commission created; procedures for establishing agricultural mutual aid teams established; legal procedures introduced to deal with war criminals, counterrevolutionaries, and bureaucratic capitalists.	First steps toward socialist-organized economy.
1952	The *san-fan wu-fan* movement launched in cities to nationalize private business sector; reorganization in government continued; commission to encourage international trade created; Chang-chun railway returned by Soviet Union.	Beginning of nationalization of private sector.
1953	First five-year plan announced; rules published for setting up agricultural producer cooperatives; first population census carried out; series of national	Beginning of socialist planning with drive to develop industry.

Date	Economic Event	Implications
	conferences held for cultural work and establishment of closer ties between industry and commerce.	
1954	Various national conferences convened to deal with labor, management of small private businesses, and to create a new constitution; conference held in Peking on Anshan iron-steel technology and its modernization.	Increased momentum in pace of nationalization of economy.
1955	Rules for simplifying Chinese characters published; Science Academy five-year plan announced; full-scale cooperativization of agriculture announced; procedures for fixing urban grain supply announced.	Move by state to socialize the agricultural sector entirely.
1956	Ten-year agricultural development plan announced; rules for operating agricultural producer cooperatives published; first automobile produced; second five-year economic plan presented by Chou En-lai.	Evolution of long-term planning.
1957	Agriculture's role in second five-year economic plan discussed at a national agricultural conference; the eighth national conference on labor convened.	
1958	Rules for national reconstruction of land announced; procedures for population registration compiled; establishment of rural communes begun; "Great Leap" for industrial production urged by the party.	New thrust by the state to establish full control over the countryside.
1959	"Great Leap" continued in agriculture and industry.	
1960	Outline of the 1956–67 ten-year agriculture plan published; strategy announced by party's Central Committee to make agriculture the foundation and to	Results of the "Great Leap" beginning to influence the economy seriously.

Date	Economic Event	Implications
	have industry take the lead and develop a spirit of self-reliance everywhere *(tsu-li keng-sheng)*; rules for managing rural communes announced; worst natural disasters in over a hundred years announced by government, and agricultural production reportedly in decline.	
1961	Procedures for work in rural communes published.	Attempts to retrench from setbacks caused by the "Great Leap."
1962	The production team to be the basic accounting unit (as reported in January 1 *People's Daily*); a number of party conferences held to plan strategy and work style for cadres.	
1963	National Price Commission established in National Affairs Ministry; educational movement for countryside launched; Chinese Agricultural Bank created.	
1964	Movement launched that "the entire country should learn from the liberation army"; rules promulgated concerning poor and lower middle-class peasants.	
1965	The village of Ta-chai becomes a model for agriculture to emulate.	
1966	Great Proletarian Cultural Revolution begun and politics assumes command; while revolution not formally announced, the party prepares itself and the country for it.	Urban industry suffering periodic setbacks, but agricultural development continuing.
1967	Great Proletarian Cultural Revolution formally begun; revolutionary committees established throughout the country;	

Date	Economic Event	Implications
	setbacks suffered by urban industry because of upheavals.	
1968	Continuation of the Great Proletarian Cultural Revolution.	
1969	Sending of urban youth to the countryside to work with peasants begun; first 15,000-ton tanker produced; irrigation projects in north rapidly developed; new agricultural schools set up in communes and counties of different provinces; May 7th Cadres schools created in northwest.	
1970	Large-scale irrigation developments in Hunan and Fukien provinces; large-scale reforestation projects in Hunan, Kwangtung, Anhwei, Honan, and Kiangsi provinces; completion of water conservancy on Grand Canal in Hopei province; spread of the "learn from Ta-chai" agricultural movement throughout Inner Mongolia; electrification and telecommunications developed in Peking and Nanking; more water conservancy and irrigation projects completed for major rivers.	Irrigation development continuing.
1971	During January entire countryside working on capital projects for improving land; numerous provincial party conferences convened; special efforts made to encourage iron ore production; movement launched by the party for all of industry to "learn from Ta-ch'ing" oil fields; 246 million tons of food grains reported by government for the tenth consecutive annual, bountiful harvest; new technological developments reported by various factories in	Decentralization of higher education to countryside.

Date	Economic Event	Implications

major cities; fulfillment of annual plan reported by steel industry.

1972   Drive launched by party to encourage linking of theory with
practice; rural communes financial savings increase of 89
percent between 1965 and
1971 announced by state; nationwide public health movement launched by party; movement pushed by party for education to be at the service of
the masses and help agriculture and industry; 500 new
kinds of greatly improved crop
seeds in use throughout the
country as reported by the government; in the 8 major cities,
new dwelling space for 145
million urban residents created—amounting to 62 million
square meters of space between 1949 and 1971—according to government report; importance of making agriculture
the basis and strengthening agricultural development further
underscored by the party.

Stabilization of the economy
and renewal of drive toward
modernity sought by the Chou
En-lai faction of party.

1973   Increase of 14 percent in production over previous year reported by Ta-ch'ing oil fields;
output growth achievement announced by many industries;
numerous provincial conferences convened concerning
youth and their activities; increasing emphasis given to
small-scale industry, particularly fertilizer production; increasing attention by party to
link industry and agriculture
through small-scale rural industry; expansion of people's
militia in countryside and in
cities; gains in hydroelectrical
energy production reported; 96

Date	Economic Event	Implications

percent of counties reported to have their own farm tool repair shops in operation.

1974 Anti-Confucian campaign in full swing (veiled attack against Chou En-lai faction in party Politburo); *hsia-fang* movement, or the sending of urban youth to countryside, continued at great tempo; 24-million-ton tanker called Ta-ch'ing 69 produced by Darien Red Flag Ship Works; all counties and villages receiving radio broadcasts according to government reports; southern Kiangsu reported to be using new, early ripening rice seeds; large increases in farm production reported by many provinces; party cadres urged by *People's Daily* to participate in production; peasantry exhorted by party to engage in winter capital projects for land improvements; 2 million more hectares of land reportedly irrigated.

Raging factional disputes, but continued improvements in agriculture.

1975 Fourth People's Party Conference held; report by Chou En-lai provided along with revised constitution presented by Chang Ch'un-chiao; continuation of Great Proletarian Cultural Revolution, although in muted form, with various campaigns waged to urge cadres to participate in labor, to place education at the service of the masses, and to emphasize importance of being more "red" than "expert"; sending of youth to countryside continued; September national conference of 5,000 representatives convened to "learn from Ta-chai" for the purpose of launching this new policy

Compromise with "Gang of Four" achieved by Chou to maintain existing economic organizations and move toward economic modernization.

Date	Economic Event	Implications
	throughout the country.	
1976	Late December national conference to "learn from Ta-chai" with stress on mechanization of agriculture; urban youth continuing to go to the countryside to work and help educate the peasantry; anti-Teng Hsiao-p'ing campaign rages throughout the country; Teng's "four moderns" principles criticized and the country exhorted by party to put politics in command; September 1 great earthquake at Tang-shan in northeast Hopei causing enormous damage; military disturbances in Fukien province; death of Mao, and "Gang of Four" arrested by Hua Kuo-feng.	Worsening of factional struggle in party, and crippling of many cities due to disruptions of industry.
1977	Series of national conferences held; decision by party to give greater emphasis to modern technology, education, and development of supply of scientists and technologists; return of Teng Hsiao-p'ing to the Politburo, and strengthening of his control in the party and bureaucracy; "Gang of Four" purged and blamed for the setbacks occurring during the Great Proletarian Cultural Revolution period; end of the Great Proletarian Cultural Revolution announced by party in December, thereby signaling a return to normalcy.	Continuing factional struggle with major disruptions of industry throughout the country, but gradual regaining of power by Teng Hsiao-p'ing.
1978	The "four moderns" introduced by Teng, and the country exhorted by his faction to learn from the United States and modernize by the year 2000; students and researchers sent abroad; leanings toward Japan and the United States for technology, credit, and trade.	Full commitment toward modern economic growth as top priority.

Index

Butterfield and Swire, 132

Campaigns, 200–201, 247, 248
Canada: economic growth in, 29, 30
Canal system, 81; and Grand Canal, 13, 74, 76, 82, 144, 145
Canton, 125, 144
Capital, 4, 5, 48, 61, 118, 119; capital funds market, 147–148; capital goods, 4, 23, 116, 140–141, 207; capital-intensive industries, 131; capital projects, 54; capital purchases, 46; and cotton production, 133–134; farm capital, 210, 230; foreign, 27, 138; imports, 206; investment, 51–52, 64, 116, 126, 128–130, 130–131, 141–143, 158, 170; and land, 106–107; replacement, 239–240; and resources, 44–45
Capital accumulation, 20–21, 55; and agriculture, 203–205, 208–210; and communism, 201–210, 233; and industry, 207–208; and socialism, 195–196; and taxation, 203–204; and trade, 205–207
Capitalism, 35; bureaucratic, 38–39, 167–168; and protocapitalism, 37–38; and putting out system, 134
Carter, Jimmy, 247
Cash-commodity nexus, 37
Cement industry, 5, 20, 143
Census: imperial, 6
Central Bank, 171
Central places: definition of, 12
Ceremonies, 14, 40, 48, 51, 73, 76, 109
Ceylon: tea production in, 135
Chang Chih-tung, 128
Chang, John K., 135
Charity, 119, 143; and charitable estate supervisors, 15
Chee Hsin Cement Company, 143
Chekiang, 127; land reform in, 163–164, 165, 166, 167; population of, 8
Chemical industry, 5, 53, 55, 140, 225, 229
Ch'en Yung-kuei, 216–217
Chiang Ch'ing, 228
Chiang K'ai-shek, 169, 200
Chien Chao-nan and Yu-chien, 143
Children: care of, 219; role of, 108
China Merchants' Steam Navigation Company, 128, 132

Chinese National Electrical and Potter Company, 141
Ch'ing empire, 15–17, 65; agriculture in, 173; economic growth in, 49–52, 65–70; economic system of, 70–75; employment in, 13; end of, 138; feudalism in, 36–37; fiscal system of, 160–161, 164; government role in, 75–87; gross domestic product of, 19; income distribution in, 5–6, 15, 17; industrialization in, 136–138; inflation in, 105–106; land distribution in, 13–14, 106; land tax reform in, 162; market towns in, 67, 69–70; population growth and distribution in, 6–8, 11–13; private sector in, 195; taxation in, 213; transportation network in, 144–145; wealth distribution in, 14–15. *See also* State
Cho-hsien, 119
Chou Hsüeh-hsi, 143
Chungking: wartime government, 182
Chung-li Chang, 17
CIA: estimates by, 22, 23
Civil war, 18, 20, 140, 151, 157, 158, 182, 186; and agriculture, 179
Clan, 91
Class struggle, 39, 43, 247
Coal production, 20, 72, 149
Command economy, 64
Commerce: premodern, 13
Commodities, 93; exchange, 38; scarcities of, 47, 51, 117; specialization, 94. *See also* Product markets
Communes, 25, 26, 208, 209–210, 215–216, 218, 220, 236–237; and production teams, 204–205; wages on, 232
Communications system, 28, 158, 195; telegraph and, 18, 129
Communism, 39, 40, 158; campaigns tactic of, 200–201; currency and, 183, 186; and economic growth and organization, 54–55, 195–196, 225–240; and factionalism, 227–228; guerillas of, 187; and Japanese war, 182; and Third Plenary Session, 247; in U.S.S.R., 64. *See also* State, socialist
Community development projects, 51
Compradores, 38, 128, 132
Confucianism, 46, 48

Inheritance, 51, 161; and land, 13, 14, 107, 165, 166, 167, 174; and wealth, 15

Inner Mongolia: migration to, 24

Innovations, 47, 52, 210

Interest rates, 51, 72, 91, 109–111, 141–142, 147, 186

Inventions, 41

Investment, 40, 51–52, 53, 61, 64, 115, 116, 172; capital, 128–130, 158, 240; communist, 225; in factories, 141–143; foreign, 17–18, 130, 133, 148–150; by officials, 128–130; private, 160; real estate, 106–107, 133, 176–177; and savings, 39

Iron production, 5, 20, 54, 65, 70, 128, 129, 140, 169, 206

Irrigation, 36, 50, 119, 181, 209, 210, 216, 217, 227, 236, 239

Jamaica: economic growth in, 29

Japan: colonial rule of, 54, 181, 186–187, 231; and currency, 182–183; and economic growth, 28, 29, 30, 48, 135–136; extermination campaigns of, 186, 187; firms of in China, 130; and industrialization, 159; and Japanese collaborators, 198; and land reform, 161, 162, 165; loans of, 168; and Manchuria, 18; relations of with China, 247, 248, 249; rice production of, 43, 238; and silk industry, 132; and Taiwan, 181; and tea production, 135; territorial losses of, 172; textile production of, 176; and trade, 66, 206–207; wars of with China, 17, 39, 52, 53, 146, 157, 158, 170, 182, 183

Jardine, Matheson and Company, 130, 132

Jung Chao-Liu, 205

Kaiping mines, 128

Kansu, 8, 24

Kee Ching Silk Filature Company, 130

Kiangnan Arsenal, 129

Kiangsi, 8; rice production in, 95

Kiangsu, 8, 127; cotton production in, 133

Kinship, 91; and business partnerships, 113

Kuang-yuan, 67

Kuomintang (KMT) party and government, 38, 53, 138, 158, 160; and entrepreneurial bureaucrats, 168–170; and land reform, 162, 163–164, 164–165; and military, 172

Kuznets, Simon, 12, 29

Kwangsi, 8

Kwangtung: cotton production in, 133; population of, 8; and opium smuggling, 13

Kweichow, 8, 182

Labor, 3, 6, 21, 42; bonded, 77, 106; and communism, 201; as factor service, 63; government control of, 25; hiring practices, 108–109; in manufacturing, 5; resources, 48; specialization, 97–98, 100, 134–135; and technology, 117–118; wage, 107–109; and wealth, 107

Labor camps, 226

Labor intensive industry, 27, 48, 118, 150, 151; and cotton, 97; and tea, 102

Lanchow Official Mining Company, 143

Land, 36, 106; and agriculture, 75; "black lands," 203; confiscation of, 77; cultivation and settlement of new land, 8, 13, 14, 42, 77, 78, 80, 103, 216, 217; government, 14; increase in value of, 50; and inheritance, 13, 14, 107, 165, 166, 167, 174; leasing of, 91, 103–107, 165–167; and military, 76; mortgages, 109–110; premodern distribution of, 13–14, 16; private ownership of, 14; productivity of, 117–118, 119; and property rights, 105; redistribution of, 22, 25, 26, 27, 49, 54, 225, 232; reform, 40, 163–164, 197–200, 203; as resource, 44, 48; tax, 78–80, 84, 105, 106, 137–138, 160, 161–163, 163–164, 164–167, 184, 203–204; and technology, 116; and wealth, 17, 63

Landlords: absentee, 106–107; agriculture and, 37; capitalism and, 38; and communism, 197–198, 200; exploitation by, 180; saving by, 114–115; and tenant farming, 103–105

Law and order, 180, 237–238; breakdown of, 177–178, 181–182

Modernization, 18, 28, 52–53, 55, 125, 128, 158, 238, 245–246, 248; under Nanking government, 165, 171; technological, 131–132

Money. *See* Currency system

Moneylending, 51, 91, 109–111; and banks, 111; and capitalism, 38; in cotton industry, 133; and exploitation, 180; and interest, 109, 111; and land, 15; mortgages, 109–110; pawnshops, 110–111

Monopolies, 76; control of, 39; copper, 83–84, 86; salt, 83, 86; steamship, 132; textile, 129

Mortgages, 109–110

Nanking government, 53, 138, 162; and economy, 170–173; and Japanese wars, 182; and military, 164, 172

Nanking Treaty, 125, 139

Nanyang Brothers Tobacco Company, 143–144, 169–170

National People's Party, 38

Nationalism, 144, 148

Nationalist government and party, 169, 170; collapse of, 186; and communists, 197, 204; and currency, 182, 183; and inflation, 184. *See also* Nanking government

Natural disasters, 21, 178–180, 227

Nei-wu-fu, 76

Net domestic product, 40

Ningpo, 125; banking, 111; handicrafts, 66, 67; tea production, 100

Nishihara loans, 168

North China: agriculture, 77; population, 11, 12; water control, 74

Northwest China: population, 11, 12

Officials: as entrepreneurs, 128, 129, 142

Opium, 132; smuggling, 13; trade, 72, 130; War, 37, 125

Opportunity costs, 112

Paauw, Douglass S., 170

Pao-chia system, 80

Partnerships, 112–113

Patrilineal system, 91, 107

Pawnshops, 110–111

Peace Preservation Committee, 186

Pearl River delta, 12

Peasant's Associations, 198, 199, 200

Peking: in Boxer Rebellion, 136; Ch'ing, 75

Peking Treaty, 125

People's Bank of China, 213, 220

People's Liberation Army (PLA), 198, 201, 203; and employment, 24–26

Perkins, Dwight, 144

Petrochemical industry, 55, 225, 249, 250

Petroleum, 55, 206, 207, 208, 218, 239–240, 250

Philippines: economic growth in, 29, 30

Philosophy, 41

P'ing-shan county, 198–199

Planned economy, 159

Po I-po, 203

Police, 138, 139, 162

Population growth, 19, 20, 21, 28, 29, 31, 44, 70–71, 117, 119, 127, 144, 181; decline and reduction in, 74–75, 237; distribution of, 23–24; Malthusian view of, 40–41, 42, 43; in premodern era, 4, 6–8, 11–13, 26–27; and living standard, 233; urban, 66, 139, 204

Ports: city ports, 53, 75, 125, 142, 150, 151, 157, 179, 182; free, 139; and trade, 37–38; treaty ports, 18, 20, 21, 47, 126–133

Poverty, 179, 182, 225

Premodern era: economy of, 3, 4–17, 26–27, 45; per capita income in, 5–6

Prices, 42, 47, 51, 63, 71–72, 142, 180; and agrarian crisis, 174, 176; cigarette, 169–170; under communism, 204, 211–212, 214–215, 220; control of, 39, 55, 159, 220; cotton, 133; deflation of, 73–74, 80, 85, 86; food grain, 76–77, 81; free market, 139; and government, 50; inflation of, 105–106, 183–186; rice, 93, 94–95; silk, 100; and supply and demand, 174–175; tea, 102, 131, 135; and tenant farming, 105

Private property, 55

Private sector, 91–119; consumption, savings and investment, 113–117; and cotton production, 96–98; and factor markets, 102–113; incentives, 80–81; interest payments, 109–111; product markets, 92–102; profits,

111–113; rent payments and land distribution, 103–107; rice production, 92–95; silk production, 98–100; tea production, 100–102; technology and development, 117–119; wages, 107–109

Privileges: special, 49, 80

Producer goods industry, 207, 212, 225

Product markets, 61, 63, 92–102; cotton, 96–98; rice, 92–95; silk, 98–100; tea, 100–102

Production: mode of, 36; and total factor productivity, 228–231

Professions, 17

Profits, 111–113; from exports, 131; foreign, 149; windfall, 47, 50, 112

Property rights, 26, 27, 45, 46, 158; distribution of, 162; pyramiding of, 164–167; redistribution of, 49, 164–167; reform of, 180–181. *See also* Land

Protests: peasant, 39; tenant, 106. *See also* Rebellions

Public works, 6, 15, 76, 119; under communism, 236. *See also* Road building

Putting out system, 98, 133–134

Railroads, 18, 20, 21, 125, 126, 127–128, 135, 137, 144, 145, 158, 165, 171, 195; under communism, 201, 207–208, 210; and guerillas, 187; and loans, 147–148

Rationing system, 233–234

Rawski, Thomas, 229

Rebellions, 37; Boxer, 136, 138, 146; under communism, 219, 227, 237; of 1850s, 6, 8, 13, 20, 52, 74, 86, 119, 126, 165; Taiping, 27, 73; and taxation, 76; White Lotus, 72

Recession, 39, 143

Record keeping, 6

Reforms, 27–28, 46, 52, 86, 125, 158, 170; banking, 171; communist, 247; currency, 182; fiscal, 167, 172; imperial, 17; and industrialization, 136–137; land, 25, 40, 54, 197–200; land tax, 161, 162, 163–164; legal, 77, 180; property rights, 180–181; salt monopoly, 86; socialist, 24

Religion, 51, 52

Rent, 91; land, 103–107, 165; reductions, 164–165

Research, 195; agricultural, 171; under communism, 220, 248 249; and technology, 247

Resources, 4, 44–45, 48, 49, 52, 61, 70, 72, 112, 229, 230–231, 239–240, 248; and households, 51; land, 119; Malthusian view of, 40–41, 42, 43; and material prices, 142; scarcities of, 102, 117, 118; specialization of, 135

Revenue transfers, 76

Revolution, 18, 151; Cultural, 24, 218–219; green, 208, 209–210; of 1911, 138, 180

Reynolds, Bruce, 134

Rice: production, 6, 43, 82, 92–95, 171, 179, 209, 238, 239; merchants, 110–111; rationing, 234

Riparian rights, 165

Road building, 36, 46, 50, 53, 119, 139, 158, 165, 171, 236

Rozman, Gilbert, 12

Rural environment: communes in, 25; migration to, 24. *See also* Villages

Russell and Company, 128, 130, 131

Russo-Japanese War, 113

Salt: merchants, 110; monopoly, 83, 86; production, 72, 76, 78, 137; tax, 76

San-fan campaign, 200

Savings, 39, 48, 54, 55, 63, 107, 109, 114–116, 170, 172, 186, 196, 213, 217, 220; of elite, 118, 119; household, 91

Scarcities, 50, 117, 118, 119; agricultural, 71; commodity, 42, 47, 51, 72; consumer goods, 64; copper, 84, 85; and market system, 98; resource, 102; silver, 85, 86

Science. *See* Research; Technology

Sericulture. *See* Silk

Services, 5, 29, 61, 63, 64, 66, 69, 70, 73; factor, 63, 91; premodern, 13

Shang pu, 137

Shanghai, 125, 129; currency flow, 177; government, 139; silk industry, 132

Shanghai Cotton Company, 128

Shanghai Steamship Navigation Company, 131–132

Shansi, 8

Shantung, 8; agriculture, 173

Shen Pao-chen, 128

169, 178; Nanking, 170; salt, 137; and scarcities, 50; surcharges, 50, 80, 137, 138, 178; surplus, 85
Tea, 100–102, 130, 131, 135, 175, 176
Team: farming, 25, 204–205, 231; labor, 236
Technology, 4, 6, 29, 44, 48, 49, 53, 55, 117–119, 131–132, 157; and capitalism, 116; Ch'ing, 126–127, 136; communist, 228–231, 237, 247, 248, 249; and cotton, 96–97; foreign introduction of, 131–132, 149, 150; innovations, 47, 52, 210; Malthusian view of, 40–41, 42, 43; and tea, 135
Telegraph, 18, 129
Temples, 15, 73, 119
Ten Year Economic Plan, 219
Tenant farming, 37, 38, 103, 166, 167; hereditary, 165, 174, 181; and land reform, 162; and property rights, 180; and rice production, 93; and tea, 135
Teng Hsiao-p'ing, 219
Textile industry, 38, 70, 77, 108–109, 129, 250. See also Cotton; Silk
Tientsin Treaty, 125
Tobacco, 38, 143–144, 169–170
Tokmakoff, Molotkoff and Company, 130
Tong King-sing, 128–129, 132
Totalitarian system, 231
Trade, 21, 27, 227; Ch'ing, 78; communist, 201–202, 205–207, 227, 237; and export profits, 131; foreign, 37–38, 47, 52, 53, 54, 55, 75, 85, 150, 175, 177, 182, 249–251; industrial imports, 249; interprovincial, 65; rice, 93–95; tea, 100–102; and war, 184. See also Foreign economic impact; Turnkey plants
Transfer payments, 64
Transportation, 28, 42, 52, 76, 171, 181, 219, 235, 249; agricultural product, 78, 144–145; and war, 184. See also Grand Canal; Railroads; Road building; Steamboat shipping
Ts'ao Ju-lin, 168
Tsinghai: migration to, 24
Tsitsihar Locomotive and Carriage Works, 218
Tsung-li Yamen, 136, 137
T'u-pu, 134
Turnkey projects, 202, 206

Union of Soviet Socialist Republics (U.S.S.R.): and China, 54–55, 130, 220, 247; economy of, 29, 30, 64, 159, 212; and energy, 208; and railroads, 148; resources, 239; trade, 202, 206, 211, 227
United States: and cotton, 97; economic growth in, 29, 30, 135; and electrical industry, 141; energy consumption, 208; income, 17; industry in China, 130; industrial revolution, 158; relations of with China, 247–248, 249, 250–251; resources, 239; steamship lines, 132; trade, 54, 140, 142, 206, 250–251
Urban environment, 23, 25, 29; Ch'ing, 65–68; communist, 25, 200, 237; and food grain, 235; migration to, 3, 212; population in, 12, 24, 75, 204; and regional cities, 66, 67
Utilities, public, 130, 138, 139, 141

Values, cultural, 44, 46, 47–48, 52, 53, 108; of elite, 118–119; probationary ethic, 161; work ethic, 48, 51, 108, 216–217
Velocity of money, 73, 183–186
Vietnam, 247, 248
Villages: and capitalism, 37; Ch'ing, 70, 75; communist, 54, 197, 198–200, 203, 204, 215, 237; and cotton, 97–98; described, 173; and land, 14, 15, 166; and market system, 42, 69, 70; premodern, 6; and rice, 93, 94; and seasonal work demand, 108; and silk, 99; and Ta-chai work ethic, 216–217; and wealth distribution, 14–15
Volunteerism, 248
Von Richthofen, Ferdinand, 74–75

Wages, 26, 73, 91, 100–101, 107–109; communist, 212, 232; and currency, 84; eight grade structure, 204–205; and inflation, 184
Wahson Electrical Manufacturing Company, 140–141
Wang Chen, 41
War, 21, 53, 187; and agriculture, 179; debts of, 38, 138, 145, 146; and foreign territorial aggression, 147–148; Malthusian view of, 40, 41. See also Civil war